THE MYSTERY OF DEATH

THE MYSTERY OF DEATH

THE NATURE AND SIGNIFICANCE OF CENTRAL EUROPE AND THE EUROPEAN FOLK-SPIRITS

Fifteen lectures given to members of the Anthroposophical Society in various locations between 31 January and 19 June 1915

TRANSLATED BY SIMON BLAXLAND-DE LANGE

INTRODUCTION BY URS DIETLER

RUDOLF STEINER

RUDOLF STEINER PRESS

CW 159

Rudolf Steiner Press
Hillside House, The Square
Forest Row, RH18 5ES

www.rudolfsteinerpress.com

Published by Rudolf Steiner Press 2023

Originally published in German under the title *Das Geheimnis des Todes Wesen und Bedeutung Mitteleuropas und die europäischen Volksgeister* (volume 159 in the *Rudolf Steiner Gesamtausgabe* or Collected Works) by Rudolf Steiner Verlag, Dornach. Based on shorthand notes that were not reviewed or revised by the speaker. This authorized translation is based on the third German edition (2005), edited by Urs Dietler

Published by permission of the Rudolf Steiner Nachlassverwaltung, Dornach

A catalogue record for this book is available from the British Library

ISBN 978 1 85584 608 1

Cover by Morgan Creative
Typeset by Symbiosys Technologies, Vishakapatnam, India
Printed and bound by 4Edge Ltd., Essex

CONTENTS

Introduction

In the course of life, death appears as the outermost limit. There are few philosophers and no religions that try to avoid thinking about this frontier, and most of them are obsessed with it. As one becomes conscious of one's own course of life, death for the most part appears abruptly but then with a sense of finality; and one understands the old saying that life exists in order to learn to die. And the many thousands who have died in the first, second and—according to certain voices—third, asymmetrical World War, which has already lasted for longer, extend the question of the significance of the 'choir of the dead', to which Conrad Ferdinand Meyer made his contribution, beyond the destiny of the individual.

There have always been voices that regarded death not as an end point but as a once-and-for-all transition. Fortified by a materialistically reductionist natural science, the twentieth century also brought forth empirical investigations which focused upon after-death states; and there arose a humane accompaniment of the dying in the context of 'the after-life' which developed into a considerable movement. Thousands of near-death experiences were collected, also those sounding a note that no one had hitherto wanted to hear. Because death has long been a taboo subject and the whole question of dying has been repressed, they thrust themselves on the threshold of people's consciousness and pose the very question of life itself.

Rudolf Steiner gave the present 15 lectures for members in the first half of the war-year of 1915 in eleven different towns or cities. He speaks here about death and the destiny of all who had died young and also about the death of three members. As he spoke the words for the members who had died that he had received in living contact with the dead at the festivals of remembrance and described the first stages of their journeys after death, he opened up wholly new horizons of understanding with respect to the death of those who had died prematurely. The forces of the etheric body of such a dead person are available for a fruitful world-evolution if only they are perceived and appreciated in an appropriate way. The destiny of young Theodor Faiß, who died under tragic circumstances in the grounds of the Goetheanum, is described in particular detail. The etheric body of the young Theo could be perceived clairvoyantly as being active in the vicinity of the Dornach building.

Rudolf Steiner strikes a second chord with the description of the task of Central Europe in the context of the influences of different Folk-souls, with frequent references to what he had said in the 'Folk-soul cycle' in June 1910 in Christiania (Oslo). He makes a point of clearly emphasizing that the working of the 'Folk-spirits' makes its mark upon the manner of life and the cultural sensibility of the individual folk but does not have any nationalistic connotations. He expresses the view that there can only be a fruitful living together of peoples if differences are recognized and accepted but not made absolute. The harmony of a point of view that transcends nationality is to be won through differentiation. Probably because certain misunderstandings had arisen, he repeatedly points out that this way of characterizing things has to do not with value-judgements but with phenomenology, on the basis of which alone it is possible to see the whole picture and work together.

The third theme that Rudolf Steiner dealt with repeatedly in these lectures relates to the understanding of the impulses and connections active in history. In looking back at the twentieth century, which is beginning to emerge as an historical phenomenon, questions may be posed such as: How did there come to be a Berlin Wall? What is the significance of the emergence of what is referred to as 'Pacific culture'? What role will China take over? How widely and how deeply can the evolutionary lines of such processes be investigated? According to Rudolf Steiner, most attempts at explaining historical dynamics—in cases where there are efforts to go beyond the workings of blind fate—do not go far enough. He himself in these lectures, for example, traces the situation of Central Europe around 1915 to the time around 860, during which a kind of 'pincer movement' through two streams arose. On the other hand, in his perspective the influence of a Jeanne d'Arc or the battle of Constantine against Maxentius around 312 can only be explained as to their deeper causes if the involvement of the Christ impulse is perceived.

While Rudolf Steiner was in 1915 undertaking six lecture-tours to Germany and Austria, a strong artistic impulse was living in Swiss-based Dornach. An initial beginning was being made to study scenes from Goethe's *Faust*. In addition, Rudolf Steiner was working intensively with Edith Maryon on the models for the sculptural 'Group'. He speaks in some of the present lectures about the significance of this Group, in a way that is clearly still wholly connected with the creative process.

In conclusion, some consideration may be given to the frequently asked question of *how*—80 years after Rudolf Steiner's death—his books and lectures should be read from the standpoint of interpreting anthroposophical texts in our time.

If one studies the lectures assembled in this volume in their successive order and interconnections, one can make some interesting observations in this regard. Although we do not have here the developmental arc that was possible in the lecture-cycles (a series of lectures over a few days devoted to a particular theme), the present collection of lectures can profitably be investigated under its particular aspects. The relatively narrow time frame of half a year and the urgency of the questions addressed meant that most themes are repeated in the different lectures. After reading—say—the first five lectures, one may have the experience that one is increasingly 'ticking off' the information given in the lecture and speedily moving on to the next. Here it is, at the very least, advisable to direct one's attention to *how* the lecture is being given: in what way is the theme being taken up, to what context is it related, how is it extended, abbreviated, intensified, how are the words formulated? Focusing on the form, however, leads one back to the content, which has now attained an expanded or new meaning that goes beyond mere information. Furthermore, it is rewarding to pay attention to themes that appear only once or twice. Was there a connection with the places or the community of the members present that came into play here; did not the *genius loci* together with the assembled members give rise to the characteristic mood and content of what was spoken?

Anyone who reads and works with the lectures of this volume in this sense will not only make interesting discoveries but also acquire faculties to come to know Rudolf Steiner's work at a deeper level.

Urs Dietler
2005

LECTURE 1

ZURICH, 31 JANUARY 1915

The Four Platonic Virtues and Their Connection with the Mysteries of Man's Being—The Influence of Spiritual Powers upon the Physical World

OUR spiritual science has the task of removing for our consciousness, and indeed for our whole inner life, that gulf which extends for outward human consciousness between the physical world, where man abides between birth and death, and the spiritual world, where man spends the other part of his existence, the time between death and a new birth.

For someone who lives in spiritual science with every fibre of his soul, such a statement is both familiar and one that he takes for granted. But in the moment when I am speaking to you now, one may well say that it acquires a particularly sacred quality. We have, after all, recently lost a number of our dear friends and members through the grave events of the war, and we are about to accompany two friends upon their last paths here on Earth. Tomorrow morning at eleven o'clock we shall have here in Zurich the cremation of a dear member, Frau Dr Calazza,[1] who left the physical plane this week, and we have just received the news that our dear friend Fritz Mitscher[2] died around 5 o'clock this afternoon near Davos. With these two members, souls dear to us have left the physical plane. However, spiritual science shows us the way to understand that, in a far higher sense than we otherwise are able to understand, we do not lose such souls but remain connected with them.

A considerable number of souls who have belonged to us since the work in our movement began have already passed through the gate of death; and from those sources whence spiritual knowledge flows to us, it can be said that they have—in accordance with their respective powers—become faithful collaborators in the spiritual world. Indeed, with the full responsibility with which one can say something that is founded firmly on spiritual knowledge, I can say that we have in them gained pillars for our spiritual movement. Many have passed through the gate of death who worked within our spiritual movement and who look down upon that to which their love is directed. In the period between birth and death they have grown attached to the kind of aspiration which is pursued in our circle. They have left something behind them in our Society which is itself on the path between death and a new birth.

Just as the nature that surrounds us is a world upon which we look back, so can we look back upon our physical life from that moment which one can compare with a person's birth. Immediately after death man passes through a condition that can be compared with embryonic life, with life in the mother's body, except that this period in the life after death lasts only a matter of days and is therefore much shorter than embryonic life in relation to physical life. Then follows what can be compared with the entry into the physical world, with the taking of the first breath. This can be called the awakening in the spiritual world, of which it can be said that it is like an awareness that the will of the soul that has crossed the threshold of death is being received by the beings of the higher hierarchies. Just as a person emerging physically from the body of the mother into the physical world initially finds himself able to take in the outside air and then experiences the gradual awakening of his senses, so after death does there come that moment when the soul feels: the power of will which during physical life was contained within the limits of the physical body is now flowing from me out into the universe. And this soul then feels how this will is indeed received through the activity of the next higher hierarchy, the beings belonging to the hierarchy of the angeloi. This is like the taking of the first breath in the spiritual world and gradually growing into one's spiritual surroundings; for this is what spiritual knowledge shows us.

I should like to speak about the destiny of those who have gone from us in the course of the years. I should like to cast an eye upon those who have developed a fondness for our spiritual movement and look down upon it as something of which they know that it speaks to human souls of that within which they are living also within physical life. To be able in this way to connect oneself in memory to earthly life is something that here in the physical world already belongs to the world of spirit. For those who have crossed the threshold of death, this is something of infinite value, of infinite significance. And when the stream that flows up to them from the physical world, which has its source in what they have experienced in our movement, is augmented by them as a tributary to a river, when the thoughts of those who were attached to them in love or from family ties are added to it, because it is based on spiritual relationships the community is far more intimate than it could otherwise be in our materialistic age.

Again we may say that in the case of many a person who has passed through the portal of death into the spiritual world, it appears to us as if he or she had done this out of intimate love for our spiritual movement, in order to be able to contribute stronger powers from the spiritual world. A considerable number of those who have gone from us have living in their souls the most wonderfully clear feelings about the need for our spiritual movement; and for someone who is able to acquire insight into the spiritual world, all those who have crossed the threshold of death and now look down at the movement with which they were connected are like the spiritual heralds of our movement, those who carry their spiritual standards before us, constantly calling to us: We were convinced while we were united with you of the necessity of this movement; but now that we have entered the spiritual world, we know that we can and must help at a time when this movement is needed.

This is something which those who remain behind on the physical plane who have lost relatives and friends will increasingly be aware of. For them what has been said can represent the deepest comfort of having everything that brings about a still deeper bond between souls, even if we are no longer in the position of being connected with those souls outwardly through physical eyes and physical words.

This spiritual movement of which we are to become participants has a great deal that it must bring. I should like today to choose a particular aspect out of the many things that it must bring to us. A time like ours, when outward culture—notwithstanding the last echoes of the old religions—is based wholly on a materialistic consciousness, can also only develop the impulses of moral life in a way that takes account solely of the life between birth and death. Among the many things that will emerge from our spiritual movement will be a new upsurge of humanity's moral life, the whole life of the virtues. For human beings will learn to regard moral life, the life of virtue, from a standpoint that extends beyond birth and death and which reckons that the human soul passes through repeated earthly lives, that just as it lives its life between birth and death it has also passed through many lives and can hope in anticipation of further lives which it will live in future. When we have extended our frame of vision from one life to successive earthly lives, we shall have a more comprehensive and more appropriate conception of life together with a more appropriate and more comprehensive conception of virtue and the moral life.

When we speak of the human virtues, we can distinguish essentially four such virtues of which we can speak in ordinary language. As we shall indicate later on, there is one virtue that lives in the depths of the human soul but of which we should—as we shall see—speak as little as possible for reasons that are held sacred. All other virtues which exist in life and which together constitute moral life can be regarded as special cases of the four virtues that we wish to consider and which were fully described in antiquity.

Plato,[3] the great philosopher of Ancient Greece, distinguished these four virtues because he was still able to derive his wisdom from the echoes of ancient mystery-wisdom. From this standpoint Plato was better equipped to distinguish the virtues than later philosophers and certainly than those of our times, where knowledge of mystery-wisdom has become so remote and so chaotic in nature.

The first virtue which we must consider if we are speaking of a moral life as it arises from a comprehensive knowledge of human nature is that of wisdom. However, this wisdom is to be understood in a somewhat deeper sense and as related more to ethics than one would normally understand it. We cannot say that wisdom is something that can, as it were, simply come to a person of its own accord. Still less is wisdom something that a person can learn in the ordinary sense. It is, moreover, not easy to characterize in a few words what wisdom should signify for us. If we pass through life in such a way that we allow what comes towards us in this life to influence us, if—prompted by the various events of life—we learn from the one event how we might have been able to respond to this or that more appropriately, how we might have used our powers more skilfully and effectively, if we take account of everything that befalls us in life, so that when we encounter something similar a second time we do not any longer respond as we did the first time but feel that we have learnt something; and if we maintain throughout our life the mood of being able to learn from life and of being able to regard everything that nature and life bring towards us in such a way that we learn from it—and, moreover, not simply by accumulating knowledge but by becoming inwardly better and richer—we will then have grown in wisdom, and what we have experienced will not have been without value for our life of soul.

Life will have been worthless for us if we have lived for several decades and continue at a later time to judge something that we have experienced in the same way that we evaluated it when we were younger. If we spend our life in such a way, we are very far removed from wisdom. Karma may have brought it about that we became angry when we were young and condemned this or that quality in other people. If we hold fast to this we will have made poor use of our life. The opposite will be the case if, in an instance where we formed a derogatory judgement in our youth, at a later stage of life we judge not disparagingly but with understanding and forgiveness, if we make the effort of wanting to understand. If we have an innate tendency to erupt with violent anger at certain things and if when we are older we are not led to blind anger as we were in our younger days, if the violence of our anger has been tempered by what life has taught us and we have become gentler, we have profited from life in accordance with wisdom. If we were materialists in our youth but have subsequently allowed the revelations from the spiritual world that our time has sought to impart to us to influence us, we will have employed our life in the service of wisdom. If we have closed ourselves to the revelations of the spiritual world, we have not lived our life in accordance with wisdom.

To be enriched in this way and to achieve a wider horizon may be called making use of life in accordance with wisdom; and what spiritual science wants to give us is fitted for opening ourselves up to life so that we may become wiser. Wisdom is something that opposes egotism in the strongest possible way. Wisdom is something that always reckons with the course of world events. We therefore allow ourselves to be instructed by the course of world events because we thereby free ourselves from the narrow judgement made by our ego. A wise person cannot actually judge egotistically, for if one learns from the world one learns to understand it, one learns to let the world correct one's judgements, so that wisdom extracts us from narrow, limited points of view and brings us into harmony with itself. Much else could be said which could gradually provide us with a description of wisdom. We should not attempt to arrive at a definition of such concepts but, rather, open our hearts, so that we can become ever wiser also about wisdom itself.

Here in the physical world everything that a person has to experience in waking life has to make use of the instruments of the outward physical and etheric nature. As human beings between birth and death, it is only when we are asleep that our soul nature—in so far as it consists of an ego and astral body—is outside our physical and etheric bodies. When we are in a conscious, waking state, we avail ourselves of the instruments of our physical and etheric bodies. When we fill ourselves with wisdom, when we try to live in our actions and thinking, in our feelings and sensations, in accordance with wisdom, we make use of those organs of our physical and etheric bodies which are in a sense the most perfect in our earthly life, those organs that have needed the longest for their development, which were already prepared by Saturn, Sun and Moon and have come into our lives as a heritage and have reached a certain culmination.

I should like to present to you from another point of view an idea of what one can understand by more or less perfected organs. Let us on the one hand take our brain. The brain is not the most perfect organ, but we can regard it as more perfect than other organs; for it needed longer for its development than these other organs. Compare the brain with our torso, for which our hands extend. When we undertake to do something with our hands, we have the thought: I stretch out my hand, I take the vase, I retract my hand. What have I done? I have extended not only the physical hand but also the etheric and astral hand and a portion of my ego; but the physical hand went with them.

If I merely think and entertain only thoughts, clairvoyant consciousness can see that something like spiritual arms stretch out from the head, but the physical brain remains in the skull. Just as my etheric and astral hand belongs to my physical hand, so does something etheric and astral belong to the brain. The brain cannot follow, but the hands can do so. At a later time the hands will also become fixed, and we shall subsequently only be able to move their astral part. The hands are on the way to becoming what the brain is already today.

In earlier times, during the Old Sun and Moon periods, that which today extends as something purely spiritual or intellectual from the brain was also still accompanied by the physical organ. It has now been covered over by the skull, so that the physical brain is held fast within it during earthly evolution. The brain is an organ which has passed through more stages of evolution. The hands are on the way to becoming similar to the brain, for the whole human organism is on the way to becoming a brain. Thus there are organs that are more perfect and have evolved into something more self-contained, and those that are less perfected. The most perfected organs are needed by what we achieve by way of wisdom.

Our ordinary brain is actually used only as an instrument for the lowest form of wisdom, for earthly cleverness. But the more we acquire wisdom, the less we depend upon our cerebrum and the more activity is—unbeknown to modern anatomy—withdrawn to our cerebellum, to what is enclosed within our skull as a smaller brain resembling a tree. When we human beings have become wise, when we have attained wisdom, we do indeed find ourselves beneath a 'tree' which is our cerebellum[4] and which then begins in a particular way to unfold its activity.

Imagine how a human being who has become especially wise extends the organs of his wisdom mightily like the branches of a tree. They have their source in the cerebellum, which resides in the hard covering of the skull; but the spiritual or intellectual organs extend outwards, and he is as a spiritual reality beneath the tree, the Bodhi tree.

Thus we see too that what we do in wisdom is the most spiritual aspect of our nature, or at least one of the most spiritual, for the organs are already at rest. When we do something with our hand, we must use a portion of our forces on moving the hand. When we make a wise judgement or decide something wisely, the organs remain at rest, no force is employed on a physical organ because in such an instance we are more spiritual, and those organs that we use on the physical plane in order to live wisely are those for which we need to use the least strength, those that are already the most perfected.

Wisdom is, therefore, something in the moral life which enables human beings to experience themselves in a spiritual way. This is associated with the fact that the wisdom that a person acquires enables him to derive the greatest possible fruits from his former incarnations. Because in the realm of the spirit we live in wisdom without any effort on the part of our physical organs, we are through a wisdom-filled life also most able to make what we have acquired in former incarnations fruitful for this life, in that we bring this wisdom over from former incarnations.

We have in German [and also in English] a good word for someone who does not want to become wise. We call him a Philistine. A Philistine is a person who resists any development of wisdom, someone who wants to stay as he is for his entire life and does not want to arrive at a different opinion about anything. But someone who wants to become wise makes the effort to bring the work that he has accomplished and accumulated in former incarnations into his present life. The wiser we become, the more do we bring into the present incarnation from earlier incarnations; and if we do not want to become wise, so that we elect not to cultivate further the wisdom developed in previous incarnations, then along comes one who gets rid of it altogether: Ahriman.

No one likes it better than Ahriman if we do not become wiser. We have the power to do so. We have acquired far, far more in previous incarnations than we think; we gained far more in the times when we were living through the old conditions of clairvoyance. Everyone could become much wiser than he does become. No one should try to persuade himself that there is not much that he could bring over from the past. To become wise means to bring forth what one has acquired in former incarnations so that one may be filled with it in this incarnation.

Another virtue—although it is difficult to describe it exactly in a single word—is that of courage. It represents the mood of soul that does not passively attend to life but is guided by the inclination towards active participation. One might say that this virtue derives from the heart. It can be said of someone who has this virtue in ordinary life that he has his heart in the right place. And this is a good expression for when we are able not timidly to withdraw from things that life demands of us but have the capacity to take ourselves in hand and know how to intervene where this is necessary. When we are in such a way inclined to press on with our activity in a confident and good-hearted manner—the expression 'good-hearted' is applicable to this virtue—we have something of the quality of this virtue. One could also say that this virtue is associated with a healthy feeling life that gives rise at the right moment to bravery, whereas its absence engenders cowardice. Naturally, this virtue can in the physical course of life be exercised only through certain organs. These organs, which include the physical and etheric heart, are not so perfected as those which serve wisdom. They are still on the way to becoming different and will in future indeed become so.

There is a great difference between the brain and the heart in their relation to cosmic evolution. Suppose that someone passes through the gate of death and then through the life between death and a new birth. His brain is altogether a work of the Gods. The brain is pervaded by forces which completely separate themselves from him when he passes through the portal of death; and for his next life the brain is built up entirely anew, not only in a material sense but also as regards its inner forces. This is not the case with the heart. The situation with the heart is that not the physical heart itself but the forces that are active within it continue in existence. These forces withdraw into the astral realm and into the ego, and also remain there between death and a new birth. The same forces that beat within our hearts also beat next time in our new incarnation. That which functions within the brain does not feature in a forthcoming incarnation. But the forces that inspire our heart also reappear in the next incarnation. When we contemplate a head, we can say: Invisible forces are working within it of which the brain is composed. But when a person passes through the gate of death, these forces are given over to the cosmos. When, however, we listen to someone's heartbeat, we are hearing spiritual forces which are present not only in this incarnation but will also live in the next incarnation, having passed through death and a new birth.

Popular consciousness had a wonderful sense of such things. That is why so much importance was attached to the feeling of the heartbeat, not because the physical heartbeat is so greatly valued but because we perceive something far more eternal when we consider a person's heartbeat. If we have the virtue of courage, of valiant good-heartedness, we can use only a part of certain forces for this virtue; and we must use the other part for the organs that serve as the instruments for it. These are organs for which we must still use a portion of such forces. If we are not courageous, if we do not develop the virtue of brave good-heartedness, if we let ourselves go, timidly withdraw from life and give ourselves over to the gravity of our own being, we cannot enliven those forces which must accompany the full expression of the virtue of courage.

For as long as we take a cowardly stance in life, the forces that should fire our heart remain inactive. They are a seed for Lucifer. He takes possession of them, and we do not have them in the next life. To be cowardly in the face of life means that one is providing Lucifer with a quantity of forces that we will lack when we want to build up our hearts, which are indeed the organs, the instruments of courage. We will come into the world with defective, underdeveloped organs.

The third virtue, which reckons with the least perfected organs that will acquire a form only in the future and of which they contain at present only a seed, is one that we may call temperance, circumspection or discretion.* It can also in one of its shades of meaning be referred to as 'moderation'. Thus we have three virtues: wisdom, courage or good-heartedness and temperance.

One can be intemperate in the most varied ways, such as overeating or drinking to excess. This is the lowest form of intemperance. The soul is totally engulfed in bodily desires, and our life is dominated by the body. If, however, we take our desires in hand, if we directly command the body as to what it may and may not do, we are then temperate or, as one could also say, acting in moderation. And through such moderation we also maintain some order amidst those forces whose task it is to prevent the organs in question from falling prey to Lucifer in the next incarnation; for the forces that we expend through giving ourselves up to a life of passion we make available to Lucifer. This is most severely exacerbated by our passions, if our consciousness becomes submerged in a dreamy, drowsy state.

When we lose our sense of temperance or moderation, we always make forces available to Lucifer. He takes these forces, but he also takes from us the forces that we need for the organs of breathing and digestion; and our organs of breathing and digestion are adversely affected if we do not cultivate the virtue of moderation. Those who like to be carried away by their desires and give themselves up to their passions are candidates for being the decadent people of the future, those who will suffer from all possible aberrations of their physical body.

One can say that this virtue of temperance is dependent upon the least perfected organs of man's being, upon the organs that are in the initial stage of development and must still essentially be transformed. When we consider our organs of digestion and all that is connected with them, we have to apply our ego, astral body, etheric body and

*The German word '*Besonnenheit*', which means more or less 'the quality of having thought through or reflected upon something', is difficult to render by means of a single English equivalent. The word 'temperance', which like many other words has become increasingly narrowed in its connotations, conveys only an aspect of its meaning.—Translator

physical body in order to set them in motion. With the organs that serve as the instruments for courage, the situation is different. In this case our ego remains more or less outside, in that we move freely; and only our astral and etheric bodies reach into the physical domain. When we come to the virtues that comprise wisdom, we keep the ego and astral body freely detached; for as we become wiser, we develop the organization of the astral body, we take hold of it. That is the essential point, that through becoming wiser we transform the astral body into the Spirit-self, and only the etheric body combines with the physical body. In the brain, the physical aspect of our being is accompanied only by the etheric; and whereas during waking life we are with respect to the rest of the body very closely connected in our physical organism at any rate with our astral nature, we retain for the brain the condition in which we are in sleep to the highest degree. Thus for the brain we are in the greatest need of sleep; for likewise when we are awake, our ego and astral body are outside the brain, and they have to make the greatest effort within themselves without having the support of the external organ.

Thus we find a connection between our human nature and the virtues. We can call wisdom a virtue that belongs to man as a spiritual being, where he is freely active with his ego and his astral body and his physical and etheric organs merely offer a kind of support. We can refer to courage as a virtue where a person is free only with his ego and has his supports in his astral, etheric and physical bodies. Finally, we can speak of temperance, circumspection or discretion where the seed within our ego is becoming free, where our ego is nevertheless bound to the astral, etheric and physical bodies and we work by means of it to free ourselves from these bonds.

But then there is a virtue which is the most spiritual of all. This most spiritual of virtues is connected with the whole human being. There is a function of human nature which we lose early and have only in the first years of childhood. I have often mentioned what I have in mind here. When we arrive on the physical plane, we are not in the position that we need for our human dignity. We crawl on all fours. I have pointed out that it is only through our own forces that we achieve the right situation of uprightness. Similarly, we develop through the forces that bring about speech. In short, in the first years of our life we develop forces which in all essentials—note the expression—draw us into the position that we have in the world as true human beings. We do not come into the world in such a way that we already find our 'right' orientation in it. We crawl. But we are rightly placed when we direct our head towards the stars. This corresponds to inner forces.

In later life we lose these forces. They cease to manifest themselves. Nothing any longer appears of a similar nature in human life to match the energy displayed in learning to walk and acquiring an upright posture. We become increasingly weary when it comes to our capacity of uprightness. If we begin early in the morning to live with our brain, we become tired when we have come to the end of the day; we are in need of sleep. When we are tired, that which gives us our upright posture in childhood itself remains somewhat weary and degenerates into feebleness; and anything comparable to the achieving of uprightness in childhood no longer happens in later life.

And how do we orientate ourselves in life when we learn to speak? Also when we are learning to speak, guiding forces are working with us. The same forces that we use in early childhood are, however, not lost in the course of later life. They remain available to us, but they are associated with a virtue, with the virtue that is connected with rightness, with what is right, with the virtue of all-encompassing justice, the fourth virtue. The same power that we use as a child when, from a being that crawls, we raise ourselves to uprightness lives in us when we have the virtue of justice, the fourth of those mentioned by Plato.

Anyone who really practises the virtue of justice puts every thing and every being in its right place, goes out from himself and into the others. This is what it means to live in all-encompassing justice. To live in wisdom means to derive the best fruits from the forces that we have stored up in previous incarnations. And if we had to point towards what was imparted to us in former incarnations, when divine forces still pervaded us, we must with justice further emphasize that we derive from the cosmos. We practise justice when we develop the forces through which we are connected, in a spiritual respect, with the whole cosmos. Justice represents the measure of a person's connection with the divine. Injustice is, to all intents and purposes, equivalent to godlessness, to one who has lost his divine origin; and we blaspheme against God from whom we spring if we do any human being an injustice.

Thus we have two virtues, justice and wisdom, which direct us back to what we were in former times, in other incarnations, in the times when we ourselves were still in the womb of the Godhead. And we have two other virtues, which may be designated as courage and temperance, which point us towards later incarnations. We build up all the more forces for these the less that we give to Lucifer. We have seen how what is associated with courage and temperance goes into the organs and how the organs are thereby prepared for the next incarnation. In the same way moral life extends into future life if we fill ourselves with spirituality. Two virtues extend their life over past incarnations: wisdom and justice. Courage and temperance shed their light upon future incarnations.

The time will come when people will see clearly that they are throwing themselves into the jaws of Ahriman if they shut themselves off from justice and wisdom; and what they had in former incarnations, what belonged to the divine world, would be made available to Lucifer through intemperate or cowardly actions. What is seized by Lucifer is taken away from the forces available for building up our body in our next life.

We cannot practise wisdom and justice without becoming selfless, as has been indicated. Someone who is self-seeking can only be unjust; someone who is self-seeking can only be wanting to remain unwise. Wisdom and justice lead us beyond our self and make us members of the whole organism of humanity. Courage or good-heartedness and temperance make us in a certain sense members of the whole organism of humanity. Only by experiencing courage and temperance and expressing them in our lives do we ensure that in the future we shall engage with humanity as a whole with a stronger organism. What we would otherwise cast away to Lucifer will not then be taken away from us. Egotism is of itself transformed into selflessness when it is extended in the right sense over the whole horizon of life and man finds his place in the light of the fourth virtue. This is what spiritual wisdom will bring to the future of humanity and will extend to include ethics and the moral life. This will then also flow into methods of education. If wisdom and justice are understood in the way that I have indicated, one will want to learn throughout one's life. One will see that one has to begin learning in the right way only when one is no longer young, whereas people nowadays think that when one's youth is behind one there is nothing more to learn. In this way even the greatest and noblest fruits of art, of the great writers and poets of mankind, are lost. We would approach them most fruitfully if we were to take up these works again in old age. When people read Goethe's *Iphigenia* or Schiller's *Tell*, they usually think: We've already read that at school. But this is not right, for it should not be forgotten that these works have the greatest effect on us when we read them in old age; for it is then that they promote justice and wisdom.

Again, the education of children will be particularly fruitful if the virtue of courage and the virtue of temperance are seen in the right light. When it is a case of educating children, these virtues must be viewed in an individual way, in that children are again and again shown that they are to take hold of life in a good-hearted way, that they should not be afraid of everything or withdraw from all manner of situations, and that they embrace life with circumspection and moderation in order gradually to free themselves from their passions. An immense amount can be done for the education of children in this way. These things will be explained further as we proceed in our spiritual-scientific studies.

So you see that the laws in moral life which otherwise only apply to the outward, physical plane, to the life between birth and death, extend through spiritual-scientific observations to an endlessly wide horizon. The situation here is the same as it is in other areas of spiritual science. And yet humanity has also had to experience an extension of its horizons with respect to natural science. Giordano Bruno[5] pointed out that there is not only one earthly life but that there are many earthly lives. Before Giordano Bruno people believed that there is a fixed boundary up in the sky. He made them aware that this is not so, that the blue of the sky does not constitute a limit.

Spiritual science shows that birth and death are as such not really there at all and that we introduce them into life through the limitations of our understanding.

Thus the gulf between the physical and the spiritual can be spanned; and for those who establish a real, true monism, the things that have their foundation in spiritual science have a real existence. It may often happen that those who call themselves monists make their monism very simple. They take one part of the world and make it into a single entity by getting rid of the other half of the world. True monism comes about through allowing both halves to intermingle in a meaningful way. This happens through spiritual science—but not only that this impresses itself on our consciousness but arises for the whole of our life. We must increasingly come to the real knowledge as we look into the world that in what is around us, in everything that lives and is active everywhere, there is something supersensible, not only in what our eye beholds but also in what our reasoning powers that are bound to the brain perceive. There are spiritual forces everywhere, behind every phenomenon, behind the phenomenon of the rainbow, behind the movement of our hand, and so on.

If you read the cycle of lectures that I gave at the turn of the previous year in Leipzig,[6] you will find how the Christ impulse worked through the Mystery of Golgotha, how Christ lives in the most important affairs of humanity and not only in what people have consciously known about. There have, for example, been quarrels about dogmas; but while people were arguing, the Christ impulse was living through everything and bringing about what needed to happen.

Let us take the figure of the Maid of Orleans.[7] This simple shepherd girl makes her appearance in European history. She appears in a remarkable way in that in her soul there live not only those forces that otherwise live within a person but that the Christ impulse is working in this personality, enlivening and sustaining her through its mighty influence. She became a kind of representative of the Christ impulse itself for her time. This she could only do because the Christ impulse had entered into her being.

You know that we celebrate Christmas at the time when the power of the Sun is at its least, in the deepest darkness of winter, because we can be convinced that at this time the inner light, the spiritual light, has the greatest intensity.

Old legends tell us that over Christmas up to the sixth of January people have had special experiences, because at this time earthly life and the inner forces of the Earth are at their most concentrated. Those who have the right disposition for this then indeed experience spiritual forces within the earthly forces. Countless legends tell of this. The best time for this is the thirteen days before the sixth of January.

The Maid of Orleans spent these thirteen days in a particular state, whereby her feeling life was not receptive to the outer world. Remarkably, the time when the Maid of Orleans was carried in her mother's womb came to an end in the Christmas period of 1411. She was born on the sixth of January, after she had spent the last thirteen days in her mother's body. Before she drew her first breath, before she saw the physical light with her physical eye, she experienced the earthly realm during the thirteen days in the sleep through which a person passes before he enters the physical world.

I am indicating something of the greatest significance that shows how the world is ruled from out of the domain of spirit, how what happens outwardly in the physical world is given its direction by the spiritual world, how the spiritual world is flowing amidst physical realities.

Thus in our present time we must ever more consciously remove the gulf between the physical and the spiritual through spiritual science. We do this in one realm of our lives when we become conscious that there are within our movement the forces of those who in the course of their earthly lives have united their soul and body with our movement and have passed through the portal of death. If we look across to the other bank of the stream where they are active and, feeling ourselves united with them, direct our thoughts towards them, we do this in full consciousness, the consciousness that we gain through spiritual science. We know ourselves to be in living connection with those who have passed through the gate of death, and we know them as the best forces among us. When we are able to do or to think this, we are regarding life as a field that is to be sown. Between what we ourselves plant, we see springing up everywhere plants that we could not have grown ourselves. And we can then know that these plants have been put there by those to whom it has been granted to be in the world of spirit, those with whom we feel ourselves to be connected, those with whom we become one.

It will be the characteristic sign of this movement, and of those who feel themselves to be members of it and reckon themselves as belonging to it in future, to be in fellowship also with those who are no longer the bearers of a physical body. Other societies founded only upon earthly things will remove many barriers between one person and another. The barriers between the living and the dead will increasingly be removed by the movement that will unite those people who want to be united in the sign of spiritual science. We all want to carry this in our souls and retain as a lasting experience the characteristic quality which unites us with this spiritual movement that has become dear to us.

[During the war-years the following commemorative words were spoken by Rudolf Steiner before every lecture that he gave to members of the Anthroposophical Society in the countries affected by the war.]

The first thoughts that we have as we meet together in our groups shall be directed towards the guarding spirits of those who are out on the battlefields, where they have to serve the great obligations of the time with their blood and soul-forces. We want to direct our pleas to the guarding spirits of these souls, in order that what we contribute through our petitioning love can ray out and unite with the power of the spirits guarding these souls on the fields of battle.

Spirits watching over your souls,
May thy wings bring
Our petitioning love
To the human beings on Earth entrusted to thy care,
That, united with thy power,
Our plea may radiate help
To the souls
Whom we seek lovingly to reach.

And for those who have already passed through the gate of death:

Spirits watching over your souls,
May thy wings bring
Our petitioning love
To the human beings in the heavenly spheres entrusted to thy care,
That, united with thy power,
Our plea may radiate help
To the souls
Whom we seek lovingly to reach.

And may the Spirit whom we have sought through the years of our striving enable the power that He carried through the Mystery of Golgotha to ray forth to thee, so that thou might have strength for the fulfilment of what the great obligations of mankind demand from thee. May the Spirit who passed through the Mystery of Golgotha, may the Spirit of Christ be with thee!*

---

*In these verses and the accompanying words, a distinction is drawn between words addressed to human beings and souls and words addressed to their guarding spirits through the use, respectively, of 'your' and 'thy', 'thee' or 'thou'. (Translator)

Lecture 2

HANOVER, 19 FEBRUARY 1915

The Passing of a Human Being through the Gate of Death—a Transformation of Life

IT is a time when man's connection with the spiritual world—that world which he enters when he crosses the threshold of death—comes to our awareness with great frequency through the many deaths occurring on a daily basis. Moreover, this rapid succession of almost simultaneous deaths is occurring under quite particular circumstances. This is because many earthly human beings are passing through the gate of death who under the conditions that ordinarily apply to human individuals would otherwise be able to live on this Earth for several decades; and whenever people die prematurely this also gives rise to circumstances of an extraordinary nature.

We know that when a person passes through the gate of death, he leaves behind, gives over to the earthly element, what falls away from him in the form of his physical body. We know that the so-called etheric body is the second element to be considered, but that this too separates from the individuality composed of the astral body and ego which passes through the spiritual realms between death and a new birth; that this etheric body continues to work further, separated from the ego and astral body. As it enters the spiritual world immediately adjoining our own, a world that we have often referred to as the etheric world, this etheric body can be thought of as manifesting itself differently in the case of someone who passes prematurely through the gate of death from the way it does with someone who has lived to a ripe old age; for an etheric body which has to pass through the gate of death where someone has died prematurely would under normal circumstances have had the strength to imbue the physical body with life for many years and even several decades. Now in the spiritual world, energies are lost just as little as they are in the physical world. This strength that otherwise imbues the physical body with life continues to exist. So we can say: If thousands are now passing through the gate of death virtually every day, etheric bodies are entering the elemental world which are still viable, which have within them different forces from etheric bodies that have become older. What happens now with these still viable etheric bodies?

Yesterday in the public lecture[8] I spoke of the Folk-soul, who is an actual being. In our time it needs quite particular forces. It needs such forces also at other times, of course, but quite especially in our time. This Folk-soul still receives these viable etheric bodies. The human being himself pursues different paths through his ego and astral body—those paths which will then prepare him for his next earthly life. But these etheric bodies separate from the human individualities, they pass over into the essential nature, the substance of the Folk-souls. Thus after such a destiny-laden time as we are now living through, we are approaching a time when the Folk-soul has within it—as living forces residing in it—the etheric bodies that have been made available to it by those who have crossed the threshold of death in battle. Thus a time is drawing near when the spiritual scientist can know that what has been sacrificed by way of etheric bodies on the altar of the great events of the time has not been lost. A time is drawing near when from the Folk-soul an effective force streams forth into the individual souls from whom at the same time proceeds what numerous human beings have received here on Earth in the first, second and third decades of their youth, what they would otherwise have been able to retain for many decades but have given over to the Folk-soul. This will in future be in the forces that the Folk-soul infuses into individual souls; and it has not been lost.

Let us take this rightly into our hearts. Let us think how our awareness of the connection with the spiritual world can be enlivened in our hearts when we record the fact that one will in future be able to speak of the Folk-soul in such a way that the fruits of sacrificial deaths reside within it as effective forces. This will be particularly important in the near future. At other times it would be different, but for the near future it will be significant for a quite particular reason.

We have been living in a dire period of materialism. Souls that have not been able to approach spiritual science have, as it were, been plunged into a strong aura of materialism. It will in the coming times be the task of the Folk-soul to combat this aura. Forces for combating materialism will flow to this Folk-soul through the fact that the etheric bodies of those who have died prematurely live on in this Folk-soul, thus making such forces available. These etheric bodies sacrificed on the altar of human evolution will be the most powerful adversaries of materialism.

Thus we must distinguish between what passes as an individual human being through the expanses of the spiritual world and remains united with the human individuality and what is channelled through the etheric body to the universal whole, what in the sense referred to here works further in the spiritual totality in the substance of the Folk-spirits.

This can make a particularly deep impression on our feeling-life if we consider two types of human beings with regard to this spiritual difference: the soldier fallen in battle, who goes through the gate of death devoted to the task of his people—who at the moment when he enters the field of battle, when he merely makes the resolve to do so, must in a certain sense also be deciding to look death in the eye—and, in comparison, the ascetic. One gains some idea of the difference between the soldier who has fallen in battle and the ascetic if one considers what the forces of the etheric body signify in human life.

The ascetic works upon himself. He tries to work upon himself in such a way that he completely overcomes his physical nature as such, that he becomes free from this physicality even during his lifetime. Because of the work that the ascetic does in this regard, a significant transformation also takes place in his etheric body. One could say that he uses the forces of this etheric body in the strongest way in order to incorporate it in his ego and his astral body. What makes the ascetic free from his physicality stands the individuality in good stead; it serves the transformation of the individuality. Thus a person who becomes an ascetic can only serve humanity by way of what he makes of himself. However, someone who makes himself free from the physical body in early youth by giving himself up to military demands gives the forces of his etheric body over to the general whole; he incorporates it in influences of a universal nature. One must feel this difference; it is a significant difference. It points us in some small degree towards what holds sway as a reality in human life; and it is, moreover, also significant to look retrospectively at what the etheric body is, at the passage through the gate of death.

In the moment when someone crosses the threshold of death, he is still united with his etheric body. We have often described what happens with it. This state of union with the etheric body gives a person the possibility of living so rightly in all the mental images which the life that is past has kindled within him as wholly to be absorbed as in a mighty tableau in all that this last life has given him. But this is a vision that lasts a relatively short time and fades with the separation of the etheric body from the ego and astral body. One can indeed say that the fading process begins immediately after the moment of death, a tendency for the impressions that derive from the possession of an etheric body to become ever weaker; and there then makes itself felt what is of particular importance after physical death.

Those who want to form ideas about life after death will only to a very small degree gain a right conception of this. It is even difficult to find words for those conditions which are so different in nature from those experienced in the physical body. People readily believe that, once someone has passed through the gate of death, he would first have to acquire a consciousness again. But this is not so. What he experiences when he crosses the threshold of death is not a lack of consciousness. With death it turns out that there is not a lack of consciousness but the exact opposite. There is a too-muchness, an over-abundance of consciousness when death comes about. One lives and weaves wholly within consciousness, and just as strong sunlight causes the eyes to shield themselves, so is one initially numbed by consciousness, one has too much of it. This consciousness must be dampened down in order that one can orient oneself in the life that one has embarked upon after death. This lasts for quite some time, in that it gradually happens that after death there are more and more moments when consciousness makes such an orientation possible; that the soul comes to itself for a short time and then enters into a kind of sleep-like state, as one might describe it. Such moments then become ever longer, the soul increasingly becomes accustomed to such conditions until there is a complete orientation in the spiritual world.

This also causes difficulties in forming clear ideas of the way that the person who has passed through the gate of death perceives his surroundings. In the last few weeks we have cremated a dear anthroposophical friend, and it was the wish of the person who has now died that I took on the task of celebrating a committal festival at the place where she died for her assembled friends. In the time when I was speaking and my words had been directed to the dead person, she was as though sleeping. Then the heat took effect, the flames, as it were, took hold of the body, and at this instant a moment of consciousness came over the soul, as a moment of orientation; and the dead person then had the whole picture of what the funeral and the funeral address consisted of before her, as one has something of a spatial nature simultaneously before one. Time indeed becomes space. One sees the past not as in life one sees the past elapsing in time but one sees what is past before one as a spatial phenomenon. So that what had already run its course, had happened, say, a quarter of an hour before, then stood before the soul of the deceased person as a first moment of enlightenment of her consciousness. Then again a state of stupefaction came to pervade the flooding light of consciousness, in order in this state to reach towards those other states in which the soul gradually learns to orientate itself in the spiritual world.

It is important if we want to form good conceptions about the life after death that we keep these wholly different ideas of time in mind; that we see that time there is not something of which one can say that it has elapsed and one recalls the things that happened in time, but what has elapsed is there before one. Just as the table stands there and this table does not go with me when I go and look back at it, so after death does what has happened, what can only be remembered, stand there, and the dead person looks back at it as in the body one looks back at spatial objects. It is very important to bear this in mind. Something further of quite particular importance that needs to be considered is that we remain in connection, our earthly life retains a connection, with what we afterwards experience between death and a new birth; at any rate it remains in close connection until the point of time that is referred to in the last Mystery Play[9] as the midnight hour.

It would be remiss of me not gradually to give our friends some idea of these conditions which are difficult to describe. The soul that has crossed the threshold of death looks upon what we as earthly human beings have experienced between birth and death—but not as if what one experienced then were simply there but much of the state of being of the dead person also exerts an influence in a particular way. The state of being of a dead person is not like that of someone living between birth and death. The state of being of someone living between birth and death is such that he feels himself enclosed within his skin and looks out at the world through his senses. As soon as one enters the spiritual world as a dead person, one flows out into the whole of the spiritual world. One gradually feels oneself filling the whole spiritual world. And what one has experienced during physical Earth-existence one senses to be something that continues to belong to one—not, of course, as a physical body but as what constitutes the form, the forces of the physical body. This one retains after death, but in such a way as the human eye inhabits the physical body. Just as one has the eye for seeing, so does one have oneself, the earthly life that one has lived through, as a cosmic sense-organ in order to perceive the world. What our eye is now for our body, our earthly life is for our spiritual life after death.

Our earthly life is used as an eye, a sense-organ. You will through lengthy meditation gradually come to realize how significant it is to say that our earthly life becomes a sense-organ for our life between death and a new birth. When a person's ego and astral body leave his physical and etheric bodies as he goes to sleep, a similar situation also pertains. When initiation occurs and he is enabled to behold the spiritual world outside his physical and etheric body, he knows: in the spiritual world you perceive as through a sense-organ with the spiritual part of your physical body, and you think in the spiritual world with your etheric body. Your etheric body is actually like your brain in the spiritual world and your former physical body is a sense-organ. But you yourself are with all your life-forces spread out over the spiritual worlds. You have spread yourself out; you do not feel yourself to be concentrated by your skin in one place, you feel yourself poured forth, spread out over the spiritual world.

It is an entirely different existence. And to it belongs the fact that someone who himself enters the spiritual world, whether through death or through initiation, lives in a state of union with the other beings of the spiritual world, with beings of higher hierarchies or with human souls who are living between death and a new birth, in such a way that he does not experience them as one outwardly meets earthly human beings, where one is spatially separated from them. Rather does he experience them as being with him in a common spirit-realm, in a state of mutual interpenetration. What another soul experiences one learns about not through this soul saying something to one, as with earthly human beings, but through one's living into the other soul and experiencing its thoughts as it experiences them. Hence it is also the case that one can only be sure of really experiencing what, for example, a dead person is experiencing when one knows that one is, so to speak, within the one who has died, one is not merely giving an account of something that one apprehends from the model of something or other that one experiences on the Earth but one is aware: the dead person himself is speaking through your being.

I should also like to explain this by means of an example.[10] One of our members recently died. Already before the cremation there was felt to be the need to apprehend what this personality had to say after death. This came about through the links that she formed with her etheric body and her capacity to express herself in, as it were, an earthly form through her etheric body, while nevertheless everything was brought together that had been interwoven with her soul through an intensive experiencing of the anthroposophical conception of the world. Thus we have to do with a personality who had reached a good old age, and who in the last part of her life had been committed really intensively and with all the forces of her heart to our spiritual-scientific view of the world. Then she passed through the gate of death. She therefore still had her etheric body.

It was still before the cremation, and the etheric body was still there as a means of expression. This gave the possibility that she could still express herself through earthly words, because the etheric body was able to have an after-experience of them. And this liberation from the body, from Earth-existence, at the same time gave the possibility of bringing together the whole being which through the heart had been engraved in the soul. And as I was shown how this personality who had passed through the gate of death wanted to express her being (approximately on the second day after her death had occurred), the words were formed that I can impart to you, words that are to be seen as words experienced by the deceased person. So that one has to imagine that here, on the second day after the death, this being of the soul that had passed through the gate of death was filled with the power of these words. And if one put oneself in the place of the soul, this being of the dead person expressed itself through one in these words. Hence I could do no better than to address these words to the dead person at the funeral, for these were the words that she herself, so to speak, spoke to the friends that stood around her earthly remains. I can give you the assurance that I have added nothing to these words, but I have tried to regard them as coming from the being of the deceased. To be sure, later there ensues what I have called the numbing or stupefying of consciousness, which one could call a state of sleep. The dead person would now not have been able to bring this being of hers to expression, because she now lacks the means of the etheric body. She will be able to do so after some time, but not immediately after death. These are the words:

In world expanses I will to bear
My feeling heart, that warm it may become
In the fire of the working of holy forces;

In world thoughts I will to weave
My own thinking, that clear it may become
In the light of the eternal life-in-becoming;

In soul-foundations I will to immerse
The sense of what has been, that strong it may become
For true aims of human working;

In God's peace I so aspire
'Midst life's struggles and concerns,
My self for the higher self preparing;

Striving for peace in joyous work,
Sensing world-being in my own being,
I would fulfil man's highest duty;

May I live expectantly in the light
Of my destiny's star, that grants me
The place in the realm of spirit.

This is, as it were, the result of many years' absorption in the world-view of spiritual science. This long absorption in the spiritual-scientific world-conception has become the essential nature of the soul itself and has expressed itself in this way.

It is a clear, vivid example of how the forces of the soul are really taken hold of when one does not merely take up spiritual science in a theoretical way but transforms it into life-forces within the soul. Then the feelings and sensations that come from the spiritual-scientific world-conception go beyond something of a theoretical nature and themselves become forces within the soul. Then one can be quite certain that no one who has not become acquainted with the world-conception of spiritual science would bring his own being to expression after death in words such as these:

In world expanses I will to bear
My feeling heart, that warm it may become
In the fire of the working of holy forces;

In world thoughts I will to weave
My own thinking, that clear it may become
In the light of the eternal life-in-becoming.

I should like to place this before your souls as a clear example of the mysterious course that the human soul takes through the point of time that separates life between birth and death from the life between death and a new birth, where in a sense everything that was for us in earthly life still an outward experience becomes an inner richness of the soul and thus lives within us. Here one still receives spiritual science as something of an outward nature. Directly after death, however, it manifests itself in the soul in the way that, say, the strength of a muscle now lives in our physical body. One must have some feeling of this if one is wanting rightly to grasp the inner meaning, the inner significance of what spiritual science can be for the human soul. One will then gradually—and for this one needs to have patience—form for oneself a concept of the totally different circumstances that pertain in the spiritual world. Whereas we formulate words and concepts for the circumstances that exist in the sense-world, we can at best give symbols for what is in the spiritual world. One must patiently work towards developing concepts and feelings that to some extent rightly and truly express the circumstances prevailing in the world of spirit.

The logic of earthly life—and indeed, it is only a logic of earthly life—is even for earthly life sometimes thoroughly unreliable. I have already spoken here of how with the logic of earthly life one can miss, fail to recognize real facts. I have often given the following example: Suppose that someone is walking beside a river. We see that he falls into it. We hurry up and discover that he is already dead. We see a stone at the place where the person fell into the river, and can now form a perfectly logical, but nevertheless superficial judgement. We can say: He stumbled over the stone, fell into the river and drowned. Drowning was the cause of his death. But this may be completely wrong. If one investigates the matter purely anatomically, it may turn out that the person had a heart attack and fell into the water as a result of that. The heart attack would then be the cause of his death. With ordinary, correct logic we arrive at the opposite conclusion. Such conclusions—this should be observed merely in passing—are continually drawn in human life and especially in science. Science is full of such conclusions, where cause and effect are confused.

But all this becomes important when questions of human destiny are concerned. In the autumn we experienced a blow of fate in Dornach which is instructive in the most significant sense. The little seven-year-old son of one of our members, Theo Faiß,[11] who was a very lovable, wide-awake child, went missing one evening. It was on an evening when there was a lecture. The mother went looking for the child, but he was not to be found. It was first heard that the mother was searching for the boy when the lecture was over, and the only thing that people could think was that the boy's death was connected with the accident of a furniture van. A member of our Society had dispatched her furniture in a van, and in the evening this van had overturned on the spot where it was found. It was 10.15 pm and we made every possible effort to lift the van. Members of the military services came to help us lift this van; and when this was done the boy was found crushed underneath it. Now imagine, there has never been a furniture van in this area before, and there have been none since. All possible investigations enabled one to establish that the boy had been at the very spot—it must have been a question of minutes or even a single moment—when the van overturned. It was at any rate remarkable that those who were at the place where the van had overturned had initially only thought of the safety of the horses. No one had any idea that the furniture van had fallen on the little boy.

So the child was dead. According to the outward materialistic view, it was purely by chance that the van had overturned at this moment when the child came by and was crushed. This is what the materialistic view will say. From the spiritual perspective this is complete nonsense. For what is of concern here is the karma of the child, and this karma of the child guided all the various circumstances. It had guided the furniture van there at the moment when the child needed to die, because the child's karma wished it so. The karma of the child had run its course. We have here to do with the need to reverse cause and effect.

Through such circumstances and their perception one can gradually find one's way to a real conception of life that brings us to the point of reversing what outer appearances present to us. We must do this many times over. But the situation becomes especially significant if afterwards there is an experience of what arises from such a circumstance. The soul of a human being passes through the gate of death. This soul had incarnated for seven years in a physical body. Why would little Theo not have been able to live for seventy, eighty or ninety years, when viewed outwardly, if karma had not made it impossible? He had an etheric body that could have supported life for decades; an etheric body that was indeed full of forces of the eternal, of the good. He was a boy with outstanding qualities.

As you know, the actual individuality, the ego and astral body, continues on its own path. But the etheric body separates out, this etheric body into which are woven all the beautiful, tender forces that have developed in the age of childhood but in which also live all the forces that come from former incarnations. Now consider what one has before one with such an etheric body. The individuality comes from former incarnations. It embodies itself in this incarnation; it brings with it what comes from former incarnations. The life in this incarnation is in a certain sense the fruit, the realization of what resided as a cause in former incarnations. These fruits would then have been able to come to fulfilment throughout the present life. Everything that derives from the fruits of former incarnations would then have passed into this etheric body. This did not happen. Thus in this etheric body everything that exists by way of causes in the former incarnations finds its place.

And what is most remarkable is this: anyone who tries to investigate the aura of our building in Dornach will find this etheric body of little Theo in the aura of this building. It is there, it hovers around and surrounds the building in Dornach with its life. Anyone who has something to do with the building or will have something to do with it since that late autumnal afternoon when little Theo crossed the threshold of death knows what was changed in the spiritual aura of the Dornach building because in this aura there has been assimilated that etheric body which contains the forces that would otherwise have been used for the sustenance of a physical human body for several decades, and this etheric body has flowed forth into this aura of the building.

So mysterious are the paths that the wisdom flowing through the world has to traverse with its creatures. The only right conceptions of the way that human life as a whole takes its course—and this eminently includes the life between death and a new birth—are those that enter into the details of these things. And since our anthroposophical movement should not be abstract in any way but should be something in which we, and also those that belong to us, are involved with our whole being, it may also be possible to speak about such things. Unlike other societies, we do not ally ourselves only with a particular programme, but we want to be engaged in our spiritual-scientific movement with our entire soul. We want to think of this spiritual-scientific movement as an actual stream to which each person belongs who really adheres to it with all his feelings. Thus we can say that we speak as one speaks here and there in an extended family about those belonging to it; for what touches us in a familiarly intimate way at the same time gives us the highest, most significant and—for us—the most important information about the spiritual world.

Out of such a mood I should like to mention another of the many deaths of our friends that have occurred in recent times. Fritz Mitscher,[12] who was an infinitely dear friend of all of us, passed through the gate of death not long ago. And it turned out that the necessity arose for me to formulate in words what my own soul felt as it inclined towards the soul that had just crossed the threshold of death. Notice the difference between the previous words that I read out to you and the words that I now want to recite. The words that I have just read to you derived from the soul of the deceased person. The words that I shall now share with you were stirred within my own soul on beholding in a soul sense the dead person, Fritz Mitscher, still united with his etheric body. It is, therefore, the impression that the dead person made which is now communicated in these words. You may perhaps know that Fritz Mitscher was already active on behalf of our Anthroposophical Society as a young teacher in many different places, especially in Berlin. And many of us also know how it was in so beautiful a way his will to connect what he had been able to acquire of knowledge and learning of the Earth with the noblest and most exemplary anthroposophical awareness. This expresses itself also after death, when in his entire being there is united what he was and what now radiates after death from his soul in its body-free state but still united with its etheric body. And it seems to me that what Fritz Mitscher was after death had to be expressed with the words that I felt obliged to send to him at the cremation.

As a hope that gladdens us,
So do you venture upon the field
Where spirit-blossoms of the Earth
Would, through the power of soul-being,
Manifest themselves to the questing spirit.

Your longing had its deep affinity
With a pure love of truth;
The goal to which you tirelessly
Aspired throughout your life
Was creation from the spirit-light.

You cultivated your fine gifts
To follow with sure step
The radiant path of spirit-knowledge,
Unswayed by outward opposition
As a true servant of the truth.

Your spirit-organs you enhanced,
That they boldly and persistently
Thrust error from you
To both sides of the path
And create for you a realm of truth.

To fashion your self that it reveal
The purity of light,
That the Sun-power of the soul
Might radiate its strength within you,
Was your concern and joy.

Other cares, other joys,
They barely touched your soul,
For knowledge, as the light that
To existence meaning gives,
Held for you life's truest worth.

As a hope that gladdens us,
So do you venture upon the field
Where spirit-blossoms of the Earth
Would, through the power of soul-being,
Manifest themselves to the questing spirit.

A loss that deeply us aggrieves,
So do you vanish from the field
Where earthly seeds of spirit
Have matured for your senses' spheres
In the womb of soul-being.

Feel how we look lovingly
Up to the heights that called you now
Away for other creating.
Extend your strength from realms of spirit
To the friends you've left behind.

Hear the entreaty of our souls,
Sent to you in confidence:
We need here for earthly work
Strong power from spirit-lands
Which to our dead friends we owe.

As a hope that gladdens us,
A loss that deeply us aggrieves:
Let us hope that from far and near,
Unforsaken for our life,
You shine as starry soul in spirit-realms.

These are the words that were sent from the one who had died to the being of this deceased person. And then some time passed after these words were spoken at the cremation. And from the being of the person who had died, sounding forth not as yet from a well-ordered consciousness but as from his essential nature, the following words could be heard; words that therefore now resounded from the one who had died in the night following the cremation.

To fashion my self that it reveal
The purity of light,

That the Sun-power of the soul
Might radiate its strength within me,
Was my concern and joy.

Other cares, other joys,
They barely touched my soul,
For knowledge, as the light that
To existence meaning gives,
Held for me life's truest worth.

Thus did the words resound. I had afterwards discovered that the two verses had been directly transmuted from 'you' or 'your' to 'me' or 'my'. I had not been aware of this before; for I had heard the verses as I first read them to you. And now they came back from the being of the person who had died, spoken by him.

To fashion my self that it reveal
The purity of light,
That the Sun-power of the soul
Might radiate its strength within me,
Was my concern and joy.

Other cares, other joys,
They barely touched my soul,
For knowledge, as the light that
To existence meaning gives
Held for me life's truest worth.

This shows that, also at the time when consciousness does not yet have the form that it has after this time from the soul throughout the period between death and a new birth, the words that are addressed to the dead person come livingly and meaningfully transformed. One must merely feel the extent to which the spiritual-scientific world-conception becomes truly alive in forming connections between the physical and spiritual worlds. For a sense of consternation may well pass through our soul if we feel through such an example that the words are addressed to the dead person—and he repeats them back to us unchanged. But our feeling is that, on the one hand, they have reached the dead person, because they have resounded back from him—though not as an echo but changed in a meaningful way.

These are things that give us the assurance, the confidence also for our present time that the souls that live here in earthly bodies have a connection with the spiritual powers working and weaving through the world, and that the earthly souls of human beings that have passed through death are interwoven with this stream of spiritual powers wherein they experience their further destiny after they have died.

If we allow the connection of the physical world with the spiritual world rightly to exert its influence upon our hearts and minds, we can indeed extend our consideration to other things. I have on a previous occasion indicated also here that in this interaction, this quite specific interplay between the physical and spiritual worlds, we find ourselves drawn quite especially towards the impulse of the Mystery of Golgotha. We well know that it is only really now that we are through spiritual science beginning fully to take into account the meaning and significance of the Mystery of Golgotha and of the Christ Being. Hitherto people have done this, and rightly, with their reasoning powers. And what has emerged from this? Well, if the influence of Christ in the earthly life of human beings had been dependent upon what they have understood of it, the influence of the Christ impulse on Earth can hardly be very great. Theological quarrelling and all manner of arguments have characterized people's understanding of Christianity. But Christ has worked out of a living power.

I have also previously referred here to the example of the battle that Constantine waged against Maxentius,[13] through which the destiny of Europe at that time was decided. With this, Christianity was first really recognized and then became the ruling power in Europe. This battle was not won through military tactics or through the armies of Constantine. Maxentius had Rome to defend. Through consulting the books of the Sybils and through a dream that he had had, he had been led to believe that his army, which was five times stronger than that of Constantine (who was marching against Rome), was to be led by him out of Rome; he would then annihilate Rome's enemies. He indeed led his army out of Rome, strategically the most inept thing that he could have done, for from a strategical point of view everything was in favour of leaving his army in Rome and letting the enemy armies approach; but he led his army out of Rome. As for Constantine, who was leading his armies against Rome, what gave him his power was not technical skill of a military nature but, rather, a dream that he had had. The dream's message was: if you let Christ's monogram go at the head of our army, you will conquer Rome. As a result of Constantine's victory with his weak army, the whole map of Europe was transformed at that time and for future times. The cultural life of Europe thereby also became different. What people in those days were able to fathom of all this would not have sufficed to accomplish what was achieved. The Christ impulse was working into the subconscious regions of human beings, into what lived in the depths of people's souls, of which they could only dream in the dream-pictures that sprang up before them.

We have a later and highly significant example of the influence of the Christ impulse in the Maid of Orleans. Anyone who really studies history—that is, not in the way that history is often studied today but through trying to recognize the actual connections—can know that again through what the Maid of Orleans did the destiny of Europe was defined in an absolute sense for the next few centuries; for what was decisive for this destiny of Europe, and especially that of France, was not military strategy or the wisdom of politicians but the deeds of the shepherdess of Orleans, in whom the Christ impulse was working through His representative, Michael. Her soul was wholly imbued with and inspired by the Christ impulse. Just as the Christ impulse was an active force when the battle between Constantine and Maxentius was decided, without people being consciously aware of this, so was the Christ impulse also a contributory factor when the Maid of Orleans sent the French armies to meet the English armies. The whole continent of Europe—including England—would have taken a different course if France had not been victorious then. England, too, would not have been what it became if it had not been defeated. But as said, what brought the victory about were the subconscious forces that manifested themselves in visions; and the abilities of the Maid of Orleans were inspired by them. Thus one can say: What the Maid of Orleans did stands under the influence of an initiation that was more or less unconscious. A pure soul-vessel—such as the Maid of Orleans was—through which the Christ impulse could work through His Michaelic representative had to be unconsciously taken hold of and encompassed.

Let us look more closely at what is involved here. When someone today consciously undergoes an initiation, there are rules for this. The rudiments of this are explained in my book *Knowledge of the Higher Worlds: How is it Achieved?* There are rules through which one can gradually make progress in this respect. The initiation of the Maid of Orleans could not, of course, have been of this kind; but a spirit not otherwise united with the human soul must have taken up its abode in this human soul and pervaded it. For this to happen there would have to have been particularly favourable circumstances. It is not always that a spirit of higher spheres can exert such an influence upon souls that have the capacity for this. Particularly favourable circumstances must be in place in order that an individual human soul may without initiation, without special work, come into connection with higher worlds. Such circumstances are present in the time when the spirit of the Earth wakes up, as it were: in the time from 25 December until 6 January. When in summer the Sun is at its highest, when the physical warmth of the Earth rays out to the greatest extent, the conditions for initiation are most unfavourable, because then the spirit of the Earth is asleep. The spirit of the Earth is most wakeful in the darkness of winter, at the winter solstice.

Hence it is no mere legend but corresponds to a truth when it is related in old legends that in the thirteen nights preceding the sixth of January certain especially suitable souls were initiated, so that they were able to enter the spiritual world, so that they were able to experience there what we call Kamaloka and Devachan. We may well recall the recitation here in Hanover of the legend of Olaf Åsteson,[14] who in the thirteen nights traversed in sleep the whole path that can constitute the path through Kamaloka and Devachan. Olaf Åsteson then relates what he has experienced in these thirteen days.

When, therefore, outward physical earthly darkness is at its strongest, the circumstances are most favourable for leading a soul into the spiritual world. For souls that are initiated—not through directly conscious work but through particularly favourable circumstances—for a deed on behalf of humanity as a whole such as the Maid of Orleans accomplished, it would therefore have been most favourable if she could have been able to sleep in the thirteen nights, and moreover in connection with the spiritual world; thus if she could have undergone all this in a kind of sleeping condition.

Now it is indeed so that the Maid of Orleans passed through such a state of sleep. This was because the Maid of Orleans spent these thirteen days until 6 January in her mother's body in a state where a person is still asleep; for a human individual only awakes to physical life when he has been born and takes his first breath. In the Maid of Orleans's case the last nights of sleep during the embryonic state fell in the time of the thirteen nights, for she was born on 6 January. Here you have the foundation of the mission of the Maid of Orleans, to whom it was given—as this pure soul before her first breath in the last thirteen nights of her mother's pregnancy—to receive initiation in this state of sleep, in the particularly favourable circumstances of earthly life. The calendar makes this perfectly plain; for if you open up a calendar you will find that on 6 January the Maid of Orleans has her birthday. Thus the calendar shows that a deeply inward connection exists between the physical and spiritual worlds. It was of course necessary for the soul of the Maid of Orleans to be prepared through its previous incarnations. But as in the thirteen nights this soul met with what was able to come through it, what ensued historically occurred in order at this point in the evolution of mankind to make the intervention of the spiritual world into the physical world possible.

Thus the spiritual world is always there with all its various aspects. The spiritual world is always among us; and the ways that the spiritual world seeks out in order to exert an influence in the physical world are many and various in nature. Our awareness of the connection with the spiritual world becomes ever stronger the more in such instances we give expression with a particular depth to the connections between the physical and spiritual world, in that such connections remain livingly in our soul.

On the other hand one must say that what happens here in the physical world can also serve as preparation for the nature of the connection between the spiritual and physical worlds. And if someone who has taken up as intensively as Fritz Mitscher[15] what flows through our spiritual science, and in the thirtieth year of his life passes into the spiritual world—his thirtieth birthday would have been on 26 February—and has impregnated his soul with the power that can pervade it through our spiritual science, we have a mighty individuality who will remain together with us in the spiritual world and who is a helper of the greatest possible stature. And when one calls to mind how difficult the aspiration towards spiritual knowledge is in our time, beset as it is with materialism, it may perhaps also be said that anyone who is connected with the spiritual world with every fibre of his being places the greatest hopes on those who can be spiritual helpers, who become spiritual helpers after laying aside their physical body.

It does of course not need to be said that this crossing of the threshold of death can never be a personal decision, but that it can be brought about only through karma. These spiritual helpers are those who give us hope and consolation, when we see how difficult it becomes precisely at this present time to bring our spiritual-scientific movement through the many hindrances. But we know that higher spiritual forces exert their influence upon the Earth, in order that the stream of the spiritual worlds may contribute to the physical purposes of the Earth. Thus the unused forces of human souls come into the spiritual worlds so that these forces may be active there in conjunction with other forces. Thus it was that I truly called out the following words to our Fritz Mitscher from my innermost heart:

Hear the entreaty of our souls,
Sent to you in confidence:
We need here for earthly work
Strong power from spirit-lands
Which to our dead friends we owe.

Then when in an honest way we try to bring our spiritual movement further towards its goal, we are conscious that the forces that are available to us here on the Earth are supplemented by those which our friends have already borne through the gate of death into the spiritual world.

We can also gather all this together for an understanding of the general world-situation. The human souls who are, because of the fateful events of the time, now passing through the gate of death bear their etheric bodies on the one hand to the Folk-spirits. On the other hand they bear everything that they have summoned up by way of sacrificial devotion, in that through the very nature of these events of the time they have passed through the gate of death with their individuality. And all this will be poured forth as an active influence into the time that is to come.

It will in this respect be dependent upon those people who live through the peace to form out of themselves a connection with what will, as it were, descend from above. Those who as mothers and fathers, as brothers and sisters or relatives of some other kind are today experiencing the decease of those dear to them on the battlefield can receive into their consciousness the fact that with the etheric body something of immense significance for the future passes over into the general affairs of earthly humanity. Not only that they can know that individualities are strengthened and fortified for a subsequent life of greater intensity through a sacrificial death, but they can also know that what the warrior who has passed through the gate of death has transmitted to the Folk-soul is a living reality. Moreover, it should be said that those who have crossed the threshold of death when they are young have fathers and mothers, sisters and brothers engaged with the common Folk-soul and with their individuality.

And this idea will only have significant value when it has wholly become a feeling, so that one will know in one's feelings: the dead are there, they are amongst us—when this bond will be so strong that death actually becomes an untruth also for our feeling. For when he can summon up all his forces and no longer has the hindrances of a physical body, a dead person is often able to manifest himself more truly than in his physical embodiment. Powerful streams of consolation, streams of an inner capacity to bring comfort, emanate from what spiritual science can give to souls in living consciousness and living feelings. Then when this is experienced in this way, especially those who ally themselves with spiritual science can look full of hope towards the future. They can experience these fateful and momentous events as something like the dawn of a time of transition which will be followed by a sun-filled time of peace. But an important part of the spiritual potency of this sun-filled time of peace will be what has been achieved by the sacrificial death of so many.

It will be made fruitful here on Earth especially if a bridge, a link is formed between the living, the souls incarnated here on the Earth in a physical body, and the souls that are above and want to ray down what they have received. And it is here where a real understanding of spiritual science strikes so truly a chord within our heart and calls on us to do what we are able to accomplish out of the awareness that we have gained through spiritual science, what we are able to do and feel in order that the great, destiny-stirring, grief-outpouring events of the present time may, to the extent that it lies within our power, turn out to be fruitful and healing for mankind. Those who know something of spiritual science can feelingly know and knowingly feel how the bridge up to the spiritual world is created: namely, that from souls that have remained below thoughts and feelings are sent which can be kindled through spiritual science. The horizon for this will be a horizon of peace. The souls that will want to send down the spiritual rays of light will be above. There must be people below who have learnt to send up from their souls such thoughts and feelings as are inspired by spiritual science. When there are indeed souls who with an awareness of the spirit direct their minds into the spirit-realm, the time will then have come when, precisely through such fateful and grievous events as are taking place in our time, an intimate bond must be woven between the physical world and the spiritual world to which we aspire through our spiritual science.

So let us summarize what our understanding and our task shall be and what shall awaken our confidence in the words:

> From the courage of the fighters,
> From the blood on fields of battle,
> From the grief of the bereaved,
> From the people's sacrifice:
> There will ripen fruit of spirit,
> If souls will turn in consciousness
> Towards the realm of spirit.
> [Translation by George and Mary Adams]

Lecture 3

BREMEN, 21 FEBRUARY 1915

Spiritual Science and the Riddles of Death—Deeper Connections of European History

In our times, what is referred to in spiritual science as the riddles of death come to our attention in a particularly meaningful way. Everything has either a close or distant connection with them. We receive above all from spiritual science not only the fundamental conviction but the basic knowledge about the world in the physical body and about the world that we enter through the portal of death. But this latter world actually also always livingly surrounds us in our sensory existence, although it is not discernible to someone who is strongly attached to the life of the senses because he is insufficiently attentive to it. When such dramatic events as now surround us are pervading the age that demand such a multitude of sacrifices from human beings, we must engage with them with our whole soul. It is in this respect clearly apparent that there are many things which can be illumined from the standpoint of spiritual science.

We wish to direct our attention to realms of life where it is evident that humanity has through a materialistic way of thinking arrived at a disastrous degree of illogicality with respect to what is going on around it. We hear, for example, the various nations reproaching one another in the manner that is familiar today: I did not want the war, it was you who started it. The question is in itself justified, and it can already now be stated (for the facts speak for themselves) where the outward causes lie.

But someone viewing this from the perspective of spiritual science will see it differently. With regard to this question he must be clear that the war is actually a final phase—or at any rate a later phase—in the course of the events that came before. One also commits an error of judgement in the case of processes of illness, where one often continues to speak of such processes when there are processes of health which need to occur in order to bring healing. The outward processes that ensue in order to paralyse the illness, in order to bring healing, and which have previously taken place, are not noticed. The war also represents an apparent process of illness. It is an endeavour on the part of mankind to reach beyond certain events which preceded it. The sickness resides in the unhealthy relationships of nations with one another. When one investigates outward causes with one's reasoning powers, one overlooks the inner causes.[16]

Where we are as though herded together as in a fortress and surrounded by a ring, there is good cause to raise the question as to the inner reasons or the nature of the sole reason that this encirclement was brought about. People speak of an encirclement in relation to recent years, to the last few decades; but when one considers the wider context one sees that it begins much, much earlier. It may sound strange, but one can identify the year 860—not 1860 but 860. The process that now comes to expression in a manner that one can designate as the most terrible war that humanity has faced since its time on Earth began has lasted as long as this.

In the deeper context of European history one finds the highly remarkable thing that in Central Europe something of the nature of spiritual substance was pressed together; and if one investigates these deeper connections one sees that this was with a particular object in view. It does not have to do with the outer determining factors of blood, of race, but with the fact that something of the nature of a spiritual substance pervades the world. Something draws together in Central Europe as in a snake-like ring that comes down from the extreme North. Two streams from the East and West reach in the form of a ring towards the South and come together again in a similar pattern.

In the ninth century the Norsemen,[17] who are related by blood with so much, move down from a centre which later comes to be in Central Europe. But they invade the Roman element which derives from Southern Europe; they intermingle with it. In 860 they stand before Paris, and the Vikings are overpowered by the Romans. The

Western territory of France owes its origin to this. The Vikings (as Normans) brought more to England from France than the Angles and Saxons were able to bring to the British Isles. In the East the Vikings migrated further,[18] they forced their way down from the North towards the Volga and the Black Sea into Slavic territory. Later the Tartar stream invades. The Slavic element racially overwhelms the Vikings and brings them the Christian religion in its Eastern form. They become slavicized as 'Ros' (this is what they are called in Finland), nothing of which remains other than the name Russia. This name is of Germanic origin. The name Rurik[19] has the same origin.

People have very dubious views about these connections. In the West of Europe many speak of how the French are called to re-enliven the old Celtic world in a kind of renaissance. There is the idea that in Central Europe there are predominantly Germans, whereas the West is the cradle of Celtic culture. But the truth is the reverse of this, in that in the French there is far more German blood and in Central Europe more Celtic blood. Nevertheless the inhabitants of the West are completely overwhelmed by Romanism. In the East the Viking element and, hence, the Germanic heritage are overpowered by a foreign racial element; and a religion that is completely alien to the Russian Folk-soul continues to hold sway there.[20] Thus people in Central Europe are confined within these encircling arcs. The Romans reach as far as Constantinople, as do the slavicized Norsemen. So we have the form of a snake or ring.

When we consider what was spiritually pressed together then, we have the impression that it has a particularly important task. Yesterday I gave an indication of something of which I have spoken elsewhere,[21] that a certain intimate association of the Folk-soul with the individual soul was to take place here and fruits of the fairest kind were to be brought forth within the best of those involved. The ego was to be directly embraced, not the particular soul-members as in the West, the ego was to be directly enlivened. It arises from this—as must already be clear from viewing these things exoterically—that in Central Europe there could never be total hostility towards idealism, that to an intense degree there was always a certain inclination towards the spiritual world.

When we began our spiritual movement,[22] karma disposed that we had initially to work in conjunction with the British movement. But outwardly, everything further was only a symptom of what had to occur with a certain necessity. When we consider what the theosophical movement from which we had to separate ourselves actually is, it will be apparent that cultural life has fallen there into two parts. Outer life takes a purely materialistic course and the spiritual element is added on to it. They always go their separate ways. Contrast with this what our spiritual life must be for us. Just as in the organism the head cannot be thought of without the body, so does our spiritual life grow out of the overall cultural life.

One needs only to begin with Tauler, Eckhardt, Angelus Silesius and then proceed to Herder and Lessing—everywhere we must develop from this what shall become a higher spiritual culture. We cannot simply attach our spiritual outlook to what we find, we must conceive of it as an organism and raise it to such a status. We must inwardly make the discovery that Christ's Second Coming is a spiritual affair. Hence we cannot make even the smallest concession. We can only approach Christ as a figure with the eye of spirit, with an inner experience. In the West He is forced into a materialized mould, made into something dogmatic. People could not but imagine that He would come in the physical body. Hence the grotesque idea[23] of putting Christ publicly on display in the body. This happened in connection with what was circumscribed at that time.

Thus this question must touch us quite objectively: How must Central European culture relate to the culture of the future? Truth is something universal, but how it arises is a different matter. In Central European culture lie the sources for the whole spiritual culture of the future. We must find the path from German idealism to a spiritual culture. To this end it is necessary that here in this central region a culture of the ego is established. On the occult plane this can easily be seen. The human ego must be enkindled by the outer world, since it first awakens and becomes inwardly conscious. Thus the ego-culture of Central Europe is inspired from without. One needs only to observe recent events, the unification of the German nature. It is characteristic that the German Reich was founded in 1871 on foreign soil. So many things could be said that show also in outer events that a culture of the ego holds sway in Central Europe.

It seems appropriate to ask: What significance do sacrificial deaths have for the spiritual world? Countless human beings are passing through the portal of death in the flower of their youth. First the connection between ego, astral body and etheric body separates from the physical body. The physical body is seemingly given over to the Earth, the etheric body to the etheric world, astral body and ego go further on their way. But it must surely occur to us that the relationship that a person has to his etheric body when he passes at a normal age through the gate of death is different from that of those young people who are doing so now. One understands this at the level of the physical body, and one now comes to understand it for the etheric body. It would still have supported the physical body for decades and been able to work upon it. It goes through the gate of death with these unused forces, is united with the Folk-soul; and the work of the Folk-soul will in future be impregnated with the unused forces of these etheric bodies. It is up to us to have an understanding of this.

There will be people who will know that the Folk-soul is an active element. Only if one knows that unspent forces of etheric bodies will work as a spiritual power in a quite specific way in the spiritual world can one understand what actually goes on. The awareness of this connection with the spiritual world becomes important. Through the engendering of such an awareness of the spiritual world, spiritual science will increasingly become something living in people's hearts and minds and not remain a mere teaching. A person knows that he is in a spiritual aura, just as he knows here that the air is all around him. Just as he distinguishes here between fresh and stale air, so will be aware of good and evil spirits in experiencing the spiritual aura.

This is indeed the right fruit of spiritual science. We see it when we observe events affecting us that we may find instructive. One such event occurred where our building is located. This concerned a child, the forces of whose etheric body were unspent. For someone to see who knows how to see, the forces have passed into the aura of our Dornach building and live there. This is something for which I can vouch. The etheric body, which as regards its forces belongs more to the commonality, continues to exert a rightful influence. Since then it has tried to do something through inspirations in the vicinity of the building. These are helping forces.

Such things come to our attention; we can let ourselves be instructed by them as to how mysterious the connections are in the spiritual world. In recent times we have had the experience in the karma of our Society that dear friends have through death been taken from us away from the physical plane. What I said in the Vienna cycle about the life between death and a new birth[24] was made very clear to many by these souls. One of these souls has found the way into our movement when the physical body was already worn out. This was a being who, since belonging to our movement, manifested herself to me in her soul-nature through a body that had become translucent. After death the image of the soul that I had formerly known was interwoven with the way that it presented itself afterwards. The following words made themselves audible approximately three days after death had occurred:

You appeared among us,
The moving gentleness of your being
Spoke out of the quiet power of your eyes—
An enlivening peace
Flowed in the waves
With which your gaze
Conveyed the weaving of your inner being
To all things and to other people;
And this being was ensouled by
Your voice, which eloquently,
More through the manner of speaking
Than the words themselves,
Revealed what lay hidden
Within your beautiful soul;
Yet wordlessly they fully revealed
A devoted love
To those attentive to it—
This being who from a quiet, noble beauty
Proclaimed to the receptive
A feeling of world-soul-creativity.

After death there is a dimming of consciousness, because it is being flooded with activity. This happens through the review that is the first thing that occurs after death—not in a case of suicide—as a kind of solar point. It is one of the most beautiful and highest of experiences. One begins by saying: This has been your life—and through this one orients oneself in the spiritual world.

Our friend had emerged from the stage of the etheric review, so that one spoke to the being who was indeed present but not conscious. Then through the heat came a moment of consciousness and she saw the cremation. Time becomes space.

There is a correspondence between what takes place in the physical and in the spiritual world. In such a case a call does not resound from the spiritual world like an echo but is transformed into a comprehensible answer from the not as yet conscious soul. Through such examples of the feeling that can be discerned in us, in the knowledge of the spiritual world apprehended by our feelings, the result must be that we experience the reality of the spiritual world. It is particularly important to acquire this definite feeling in our time in order that healing for the whole of humanity in both its physical and soul aspects may grow out of the grave nature of the present; for great events of world significance have always also been, for a superficial spiritual knowledge, the clear expression that in the world of the senses we have not only sense-perceptible beings but that spiritual beings are involved with them.

It is difficult to break through the veil that separates the physical from the spiritual world. This makes self-knowledge difficult in the broadest sense; people often take too facile a view of it. Even in an outward physical sense it is sometimes difficult. The notable philosopher Professor Ernst Mach[25]—not Ferdinand Maack,[26] I would not otherwise have spoken of a notable philosopher—has given a grotesque example of this.[27] In one of his works Mach says that when he was a young man an unpleasant, somewhat repugnant face had once appeared to him reflected in a shop window which to his consternation he was obliged to recognize as his own. He experienced something similar again on a subsequent occasion. On boarding a bus he saw a man with an ugly face approaching him from the other direction, and belatedly recognized that he had seen himself in the mirror. People have a great deal of unclarity about the nature, the form of the soul; and all that one has to go through in order to come to self-knowledge is something that they can scarcely dream of. To a considerable degree, maya is a present reality in the depths of the soul. A person has the drive towards cruelty; he lives with people whom from time to time he torments and so on. He searches for an outward cause for this; he often invents brilliant reasons for casting a veil over the whole fabric of the soul. I myself knew someone who always spoke of how he had accomplished what he had through great sacrifices. But I had to say that it was only an inner sensuality that satisfied him. When he spoke of sacrifices, egotism alone stood behind everything. True self-knowledge can be attained only if one gradually advances in spiritual knowledge, in so far as one experiences through oneself what is in the world.

There are in the world people who love to organize opportunities for gossiping. This even occurs among men gathering for their evening drink. When they are asked why they gossip, people have all kinds of important reasons for it. But if we run our fingers through all the finery, we have a feeling of pleasure. When one gossips, the etheric body constantly comes in contact with the air that is set in motion, it is thereby stroked. There is nothing baneful in this. One only understands what happens when people gossip if one knows that man has an etheric body.

Humanity is approaching a time when it must increasingly look such things in the face. It will then occur that the people who maintain today in their materialistic outlook that everything spiritual is sheer fantasy will look as they would if someone wanted to say that where the air is there is nothing but empty space. Just as one discovers that the air is real, so will humanity discover that the spirit is a reality. When one considers the greatest of all mysteries, the Mystery of Golgotha, one can believe that Christ had mainly influenced mankind through a teaching once He had passed through the Mystery of Golgotha. But what people have known about Christ is the very smallest part. Theologians have squabbled with one another, but the least of them have understood something right. Only a part of what happens in history forms part of one's conscious understanding.

One example of this is the battle between Maxentius and Constantine at Milvian Bridge on 28 October 312, which was decided not through outward circumstances of whatever kind but through influences of a non-physical nature. With an army that was far stronger than that of his opponent, Constantine, Maxentius had Rome to defend. On consulting the books of the Sybils it was indicated to him that he should lead his troops out of Rome; in this way he would destroy Rome's enemies. He was further confirmed in this by a dream. Constantine also had a dream: he was charged with having his soldiers preceded by a banner with Christ's monogram instead of the old standard. Thus it happened, and the army of Maxentius, which in defiance of all reason was led out of Rome, was defeated by Constantine's weaker military forces, and Maxentius himself met his death in his flight. The Christ impulse had here worked right into the subconscious of human beings.

The impulse lives in the subconscious in the same way that, while ships are voyaging on the sea, what really matters is enacted in submarines. In the fifteenth century there was another important moment. At that time the Maid of Orleans entered into the course of history in such a way that everything that happened subsequently was determined by this. The whole map of Europe—and also its cultural life—would have been different if the English had been victorious. The Maid of Orleans was a servant of Michael. Schiller was deeply moved by the figure of the Maid of Orleans: 'The world loves to besmirch what is radiant'. Whereas Voltaire spat poison and gall at her, Shakespeare himself could not understand her, Anatole France dragged her into the morass of materialism and all Western cultural figures failed to understand her, Schiller embodied this noble figure in his drama.

In order that the Maid of Orleans could fulfil her historical mission, it was necessary that she underwent a kind of unconscious initiation. This was an initiation of the kind that is described in the legend of Olaf Åsteson. Such initiations, for which certain karmic preconditions had to be present, could take place in the time of the thirteen nights between 25 December and 6 January. When the outer light has the least strength, an inner enlightenment is most possible.

Thus Olaf Åsteson had real spiritual experiences in the state of sleep during the thirteen nights, which he then related before the church door, as it says in the 'Dream Song'. The Maid of Orleans also in a certain sense spent the thirteen nights in a state of sleep, namely in the body of her mother. In the last period before birth a person is especially accessible to unconscious influences from the spiritual world. The Maid of Orleans was born on 6 January. On this day all the inhabitants of her place of birth came together, because something quite extraordinary could be felt in the aura of the village. It was the birth of the Maid of Orleans, in whom the Christ impulse had been implanted immediately before she perceived the physical light of the Sun.

The true goal of all our endeavours and what really matters to us is to discover the living aspect of the connection between the physical and spiritual worlds. It will come to be recognized that the twilight period of this war signifies a turning point of time. Human beings shall know that the souls of those who have sacrificed themselves work further and that this war has the task of bringing the age of materialism to an end.

It is necessary that there are souls who send thoughts up into the spiritual world like outstretched hands and bring down the consciousness from the spiritual world, souls with a spiritual consciousness. The more such spirit-conscious souls send forth their thoughts (and much is dependent upon our spiritual atmosphere being pervaded by such thoughts), the more will the fruits deriving from sacrificial deaths be able to ripen. Thus we may summarize our considerations today in these words:

From the courage of the fighters,
From the blood on fields of battle,
From the grief of the bereaved,
From the people's sacrifice:
There will ripen fruit of spirit,
If souls will turn in consciousness
Towards the realm of spirit.

LECTURE 4

LEIPZIG, 7 MARCH 1915

The Intimate Element of Central European Culture and its Aspirations

WE live in difficult, destiny-laden times. And what these destiny-laden times will bring to us earthly human beings is something that very few souls anticipate with full confidence; moreover, the significance of what comes to expression through the events of these days does not speak to souls with any degree of clarity. However, it is precisely those who try as human souls increasingly to enter into what should be assimilated by way of impulses into the cultural evolution of humanity, into the spiritual evolution of culture, through the demands of spiritual science who should know themselves to be connected in their deepest, innermost feelings with what is taking place around us on the one hand on so vast a scale and, on the other hand, so painfully and so distressingly.

What is taking place is something that not only in its nature but also in its degree is indeed without parallel in the conscious history of human evolution, that enters deeply and decisively into every living aspect of earthly evolution. One needs but to gain an inner sense of what it means—and this applies today to every person in Europe—to stand amidst the course of events of such significance in order to feel that this is a time when it is not only eminently right, but also eminently necessary, that the soul frees itself ever more and more from a mere life within its own self, within its own ego, and to try to share in the experience of the common fate that has befallen mankind. The soul will in our present time be able to learn much if it knows to connect itself in the right way with the stream of events; and it will be able to free itself from much pettiness and selfishness if it knows how to do this. Things of such magnitude are happening that virtually any thinking purely of oneself in this time of ours must be seen as a robbery that our soul commits with respect to living in association with common destinies.

And what immense questions especially those living in Central Europe must be asking themselves about things that they can really only learn now! Such people can become aware that they are misunderstood and, indeed, hated. These misunderstandings, this hatred, did not really emerge since the beginning of the war; it is only that they became apparent from that time. Thus the beginning of the war and the course of the war are also merely that which makes Central European souls aware that they must feel themselves in a certain sense more or less increasingly isolated with regard to the feelings of those people who surround the inhabitants of Central Europe with feelings and sensibilities that are thoroughly lacking in understanding.

How desirable it would be, especially now, if in the souls that are dedicated to spiritual science one could kindle an intensified interest in the great events of life, which lead the soul out from the horizon of its ego to the great horizon of human and earthly events! What benefit there would be if, precisely in the souls that have embraced spiritual science, their vision and mental outlook could be extended to a knowledge of the wider forces involved and thus bring them out of an interest in narrower forces concerned merely with the human individual! For indeed, when one hears today what the world—and especially the world around us as Central Europeans—is saying, when one reads what strange things are being said about the impulses that are supposed to have led to this war, one has the feeling that mankind has completely lost the obligation to judge in accordance with wider viewpoints in our materialistic age, to the extent that one sometimes has the impression that people had learnt nothing whatsoever but that for them history really began on 25 July 1914.[28] It is as though people knew nothing of what has taken place in the interplay of forces among the Earth's population and what has accordingly led to the problematic complications that finally ignited and flared up in the flame of the war. Hardly anything is said of the encirclement tactics of the former English king,[29] who has united the European powers around Central Europe, so that in the end—because of this union of the surrounding human forces—the only possible consequence was what has arisen. Hardly anyone is likely to go back a few years or at most decades and endeavour to form some ideas of how what now so painfully and fatefully surrounds us has come about.

But things lie at a much, much deeper level. When one speaks of encirclement, one must say: What has been accomplished as regards the encircling of the Central European powers in recent times has been the last stage, the final step of an encirclement of Central Europe which began a long, long time ago and already in the year 860.[30] At that time, when the Norsemen or Vikings who swept down from the North of Europe were gathered before Paris, a part of the power which was to come to full expression in Europe entered in the West of Europe into the Roman stream that had flooded into Western Europe from the South. We have a stream of human forces that pours from Rome by way of Italy, Sicily and modern Spain and through what is now France; while the Viking invaders who came from the North and in 860 were before Paris are overwhelmed by the Roman stream deriving from antiquity and are absorbed in this Roman stream. The vigour possessed by this stream derives from the Viking element that is absorbed within it; and what arose in the West as something alien to Central European culture derives from the Roman stream that had flooded into it.

This Roman stream did not simply come to a halt in modern France but through its dogmatically rationalistic nature, through its inclination towards a materialist manner of thinking, it proved itself well capable of overwhelming not only France but, when the Normans then reached out their hands to what are today the Anglo-Saxon lands, of causing the decisive element in what came to the Anglo-Saxon world to lie not in what the Vikings had brought from the North to the South but in what they had received from the South. Also in the British element it is the Roman element that thereby opposes without understanding what lives in Central Europe. And this Norman element infiltrated by the Roman element has further extended beyond the coasts of Greece to Constantinople. So that we see a flood of Viking-imbued Roman culture moving down from the European North to the West, encircling Central Europe in a snake-like form and extending its tentacles as far as Constantinople.

The other migratory movement emanating from the North we see flowing to the East and penetrating into the Slavic world. The first Viking invaders were given the name of 'Ros' by the largely Finnish inhabitants of what is now modern Russia, hence the name 'Russians', which is therefore reminiscent of the name that the Finns gave to the Viking population. We see these Nordic peoples extending into the Slavic element, entering ever further into it; and at the same time when the Vikings had gathered before Paris and began the process of their Romanization, we see the Viking element becoming immersed in the Slavic stream and, on the other hand, moving down to beyond Kiev and on to Constantinople. And the circle is closed!

The Norse or Viking forces move down on the one hand to the West and become Romanized, and on the other hand to the East where they are Slavicized, and as they approach from East and West they collide with one another in Constantinople. And in Central Europe there is enclosed as in a kind of cultural basin what remains of the primal Germanic world fructified by the ancient Celtic world; and this Germanic world then finds expression in the most diverse ways in the populations that manifest themselves as the inhabitants of Germany, Holland and Scandinavia. Thus we see how old this encirclement is.

In this Central Europe there is now being prepared what we can call an intimate culture, a culture that was never in a position of developing as does culture in the West or in the East but which had to take a completely different course. If we compare the culture that had developed in Central Europe with what has developed in the West, we would be bound to say that in the West there developed—and this can be seen from the smallest and most prominent characteristics of this culture—a culture whose basic character can be traced from the British Isles by way of France and Spain to Sicily and Italy and to Constantinople. The basic feature of the culture that developed was a certain dogmatism, a rationalism, a longing to clothe all the knowledge that one acquires in simple rationalistic formulas.

There developed an impulse to view things in the way that reason and the senses must see them.

Let us take an instance that, as students of spiritual science, is familiar territory to us, the structuring of our human soul in three members: sentient soul, intellectual or mind soul and consciousness soul. The human soul can actually only be understood when one knows that it consists of these three members. Just as little as light can be understood without discerning the various colours in their origin, and without knowing that it is divided into the various nuances of colour that we see in the rainbow—on the one side the red and yellow rays and, on the other, blue, green and violet—and that if one does not know this one cannot as a physicist study light, so would one be equally little able to study the human soul (which is infinitely more important) without making a comparable discernment; for each person is a human being and should know about the soul. Anyone who does not feel in his soul that it finds expression in the three members of sentient soul, intellectual or mind soul and consciousness soul will end up becoming totally confused about it all. We see this in modern university psychologists who muddle everything up when they speak of the soul, just as people get into a tangle about the nuances of colour in light; and in their immense arrogance and their scientific sense of superiority they regard themselves as quite especially learned when they create the utmost confusion in the soul-life, whereas one can only come to know the soul if one is in a position to really know about this threefold nature of the soul.

Whereas the sentient soul is initially also what makes manifest a person's desires, the more feeling-related impulses, in earthly existence, what we may call the more sensory aspect of man's being, this sentient soul nevertheless at the same time contains in its deeper parts the eternal motivating forces of human nature, those forces which go through birth and death. The intellectual or mind soul contains in equal measure a temporal and an eternal aspect. The consciousness soul, as it is now, contains primarily man's orientation towards things of a temporal nature. Hence it is understandable that the people which its Folk-soul forms through the consciousness soul, the British people, has—in line with a very beautiful remark made by Goethe[31]—nothing of the quality of profound reflection but is oriented towards the practical, towards outward competitiveness. It is perhaps not bad to call such things to mind, for those who have participated in German cultural life have not been blind to these things but have always spoken about them very clearly.

Thus to Eckermann—it was some time ago, but one can see that great Germans have always seen things in their true light, when it was a question of philosophers such as Hegel, Fichte, Kant and also several others—Goethe said: Yes, yes, whereas Germans torment themselves with solving the deepest philosophical problems, the English are oriented primarily or even solely towards the practical. They lack any sense for reflection. And even when—said Goethe—they make declarations about the morality of liberating slaves, one has to ask: What is 'the real objective' behind this? And on another occasion[32] Goethe wrote something that is highly significant and speaks more than many volumes, that even Walter Scott once admitted that even though the English* had taken part in the battles against Napoleon it was more important for them 'to keep a British objective in view' than all the liberation of peoples that was being spoken about at that time. A German philologist[33]—and there is little that the industry of German philologists cannot unearth—has discovered in the nine thick volumes of Walter Scott's biography of Napoleon the place to which Goethe was alluding, where Walter Scott admits that the British did indeed participate in the battles against Napoleon but that there was behind this the wish to gain a British advantage, that is, as he puts it, 'to secure the British object'. It is a typically English remark, one has only to look for them. These things are interesting as a means of somewhat widening our perspective today.

Thus one needs to know, as I said, that the human soul consists of these three members, or rather that the human self works through these three soul-nuances, just as light works through the various nuances of colour, primarily in the three kingdoms of mineral, plant and animal.

---

*Here and elsewhere Rudolf Steiner seems to use the terms 'British' and 'English' interchangeably. They are reproduced here in accordance with the German text.—Translator

One then comes to see that, in that he has these three soul-nuances man can assign a great deal to each of them and must do so in the course of human evolution, that the ideal of these soul-nuances is a great ideal, but each of these ideals is only one of the soul-nuances and is not for the whole soul. And only when, through spiritual science, people come to the point of attributing to the individual soul-members the respective ideals will what can be the true ideal of healing for humanity and of a harmonious interaction between human beings on the Earth become a reality. For man must aspire to what is associated mainly with his sentient soul, to what he gives expression to in the context of the physical plane, which is a different ideal from which he expresses through the intellectual or mind soul; and he must again aspire to a different ideal for that to which he gives expression through the consciousness soul. Through one of these ideals the one soul-member is ennobled, through the other another soul-member is ennobled. If one develops the one soul-member especially through the brotherhood of human beings on the Earth, one must develop the other through freedom and the third through equality. These three ideals each relate to one soul-member.

In the West of Europe everything is muddled up, and what the rationalists did was to simplify everything in the smooth formulas and dogmas that rationalism likes to make everything clear and reasonable. Through this dogmatism the whole human soul was simply regarded as one, and freedom, brotherhood and equality were spoken of as simple entities. So we see that in the West a fundamentally rationalistic cultural trend lies hidden. And we could extend this scrutiny into the details. For example, well-educated French people can spend time pondering if, shall we say, the lines in my Mystery Dramas[34] are iambic pentameters but do not rhyme. The French mind cannot understand that the inner impulse of language at this level does not require rhyme. It stands for sophistication, for what outwardly forms a framework, and it says: One cannot have lines that do not rhyme!

Thus it is also with outer life, thus it is with everything. In the West there is this insistence on dividing, systematizing putting everything nicely in boxes. But just consider what a terrible thing it was that at the beginning of our spiritual-scientific endeavours, through the fact that many of our friends were still influenced by the English theosophical movement, in every branch or group that one entered one could find as one looked up all manner of systems nicely written on cards, blackboards and so on: Atma, Buddhi, Manas, then all sorts of horizontal and vertical lines representing various systems and categories. Consider how one has bowed beneath the yoke of this dogmatism and how difficult it was to put in its place the methods of inner development that we must have in Central Europe: that the one arises from the other, that concepts are developed further in inner experience! One cannot use systemization, these donkey-bridges of the mind that bring everything into quite definite formulas. What an effort it cost to show that it is a question of going from one thing to the other, of a consequential sequence of division and development, of a living, organic formative process! I could extend this description to all areas of life, but we would have to stay here all day.

So we find this in the West as the one part of the stream that encircled Central Europe. And if we turn to the East, we must say: Here we have to do with a longing that expresses the exact opposite, with the longing to let everything today disappear in a mist of indistinctness, in a primitive, elemental mysticism, in something that does not present what is being directly expressed in clear ideas and clear words. We indeed have two snakes—the symbolism is absolutely appropriate, one of which extends from the North to the South-East and the other from the North to the South-West and which become entangled with one another around Constantinople. And enclosed in the midst of them we have what we can call the intimate Central European cultural stream, where—if it appears in its primal distinctive quality—the head can never be separated from the heart and thinking can never be separated from feeling.

One does not as yet completely see this in our spiritual science, because there has to be an effort in the direction not of conceptual systemization but nonetheless of concepts of evolution. People do not yet see that everything that is striven for there is not merely intellectual stimulation but that the heart and the whole soul are connected at every level, that the heart is intimately engaged when, for example, the head describes the transitions from Saturn to the Sun, from the Sun to the Moon, from the Moon to the Earth and so on, that the heart is at every point involved in the description, and one can be moved at the deepest level as one ascends with one's heartfelt feeling into the highest heights and dives down into the deepest depths and can again rise up from there.

It is not yet noticed today that what is only seemingly described in concepts must at the same time be inscribed with one's heart's blood if it is to correspond to Central European spiritual life. This intimate element of Central European culture cannot conceive of the spiritual without the ideal, or the ideal without the spiritual. To come to know the spirit in order at the same time to enter with the spirit into a kind of marriage of the soul is a moment that characterizes to the most intense degree the essential nature of Central Europe. Hence this Central European nature can use that which descends into the deepest depths of sensory experience and sensory feeling in order to become a symbol for the all-highest; and it is deeply significant when Goethe, after he had let the life not only of a typical German but of a typical human being, the life of Faust, pass by before his soul, concludes his poem with the words:

> Everything transient
> Is but a semblance,

and ends with these last words:

> The eternal feminine
> Leads us onwards.

Here a cosmic mystery is expressed through a sensory image, and in this sensory image there comes to expression the intimate character of Central European culture, this wonderfully intimate character that we find so beautifully and tenderly expressed and at the same time rising spiritually to the heights in, for example, Novalis. If you look at the translations that have been made here and there of this last phrase 'Das Ewig-Weibliche/Zieht uns hinan', especially the French translations,[35] you will see what has been made of it! It has often not been rendered very lucidly by Frenchmen, but they do not count on this when it is a matter of understanding *Faust.*

Intimacy of the spiritual life is in the most eminent sense what Central Europe in its essential nature is orientated towards, and it is what is enclosed in both East and West by the Midgard Serpent. And we must go to these lengths in order wholly to connect ourselves in our feeling with what is actually going on! We shall acquire from this Central European nature some objectivity for ourselves in order not to be judged by the same impulses from which things are judged in the East and West but to be able to stand before the great events of the present that we are experiencing out of truly super-national human impulses. Then we shall understand something of why Central European people are so misunderstood and even hated by those who surround them. Of course, we must be able to regard what is present in Central Europe as a mission for humanity as a whole with all humility. We must be able to arrive at a mood that avoids any kind of arrogance, but we must also safeguard for ourselves the free awareness of what is to be carried out in Central Europe.

The people of Central Europe have been imbued with a power emanating from their Folk-soul that has a constantly rejuvenating quality. It reached a high-point in the ideals of Lessing, Schelling, Hegel, Fichte, Goethe and Grimm. However, everything at that time was living more within an aspiration towards idealism. This must now be developed further in a more concrete way. The profound ideas of German idealism must gain further substance through what can come from the spiritual domain, enabling them to be raised from mere ideas to living beings of the spiritual world. It is the greatness of the task of Central Europe that must now ensoul German hearts, together with the awareness of what needs to be defended from all sides, from where the Midgard Serpent keeps the circle in its firm embrace. It is especially fitting that we who stand on the ground of spiritual science study in such a more elevated sense what is actually going on today. Moreover, we cannot be taking the innermost impulse of our spiritual science seriously enough if we do not feel how this spiritual-scientific aspiration in each single person is connected with the aspiration of Central Europe as a whole, how it must be connected with the whole substantiality of this aspiration. We must be clear that much of what we have in mind is only present in a seed-like form, but that it is the task of Central Europe to enable these seeds to unfold in blossoms and in fruits.

Just one example will be given to illustrate this. If a person tries gradually to engage in self-development through his meditation and concentration, through intimate work on his soul, all soul-forces take on a different form than they have in ordinary life. The soul-forces then, as it were, acquire a different quality. If he works really industriously on his development, as is described in the book *Knowledge of the Higher Worlds: How is it Achieved?*, he comes to the point of understanding, understanding in a living way and, I would say, livingly taking hold of the idea that in the moment when he approaches the actual spiritual world he no longer thinks as one has to think in ordinary life. In ordinary life one thinks in such a way that thoughts begin to live within one. When one confronts the world of the senses, one is aware of one's ego, and that this ego is having the thoughts. One connects one thought with another and thereby forms for oneself a judgement; one brings the thoughts together and lets them go their separate ways.

In my book *The Threshold of the Spiritual World*,[36] I have compared the development of thoughts with putting one's head in a world of living beings. Thoughts begin inwardly to swarm about, they become—if I may say so—living beings, and *we* are no longer the ones who lead one thought to another; *they* go from one to another, the one takes hold of the other and sets itself free from the other, the life of thoughts begins to become alive. Only when the thoughts, as it were, start to become vessels and containers that contract in the small space and then again become more extended like sacks or bags can the beings of the higher hierarchies draw into our thoughts, only then! Thus our own life, our whole thinking changes when we enter livingly into the spiritual world. One then begins to perceive that on other planets there live not human beings as on the Earth but other beings, that the other planets are inhabited by other beings. These other beings of other planets penetrate into our thinking that has become alive, and we no longer think about the beings of other worlds and cosmic spheres but they live in us, they live united with our self. Thinking has, therefore, become a completely different soul-quality; it has developed from the point where it was formerly into another soul-quality, into a quality that extends its influence and activity above us and becomes identical with the world which is the world of spirit.

Here we have an example of what must arise within humanity if it is to develop the state in which it is now living into a higher one for the future of the Earth. It must indeed become something that people all share that such thinking is possible, and that only through such thinking is a person able to make his acquaintance with the spiritual world. This does not mean that everyone needs to become a spirit-researcher, no more than anyone wanting to understand the achievements of chemistry needs to become a chemist. After all, even though there can be only a small number of spirit-researchers, anyone can through unprejudiced thinking see and understand the truth of what the spirit-researcher says. But it must become clear that in the course of life there reside within a person soul-capacities which, once he has passed through the gate of death, likewise of themselves become what they become in an initiate. When someone crosses the threshold of death, thinking becomes a completely different capacity of soul: it reaches out into the world of being. It is a continual extending of feeling-antennae, and the higher worlds are embraced within these feeling-antennae and one experiences them directly.

Now there was a highly characteristic figure in the nineteenth century who through his wit and erudition—for he was indeed clever—contributed to the forming of the materialistic world-conception: Ludwig Feuerbach.[37] He wrote a book entitled *Thoughts about Death and Immortality*, and it is interesting to read the following from this book. Feuerbach says something along these lines: The highest things that a person can develop out of himself are his thoughts. He cannot develop soul-capacities higher than thoughts. Were he to be able to develop soul-capacities higher than thoughts, that which originates from the dwellers of the starry worlds would be enabled to penetrate his head, and instead of thoughts he would have in his head the deeds and activities of the beings who are on the planets. This seems so absurd to Ludwig Feuerbach that he naturally considers anyone saying something of this kind to be ill. Think how interesting it is that a person who becomes a materialist because he rejects the idea of higher soul-capacities comes to understand the nature of the soul-capacity that represents the higher development of thinking. He even describes it, but he has so terrible a fear, so terrible a dread of this development that, precisely because it would have to take the course that he suspects, he rejects this soul-capacity as an impossibility, as sheer fantasy.

The trend of intellectual development in the nineteenth century is so close to what needs to be striven for and at the same time so distant from it, because it is indeed, as it were, thrust forth from the inner consciousness towards what is being sought but is unable to enter into the depths, since it must be regarded as absurd, since it is truly feared, quite massively feared. Central European cultural life must come into its own, and we shall then find that from this Central European cultural life precisely that which overcomes this fear will develop. What seeks to suppress this spirit-light of Central Europe has become too strong.

Some examples of this may also be given. Hegel, the German philosopher, raised his voice in vain against the over-appreciation of Newton. When you hear physicists speaking today (you can read about what I am saying in many popular works), you will hear: Newton is the great exponent of the theory of gravity, a teaching through which alone the cosmos can be explained. Hegel said:[38] What did Newton actually do? He clothed what Kepler, the German astronomer, had expressed in mathematical formulas. For nothing is contained in Newton's works that Kepler has not already said. Kepler worked out of that outlook whereby the whole of the soul is active, not only the head. Newton, however, brought everything into a system and thereby made all sorts of errors of judgement, for example the idea that the Sun's influence is extended into the wider periphery, which is not applicable to the movement of the planets. For Newton it really is as though the Sun had physical arms, and that it stretches out these arms and attracts the planets. But the German philosopher's warning that Central European culture would be overwhelmed in this area by British culture was in vain.[39]

To mention another example: Goethe formulated a theory of colour that arose wholly out of Central European thinking and which one will only understand if one recognizes to some extent the connections of the physical domain with the realm of spirit. The world did not accept Goethe's theory of colour but preferred that of Newton. Goethe also established a theory of evolution. The world did not understand it, and it was only prepared to accept what was promoted in a popularized, materialistic way as a theory of evolution in Darwinism. One can say that becoming aware of the forces that people of Central Europe, encircled as they are by the Midgard Serpent, have is what is needed so as not to give way to the influx of rationalism and empiricism!

You see the colossal task that lies before us, you see the greatness of the ideal. Because things continue to flow, as one might say, in the stream of appearances, people do not pay attention when one asserts the Central European identity. I do not know how many have noticed the following circumstance. When from the reasons that were specified yesterday in the public lecture,[40] our spiritual-scientific movement had to free itself from the specifically British movement of the Theosophical Society and when long ago what is now taking place in the war was in a certain sense anticipated in the realm of spirit (and which for good reasons preceded or anticipated it), I spoke about and explained the whole affair in terms of its symptoms. There are foolish people who want to pass judgements about our spiritual-scientific movement and have often said: After all, this Central European spiritual-scientific movement has likewise derived from what it has received from the British theosophical movement. I should like to recall that I said—I say this not out of personal reasons but because it is the situation, the whole crux of the matter characterized in one symptom—that, before I had any outward connection with the British theosophical movement, I gave some lectures in Berlin that were subsequently printed in my book *Mysticism at the Dawn of the Modern Age*.[41] No one will find any influence from the West in this book, and everything in it is developed purely out of the intellectual life of Central Europe, out of the spiritual, mystical movement from Meister Eckhardt to Angelus Silesius. And when I came to London for the first time,[42] one of the leading lights of the Theosophical Society, Mr Mead,[43] who had read the book following its translation into English, said that the whole of theosophy could be found in it. To the extent that people have admitted that they can go along with us, we could of course unite ourselves with the whole affair; but it has not really altered the situation.

This is what it amounts to: that we are aware of our tasks within Central European spiritual culture and that we never deviate from them! Awards and medals of one kind or another have been sent back to the English, diplomas and the like. This is perhaps of less importance. What will be really important is that one sends back Newtonianism and the distinctively English Darwinism, that is, liberates Central European cultural life from them. And in this connection something can be learnt from the way that—free from all other influences—Central European cultural life has made its mark in the form of spiritual science. But one must take this to heart, consider what is essential, and stand firmly on this ground. It is quite extraordinary how mysteriously things actually work.

Consider the following case. Ernst Haeckel has actually endeavoured throughout his life to guide the German conception of the world along tracks that are wholly influenced by British thinking, by the British nature and character. His writings are completely pervaded by British thinking, British empiricism. And now he is the first to denounce everything about England. These are processes that are enacted in the unconscious regions of the Central European soul; they are also things which in such a soul are closely connected with karma. Just think what it means when Haeckel stands before the world[44] and says that he has himself brought to fulfilment the first great deed of the great scientist Huxley, in that he coined the proposition that human bones are similar to animal bones; that he, Haeckel, has then referred to the great change in the conception of the descent of man, and that he introduced nothing into the theory of evolution other than what came from the West—and when one then sees that he is now compelled to denounce what his entire intellectual life has built up. It is the most tragic present outcome for such a soul that can be imagined. It is spiritual dynamite, for it shatters all the foundations on which such a soul stands.

And so one sees into the depths of what is actually going on at present, but also into the awful side of it that we need to be aware of. Only when one really studies things in this way will one come to be able to broaden one's conception of them beyond the narrow horizon that often prevails today. One will before all else be able to discern a great teaching—and this will be the most beautiful and at the same time the most humbling and sublime teaching, the teaching of that to which the all-prevailing might of the world-spirit has destined the people of Central Europe, who now, surrounded by the Midgard Serpent, are enclosed as though in a fortress surrounded by enemies on all sides. Only if what is happening becomes a great symbol of the deepest weaving and working of worlds will we be freed from a limited conception of the difficult, destiny-laden events of the present. And only then will we feel that we must make ourselves worthy of what, say, Fichte has said—also at a time when Germany was undergoing great challenges—in the *Addresses to the German Nation*, where—as he says—he wanted to speak 'quite simply for Germans and by Germans'[45] and spoke in the way that a German had to speak at that time to a German.

But just as Fichte spoke at that time of everything that has to do with the German mission, the German circle of duties, so are the difficulties that we are experiencing today within the encirclement by hate-filled enemies that which we have to experience as the dawning light of Central European consciousness. Indeed, something that can be found at the end of Fichte's addresses[46] can be reformulated today so that it says: For the healing of mankind, the spiritual world-conception must flow into human souls. And the world-spirit looks towards those who live in Central Europe, so that they become a mouthpiece for what it has to say and to bring to mankind in an on-going process of revelation.

One can therefore look upon what the sons of Germany and Central Europe have to defend with body and blood and soul without arrogance and without national egotism. Nevertheless one must also become conscious of this. Then alone the huge sacrifices that have to be made and the sufferings that follow can give rise to something that brings healing to mankind. For we stand at an important threshold, at a significant threshold; and one could characterize this threshold in human evolution by saying that in the future the abyss between the physical and the spiritual realms, between the physically living and the spiritually living, between the earthly and that which lies beyond earthly death must be bridged. The time must, as it were, come upon us when not only are the souls who go about in a physical body alive to us but when we feel ourselves to be part of that greater world to which the souls belong who live disembodied between death and a new birth in the world that in great style we call our own. The attention of human beings must be directed beyond what only our physical eyes can see. We indeed stand at the threshold to this new experience, to this new consciousness. And what I said to you of the widening of consciousness, of the raising of consciousness to a higher world, must become a familiar way of looking at things. Central European culture is prepared for making this a familiar experience; it really is prepared for this.

I have shown you that the best minds of the nineteenth century still had a fear of having an awareness of what lies at the depths of the soul; and in any case out of earthly forces the soul is unable as yet to devote attention to this. To be sure, that thinking to which supersensible forces and supersensible beings extend their influence is a present reality, and it makes itself manifest at that time when a person passes through the gate of death. Materialists are fearful of admitting that human consciousness could be thus extended, that the barrier between physical and spiritual experience, between what lies on this side of death and beyond it, can fall away. And because they are afraid, they reject it as fanciful, fantastic and even as a sign of mental illness. But it will come to be recognized that, when a person has passed through the portal of death, the forces that he develops are those that he has already now between birth and death. However, they work at such a deep level that he does not perceive them. They cause things to arise within him that are indeed enacted in him but which he does not attend to in the ordinary course of life. With the forces of which a person has knowledge—with these forces of thinking, feeling and will alone—physical, earthly life would not be possible. If he could only think, feel and will as he is able to now, he would never be capable of, for example, forming his body in such a way that the brain functions as it should. To this end, formative forces of a sculptural nature had to play their part. However, they already belong to what the soul no longer perceives in physical experience, to what forms part of a wider consciousness as a segment of the consciousness that we have in ordinary life.

When someone passes through the gate of death, he does not have a lack of consciousness but lives initially in a consciousness that is much richer and more full of content than the consciousness here in physical life; for the body carves out a portion of a more extensive consciousness and shows everything that can be shown, but everything is still only in the form of a reflection. Nevertheless, what is in the body and what a person carries across the threshold of death does indeed have a wider consciousness. And when someone has passed through the gate of death, he is within this wider consciousness. He has not too little but, on the contrary, too much, too rich a consciousness when he crosses the threshold of death. I have spoken about this in my Vienna cycle at Easter 1914.[47] A person has a richer consciousness after death, and when—after that backward review which has often been described is over—he enters for a time into a kind of sleeping state, not an actual state of sleep but a condition which is brought about through the fact that he is in a richer state of consciousness than he is here. And just as our eyes are dazzled by an excess, a surfeit of light, so is a person overwhelmed by the excess of consciousness, and he must first learn to orientate himself. The apparent sleep consists only in that, in this excess of consciousness; he is orientating himself in such a way that he can attune it with what he can bear after the events of his life. It is therefore a process of dampening down the excess of consciousness which manifests itself after death to an endurable level. You must clarify these things through the details given in the Vienna cycle.

I should like to illustrate this by means of two pertinent examples. I could give many such examples, for recently and also already earlier many of the friends from our circle have passed through the gate of death. But through the particular nature of the circumstances—simply because these deaths occurred recently—these considerations are more immediate in nature; and I should like to begin with such examples in order to speak to you of what can come so close to our hearts, because this has happened among us from the circle of our spiritual-scientific movement.

We recently lost a dear friend from the physical plane, and it was my task to speak for the soul who had passed through the gate of death. The impulses of the spiritual world that spoke to me sufficiently clearly in this case rendered it a clear necessity that I should characterize the particular soul-qualities of this befriended soul. It was in Zurich; and we were in attendance at the cremation of a dear member of our spiritual-scientific movement. In the relatively long time that had elapsed between the onset of death on a Wednesday evening and the cremation on the Monday morning (it is understandable that the backward review by the etheric body had already ceased), the necessity came to me quite involuntarily from the spiritual world to begin and end what I had to say beside the coffin with words which sought to characterize the inner nature of this soul. This inner nature of the friend who had departed in the midst of life was such that one had to immerse oneself in this being and, through becoming identified with it, inwardly create it spiritually, that is, one had to enable one's thinking to dive down into the soul of the dead person and to make it possible for what was weaving in the soul of the deceased to flow into one's own thoughts. One then acquired the possibility to say, as it were, with respect to this soul, how the soul was in life and how it is now after death. And this resulted out of itself that it was clothed in the following words. I had to speak the following words at the beginning and at the end of the cremation:

You appeared among us.
The moving gentleness of your being
Spoke out of the quiet power of your eyes—
An enlivening peace
Flowed in the waves
With which your gaze
Conveyed the weaving of your inner being
To all things and to other people;
And this being was ensouled by
Your voice, which eloquently,

More through the manner of speaking
Than the words themselves,
Revealed what lay hidden
Within your beautiful soul;
Yet wordlessly they fully revealed
A devoted love
To those attentive to it—
This being who from a quiet, noble beauty
Proclaimed a receptive awareness
Of world-soul-creativity.

This is how the being of this soul presented itself through my becoming identified with the soul in the days before the cremation, once the backward review by the etheric body was over. The soul had not yet found the possibility to orientate itself in the overwhelming intensity of consciousness. It was in a certain sense in a sleeping state when the body was about to be cremated. The cremation address was spoken, with these words at the beginning and at the end. What then happened was that the flame—what seems like, but is not actually, the flame—took hold of the body, and while the body was being engulfed by this flame-like element which is, however, only the rising warmth and heat, a moment of awakening came over the soul. And now one could see how the soul was looking back at the whole scene which had taken place among the people who were at the cremation. It was looking back quite especially at what had been spoken; and there then began the natural sinking back into the state of excess consciousness, or, as one might say, into unconsciousness. Later one could perceive a moment when there was again such a looking back. This then lasted ever longer, until finally there would be a complete orientation in the excess of consciousness.

But something important can be discerned from this. It was apparent that, because words had been spoken at the cremation that came from her own soul, these words enkindled the backward review within it, it found something awakening in these words. From this one can learn that one of the most important things after death is to oversee one's own experience. One must, as it were, begin after death with self-knowledge. Here in earthly life one can indeed do without self-knowledge, even to the extent that it is true that someone who is no ordinary person and also no ordinary literary figure but a renowned professor of philosophy, Dr Ernst Mach[48]—not Ferdinand Maack, I would not even mention him—in his *Analysis of Sensations*, a very famous work, makes a confession along these lines: When I was a young man I was walking along the road when I suddenly saw someone coming towards me. What an unpleasant, repulsive face, I thought. How astonished I was when I discovered that I had seen my own face in profile. So he had seen his own face, which he knew so little that he could return the verdict that he did. And the same professor relates a later instance of something that occurred when he was already a famous professor of philosophy, namely that after a long journey he boarded a bus as a man also got on from the other direction—a big mirror hung opposite him—and he expresses his thoughts quite correctly when he says that he had thought: What is this down-at-heel, unkempt schoolmaster doing here? And again he recognized himself, and he adds: So I knew the demeanour of the type of person better than my own. This is a beautiful example of how little a person knows even his outer form in life, unless he is a coquettish woman who is always looking in the mirror. But people have far, far less knowledge of their soul-qualities, far more of which goes right past them. One can become a famous professor of philosophy without this self-knowledge. But one needs this self-knowledge when one has passed through the portal of death.

A person must therefore look back to that point in his development from which he passed through death, and he must recognize himself there. Just as someone who is in physical existence and looks back with the ordinary forces of life is unable to perceive his own birth, in that this is never accessible to the ordinary powers of his soul (there is no one who can look back to his physical birth with his ordinary soul-forces), it is equally necessary that in every instant the moment of death is a present reality to which one looks back. Death is always something that one keeps in view as the last significant event. When viewed from the other side, from beyond death's threshold, death is something altogether different than from the physical side. It is the most beautiful experience that can be perceived from the other side, from the side of life between death and a new birth. It is that which appears as the glorious picture of the eternal victory of the spiritual over the physical. Thus death is viewed as such a picture, the constant awakener of the highest forces of human nature, when this human nature is living in spiritual experience between death and a new birth. It therefore means that when the soul looks back, when it tries to look back, it must initially contemplate itself. Precisely in these cases that we have had to experience recently, it was so clear whence the impulse originated to characterize this soul in a particular way, so as to approach it in this impulse of gaining knowledge of itself in looking back. Thus the so-called living works together with the so-called dead. And such a correspondence between the so-called living and the so-called dead will arise with ever greater frequency.

Another case which we experienced recently is that of our dear friend Fritz Mitscher.[49] Although Fritz Mitscher is less known to the friends here, his influence has spread among many other anthroposophists through his lectures, through what he has in a wonderful way achieved from friend to friend through the way that he engaged with anthroposophical life, an engagement that must be regarded as exemplary for the reason that he, whose inner inclinations were forged by undergoing and receiving the benefits of a learned education, sought—in accordance with his disposition—to imbue everything that he endeavoured to do with a scholarly quality, to encompass it with the intimate nature of his soul-life, but then to make it part of his anthroposophical conception of the world. We need this way of working, especially in that we want to bring to the future the benefits of spiritual-scientific ideals. We need people who try to penetrate with understanding the culture of the time in order to immerse it in the stream of spiritual culture; who in a certain sense make the sacrifice of pervading the culture of the time with the stream of spirituality. In this case too—and I am speaking only of things which have arisen through the karma of necessity—karma ensured that I had to speak at the cremation. And here, too, it arose from inner necessity that I characterized the nature of our dear friend at the beginning and at the end of the cremation address. And this is the characterization that I gave:

As a hope that gladdens us,
So do you venture upon the field
Where spirit-blossoms of the Earth
Would, through the power of soul-being,
Manifest themselves to the questing spirit.

Your longing had its deep affinity
With a pure love of truth;
The goal to which you tirelessly
Aspired throughout your life
Was creation from the spirit-light.

You cultivated your fine gifts
To follow with sure step
The radiant path of spirit-knowledge,
Unswayed by outward opposition
As a true servant of the truth.

Your spirit-organs you enhanced,
That they boldly and persistently
Thrust error from you
To both sides of the path
And create for you a realm for truth.

To fashion your self that it reveal
The purity of light,
That the Sun-power of the soul
Might radiate its strength within you,
Was your concern and joy.

Other cares, other joys,
They barely touched your soul,
For knowledge, as the light that
To existence meaning gives,
Held for you life's truest worth.

As a hope that gladdens us
So do you venture upon the field
Where spirit-blossoms of the Earth
Would, through the power of soul-being,
Manifest themselves to the questing spirit.

A loss that deeply us aggrieves,
So do you vanish from the field
Where earthly seeds of spirit
Have matured for your senses' spheres
In the womb of soul-being.

Feel how we look lovingly
Up to the heights that called you now
Away for other creating.
Extend your strength from realms of spirit
To the friends you've left behind.

Hear the entreaty of our souls,
Sent to you in confidence:
We need here for earthly work
Strong power from spirit-lands
Which to our dead friends we owe.

As a hope that gladdens us,
A loss that deeply us aggrieves:
Let us hope that from far and near,
Unforsaken for our life,
You shine as starry soul in spirit-realms.

During the following night, the soul that had not wholly come to the point of orientating itself gave back out of itself something by way of an answer which has a connection with the lines that had been directed towards its being at the cremation. Such words as these are spoken in such a way that one's own soul faithfully writes them down without any further ado. They are written as derived from the other soul to whom an orientation has been made. And I was utterly unaware that two verses are constructed in a quite particular way, until I heard these words from the soul of the friend who had crossed the threshold of death:

To fashion my self that it reveal
The purity of light,
That the Sun-power of the soul
Might radiate its strength within me,
Was my concern and joy.

Other cares, other joys,
They barely touched my soul,
For knowledge, as the light that
To existence meaning gives,
Held for me life's truest worth.

Only now could I know why these verses are constructed as they are; I had myself spoken them in exactly the same form:

To fashion your self that it reveal
The purity of light,
That the Sun-power of the soul
Might radiate its strength within you,
Was your concern and joy.

But every 'you' came back as 'me', every 'your' came back as 'my'; they came back thus changed by the soul speaking about its own being.

This is an example of how there is a correspondence, how there is already a mutual relationship between the world here and the world there in the time after death. That this awareness penetrates into human souls is an essential part of the significance of our spiritual-scientific movement. That the world also of those who live between death and a new birth becomes a world in which we know ourselves to be together with them is something that spiritual science will give to humanity and so expand the world from the narrow sphere of the reality in which man provisionally lives. However, this is intimately connected with what needs to happen in Central Europe. And anyone who has listened well will find in the words directed towards Fritz Mitscher's soul what is deeply connected with this significance of our spiritual-scientific movement, for these words are spoken out of a deep inner necessity:

Hear the entreaty of our souls,
Sent to you in confidence:
We need here for earthly work
Strong power from spirit-lands
Which to our dead friends we owe.

It can sometimes be that—and even though this is not really the case, it may appear to be from a recent perspective—people may doubt whether the souls that are incarnated in the flesh here on the Earth will actually do what must necessarily be done from a spiritual conception of the world for the well-being of humanity and the Earth. But anyone who is fully and livingly involved in the spiritual-scientific movement cannot have such doubts, because he knows that the forces of those who have ascended into the spiritual worlds after they have felt themselves strengthened through having absorbed spiritual science into their being are working into the stream within which we stand in life. And it is like coming to an understanding with the soul of a friend who has passed through the gate of death when one recalls its life, calling to mind what a spiritual movement can owe to the power of the friend; when one is able to come to an understanding with it to remain united with its forces, so that we always have it among us, so that it continues to be active among us. It is not merely a matter of receiving ideas and concepts of a spiritual-scientific nature but that we create a movement, a spiritual movement here on Earth that we truly imbue with spiritual forces.

It is in this moment appropriate that, out of the feelings that will doubtlessly be living in the souls of the friends who are present, to direct thoughts towards the soul of someone who has always devoted his forces to this branch or group. As an indication of our wish to feel united with him, of our wish to know ourselves to be united with his forces after he passed through the gate of death, we are rising from our seats. The Leipzig friends all know of which befriended soul I am speaking, and they have directed their thoughts to this soul with moving hearts.

These have been the ideas which it has been my task to bring to your attention today in the time that we have been able to be together. These words were ensouled by the awareness that the weight of the difficult and destiny-laden days in which we are living must be removed from those who will walk peacefully over the Earth, in whom the forces of peace will be active. But because of the way that a great deal will, and indeed must, be strongly transformed by what is now happening in the life of earthly humanity, we who feel an allegiance to spiritual science must be especially mindful how much it matters that on the ground for which so much blood is flowing, for which souls are so often going through the portal of death, on which so many fathers and mothers, brothers and sisters, sons and daughters are mourning, what can be accomplished by those whose souls can be illumined by the future-assuring thoughts of spiritual science must indeed be brought about.

Yes, those thoughts which come from the consciousness of the living connection of the human soul with the spiritual world must be in the ascendant. These spiritual worlds will now pervade souls, and there will be spiritual forces that are brought forth by our destiny-laden days. Just think how many are going through the gate of death in this time in the flower of their youth! Consider that the etheric bodies of these people who are crossing the threshold of death between their twentieth and fortieth year are etheric bodies which could have maintained the body here in physical life for decades. These etheric bodies are being separated from the physical bodies, but they still retain forces within themselves to work here for the physical world. These forces will work further in the spiritual worlds, separated from the unspent etheric bodies that have passed through the gate of death. The spirituality from the unspent etheric bodies of heroic fighters becomes a source of radiant brightness for the spiritual salvation and advancement of mankind.

But that which streams down must meet with the thoughts that can stream forth from the souls that will be able to receive them in spirit-consciousness through spiritual science. We shall therefore summarize the thoughts that we have brought before our souls in some words which represent the connection of the awareness that has been brought by spiritual-scientific thoughts with the events of the present time, which express how the space for the coming time of peace must be filled with thoughts that have reached up from souls into the spiritual worlds, from souls that have been imbued with spiritual science. Then will that which is struggled for in our time with such great sacrifice, with blood and death, will be able in the right sense to bear blossom and fruit when souls are found that turn their minds to the realm of spirit. Hence we who are mindful of days of such grievous destiny today may say:

From the courage of the fighters,
From the blood on fields of battle,
From the grief of the bereaved,
From the people's sacrifice:
There will ripen fruit of spirit,
If souls will turn in consciousness
Towards the realm of spirit.

Lecture 5

NUREMBERG, 13 MARCH 1915

The Entry of the Christ Impulse into Historical Events—The Bridging of the Gulf between the Living and the Dead

IF spiritual science really is to be a kind of living draught for our souls, as it can indeed become, this spiritual science must also on the other hand prove to be a powerful and suitable means of widening the spiritual vision of the souls that have dedicated themselves to spiritual science in times when so much is being prepared and which are of such significance as ours. In this way, what is happening can be seen in a somewhat wider light than is possible today for those of our contemporaries whose vision is limited to materialism. In what has over the years been cultivated within our spiritual-scientific movement, it has been possible to see that one of the aims has been to expand the nature of the soul's experience, so that one can be emancipated from merely thinking about the narrow limits of one's own self and one's surroundings and is enabled to look somewhat more widely at the great impulses, the great manifestations of forces that pass through the whole evolution of earthly humanity. And when we have thus endeavoured to broaden the scope of our feelings and sensibilities, we should—specifically in such times that on the one hand make so deeply painful an impression on the soul with their tempestuous waves and, on the other, elevate it to a quite particular height, because so much of significance is concealed within them—be able to render the forces that we have acquired through spiritual science capable of seeing something that is not so outwardly visible in the events, something that the ordinary intellect is unable to perceive in them.

We should, above all, be able to raise the question: Does the terrible torch of war that has been set alight and is burning over our heads have any significance of a prophetic nature for our earthly evolution as a whole?

Only those who view these events in so significant a light as to glimpse the possibility of this can rightly play their part in them. Friends within our ranks have often asked why in recent years it has been said in our circles that in the decades of the twentieth century there will be times towards which we must look with a particular attentiveness, because the children and grandchildren of those who are now living will have to live through events that are great and important but also tragic and painful. Those who are entrusted today with the task of giving something to enable the souls of children and grandchildren to remain upright in the face of what will descend upon humanity in the twentieth century must be aware that a strong inner power must be given to their children. Our descendants in the twentieth century will, to a far, far greater extent than we can imagine today in ordinary life, need strong inner forces as a support for their souls in order to carry with them the precious legacy of human culture that has been accumulated over the decades and centuries of human evolution. Moreover, the descendants of those now living on Earth will be exposed to additional storms of life. I said that people may sometimes have been surprised that such things have been spoken of in our ranks. Perhaps, however, a sense of this may arise when we consider that we are living in the midst of the greatest and most terrible military conflict that has ever befallen mankind since recorded history on this Earth began.

Indeed, it would be quite wrong if we did not concern ourselves as fully as possible with the significance of the present moment and consider the question: What does the spiritual knowledge to which we aspire with our deepest longing have to do with what is to enter into the evolution of mankind? Even if we look only superficially, do we not see a storm that arose in the East some time ago threatening to engulf the modern culture and civilization of Europe? One should at least know that very powerful forces reside in the East, of which it can be seen that, in the way that they are now making themselves felt, they have the aim of breaking up and destroying European culture. To what extent this is the case can only be surmised at present.

With what we may call European culture and civilization, we are living in the fifth post-Atlantean cultural period. It is the culture of the consciousness soul, in whose midst souls are among us who have something to give to mankind. If we look back upon Graeco-Latin culture, this Graeco-Latin culture is essentially—albeit in a quite different form—an echo, a repetition on a higher level, of what existed on Ancient Atlantis. Although it previously appeared there in a different form, in the fourth post-Atlantean cultural period there was something of the nature of a repetition of it. The fifth post-Atlantean cultural period in which we are living is a new form, it is something entirely new that has been added to the existing evolutionary course of mankind. We should understand this not merely as an abstract truth, as a theory, but with the deepest and most intense feeling of responsibility, and we should also be clear that long periods of time in earthly evolution will have to elapse until everything that the divine world-order has to give to earthly humanity through the fifth post-Atlantean cultural period has been brought to fulfilment from the hearts and souls of human beings.

The most significant event of earthly evolution, the impulse of the Mystery of Golgotha, occurred in the fourth cultural period. The Mystery of Golgotha will not simply continue to exert an influence in the fifth cultural period in the way that it did in the fourth cultural period. The fifth cultural period has the task of gradually approaching the Mystery of Golgotha with full spiritual understanding, with all the cognitive forces of the soul (and not merely with the forces of the intellect, or of a piety based wholly on feeling); the task of gradually understanding the Christ who went through the Mystery of Golgotha with all the forces of knowledge and understanding that the soul is able to bring out of itself. Thus the words of St Paul, 'Not I, but Christ in me'[50], will become a reality in a new way. And indeed, everything that we develop through spiritual science is the preparation for understanding the essential nature of Christ with all the inner cognitive forces of the soul. This is a significant and important task of the fifth cultural period.

Let us now enter somewhat more deeply into what is being asked of the fifth cultural period by bringing before our souls the way that the Christ impulse has influenced mankind since the Mystery of Golgotha. If the influence of the Christ impulse had been confined to what human beings have understood of it over the centuries since the Mystery of Golgotha was accomplished, the Christ impulse would have had little effect on them. However, it is not an impulse that has merely been imparted conceptually to the human intellect or to an understanding based on feelings, but it is a real impulse that has entered with living forces into the course of history. What is symbolized outwardly by the blood that flowed on Golgotha is the source of a living power that streams into the history of humanity.

We shall try to understand through a historical event how this Christ event has exerted an influence without human beings having understood it; how it has been working as a livingly active force in human evolution. It is the task of the fifth post-Atlantean cultural period to bring the whole inner nature and essence of the Christ impulse to consciousness. However, it had already been working as a living force in the subconscious regions of the soul before it could awaken to full consciousness within humanity. One of the figures whom the Christ impulse sought out in order to exert an influence—and an influence of significance—through her is, for example (and I could have chosen other examples), that of the Maid of Orleans.

When we trace the history of Europe back to an event which was enacted in connection with the personality of the Maid of Orleans, we must say—even if we observe history only from an outward perspective: What she accomplished at that time, when by rising up amidst the French people she drove back the English forces (for she did indeed achieve this), was the initial step in giving the form to the map of Europe that it has gradually acquired. Any other view of the history of the last few centuries, in so far as it relates to the arising of European nations and states, is a fabrication, a view that does not take into account the fact that the Christ impulse, which was at the time a living force in determining the boundaries and identities of the European nations, was working actively with the Maid of Orleans. One might well say that while learned people have disputed about many things, beginning with arguments about the question whether the Last Supper was eaten in this or that form, whether this or that should be interpreted by this or that formula, and while learned people have shown that with their conscious minds they have not arrived at an understanding of the nature of the Christ impulse, this same impulse was working through the simple country girl, through the Maid of Orleans, it has been moulding the shape of European history; for the influence of the Christ impulse is not dependent upon the understanding that one has for it. It was through its Michaelic representative that the Christ impulse exerted an influence on the Maid of Orleans.

However, the Maid of Orleans had to pass through something similar to an initiation for this to happen. We speak today of initiation and for this purpose we give to human consciousness the rules that are put together in the book *Knowledge of the Higher Worlds: How is it Achieved?* But such an initiation could not of course apply to the Maid of Orleans. In her case one can only speak of an initiation that was in a certain sense a remnant of an older initiation and which was enacted more in the subconscious regions of the human soul. These old initiations have continued to exist as elemental forces even until modern times; and in old legends and fairy tales much is said about things that happened to one or another person which evoked within him the inner soul-capacity enabling him to perceive certain aspects of the spiritual world. This is merely an indication that, independently of human involvement and by virtue of the influence of divine-spiritual forces that pervade the world, certain people who are suited for this through their karma are natural initiates, thanks to the place given to them by the karma of humanity, where this karma of humanity flows together with their own karma.

A very beautiful echo of such a natural initiation, as one could call it, is given to us in a poem which speaks of how the 'son of the Sun', Olaf Åsteson,[51] abided during the thirteen nights and days that elapse from the birth of Jesus* until the appearance of Christ, until

*The German text here refers to the 'birth of *Christ*'; but this is difficult to reconcile with numerous indications given in Rudolf Steiner's studies of the Gospels and elsewhere.—Translator

the sixth of January, in a kind of sleep-condition. Olaf Åsteson's very name indicates that he possessed hereditary cognitive forces of a subconscious nature, for Olaf Åsteson actually means: someone through whom flows the blood of his ancestors. Olaf Åsteson, the son of the Sun, sleeps and dreams through the thirteen nights that are the darkest of the earthly year, or at any rate contain the greatest power of the year's earthly darkness, from the first day of Christmas until 6 January, the festival of Epiphany.

Now the connection with these nights that features in such legends is not the result of some crazy superstition. The fact is that there are two times in the year that relate cosmically as two opposite poles to the life of the human soul in the body. The time of the year that lies in summer around the festival of St John's is the season which is especially suitable for the human soul, together with all its passionate impulses, to be drawn up into and to be united with the cosmos through the outward physical power of the Sun, which then attains its greatest strength. Thus when in ancient times people forgot themselves and were drawn up in the course of this festival into the strong outward physical forces of the cosmos, the St John's festival had the task of imbuing the human soul with the divine-spiritual forces with which the cosmos is pervaded. But when the power of the Sun reaches its physically weakest point, in the middle of winter, the spiritual forces that are active in the darkness attain their greatest strength; and one would be right to say that the festival of the birth of Jesus of Nazareth is celebrated at this time in accordance with cosmic laws. When the outer physical world is at its darkest point, the soul can have the most powerful experiences when it feels united with the forces that spiritually pervade the aura of the Earth.

Hence it is during those days that Olaf Åsteson sleeps and sleeps and experiences all that we call kamaloka, then what we call the spirit-world and, finally, the world of spirit. And the Norwegian legend tells us how, once he has awakened after the thirteen nights, Olaf Åsteson is able to relate what he has experienced, how he has met with souls in the worlds of soul and spirit. These are pictures that correspond to an imaginative knowledge, but they are indicative of living realities accessible to human souls when they feel themselves to be transported at that time of physical darkness (which is, however, a time of spiritual enlightenment) to what is working and weaving in the Earth's aura. At the end of the legend we see the forces of the Christ impulse, which powerfully enthral Olaf Åsteson in his subconscious mind. Such legends speak, as it were, of natural initiations which were still possible in ancient times, of a direct perception of the spiritual world. At these times the aura of the Earth has, indeed, a power that it does not have when it is flooded and irradiated by the physical power of the Sun; and as Christ has since the Mystery of Golgotha been united with the Earth's aura, the power of the Christ impulse can exert a particular influence in the course of these days upon human souls, if they are receptive to it.

Thus before investigating anything historically, one might presuppose that, also in the case of a figure such as the Maid of Orleans, the Christ impulse must have been working subconsciously in her soul for thirteen days; that she must have experienced an enlightenment through the Christ impulse similar to what Olaf Åsteson underwent in a state of sleep in the thirteen days and nights. The Maid of Orleans must then have been in a condition resembling sleep in the thirteen days that lie between 25 December and 6 January; and on 6 January, after her soul had been entranced in a kind of sleep, the Christ impulse must have taken hold of her soul. What can be thus presupposed did indeed take place in a particular way, albeit during a special time when a person is abiding in a state of sleep.

Before a human being takes his first breath in earthly life, before he is delivered from his mother's body and receives the first ray of earthly, physical light, he spends a period as a developing human being in a condition which can truly be termed a state of sleep. Just as in the evening one enters into a state of dream-like sleep, so is one in such a condition in the body of one's mother; and those days when dream-like sleep is most receptive to the unconscious influences of the spiritual world are the last days that a person spends in the body of the mother. Thus it could also well be that in the case of the Maid of Orleans these days would have been used to implant the Christ impulse into her being, before she perceived the physical light of the Sun with her physical eyes and took her first breath outside her mother's body.

This did indeed happen, for the Maid of Orleans was born on 6 January. On the sixth of January, the whole village came together because something of an indeterminate nature could be discerned in its aura. This is a historical fact. The people did not know what had occurred: the Maid of Orleans had been born. Much lies hidden behind such things. And only when humanity comes to be able to see this mysterious fact in its true light will there also be any understanding of what is actually going on beneath the surface of outward events. The divine forces seek the most manifold ways of making their approaches to the human soul. Of course, the karma of the Maid of Orleans had to be suited to something of this kind; but because her karma brought it about that she was born on 6 January, this provided historically for making it possible for the Christ impulse to work in a particular way upon this figure of history and gave Europe a completely new form.

These are things which one can examine if one studies the course of history with a certain understanding. These are the things with which a spiritual understanding will connect in future when this present fifth post-Atlantean cultural period has brought forth from human souls all their forces of cognition. Human souls will then experience the existence of the Christ impulse with an ever greater degree of consciousness. But they will only do so if humanity enters into a state where spiritual science is no longer regarded as a mere theory but is felt to be something living and is inwardly experienced. Spiritual science will then be able to fulfil its true mission in the evolution of mankind.

In a time such as ours, we must be especially conscious that it is necessary to bridge the abyss that in a materialistic age increasingly opens up between the human souls that live incarnated here in a physical body and those that have already passed through the gate of death. And one will increasingly come to regard the souls living between death and a new birth as just as much belonging to humanity as a whole as those who are in the physical life between birth and death. The awareness that we are all united in the earthly realm—also those who have gone before us into the supersensible regions, who are still active among those of us who are in physical bodies, albeit with different forces—must become ever stronger and more intense. But for this an understanding of the spiritually active forces is necessary; it is necessary that we learn to see the connections between earthly phenomena in that new light that spiritual science can give.

Because spiritual science is intended to be something that moves our hearts, while at the same time bringing our minds further on their path of knowledge, I want to speak to you of something that occurred in our circles in recent weeks. This is also a way of relating to and shedding light upon much that we have been preoccupied with recently in the wider context of our spiritual-scientific stream of knowledge. I could, to be sure, also choose other instances, but these cases are linked so directly with our karma that I am again able to speak of them today. You can extend what I shall say to others both within and outside our spiritual-scientific movement whose destiny and its relationship to their death bear a similarity to the cases of which I wish to speak.

Last autumn we experienced a deeply moving event in the vicinity of our building in Dornach.[52] Some dear friends had moved to Dornach with their children and had found somewhere to live near the building in order to look after the gardens. The eldest of the children, a boy of seven who was wide-awake intellectually but also had quite particular heart-qualities, was indeed something of a Sun child. One felt deeply drawn to the soul of this child, even if one saw him only fleetingly every now and then. When the father had to enlist in order to fulfil his duty as a German citizen, the seven-year-old boy was, I might say, whole-heartedly in the life-situation of doing his best to replace his father by helping his mother in whatever way he could. He went to town by train and did the shopping completely on his own, despite being only seven. One evening he did not return. It was an evening when there was a lecture. Someone who knew us well came at about ten o'clock and said that the boy was missing. There seemed in the end little doubt that the boy's absence had something to do with the accident of a furniture van, which had overturned near the building at a place where most probably no such van had ever been before and had not done so since and in all likelihood would not for quite some time to come. It had fallen down a small slope into a field in such a way that the drivers said that there could be no question of lifting the van that evening. They unharnessed the horses because they were very concerned about them, and left the van where it was with the intention of lifting it the following day, thinking that it would take a whole day to restore the heavy van to an upright position. It was now ten o'clock in the evening. We had to connect the boy's disappearance with the accident involving this van. All possible implements were fetched and everyone able to work helped, and in two hours the van had been lifted. Around midnight we found the dead boy beneath the van.

Now if one considers the external facts, namely that shortly before this happened many different strands came together, so that the boy, who otherwise always took a somewhat different path which would have led him to pass the van on its right side, on the occasion in question chose a path which led him past its left side at the moment when it overturned; that he had been detained by some well-wishers for roughly a quarter of an hour (he had had some supper in the so-called canteen), with the result that he had come away later than he would have wished; that the incident took place in such a way that it was only a few minutes later that the boy was at the spot where the van toppled over, and no one noticed what happened to him (some people who were not far away saw the van overturning, but they had not seen the boy)—if one considers all of this, one recognizes this outward scenario as an excellent example of the kind of logical deception that one can so easily fall prey to.

I have often spoken to you about this and have shown that people can be subject to delusions in ordinary life, so that they become confused about cause and effect. I have given the example of seeing someone in the distance walking beside a river. One sees that he suddenly staggers and falls into the river. Shortly afterwards his dead body is pulled out of the water. Now one would have good outward reasons for supposing that the person concerned fell into the river and was drowned; and if one does not investigate further one would adhere to this judgement. In this case one only needs some external means to be convinced of this or a different point of view. One's initial judgement is strengthened by finding a stone at the place where the person fell into the river; but when the body is opened up it is discovered that he had had a stroke, that he had fallen into the river as a result and that he had died not because he had fallen into the river but had done so because he was dead. Thus cause and effect are completely muddled up. For those with the requisite insight, this happens particularly in the realm of science. In our present case, where we are considering the death of this boy, we must say: The van conveying the furniture had been ordered by this boy's karma, his karma brought the van to this very spot. It is wrong to think that it was an accident. In this case, the boy was only to reach his seventh year in this incarnation. I might even say that the whole event was arranged accordingly. We must get used to viewing cause and effect altogether differently to the way that they are seen in ordinary life.

When we look with the eye of a seer at the life of this soul, we will be deeply moved by a significant fact which at the same time sheds light upon the spiritual mysteries of the world. Not long after the boy's death, the whole aura of the building in Dornach changed. In saying this, I am telling you something connected with my own experiences. If one has oneself to work for this building of the Anthroposophical Society, if one has to arrange what is to happen there, one knows what one owes to the helping forces that stream into one's soul from such an aura. Since the event that I have described, the unspent etheric body of the boy has actually been connected with the aura of the building in Dornach. The etheric body is what is laid aside by a person. The individuality, consisting of the ego and astral body, goes further on its way—that is something quite different. But when an etheric body of a child of so tender an age is laid aside, it has forces within it which could have sustained the physical body and physical life for decades. These forces have now passed through the portal of death unused. They are laid aside after a few days. These forces are now active in the aura of the building. One cannot therefore say that in the case of this individuality it is the soul that is involved but, rather, the unspent etheric body. Nothing is lost, even in the spiritual world. The physicist knows that nothing of physical forces is lost, that the forces are simply transformed.

Similarly in the spiritual world we must look for transformed forces, unspent etheric forces that rise up into the spiritual world from people who have died young. We come close to these things when we observe them by means of actual instances. It is only for this reason that I am speaking to you today about them.

A dear anthroposophical friend[53] died some weeks ago in Zurich after a life which had brought her much testing, and the karma of our movement brought it about that I had the task of speaking at the cremation. The time from her death until the cremation lasted from six o'clock in the Wednesday evening when her death occurred until the following Monday at 11 am. Thus a longer time than normal. The separation of the individuality from the etheric body had already happened by the time of the cremation. The remarkable thing was that during the time when the soul had released itself from the etheric body in the interval between the onset of death and the cremation, I was confronted with the necessity of speaking certain words both before and after the address at the cremation. My own verbal faculties had very little to do with the way these words were formulated, but by identifying with the soul that had crossed the threshold of death the necessity arose of characterizing this soul, but in such a way that the characterization was given as an inspiration, an illumination that came from the soul itself. It was as though the soul said: Formulate words whereby that which characterizes my soul appears in the words that sound. But there was in my mind still a certain unconsciousness. The words did not have a conscious origin but they derived from the being of this soul. I had to characterize it as it wanted to be reflected, not in an egotistic way but as it appeared to itself when another soul contemplated it. And this other soul was obliged by necessity—even in the way that particular words were formulated—to speak what follows at the beginning of what one might call a funeral oration. The following words had to be spoken as though addressing the soul that had passed through the gate of death:

You appeared among us.
The moving gentleness of your being
Spoke out of the quiet power of your eyes—

An enlivening peace
Flowed in the waves
With which your gaze
Conveyed the weaving of your inner being
To all things and to other people;
And this being was ensouled by
Your voice, which eloquently,
More through the manner of speaking
Than the words themselves,
Revealed what lay hidden
Within your beautiful soul;
Yet wordlessly they fully revealed
A devoted love
To those attentive to it—
This being who from a quiet, noble beauty
Proclaimed a receptive awareness
Of world-soul-creativity.

As said, these words had to be spoken at the beginning and at the end of the funeral. Now this soul was in a certain sense sleeping during the whole event, during the funeral ceremony. Then followed the cremation. The remarkable thing was that the first moment of a lighting up of consciousness—later gradually to fade again—occurred for the soul at the moment when not the flame but the warmth took hold of the corpse. Thus one could say: This soul has now passed through the gate of death, it had put aside its etheric body, and now it could be seen how such a soul looks back. In this backward review the whole funeral ceremony stood before this soul, that is, it perceived what had been said. And one could see the mystery of the working of time for the soul once it has passed through the gate of death. This could always have been seen in such a case.

When one is here in the physical body and looks at something in the spatial realm and then goes away from it, this object does not go away but remains where it is, and one can continue to look round it—one sees that it is still there. This is not how it is with what we experience in a temporal sense in physical life; we have only a memory-picture of events. But when one looks back at events after death, they continue to be there; one looks at the sequence of events as though through space. Thus what had been spoken had continued to be there, and the soul looked back at it through the passage of time as at an object in space. This is what perceiving the phenomena of the Akashic Record is like. Then there again ensued a kind of sleep. But especially in this case it was so clearly apparent that the materialistic soul's fear that, when the soul crosses the threshold of death one's consciousness would be diminished, is without foundation; for when we sink into a kind of sleep after death, we do not have no, or too little, consciousness until we subsequently awake but we have too much consciousness.

When we have laid aside the etheric body and when the life's tableau has come to an end, we are initially so filled with consciousness—I have spoken about this in the cycle entitled *The Inner Nature of Man and the Life between Death and a New Birth*[54]—that the consciousness becomes dazzlingly bright, and the human individual has first to orientate himself; and he orientates himself by looking back upon his own earthly life and his character in this earthly life. He has to orientate himself through self-knowledge, it is there that the power of orientation can gain a foothold; and through this what is in a certain sense an excess of consciousness is dampened down to the extent that he is able to come to terms with whatever he may have undergone in this last incarnation. It is therefore a dampening down of the excess consciousness that was present to the extent that the person can bear it. But this can occur in stages. And under the impression of the warmth, the heat, taking hold of the body, there arose a first lighting up of real consciousness in the soul of this personality with whom we were befriended.

That a soul that has passed through the gate of death does, however, endeavour to bring together what resides within it manifested itself to me especially clearly through another case. I said that these things can be experienced with every death, but I am giving you characteristic examples from the most recent time. I was able to see this with quite particular clarity in another instance, when a personality well-known to us crossed the threshold after she had reached old age. During the last years that she spent on the Earth, she had devoted herself in a quite unusual way with all her feelings and sensibilities to what one may call the impulses of spiritual science. She embraced all the different aspects of spiritual science more with her feelings than with her intellect; she united with her soul the kind of sensibility that results from a non-theoretical, true-to-life conception of spiritual science.

Now the situation with this personality was that shortly after her death, during the experience of the tableau of her life associated with her etheric body, there radiated from the soul with which one then identified that which this soul was now seeking to take hold of as its self when it had laid aside its body. And shortly after death had occurred, when the soul was still united with the etheric body, I had to write down some words which, again, I had not formulated through my human knowledge but which are none other than an account of what the soul was working on within itself in order, as it were, to bring together as though in a kind of résumé what it had been able to receive from spiritual science in order to come to an inwardly full self-consciousness. This resounded in the soul with words that in accordance with an inspiration, I also had to speak before and after the funeral address. You will immediately notice the great difference between the whole tone of these words from those that I previously cited in connection with the other personality:

> In world expanses I will to bear
> My feeling heart, that warm it may become
> In the fire of the working of holy forces;
>
> In world thoughts I will to weave
> My own thinking, that clear it may become
> In the light of the eternal life-in-becoming;
>
> In soul-foundations I will to immerse
> The sense of what has been, that strong it may become
> For true aims of human working;
>
> In God's peace I so aspire
> 'Midst life's struggles and concerns,
> My self for the higher self preparing;

Striving for peace in joyous work,
Sensing world-being in my own being,
I would fulfil man's highest duty;

May I live expectantly in the light
Of destiny's star, that grants me
The place in the realm of spirit.

Self-characterization of the soul in a personal form! In the former case you have the clear character that the soul that is observing must delineate the other soul out of a mutual mental association with it. Here the observing soul had nothing to do other than put itself wholly in the place of the soul that was still seeking to understand itself in its being—enriched as it had been by spiritual science—with the forces of the astral body, in order to gain some degree of clarity as to how it had now to orientate itself in the spiritual world.

There are cases where it becomes so fully clear that, when a person has gone through the portal of death, he is instructed to look back at his self in self-knowledge. Moreover, it has been clearly apparent that it is to a certain extent helpful for the dead person if someone still dwelling in a physical body helps him to formulate in words what is living and weaving within him. Of course the times when the individual concerned perceives his weaknesses and his errors in the soul-world are still to come. But we must state that to the extent that death is at times feared by those who still abide in the body, death takes a very different course when viewed in retrospect from the other side.

Here in the physical body, no one can look back with ordinary human forces to the hour of his birth. Indeed, there is no one who does not have clairvoyant powers for whom it is possible to look upon his entry into the world; only later does the point of time arrive to which one is able to look back. The precise opposite is the case with that birth into the spiritual world which we call death. A person perceives this moment constantly in the life between death and a new birth. This moment alone is one of the most glorious, most wonderful and most beautiful things that one can see in the spiritual world. Viewed from the other side, death is always the direct proof that the spirit unremittingly celebrates its victory over physicality, something that one experiences through one's own being: hence this aspiration to experience within the soul after death what one is able to be. It is therefore a help if a soul living in a body formulates in words that towards which the soul is aspiring, so that what it is appears—together with all the best that it has—before its own spiritual sight after it has passed through the gate of death. One could precisely in this case see so rightly how such words that relate to the self of the soul in question come to one with an inner necessity when one has to speak at the funeral, and where one speaks not arbitrarily but obeys the divine voice that bids one to do what one has to do.

This became apparent to me through the karmic course of recent times in yet another case, when one of our friends in whom great hopes for the future of our movement were invested died in his early youth. He died in his thirtieth year. He would have been thirty years old on 26 February and died shortly before. This friend, our dear Fritz Mitscher,[55] was someone who with infinite, self-sacrificial devotion infused out of his scholarly nature what he was able to attain in his scholarly pursuits with spiritual science and, hence, indeed had something in his sights that is so necessary for our movement: embracing the full extent of our modern science in such a way as to imbue it with spiritual science and to express it in spiritual-scientific terms, so that one stands fully on the ground of scientific understanding. He was well prepared for this. Even if the course of karma is such that such souls pass prematurely through the gate of death, this has its significance in the course of the world as a whole. And just as in the other cases (because I had been urged through karma to speak at the funeral), it also happened then that I had to speak words at the beginning and at the end of the funeral address which had likewise to be spoken in the same way by putting oneself in the place of the being of the soul, so that the words were again not formulated arbitrarily but were composed in living association with the soul that had crossed the threshold of death. This is what I was obliged to say:

As a hope that gladdens us,
So do you venture upon the field
Where spirit-blossoms of the Earth

Would, through the power of soul-being,
Manifest themselves to the questing spirit.

Your longing had its deep affinity
With a pure love of truth;
The goal to which you tirelessly
Aspired throughout your life
Was creation from the spirit-light.

You cultivated your fine gifts
To follow with sure step
The radiant path of spirit-knowledge,
Unswayed by outward opposition
As a true servant of the truth.

Your spirit-organs you enhanced
That they boldly and persistently
Thrust error from you
To both sides of the path
And create for you a realm for truth.

To fashion your self that it reveal
The purity of light,
That the Sun-power of the soul
Might radiate its strength within you,
Was your concern and joy.

Other cares, other joys,
They barely touched your soul,
For knowledge, as the light that
To existence meaning gives,
Held for you life's truest worth.

As a hope that gladdens us
So do you venture upon the field
Where spirit-blossoms of the Earth
Would, through the power of soul-being,
Manifest themselves to the questing spirit.

A loss that deeply us aggrieves,
So do vanish from the field
Where earthly seeds of spirit
Have matured for your senses' spheres
In the womb of soul-being.

Feel how we look lovingly
Up to the heights that called you now
Away for other creating.
Extend your strength from realms of spirit
To the fields you've left behind.

Hear the entreaty of our souls,
Sent to you in confidence:
We need here for earthly work
Strong power from spirit-lands
Which to our dead friends we owe.

As a hope that gladdens us,
A loss that deeply us aggrieves:
Let us hope that from far and near,
Unforsaken for our life,
You shine as starry soul in spirit-realms.

Already during the following night I could experience that these words resounded from this soul from out of the spirit-realm:

To fashion myself that it reveal
The purity of light,
That the Sun-power of the soul
Might radiate its strength within me,
Was my concern and joy.

Other cares, other joys,
They barely touched my soul,
For knowledge, as the light that
To existence meaning gives,
Held for me life's truest worth.

I can assure you that when I had written these lines down I had not even remotely thought that the two verses were as they were, with every 'you' changed into 'me' and every 'your' into 'my'. I only became aware of this when the two verses sounded back to me from the other soul as an answer during the following night. Thus the verses remained exactly as they were, except that they were transposed from the second person to the first.

If I mention this, it is because a heart understanding can arise within us of how the possibility will remain in the future of human evolution of speaking from soul to soul when the mouth can no longer be used as an instrument. For just as we receive an answer through the mouth of the other soul for everyday life, so was it exemplified here where the soul gave an answer even from the unconscious part of its being, as if it were saying: I have understood, for this is indeed how it was with me in life; now that I have laid the body aside, I can understand what I was striving towards in life.

It is not only a question of receiving concepts, thoughts and ideas about the spiritual worlds but of living as a human being in a certain way in a particular life, in that as people of the fifth post-Atlantean cultural period we are approaching the sixth and seventh cultural periods. It is essential that the abyss separating the living from the so-called dead is bridged, that humanity increasingly becomes one, not only in so far as it is incarnated in the body but also in so far as it has acquired those forms of existence that people experience between death and a new birth. Spiritual science has the task of not merely bringing this to mankind but it is the first, I might say still stammering attempt to do so for the life that the Earth needs for the rest of this post-Atlantean evolution; for what can be given in spiritual science is indeed now still merely a tentative beginning to what future generations of humanity will experience through spiritual science.

I wanted by means of this description, which seeks through the power of the heart to shed some light upon circumstances relating to life and death, to give some indication to you today of this focus of spiritual science upon life, so that you may develop an understanding different from one oriented around the head—namely, an understanding of the heart—such as we seek in a living way through spiritual-scientific study and is accordingly the task of the fifth post-Atlantean cultural period. It will be followed by the sixth and the seventh periods of culture. However, one will only rightly grasp what it is about Central-European culture that is to be defended if one intimately feels its connection with what mankind has to achieve in the fifth cultural period. A start can then be made with what I referred to at the beginning of today's lecture: a broadening of the perspective of what lies hidden within our destiny-laden times.

In the East, a kind of human life is being prepared which will have a significance for the future. You need only to read about this in the cycle about *The Mission of Folk Souls* that I gave in Christiania.[56] But the soul-nature of the East-European—not to speak of the Far East—is fundamentally different from that of someone from Central Europe; and we must through what spiritual science shall represent for us come to have an open mind for such matters. It is a familiar story[57] that the Varangians were summoned by the Russian Slavs and that they were told: We have a wonderful country, but we cannot create order in it—come to us and bring us order! Establish some kind of government for us!

This is a nice story about the origins of Russian history, but it is no more than a legend without any historical basis. Things did not happen like this. The truth is that these Varangians went out as conquerors, and no one asked them to come. Nevertheless, what is thus related in the story has a greater significance than it would have if it corresponded with a historical truth for it has a truly prophetic significance: it represents something that has not happened but will happen in the future. What is to develop in the East will have to unfold in such a way that the capacities of the Eastern peoples are used for taking up what the culture of the West has created and allowing it to be elaborated further and fructified with what originates in the West. This will be the task of the Eastern peoples at some point in the future.

The actual nature of the Russians of Eastern Europe can be briefly characterized by looking not at that mendacious group of individuals that now rules the Russian people but at the people themselves. Then we must be quite clear that the Russian soul has an immense range of gifts, that it is, so to speak gifted in all sorts of ways; but as it increasingly unfolds its mission in the evolution of the world and of humanity it will become apparent that the phenomenon that it presents is one of gifts without the power to realize them. The range of gifts will grow increasingly and will become ever greater.

But what, for example, distinguishes the Central European is that he has united his gifts with spiritual power, that he evokes that quality of 'endeavouring constantly to strive' and lives intimately with his Folk-spirit; that he wants to make a reality of what he seeks to understand. This is magnificently apparent in Fichte's philosophy, where the ego, in order to understand itself, seeks constantly to create itself (the greatness of this philosophy will one day be appreciated); and this so characteristic quality of Central Europe is present in a polar opposite form in Russia, in the East of Europe.

These Russian souls are receptive to an extreme degree: they have the greatest gift for absorbing things, but if one attributes to them a productive capacity one is under an illusion. They are called upon to develop gifts without the capacity to realize them. The very idea is difficult to grasp, because this is something that has not existed before in human evolution but it must gradually take this course. And in the future it will indeed happen that the call will go forth from the East to the West: We have a wonderful country, but no order—for the disorder will become even greater; come and create order! Central Europe is called upon to bring the productive capacity of the spirit to the East. What is happening at present is an unreasoning resistance to what must occur in the future. People try to stamp out what has to come about, only to say: Come to us and create order! In the history of human evolution, what is most strongly resisted and rejected is that which in the end is most longed and striven for.

The greatest misfortune that could arise is that Eastern Europe, that Russia should be victorious in this process, it would be the greatest misfortune not for Central Europe but for Russia itself, the very greatest misfortune from an inward perspective; for this victory would have to be reversed, its effects could not be allowed to remain. Thus we are facing a tragic moment in human evolution, that the East is defending itself against something for which it will long in future and with all its forces; for it would be doomed to disaster if it does not allow itself to be fructified by the spiritual and intellectual life of what is for it the West, the peoples immediately adjacent to its Western boundary.

And the West in this context must itself, in the further course of its cultural development, bring forth not merely idealism but a living spiritual life. This living spiritual life will be like a spiritual Sun which will move from West to East, in a direction opposite to the course of the outer Sun. And in an outward sense Russian people will increasingly see how little they are able to achieve through their own forces, and that they must set about finding their true place in the whole evolutionary process of mankind; and that they would be committing the greatest sin if they repudiated or misinterpreted the culture developed by the peoples on their Western fringe.

We have been able to experience what I might call some strange anticipatory indications of this. Did not something arise in Eastern Europe which would have been an impossibility in the West, the so-called world-conception of the bare-footed? This is a kind of philosophy that has quickly become widespread, although a few years ago it did not exist. The bare-footed! The world-conception of those who make a lack of faith in man and in humanity into a philosophy, since they cannot believe that man is actually anything other than a being who wanders about between birth and death amidst toil and fear, such that the words freedom, brotherhood, compassion, pity and love are empty clichés, and that the only wisdom consists in wandering through the world as a pilgrim with bare feet, who looks upon the whole degeneracy of Western European culture (to express it in bare-foot terms) as a great illusion, and who considers the ragged clothes, the bare room and the broad road to be the path that a person follows when he has attained the heights of bare-footedness. And when a writer gives expression to this world-conception of the bare-footed in significant words spoken by one of his characters, it must make a strange impression on us, inasmuch as we try, out of our Central European world-conception, always to discover what may kindle for mankind the light of the future. When a writer lets one of his characters express what is actually a kind of summation of the bare-foot world-conception and of the philosophy of those who adhere to it,[58] what do we make of it?

'Indeed, what does man mean to you? Do you understand? He takes you by the scruff of the neck, he squashes you like a flea with his fingernail! Then you are to take pity on him!... Well now! You can then show him how foolish you are. In return for your pity he will stretch you with seven tortures, wind your intestines round your hand and tear every vein out of your body, an inch every hour... You fool... pity? Pray to God that they may whip you without mercy, and there's an end to it! Pity?... What nonsense!'

And Gorky, of whom you will have heard much, says of such words: 'Cruel, but true', in that he is not only recounting the world-conception of a fictional personality as the writer expresses it but his own world-conception, which is the way that he views the world. This is the world-conception of a bare-footer, a world-conception that one can speak about as one might of any other current world-conception. It is the world-conception that has lost the possibility of transcending itself, of reaching beyond itself to something that sends light into life; that has to wait until it is fructified by this light and is then able to fulfil its mission; but is now rebelling against what it should be doing. Many are the slogans that one will have encountered in the world, but one of my most painful experiences has been of the empty words that were bandied about by the various parties in August 1914, at the war-assembly of the Russian Duma; such a mountain of clichés surpasses everything in its empty verbiage. Such things as this are spoken only when all living creative power of the soul has been exhausted. The East is truly standing at the threshold of things to come, and it is developing a force that is opposed to what will one day be the source of its greatness. And we in Central Europe must say to ourselves: The East is waiting for the spiritual wisdom which must rise up from Central Europe.

My dear friends, try to transform into feelings what I have sought to characterize in a few words with, if I may say so, a heavy heart, so that this can shed light upon what we as spiritual scientists are able to encompass with an extended awareness and into which we may penetrate, in order to grasp the true, present necessity of the spiritual-scientific conception of the world. We shall then be imbued with thoughts filled with understanding which rise up from our souls into the cosmic expanses, thoughts which will then encounter the forces that will send their influence down from these worlds of spirit when peace will once more reign in the earthly domain.

Today I have shown you how the influence is extended of those etheric bodies which, as unspent etheric bodies, are separated from souls and could have continued to work on behalf of physical life for years, even decades, here in the physical body. We cannot help thinking of the many unspent portions of etheric bodies rising up into the spiritual world, in addition to what those people passing on the battlefields through the portal of death bring into the spiritual world through their individuality. These etheric bodies will form a great quantity of spiritual forces; and these forces can work from the spiritual spheres on developing a spiritual world-conception that will gradually take hold of humanity. However, in order that these forces deriving from the unspent etheric bodies can send down their influence from the spiritual spheres, they must be met with thoughts that likewise ascend into the spiritual spheres from earthly human beings, thoughts that bring understanding for the secret influences of the spiritual world, imbued as they are with the forces of these unspent etheric bodies.

This should be for us a source of encouragement that we fully explore the great truths of spiritual science; for these truths will stimulate within us thoughts which will then go on working in other people. And as the destiny-laden content of our present time takes its course, a time of peace will ensue when that which has come to pervade our souls from spiritual science will rise up and meet with the forces that have gathered and now stream down from the etheric bodies of those who—on the battlefields of the present—have passed through the gate of death. And then will occur something that I should like to summarize in a few words which arises as an outcome of spiritual-scientific research. If we rightly bring the fruits of spiritual science to bear upon what is taking place in our time, the result will be something that I should like to express in the following words:

From the courage of the fighters,
From the blood on fields of battle,
From the grief of the bereaved,
From the people's sacrifice:
There will ripen fruit of spirit,
If souls will turn in consciousness
Towards the realm of spirit.

Lecture 6

NUREMBERG, 14 MARCH 1915

Moral Impulses and their Results—The Relationship of the European Peoples to their Folk-Spirits—The Cultural Impulse of Eurythmy

It might at first seem, and also does seem to many people, as if that which one calls, in the true sense, clairvoyant powers through which the beings and processes of the spiritual worlds can be recognized, are not available to people in everyday life and are not developed within their souls. But this is not so. Clairvoyant powers are not forces which are necessarily unfamiliar and alien to people in their daily lives. This is not the case; on the contrary, what we develop in order to gain insight into the spiritual worlds, what we must draw forth from the deep foundations of the soul, is, with a certain soul-activity, also present in a person's ordinary life. It is present in what one calls man's moral impulses. A truly moral deed, a truly moral impulse derives from the same faculties of the soul that lead through the corresponding development to clairvoyant faculties.

As far as ordinary life is concerned, the fact is that everything that a person does can come out of what resides within his bodily nature or what he has acquired in the course of life for and through his body. When someone develops desires, when he does this or that which he is induced to do through his education or his other life-circumstances, it is the bodily nature from which the corresponding impulse proceeds. But there are in human life impulses that do not come from the bodily nature, where only the soul is involved when a person takes hold of these impulses: these are moral impulses. A truly moral deed is one for which the body is called upon for help in order that one can have a conception of the moral deed, but the impulse, the drive towards the moral deed lies in the soul-spiritual realm; and this is independent of the body. One will never be able to give a definition of morality with mere philosophy, and it is characteristic of any philosophy that seeks to be a moral philosophy that it does not come to a right, satisfactory definition of morality if it does not start from the premiss that it is possible for man to experience his soul-spiritual nature independently of the body. The only right way to define morality is to say that something is moral where a person decides what he does through forces that are independent of his body.

Now we know that human life is composed of moral, less moral and immoral actions. The difference that exists between moral and immoral actions manifests itself in its true light only to occult investigation. In the smallest cycle of his life—the twenty-four hour period—a person enters into the state of sleep. This state of sleep consists in that the ego and astral body essentially leave the physical and etheric bodies and then live outside this physical and etheric organism. Now it is not enough simply to state that the ego and astral body leave the physical and etheric bodies; for one must also be clear that, in that the ego and astral body depart from the etheric and physical bodies, they are received into the spiritual worlds that supersensibly hold sway around us. We enter the supersensible worlds with our ego and astral body.

If during the day, in our waking state, we have had a moral impulse and have accomplished a moral deed, there is the following situation: we must, as regards our ego and astral body be received by the spirits of the next-highest hierarchies, by the spirits that we include among the hierarchy of the angeloi, archangeloi and so on. They must receive us, we, as it were, enter into them when we go to sleep. Just as by day we live in the body, so while we are asleep are we within the beings of the higher hierarchies. Thus we have this clearly in mind. Now if we have accomplished a moral deed or have had a moral impulse, the possibility exists for the beings of the next-highest hierarchies to receive our ego and our astral body, together with our moral impulses or whatever has continued to exist of them in our soul, in accordance with spiritual, cosmic laws. If we have committed an immoral act or had an immoral impulse, we cannot enter during sleep with it, and with the residue of what has been formed within us as a result of the immoral impulse, into the beings of the higher hierarchies. That within us which is immoral is indeed thrust back again into our bodily nature.

The consequence of this is that everything that we bring into the spiritual worlds during sleep that is an after-effect of something moral does not work within our physical and etheric bodies, for it is taken away from them. On the other hand, immoral thoughts, immoral impulses and immoral actions become something that is thrust back into the etheric body and physical body; it continues to work within them. Thus there is the possibility that when someone is in the state of sleep, between going to sleep and waking up, the results of his immoral actions are working within his physical and etheric bodies. In this respect it is easy to recognize something that I have often spoken about in lectures, namely that language has a wonderful genius, that it works in a wonderfully genial way. When we speak of guilt, the German word '*Schuld*'* conveys the precise meaning of what is involved here. We equate what we owe to the spiritual world with our moral actions, but we remain in debt to the spiritual world with respect to what we have to leave behind in the body, our immoral thoughts, our immoral impulses, our immoral actions.

Now consider the following: if we were to spend our life in such a way that we would perceive and think about only the things of the outer world, the processes in our physical body would themselves be quite different than they are, since we do not only think and perceive but also remember what we have thought, perceived and experienced. What we think, imagine and feel goes right down into our etheric body; but the etheric body imprints it on the physical body, and that which the etheric body creates in the form of impressions in the physical body is memory. When in later life we recall something that we have previously experienced, this means that our astral body, which has then united itself with the etheric body, is directly juxta-

*This word combines the shades of meaning conveyed by the English words 'guilt', 'blame', 'fault' and also 'debt', together with the concept of 'owing' something.—Translator

posed with what has remained as an imprint, as a seal's impression in our physical body. The materialistic conception that has developed is naive: it is, so it is thought, as though one memory would be sitting here in the brain and another one there, as though arranged in little boxes. This is not true; every memory has an impression which fundamentally corresponds to the whole head and to much else besides in the human form, and memories are intertwined rather than next to one another, as the naive materialist notion supposes. The activity of the memory is, therefore, dependent upon our astral body and etheric body being able to bring about impressions in our physical body.

It is actually the same activity that occurs outwardly when we make a note of something for ourselves. When we look at our notes, what we have in our soul does not, of course, bear the least similarity to the signs that we have on the paper. On the paper are signs of some form or other, but through what we then make of them we are stirred in our soul to re-enliven what we have noted down, a mental process takes place. And so it is with memory. What remains within us actually has essentially no more similarity to what appears in the soul when we recall it than what is on the paper has to what appears in our soul when we read what we have written.

When beheld clairvoyantly, the situation where someone recalls something that he has previously experienced is like this. What lights up in his physical body is a sign that is in some way a copy of the human form beginning from the head and extending a little below it. These are signs. It is something else that appears in the memory, but these are signs. And what we experience as we remember is what the soul makes out of the signs. It is truly a subconscious reading that appears as memory. When natural science makes somewhat further progress and investigates the physical processes, it will come to be a help for spiritual science in that it will show that what remains in the body must first be subjected by the soul to a process that in the soul is fundamentally similar to reading. This process of remembering is a regular activity of the human soul.

However, if we now send down into our body when going to sleep the results of immoral impulses, thoughts or actions, we do not bring the immoral impulses that we have had forth from our physical body.

As a result, something happens similar to what ordinarily happens in memory. The work on the physical body is imprinted there; and when a person now wants to go to sleep and his ego and astral body want to leave his physical and etheric bodies, this process begins. What he has to leave behind makes its impression in the way that memories do, and then come the pangs of conscience. Thus they are reflected back from that which was imprinted upon our physical body and also our etheric body through the events in question. This then remains. And because it remains like ordinary memories, these pangs of conscience remain and develop in intensity and then appear in the form of self-reproaches throughout our further life. That is the important thing that we come to—to see that moral behaviour is a real process, that it is not something abstract but that this moral behaviour is a matter of bringing what we do here on Earth up into the spiritual worlds. And as we surrender the results of our moral conduct to the higher hierarchies, they also in a certain sense remain within these higher hierarchies. But what we cannot take with us and goes on working within the physical and etheric bodies remains here on the Earth, it is within the earthly process. When someone has passed through the gate of death, he must always look back at this; and in that he does so, the impulse must arise within him to clear it away from the earthly process. This is the basis of the working of karma between death and a new birth.

Thus we do indeed take the results of our moral impulses into our karma; but in that we bring them up into the spiritual worlds during sleep, they also make an impression there. We can say that the angels, the archangels and also the Spirits of Personality now have that which we bring to them by way of moral impulses. What do they do with them? These moral impulses that are henceforth in the spiritual world are for the evolutionary course of the Earth, they are the real fructifying seeds for later periods of the Earth. It is not only that we preserve these results in our karma but we bring up the impressions, and in future earthly epochs the spirits of the higher hierarchies bear them down again; and these results of the moral impulses then in later earthly epochs form the fructifying seeds for the creative thinking of human beings and for human thinking as a whole. One may think that a period in earthly evolution is completely immoral, so that no impressions of moral impulses would be borne aloft into the spiritual worlds. A period would accordingly follow in earthly evolution when little would occur to people in relation to earthly life, when they would have few ideas and concepts, when there would be a poverty as regards what can pervade and inspire life with soul-qualities.

Thus we stand with our moral impulses in a real cosmic process; and spiritual science, which makes this apparent to us, is therefore well able to heighten and energize our self-responsibility, for it is only through it that we are aware what it means to be moral or immoral in human life. To be immoral means to take away from the Earth its seeds of future life, to incorporate them in the physical earthly process in which they then become seeds of destruction for forthcoming earthly epochs; for of course they continue to be preserved there, because nothing is lost. They then obliterate what should continue to live vitally within human souls. Let us suppose that a significant number of people would decide to live immorally in a certain epoch. This would then bring about a later epoch that was impoverished in thoughts, and souls would come down to the Earth and find a poverty of thought on the Earth; they would be condemned to a barren life.

Now there is the possibility that we not only become aware of the nature of morality. If we do not take active account of the true reality of morality, we create desolation on the Earth. But we need, and we have the possibility, to receive something else into our soul-development, and that is the knowledge of the supersensible. The Earth has actually never been wholly without knowledge of the supersensible. We know that in ancient times humanity received a certain inheritance of clairvoyant capacities and faculties and, hence, also of clairvoyant knowledge; and it is not so long ago that the after-effects of this clairvoyant knowledge still existed on the Earth. We also know that we live in a time when this clairvoyant knowledge has for some centuries been depleted to the point of disappearing altogether, and it must be replaced by clairvoyant knowledge that is consciously attained. We are living in this important time. And yesterday we called to mind the fact that the fifth cultural epoch and those who are its bearers have the task of consciously re-establishing clairvoyant knowledge in human souls. The fifth cultural epoch will not come to an end before a certain amount of clairvoyant knowledge has taken hold of a relatively large portion of humanity. It is true what Herder says, that enlightenment will spread over the Earth.[59]

All knowledge that we acquire from the purely sensory outer world, all thoughts that we have purely as after-images of this outer world, cannot be brought so unconditionally into the spiritual world while we are sleeping. It is true that the thoughts, the ideas that we have extend to a certain degree to the beings of the higher hierarchies—with the exception of immoral impulses; the images of the outer world that we acquire do indeed reach into the spiritual world to some extent. But they do not extend very far, and above all no further than the sphere of the archangels. Thus if a person is full of ideas that derive from the sense-world, he cannot bring ideas developed solely from the world of the senses very far into the spiritual worlds. However, such supersensible ideas as we may experience are brought far into the spiritual worlds, and those beings who belong to the hierarchy of the archangels receive their impressions and bear them into later times; and this supersensible knowledge that is borne aloft into the spiritual worlds through the ego and astral body of human beings is subsequently related to the process of earthly evolution. What is now formed is not the active influence associated with moral impulses, the fructifying seeds, but the seeds for what we call the advancement of the Earth.

The rejection of supersensible ideas by an age signifies the condemning of a future age to make no progress in earthly evolution. Someone who rejects supersensible ideas hinders the progress of future ages, in so far as it is up to him. If a whole people became completely materialistic, this materialism of a whole people would condemn the Earth to come to a standstill in its evolution for a future age—naturally to a certain extent, because the other peoples would not necessarily reject supersensible ideas. Thus here too we see again that the acquisition of supersensible ideas has a significance in the earthly process itself. Causes and effects therefore have a connection with the earthly process as a whole. Those people who are in a certain sense conscious materialists in our present time have actually been seduced by ahrimanic spirits, for Ahriman has a great interest in obstructing rightful progress.

Again we see that spiritual science is in a position to intensify the individual human soul's feeling of responsibility towards the totality of the world. We see that spiritual science draws us away from the self and makes us participants in the whole unfolding process of humanity, that spiritual science is in its very nature a selfless activity of the human soul.

In a certain respect, everything living in supersensible ideas is reflective of the moral life. Thus there is nothing more disturbing for knowledge of the supersensible worlds than filling the human soul with immoral impulses. Basically we see from this what a deep foundation there is for saying that as preparation for clairvoyant development an eminently moral way of thinking is demanded of human beings. It is indeed the task of the fifth epoch to ensure that human beings undertake to develop spiritual knowledge in a conscious way, so that in the post-Atlantean age that is still to come the further advance of humanity is not impeded, so that such an advance may truly take place. And if after all that has been spoken of now in recent days we have to a quite particular degree ascribed the predisposition for spiritual knowledge to the Central European peoples, it must be clear to us that the further existence of the undisturbed development of Central European culture is of considerable significance.

If in the context of what has been said we now turn our attention to the horizon of specifically European life, what do we find? There is, in the first place, a connection between the life of the various peoples and the life of the higher hierarchies. You need only to study the cycle about the development of the Folk-souls that was held in Christiania[60] and which is especially important at the present time; you need only to give it your serious attention and you will see how archangelic beings influence the life of peoples; how this life of the various peoples as it interacts with the higher hierarchies is made manifest in what takes place here on Earth. When we consider an individual human being, we know that his ego-development is a slow and gradual process. It is true that consciousness of the ego begins in early childhood, from the time back to which one can remember. But this ego becomes ever more mature, it advances in its development. In our time there are considerable errors with respect to this ego-development. There is far too little awareness that such a development of the ego is taking place in life; and one may have the experience that people today reckon themselves sufficiently mature in their earliest youth to judge everything, because they do not know that a certain age must first be reached in order to judge particular things, since only through this will the ego have reached sufficient maturity.

As it is in a person's individual life, so it is also with the life of peoples. However, we must bear the following in mind if we want to understand the life of peoples in relation to individual human life on the physical plane. A human individual matures with respect to ego-development by becoming more and more mature in himself; he also learns to have a better overview of the outer world. What do we know of the outer world when we have reached the age of twenty or twenty-five, and what can we know—if we spend our lives in a proper, orderly way—if we have lived for a further ten years! A spiritual scientist has to acquire a sense for such things. Thus this is how the ego stands in relation to the outer world, in relation to what surrounds this ego.

It is different with the beings of the higher hierarchies. These beings of the higher hierarchies stand for their part in such a relation to our ego as we do to the things of the outer world. For us, the phenomena and beings of the mineral, plant and animal kingdoms are the object. For the beings of the higher hierarchies, for example, our egos are the object. However, the relationship of the beings of the higher hierarchies to our egos is not one of perception, as we have with respect to the outer world, but it is more an irradiating of our ego with the will of the higher hierarchies, an influence of the will of the higher hierarchies.

Those archangelic beings that have the task of guiding the peoples truly stand in such a relation to the human individuals belonging to the peoples as we stand with our faculties of perception towards the things of the outer world. We are the objects for these archangelic beings. What for us is the outer world, we are as human beings for the archangels, except that with us it is more a process of perception and with the archangels more a process of will. But with regard to this will-process the archangel also undergoes a development. This archangel likewise undergoes a maturation of his soul, though not with respect to his ego but with respect to deeper forces of his soul. He undergoes a development through which he then gradually attains a different relationship to the human individuals belonging to his people; just as with our more mature ego we achieve a different relationship to our surroundings.

Let us, for example, take the archangelic being to whom the guidance of what we know as the Italian people has been assigned in the course of history. This archangelic being has for a long time had a relationship to the Italian people such that it has essentially come to influence the higher parts of the soul. In its further course of development, however, this archangelic being has been working not only into the higher regions of the soul but also into its lower aspects, into the passions and impulses of the soul that are still connected with the body. Thus the development of the archangelic being goes further: firstly it works more upon the soul-nature itself, in the later course of its development it becomes more powerful and works into that aspect of the soul that is more connected with the body. And we can with respect to the Italian people state that around the year 1530 the archangel underwent the stage in his development which can be characterized by saying: Formerly he worked more upon the soul, now he begins to impregnate with his will the soul in so far as it pervades the body. And now for the first time the Italian people really begins with respect to its outer world to set about developing its national character.

Study the history of the Italian people before the period specified (around the middle of the sixteenth century), and you will see that the archangel has still been influencing the inner soul-qualities of the people in the Italian peninsula; but that then the outward national character as we know it at present really developed for the first time. Before this time—and such a point of time exists for every people—the soul-life of the people is still vitally alive. This is so that the soul-life of a people can receive this or that quality. The qualities are not yet so energetically imprinted. After this time, when the archangel has developed his will-relationships to the deeper qualities of the soul, the character of the people becomes fixed, it enters into actual physical qualities; and the time begins when one can hardly approach the people with something that does not correspond with the national character, when a certain nervousness becomes apparent if one comes with something that does not wholly lie in the national line or stream.

For the French people, this point of time can also be determined fairly accurately. It is of course only approximate, but for the French people it can be assigned to the period around the year 1600, at the beginning of the seventeenth century, and for the English people in the middle of the seventeenth century, around the year 1650.

If you go back before this period to the time of the Middle Ages, you will see how much of a sense of community the peoples of Europe still have, and that the forming of the national characters of the various peoples begins in the periods that I have indicated. The archangel undergoes a development such that one can say: Formerly his forces were still weaker, so that he could only influence the inner regions of the soul; subsequently the forces became stronger, he is able to extend his forces to the physical realm and thereby brings about the sharply delineated national character. Certain phenomena begin to become understandable if you apply such insights to historical study.

Consider that at the time when the English people had its Shakespeare, the national character had not yet been formed in this way, so that the fact that Shakespeare could no longer be understood precisely on the part of the English people has its origin in that the archangel has bound the differentiated national character in his firm embrace. There will only be a real study of history in the future if people no longer, as was generally the case in the nineteenth century, base their study of history on the premiss that ideas are effective elements in history. A person can have ideas, but ideas cannot work as forces in history. Angels, archangels and Primal Forces can also have ideas, but ideas must always proceed from beings; what exerts an influence must be a being. The whole study of history of the nineteenth century, in so far as it speaks of ideas in history, is a chimera, because it is based on the belief that ideas are able to develop and freely move in a continuous stream of time.

We can now raise the question: How is this with the German people? Was there also a specific time when the archangel reached a particular stage? Such a time has already come. But there is a certain difference between the German people and other peoples. We know that the human soul consists of the sentient soul, intellectual or mind soul and consciousness soul. You can also see from the lectures about the Folk-souls that the archangel of the Italian people dedicates the forces available to him to working mainly upon the sentient soul, in the case of the French people upon the intellectual or mind soul and in that of the British people upon the consciousness soul; and with the German people the influence is upon the ego, which extends its authority over the three soul-members. Thus the relationship of the archangel to the individual egos of the German people differs from that of the Western peoples. A point of time has already come when the archangel of the German people has taken hold of physical life or the lower aspect of soul-life, in so far as it enters into the physical domain. This is approximately the time between 1750 and, say, 1830. If one cares to study these things properly, one will discover some amazing insights into the course of development of various peoples. And if someone would but involve himself in studying the truly immense difference that exists in German life between people of the nineteenth and twentieth centuries and those who lived two hundred years earlier, he would see how considerable this difference is.

At that time the archangel exerted his influence upon the national character of the German people, just as the archangels exerted their influence upon the other peoples at the times that I have indicated. But one could say that he withdrew it again; he did not leave his mark so energetically and so thoroughly upon the physical organism as happened with the other peoples. Hence it came about that what occurred in the second half of the nineteenth century was that the German people unconsciously received all manner of influences from the other peoples; and this has in our time already led to tragic conflicts. Just think of something such as the fact that in his whole world-conception, in so far as he has based this world-conception on science, Ernst Haeckel is utterly English, completely anglicized, that he has embraced English thought-forms.[61] Everything that he thinks is influenced by English nature. He takes Darwin and Huxley as his starting point. He regards Spencer as his philosophical god. And whereas one cannot really translate a book by Hegel or a book from our spiritual science into English, it is very easy to translate Haeckel into English. You will be astonished that I say this, because you are well aware that spiritual-scientific books are translated into English. But what is in the books can only approximately be rendered in English translation; it is not really there but only approximately.

One cannot, for example, ever really translate into English the archetypally German sentence that belongs together with the sensibility of Meister Eckhardt and everything that has developed in German culture in relation to Meister Eckhardt.[62] One cannot really translate this sentence into English: '*In dem Gemüte lebt das Fünklein, in dem sich in der Menschenseele die Weltseele offenbart*' (The spark wherein the soul of the world manifests itself in the human soul dwells within the heart). It is impossible to translate it properly into English, since there is no equivalent for what is experienced in the word '*Gemüt*'. It is similar with the Hegelian dictum that forms a basic nerve of German philosophy—*Sein und Nicht-Sein vereinigen sich zur höheren Einheit im Werden* (Being and non-being are united in a higher unity in becoming)[63]: impossible to translate into English. Of course, one can translate everything, but that which is experienced through such a sentence cannot be reproduced in this language.

The German language also has the particular property that it permits a certain fluidity. Think how infinitely easy it is to say when something is translated into English or French: This is wrong, one does not say such a thing! We Germans may not develop the bad habit of saying that something is wrong, but we must keep our language fluid—that is a radical way of putting it, of course. But if you go through our lecture-cycles, you will see how much effort is devoted to finding ever new word-structures, also word-structures from which new words are formed. This derives from the fact that the activity of the archangel of the German people has ceased to be so sharply defined. He merely made an approach in the course of something less than a century, and then left the people free again. There is infinitely much substance in what I am saying. But this also has to be so, for the German people has the task of transforming its idealism into spirit-knowledge. Fichte, Schelling and Hegel, who are so attacked today, have created a thinking which, it is true, is not spiritualism or spiritual science but which, if one inwardly meditates upon it, does indeed lead to spiritual science. But if this is to happen the German national character must continue to be fluid; it must make it possible for one to say that, whereas one can *be* an Italian, a Frenchman or an Englishman, one is constantly *becoming* a German. In the case of the German people the archangel has only established the basis for forming the national character. And in the same way, being nationalistic or chauvinistic in the way that the West-European peoples are would be an untruth for a German, something that he cannot be—of course, one can do anything, but it does not correspond to the true nature of a German person.

Something entirely different applies to the Russian people. With the Russian people, it must above all be clearly perceived that the archangel relates to the individual egos of the people quite differently than is the case with Western and Central European peoples. The situation with the West-European peoples is that the archangel influences with his will-emanations the sentient soul of Italians, the intellectual or mind soul of the French, the consciousness soul of the British and the ego of Germans. But with the Russian people the Folk-spirit does not directly influence human souls. He, as it were, hovers over the people like a cloud, and the soul can only have a dim sense of and a yearning for him. He has in a certain sense remained a group-spirit; and there is no inward interaction of the Folk-spirit with the individual human egos.

One can hardly have a more tragic, more serious impression than if one is present at a Russian Orthodox service, where the human ego of those who participate in it as believers is almost completely excluded. A totally impersonal universality that disregards the individual personality pervades everything that happens.

A quality not addressed to a human nature holds sway in this service. This is a direct expression of the fact that the Russian soul has not yet awoken to that enlivening quality deriving from the contact of the individual soul with the Folk-spirit. Everything tends towards rigid patterns and stereotypes, as exemplified both in the way things are done and in icon painting. We are confronting an entirely different phenomenon from what is the case in Western Europe. We find that the archangel has not as yet come to the point of influencing the national character. Nationality is, therefore, still a dream of the soul for Russians. They do, of course, constantly speak of the 'truly Russian man', and Russian writers do the same; but this is a dream of the soul which is especially emphasized because the Folk-spirit is not embodied within human beings and because the Russian has a longing for a Folk-spirit that lies above the purely personal.

One must look into these deep mysteries, and one will then understand how the cultural realms of Europe relate to one another. It would, of course, never occur to me to see in this interface between these cultural realms the cause of present events. But indirectly it does indeed play a part. In particular, one must be quite clear that the flames of war that are now burning are a mighty sign that we must make ourselves familiar with what is working and weaving within the cultural life of Europe.

We look up to beings of the higher hierarchies; we also see these beings of the higher hierarchies in course of development. While we as individual human beings develop our ego, we see these beings develop in such a way that they acquire more and more power to imbue the ego with the will. At first they still keep themselves distant from the ego; they over-light it from above, as with the Russian people. Then there is simultaneously a more intimate over-lighting and living with, as is the case with the German people. And then there is a stricter and more inflexible working of the national character into single human individuals, as is the case with the three West-European peoples that have been characterized.

From this you also see how the present phase of human evolution has come about. If you but look at European history, you will find—if you disregard Russia, where the circumstances are quite different—how similar especially the life of the West-European peoples and in a certain sense also of the Central European peoples is, how a European internationalism reigns. And then we see that from the fourteenth century onwards a new age dawns for the various peoples. We see that with the coming of this more recent age the peoples are gripped with a distinctive national character. We see that so much is given to the German people by way of national character at the turn of the eighteenth and nineteenth centuries that German people feel something of a national character but do not receive as much in this respect that they ever become absorbed in an inflexible national character. One will find that it lies deeply in the German nature not to need to be absorbed in matters pertaining to national character; that it really has a deep significance when Fichte says: All that freedom wishes of the human soul, all that aspires to the most universal aspect of mankind, belongs to us.[64]

Herein lies a free possibility for development of the Central-European German character. But there is also that which leads directly to the 'insight' that the West-European peoples must indeed reckon with this national character—this fluid national character—of the German people. I am well aware that the fluid national character can precisely in our time lead to a tragic outcome. Let us think again of Ernst Haeckel. We have seen that in the second half of the nineteenth century—because the development of the national character was again freely bestowed—he could be influenced so strongly in an English way. And now we come to our own times. This man Ernst Haeckel, who bears the whole English nature within himself, has hurled the strongest possible words of hatred at the English people. He was the most prominent of those who have returned all English diplomas, prizes and awards. It would be far more important that people in his position sent back materialistic Darwinism, materialistic Newtonism and everything that has issued from them. In this respect we must also simply learn to understand ourselves rightly; we must be able to learn to see things objectively without nationalistic hatred.

It was essentially a kind of cultural prelude of things to come[65] when a few years ago the split necessarily took place between our anthroposophical movement and the theosophical movement with its Indo-English character. This had to happen. Those whose task it is to develop the spiritual view of reality cannot ally themselves with the materialism of a Christ embodied in the flesh; and within our ranks it had to emerge that the Second Coming of Christ will in reality be the reappearance of Christ in the etheric. This has already been spoken about frequently and can be heard from the mouth of Theodora in my first Mystery Play.[66] To be sure, we now read in an English theosophical journal[67]—I am not making this up, and it is, moreover, the President of the Theosophical Society who writes this—that the way that the Germans are conducting the war shows what was actually hidden behind the German theosophical venture at that time, for it is now—according to her—apparent that it had been taken amiss that the President (Annie Besant) had always allied herself with the prince of peace who had such good intentions towards Europe, Edward VII. We are said to have regarded this with immense aversion, and therefore sent to England the agents who were to present our version of theosophy in order to lay our hands on the theosophists there. If we had succeeded, relates the President of the English theosophical journal, in getting as far as laying our hands on the whole 'rich administrative machine' (as she puts it) of Indo-English theosophy—of course, we wanted nothing of the kind—our plan to bring the poison of our views to India and thereby gain influence over the British Government would have come to fulfilment, as would our plan thereby to cause the British people to acknowledge German sovereignty over England! This is the explanation that is now given to theosophists in English theosophical journals.

Now see the truth! We must bring it to consciousness, for it does not work if we think about these things as though in a dream. The truth is actually that all that I have written in my book *Mysticism at the Dawn of the Modern Age*[68] is written solely out of the way that spiritualism lives in the cultural stream of Central Europe. The book was at once translated into English, and it was said to us at the time—to me, at any rate—that in this book the whole of theosophy can be found. We could now say: If people in London find that the whole of theosophy is to be found in the book, they can go along with us. But we have not taken a step that was anything other than an expression of the evolving spiritualism of Central Europe. And a few months before the outbreak of the war[69] I was quite particularly touched—it is appropriate that I mention this today—that some of our ladies who are eurythmists came over to London in order to give a course there. People liked eurythmy. That is good; it should give pleasure. But they did not notice that eurythmy is something spiritual, the polar-opposite of materialistic sport; that on the one hand one has something sweeping through Europe that belongs wholly to materialism and brings materialism right into the movement of human beings through sport, which serves people's amusement and the craving to make oneself healthy, which is completely materialistic, whereas with us every movement is the expression of the spiritual and corresponds precisely with Central European spirituality. It is always a matter of working on this foundation and deriving the fruits of spiritual development from it.

How sport, too, has invaded Germany in the second half of the nineteenth century! We also have more refined sportive activities (the method of Dalcroze[70] is especially worthy of note): how these things have taken hold! One will not now be especially warmly inclined towards him, because he is one of those who so dreadfully mock 'German barbarism'. But the movement discipline that belongs to the German spirit is eurythmy, whereby the spiritual element that resides in the movements of the etheric body, that belongs naturally to the etheric body and works within man's supersensible being, is brought to expression in the movements of the outward physical body.

Eurythmy rests on the following principles: we have an organ through which the etheric body is prompted into activity, so that the physical body becomes an image of the etheric. This is the case when we speak. But it is not the whole physical body but the air that is an image of the etheric. The sounding word in the air, the way that the air vibrates, is a direct expression of the etheric. If one now takes hold of what lives in the sound, in the word, and extends it to the whole etheric body and then lets both hands and feet move as the air is moved quite naturally in speaking and singing, then one has eurythmy. For eurythmy is a speaking of the whole human being, so that the help not only of the moving air but of the human organs is called upon.

You can see from such a matter on how universal and all-encompassing a scale the involvement of spiritual science in modern culture is conceived. In order to understand the essence of this, we have been hearing certain things that people do not even think about today; and if through these two lectures that I have now given in this intimate circle I have achieved nothing more that awakening within you the awareness that one should look still further at what spiritual science wishes in a universal respect for human life as a whole, that is already sufficient. For the task of spiritual science will not really be fulfilled by our familiarizing ourselves with specific theoretical concepts. This task of spiritual science will be fulfilled when it enters into everything, into the whole of life, and imbues this life with spirit; and in our fifth cultural epoch it is necessary to bring about the spiritual awareness to understand these things within that people to whom this task especially falls, to bring about a sense of responsibility with regard to evolution. It is easy, really easy, to criticize the evolution of humanity. But this is not the point, for the things that happen occur with necessity, even if they are at variance with what the good progressive forces want with human beings.

We now have in a certain sense to have living on an on-going basis within our culture something opposed to these good progressive forces. Among the many things in this category is, for example, this, that because of the present cultural standpoint of our time we are—for the sake of progress, as one says—really beginning to maltreat our children from the most tender age; for there is indeed nothing more contradictory to human nature than to let children from their seventh year to begin to learn school subjects and to teach them in a school environment, as one does at present. It would be the greatest fortune for someone to grow up quite differently, and to receive what is being brought to people in their seventh year only in their ninth or tenth year. But this is not, be it noted, said with the intention that it should not happen, for general cultural progress demands it; it must be so. Nevertheless, the counter-pole must be created. And whereas, on the one hand, we badly maltreat the etheric bodies of children through having certain kinds of schooling, because we inculcate something in them that is entirely unsuitable for them in these years, we must create a counter-pole by introducing eurythmy and bringing to the children what eurythmy represents, so that the etheric body has the balance in these movements that are innate to it. Eurythmy will become something that is quite general, for evolution does not reach its goal through moving forward in a one-sided way but through moving forward by means of opposites. One must always create the counter-pole, assert the value of the counter-pole. Evolution is motivated by opposites. And a counter-pole must be created to the maltreating of the etheric body through modern schooling by making the etheric body more elastic, by bringing it naturally into movement in the sense that this is attempted in the first rudiments of our eurythmy. Thus, something that perhaps many people today still refer to as 'our eurythmy' is indeed connected with what I have to call the universal character of our spiritual movement.

When, on the one hand, we see how this enters into the fabric of outer life and, on the other, we become deeply aware that the depths of the Christ impulse are connected with what we bring together in spiritual science, we have a full range of knowledge of the universal character of spiritual science. A great deal depends on our capacity to form for ourselves a sense for this universal character of spiritual science. And I have to say that it is at this time an experience of the weightiest kind that the present destiny-laden events are not felt at a deeper level, that they do not make stronger impressions on our contemporaries; for quite apart from everything that one can observe outwardly, these fateful events are a warning signal, a warning against perpetuating what the last centuries have brought to humanity by way of materialism, a warning to make an abrupt change in the evolutionary path of mankind. And all that is being undergone in terms of blood and death should be experienced as if it had been sent to the Earth from the Gods, in order to teach us how necessary spirituality is to the further evolution of mankind.

It is, for example, really lamentable when we experience in these times that people give lectures and also write articles where they say: If only the time might soon come when free contact and communication of the peoples is restored to its former state, since otherwise the Germans could succumb to the delusion of returning again to the metaphysics of Fichte and Hegel and developing metaphysical impulses. Even in these fateful days it is presented as a fear that something of the nature of metaphysical impulses might reappear!

These months *should* be awakening metaphysical impulses! We see in so many cases—to the sorrowful experience of mothers, fathers, sons, daughters, sisters, brothers and further human connections—that an unconscious belief in the significance of the supersensible is passing through the world like a breath of magic. Thousands and thousands of people are sacrificially crossing the threshold of death; and when peace is restored to our Earth, should people be allowed to go on preaching that human life is circumscribed by birth and death? The sacrificial deaths would then have been offered for nothing, for these sacrificial deaths derive—even though not with any clarity for many—from the firm belief that these deaths are the dawn of a new age. Anyone who dies on the battlefield truly wants to affirm something other than merely saying: Here ends my body. How meaningless it would be to fill European earth in our time with corpses if the materialistic world-conception had even only a smattering of legitimacy. We must inscribe this in our souls above all else.

Those who will survive this time will live in the period when peace will again reign; and they will be betraying those who have died if they do not work on the spiritualizing of human evolution. For not to work on the spiritualizing of mankind actually signifies none other than saying to those who have shed their blood and lost their lives: You died for nothing! For if materialism is right, they have all died for nothing.

A spiritual scientist must be especially imbued with this feeling. I have during these days been able to read again that there are people today—and in the nineteenth century these people became increasingly numerous—who maintain: It was a prejudice of St Paul that he said that if Christ had not risen, our words and our faith would be in vain.[71] But these words of Paul are true! For only through what happened through the Mystery of Golgotha has the human soul again been invested with powers that lead it into the spiritual world. We have spoken of these powers. But our time calls us with clear tones: The death of so many is in vain if materialism is right! If materialism is right, they will have all died for nothing.

If we imbue ourselves with such thoughts, those who have made their forces available to the great advance in human evolution in a death that occurred in the flower of youth will have their forces strengthened by the thoughts that rise up from our souls. If human souls direct spirit-wards what they have by way of spiritual thoughts and feelings, then—as I said also yesterday at the end of my lecture—the forces from above that have gathered, the unspent etheric forces, will meet with the spiritual thoughts of human beings and usher in a new age. We shall therefore conclude also today with the words that have during these days given us the meaning, the felt significance of the position that we occupy as spiritual scientists in our time:

From the courage of the fighters,
From the blood on fields of battle,
From the grief of the bereaved,
From the people's sacrifice:
There will ripen fruit of spirit,
If souls will turn in consciousness
Towards the realm of spirit.

Lecture 7

VIENNA, 7 MAY 1915

Cosmic Influences upon the Members of Man's Being—The Occult Foundation of the Christmas Festival—The Significance of Sacrificial Death

It is my intention in the course of these days to bring you something from the standpoint of spiritual science that can shed some light upon the great events of our time. This coming Sunday, therefore, it will also be my task to direct our attention towards certain themes which can cast light upon these events that so deeply move our hearts and souls at this present time. My purpose today is to establish a preparatory foundation by guiding you towards an awareness of certain powers and forces that are active in the historical life of humanity but which can only be recognized through those insights that spiritual science is able to give and are not directly perceptible to ordinary, everyday consciousness. I shall make reference today to certain facts of human development working at a more or less subconscious level as they come to expression in the course of human history. But as you know from what is described in my book *Knowledge of the Higher Worlds: How is it Achieved?*, we should be aware from the outset that what takes place in the hidden depths of every human being can be discerned in successive stages of supersensible knowledge, in so-called imaginative knowledge, inspirative knowledge and intuitive knowledge. In yesterday's public lecture[72] I have already emphasized that it must always be borne in mind that the spiritual scientist who reveals something about the spiritual worlds as a result of imaginative, inspirative and intuitive perceptions does not bring anything that does not already exist—even without his knowledge—in those spiritual regions in which every human soul dwells. The spiritual scientist only draws attention to what lives and weaves in the world and to how the individual human soul finds its place there. Hence such knowledge is important not only for those who intend to penetrate into the stream of occult experiences but also for every human soul, in that it constitutes an inner reality under all circumstances, albeit one that cannot be recognized by ordinary, everyday perception.

I should like to begin by mentioning a few facts about human nature that have arisen from imaginative perception. We observe on a daily basis an enigmatic process—enigmatic, that is, to ordinary science—that takes place in our life in rhythmic alternation: waking and sleeping. We are well familiar with the idea that in the waking state we belong to the physical earthly world with our four bodily members, the physical body, the etheric body, the astral body and the ego. We know that while we are asleep, thus from going to sleep until waking up, we are in the physical world only with our physical body and our etheric body and that our astral body and ego have, as it were, withdrawn into the purely spiritual world. We can characterize what presents itself to the spiritual perception of the spirit-researcher by saying that the spirit-researcher sees what, for example, takes place whenever a person leaves his physical and etheric bodies on going to sleep and enters into the region of the higher world with his astral body and ego. The spirit-researcher simply perceives what happens every time that someone goes to sleep.

We can therefore say that the spirit-researcher only observes what would present itself to every human soul if it could look down upon the world not in a dreaming state but in the state of dreamless sleep, and thereby find among the things of the world its physical and etheric bodies as something existing outside the sleeping soul.

Now we should not imagine that from the standpoint of sleep we see our physical and etheric bodies which we have left behind in the same way that we perceive what surrounds us in the physical world with our physical eyes. In order to see what surrounds us in the way that we perceive it from waking up until going to sleep, we have to use our physical eyes, our physical sense-organs. We do not use them when we are outside the physical and etheric bodies. If we were suddenly to become clairvoyant while we were asleep, we would not perceive anything of what we see while we are awake as it is in our waking state. Moreover, we do not perceive our physical and etheric bodies in the way that we behold our physical form when we look at a mirror. It is totally wrong if one thinks that one perceives the physical and etheric bodies as if one's astral body and ego were bending over them. This is not the case. What presents itself to imaginative knowledge—and I really mean imaginative knowledge—is that everything that we are accustomed to seeing in the waking state ultimately disappears, it momentarily vanishes. Moreover, as we perceive our physical and etheric bodies, they appear to us not as they are in the waking state but as though expanded into a world; they appear to us as connected with the whole of the earthly world. We behold them; we are aware that we are looking at our physical and etheric bodies. But we behold them in such a way that they initially, as it were, constitute for us the only world there is. Just as in our waking state we are surrounded by mountains, rivers and clouds, Sun and stars and so on and look upon them as our environment, so when we are outside our physical and etheric bodies and look upon our surroundings, we behold these physical and etheric bodies of ours as though extended into a world. We do not perceive anything else. We behold this as we otherwise look upon the various objects of our Earth. We look upon our own bodily nature as upon a whole world.

Remarkably, this world that we behold is such that, when we fall asleep, we experience it as we experience the Earth in spring, when after it has been liberated from its winter mantle of snow it brings forth green shoots, when it once more prepares itself for growth, when everything begins to sprout and germinate again. As when we fall asleep we behold the physical and etheric bodies enlarged into a world, we see them in such a way that we experience them as a planet that is awakening in the spring. This continues throughout the state of sleep. The mighty pictures that appear to us in their extension as a planet prepare to pass over into summer, just as the Earth prepares to pass into summer when spring comes to an end. This is how we experience sleep if we live through it in the right way. While we are asleep, we reach that point where we feel that our physical and etheric bodies are bringing the process of budding and sprouting to the blossoming state and indeed to the forming of fruit; everywhere we find everything growing and flourishing. To be quite specific, I have to say that what presents itself to imaginative perception has something paradoxical about it.

Whereas with our physical perception we survey the surface of the Earth and we are aware that what is growing there reaches upwards from below, when we observe from outside what is going on with our body and compare this with the plant world it is as though its roots were penetrating into our body from above and its blossoms were growing into it. We therefore experience a world that is completely upside down, and fruits grow into us. We then discover that these fruits which penetrate into us are bringing to expression the strengthening that we are aware that sleep brings to us. Through this we know—and indeed, what we behold thus in Imagination are actual forces—that our physical and etheric bodies receive forces from the whole cosmos while we are in a state of sleep. We behold how forces that express themselves in the forming of plants growing forth from the world come from the cosmos. We see that the cosmos transmits a whole vegetation into our bodily nature; and we then acquire the sure knowledge that when we go to sleep we leave our body, because from waking up until falling asleep our astral body and ego withdraw our physical and etheric bodies from the influences of the forces of the cosmos. By going out in this way, we free up our physical and etheric bodies for the influences of the whole cosmos, which sends these forces—whose nature is elemental rather than physical—into us as expressed in the imaginations described. Thus every time we go to sleep, a connection is formed between the physical and etheric bodies and the whole cosmos. Whereas in the waking state we live in the physical world, during sleep our physical and etheric bodies live in what we call the elemental world, the world of pure forces that is represented in the imaginations that have been described.

And where are we ourselves with our ego and astral body? This has been frequently described, and it has also been recounted in several of my books: with our ego and astral body we are in the world that has been referred to as the world of the higher hierarchies among the beings whom we call angeloi, archangeloi, archai and so forth. The ego and astral body immerse themselves in these beings and their world. Just as during our waking state we know of the beings of the animal world, the plant world and the mineral world and, as it were, preside over this world as human beings by taking them into our thoughts, so are we received as thoughts by the beings of the higher hierarchies. Just as we think nature, so do the beings of the higher hierarchies think us. Hence to be precise, it is not correct to say that when we leave the physical body we bear the world in our thoughts. A more correct way of describing our experience is to say that we are being thought by the world of the higher hierarchies. As a thought would experience itself during waking life if it had consciousness, so would we have to experience ourselves as the thoughts of higher beings when we are outside our physical body.

And how is the moment of waking up experienced by our imaginative knowledge? As we gradually approach the moment of waking up, we do indeed experience it—and we can again compare the imagination with outward nature—as the arrival of winter, with its destructive and paralysing effect on the budding and sprouting life of summer. And just as winter brings frost and cold over the Earth and destroys the glory of summer, so do we immerse ourselves into our physical and etheric bodies. In the same way that winter brings the destruction of the glories of summer, so as we wake up do we bring the destruction of the forces that entered into our physical and etheric bodies from the elemental world of the cosmos as vegetative growth or from the animal world. And while we are awake, our presence in our physical and etheric bodies brings them into a state comparable to the conditions in which the cosmos places the Earth when it is winter. We spread winter over our own physical and etheric being when we enter into it. You also see from this that what is often used as a comparison derived from physical circumstances is not applicable to a spiritual perception. To be sure, people have the feeling that they are connected with the whole cosmos and that in a certain sense what they experience is a microcosmic reflection of the macrocosm. But when they actually want to compare something in their microcosmic lives with the life of the macrocosm, they like to say that waking up is like the arrival of spring into our life, waking life is like summer. And autumn is like the fatigue that descends on us in the evening, sleep is like winter. The reality is the exact opposite. Summer is the life of sleep, winter is waking life. That is the truth of the matter.

When the spirit-researcher really investigates these relationships, he finds that, while his ego and astral body rise into the regions of the higher hierarchies and are thought by higher beings, not only does that which derives from the elemental world influence his physical and etheric bodies but certain beings of the higher hierarchies also work right into our physical and etheric bodies. Not only is it the elemental world, consisting of forces, but actual beings, beings of the higher hierarchies, that are active in our physical and etheric bodies. And what is remarkable is that we can be aware that at the moment when we go to sleep, we enter into conditions that are quite different from those that prevail while we are awake. As said, everything that can be expressed in this way is based upon the fact that spiritual research enables us to contemplate the processes of going to sleep and waking up. And it then becomes apparent to it that that being from the higher hierarchies whom we must experience as the Folk-spirit, the Folk-soul to whom we belong is influencing our physical and etheric bodies. When a person wakes up, he not only dives down into his physical and etheric bodies but also into the processes that take place in his physical and etheric bodies as a result of what his Folk-spirit brings about. The remarkable thing is that—I beg you to note this well, for it behoves those of us who want to penetrate into spiritual science to study the connections between things more deeply than is possible for ordinary, outward perception—when someone goes to sleep he not only dives down into those beings of the higher hierarchies that correspond to his individual development but also into such spiritual beings as we must regard as Folk-spirits. Moreover, from going to sleep until waking up he immerses himself in the connections of all Folk-spirits other than his own.

So let us note this carefully. While we are awake we live immersed in the spiritual facts that our own Folk-spirit enacts in our physical and etheric bodies. We live, as it were, together with our own Folk-spirit from waking up until going to sleep. But in addition to our Folk-spirit there are all the other Folk-spirits of the other peoples. When we go to sleep we become immersed in the connections of the other Folk-spirits, not in one other individual Folk-spirit—bear this strictly in mind—but in what they accomplish together, what they accomplish in association, as a community. Only our own Folk-spirit is excluded from this context during the night. We cannot avoid having a connection with all those Folk-spirits belonging to the other peoples in which we are not incarnated in a particular incarnation. For in that we belong to our Folk-spirit when we are awake, we belong to the other Folk-spirits when we are asleep, though only to their interaction with one another. When we are awake we belong to the intentions of the particular Folk-spirit in whose realm we were born in a specific incarnation.

But there is a means, also during sleep, of becoming immersed in the being of one other particular Folk-spirit. Whereas we normally live within our own Folk-spirit together with his activity when we are awake and, in sleep, in the interaction between the other Folk-spirits, we can dive down when we are asleep into one particular Folk-spirit if we acquire in life a really burning hatred of what this other Folk-spirit brings about. However grotesque it may sound, it is nevertheless true (and in our movement we must be able to cope calmly with such truths) that if someone feels from his innermost being so intense a hatred towards another people, he condemns himself to sleeping with the Folk-spirit of this people during the night, to being together with it.

Here we are dealing with truths with respect to which we can see that, behind the veil that conceals the spiritual worlds for ordinary observation, life begins to acquire a deeply serious character, and that it is in a certain sense uncomfortable to be an adherent of spiritual science. For spiritual science begins to approach with a considerable degree of seriousness certain matters from points of view that people find uncomfortable and from which we are mercifully spared through the fact that life in the ordinary sense does not reveal them to us. Although we must, of course, stand fully in outer life on the ground that this outer life demands of us, we must regard such a principle with full seriousness if we raise ourselves in the realm of spiritual science to those realms where other facets of life begin to reveal themselves.

In the book *Knowledge of the Higher Worlds* it is stated that in the moment when one rises into the spiritual world (and every human being is in the spiritual world, it is only a question of acquiring knowledge of what is always there) that comfortable unity of human nature in which we live in the physical world ceases to exist. Divisions arise within it; but apart from those divisions that are mentioned there and which one can observe after the meeting with the Guardian of the Threshold, many other divisions appear, including one that is of deep significance for our whole life of feeling. We should recognize that, while in a particular incarnation we must fully do our duty towards the people to which we belong and offer it our unstinting love, this national entity plays its part in the whole evolutionary process of the Earth. We must be clear that, in that we are through our ego and astral body also spiritual beings, we belong to the whole of mankind and should share our impulses with humanity as a whole. It is not the case that spiritual science allows us to live in a one-sided attitude; we must be able to bring the two sides of our being into full harmony with one another.

We must be clear that—even though as people of our present incarnation we can, while being spiritual scientists, identify lovingly with our own people, just as anyone can love his national heritage—we must bring this feeling into harmony with what unites us with the whole of mankind. Spiritual science emphasizes in a particular way this leading us into ever greater unity with humanity as a whole, because it reveals to us that through our ego and astral body we are connected with the whole of mankind. It increasingly demands of someone who dedicates himself to it with heart and soul that he creates harmony between opposites. It would be disastrous if one were to confuse true spiritual science with that vague mysticism that would forever like to combine the needs of outward physical life with that to which we must aspire by reaching into the spiritual world. For that vague mysticism which would seek to bring into ordinary life the things which spiritual science reveals in their true light will, for example, never be able to bring the love for one's own nation into harmony with love for the whole of mankind and will lead to a vague mystical cosmopolitanism.

One can, as I have already done, compare this with what nebulous-minded theosophists are forever saying about equality and about the equal values of all religions of the Earth. To be sure, one can say in abstract terms: All religions of the Earth contain the truth. But that is exactly the same as saying that on the table there are pepper, salt and paprika and all sorts of other things, and all these are condiments. Sugar, pepper, salt and paprika—they are all the same; so I put paprika in the coffee and sugar in the soup, because they are all condiments. Those who blather in a vague mystical way about the unified essence of all religions instead of penetrating into the true nature of each one as it appears in our earthly evolution are basing themselves on the same point of logic. It is not a question of constantly saying that all peoples are merely the expressions of the universally human but, rather, that we recognize the specific tasks that the various peoples are given by their Folk-souls. Some indications in this direction were given in the lecture-cycle which was printed some time ago and was held several years before the outbreak of the war; and since the lectures were not given under the influence of the war it cannot be said that they resulted from impressions of the war: *The Mission of the Individual Folk-Souls in Connection with Northern Germanic Mythology.*

It is important especially in our time to reflect about such serious things as this, so that harmony between universally human love and the love of one's own people can be found. One does not need to shy away from characterizing the particular qualities of an individual nation, in so far as it is a nation—the individual human being always rises above his nation. However, as is apparent from the observations that I have already made, this must of course be done without any hatred. Just as little as one recognizes the true nature of individual plants if one hates the plant and describes the hatred that one feels, so is one unable to recognize the qualities of a nation if one describes what one hates about this people, or if one incorporates in one's description what comes out of feelings of hatred.

Moreover, it must be the constant endeavour of those who are able to rise to the viewpoints of spiritual science not to see the nature of the world in a uniform singularity but in the harmony of its manifold characteristics. A person must be able to feel every possible warmth for his own people, a warmth that does not need to be any less than that of someone who does not aspire to spiritual science, while on the other hand he should be able to unite this with everything that brings us together with the whole of mankind to which we belong as one great all-encompassing being.

As already stated, we shall turn to matters such as this the day after tomorrow. What I want to say now is that as we pass from our waking state into that of sleep and are therefore received by the beings of the higher hierarchies, we at the same time cast off that which connects us with our particular incarnation through our physical and etheric bodies. In sleep we therefore also cast off our national character. Through sleep we become simply human beings, human beings with all the qualities that we must have through the experiences that we have had as human beings. If as spirit-researchers we observe what is happening with a person both when he is awake and asleep, we perceive that when he is asleep his ego and astral body are living in the spiritual world, just as his physical and etheric bodies also belong to the great world; that this personal life which, as it were, takes its course within our skin ceases, and that we extend our self to the great self.

Now consider that in the course of twenty-four hours we actually experience a summer and a winter state. The Earth also passes through these summer and winter states, but the Earth traverses them in the course of a year. Why does the Earth pass through these states over a year? Because the Earth is a being as we ourselves are, though at a different hierarchic stage. The whole Earth, if we observe it physically as it is around us, is the body of the Earth; and just as we bear within ourselves a soul and spirit, so does the Earth also have its soul-spiritual aspect. The difference is merely that we wake up and go to sleep in the course of twenty-four hours, while the Earth wakes and sleeps in the course of the year. It is awake from autumn until spring and sleeps during the summer. Thus we can say that during the summer we are living embedded in the sleeping Earth; and during the winter we live embedded in the waking Earth. It is not true that the Earth is awake in summer and asleep in winter, as we can say in the trivial comparison taken from ordinary life. The truth is that when autumn comes, the Earth wakes up as a soul-spiritual being and is most awake in the middle of winter. The Earth spirit is most deeply immersed in thought in the middle of winter and it begins gradually to cease thinking with the approach of spring; and it sleeps when outer life is budding and sprouting—the Earth spirit is asleep during summer.

As human beings we are not only connected through our physical body with the body of the Earth, but we are also connected with the spirit of the Earth. We know through various lectures that through the Mystery of Golgotha the Spirit whom we call the Spirit of Christ united Himself with the spirit of the Earth. Since the Mystery of Golgotha the Christ Spirit has lived within the spirit of the Earth. Consequently, if people want to celebrate a festival that would express to them that the Christ Spirit is within the spirit of the Earth, at what time would they have to mark this festival? They would have to place the festival not in the summer but in the winter. This is the Christmas festival. It is for this reason that the Christmas festival and what develops from it is celebrated in winter. This derived from a true knowledge which in former times fixed the ordering of the Christian year. The Christmas festival was laid down in accordance with occult truths and not with historical facts; because as regards what now constitutes humanity, man is united with the most fully awake condition of Earth existence—in that his soul-spiritual aspect is embedded in the soul and spirit of the Earth—during the winter. In the winter he lives together with the waking Earth.

And what will people in former times, who as we know based their service and knowledge of the world upon a kind of dream-like clairvoyance, have done? They must primarily have appealed to what lives in the sleeping Earth spirit, to when the Earth spirit is for the most part asleep and has withdrawn into a state of sleep. In contrast to people of modern times, they must have been inspired by the truths that flowed to them in an unconscious way as best befitted them. Among the peoples whose cults and knowledge were drawn from a more sleeping, dreaming state, we therefore find in the middle of summer the St John's festival, the summer festival in contrast to the Christmas festival, which is suited to a more modern humanity.

What has been continued outwardly and what our materialistic age no longer understands has its deep foundation in a spiritual reality. Now we live in an age when people must again begin to think and feel in a completely different way from what was the case in the former period. This former period had the task of making the realm of materialistic thinking and feeling accessible to human beings; and the last few centuries that human souls have been living through have indeed brought this about. Earthly evolution had to pass through this materialistic epoch. It is not good if we only have harsh criticism for materialism; for it had to make its appearance in earthly evolution. But now we are living in a time when materialism must be overcome, when spiritual perception must come once more to human souls. This is the more or less clear and indistinct feeling of all those who feel drawn in their own soul to our spiritual-scientific endeavours, to our spiritual-scientific world-conception: that they feel that now is the time when the spiritual world—which had formerly to be perceived in a dream-like way—must be grasped consciously. Spiritual science exists for this very purpose.

The period that has now elapsed was that of materialism. And because humanity had to immerse itself in materialism, the strong impulse that leads it up again had to be active quite specifically through the age of materialism. This is the Christ impulse. When the Christ impulse entered into earthly evolution, the preparation also began; it entered its most active stage in the fourteenth and fifteenth centuries. But when the Christ impulse approached, humanity was preparing to immerse itself in materialism. The Christ impulse existed as an objective fact in world evolution, but the people living in the time when it appeared were least of all able and ready to understand it. We now live in a time when we need to begin to understand what took place then.

What do we see from this? We see in evolution to this point that the Christ impulse has followed a remarkable course. We see that once it entered into human evolution through the Mystery of Golgotha, this Christ impulse was not understood by those living at the time. Let us try to form for ourselves a picture of what people did in their cleverness. In the first and following centuries after the emergence of the Christ impulse, we find that all manner of theological systems are formulated, that people argue about how they should think of the Trinity and so on. We see an endless amount of theological quarrelling and disputation over the centuries, and it would be the worst possible path to take if one sought from all these theological arguments to understand today how the Christ impulse was exerting its influence. The people who were arguing about their understanding of it did not understand anything of the way in which the Christ impulse belongs within evolution.

Let us try to form a clear picture of how its influence became apparent. I should like to present some facts in this connection. Let us take an event that occurred in the fourth century, in the year 312 and on 28 October, and which completely determined the future map of Europe. This was when Constantine,[73] known as 'the Great', the son of Constantius Chlorus, marched against Maxentius, the ruler of Rome, and won a victory over him which led to Christianity also becoming outwardly victorious in the Western world. Constantine then made Christianity the official state religion. But did he manage this out of his own cleverness? Did what occurred at that time happen out of cleverness at all? We cannot say that this was so. What actually happened?

When Maxentius, the Roman Emperor, had learnt that Constantine was on the march, he first consulted the Sibylline Books. He therefore set about trying to understand world phenomena in a dream-like way. What he derived from these books was interpreted to him as follows: the right deed would be done by the one who, as the ruler of Rome, would leave the city and fight the battle outside its walls. This was the most improbable advice that could be imagined; for Constantine had a much smaller army than Maxentius and would not have had much success if Maxentius had stayed in Rome. Moreover, it was not the generals in Constantine's army who won the victory. The situation was, rather, that Constantine had a dream where the symbol of Christ appeared to him; and in response to this dream he ordered that the Cross, as Christ's symbol, be carried in front of his armies. He made his subsequent deeds dependent upon the revelations of his dream. This battle, through which the map of Europe was determined at that time, was not decided by the cleverness of human beings, or won by the generals, but by dreams and prophecies. Everything in Europe would have taken a different course if things had turned out in accordance with human consciousness and not in accordance with what emanated from unconscious influences that people were not even aware of.

Theologians have argued about the nature of Christ, whether He was born in eternity together with the Father, whether He was born in time, whether He is equal to the Father and so on. In all their thoughts, nothing of the Christ impulse is contained; rather was its influence to be found in the subconscious minds of human beings. It worked not through the ego but through the astral body. The Christ impulse was a reality, and it was active without people needing to understand it. That is the important and essential fact. The way in which Christ has been working is as independent of what people have understood of Him as the course of a storm is independent of what people have learnt about electric machines or other such things in physical laboratories. The time has now come when we must immerse ourselves consciously in the influence of the Christ impulse. Nevertheless, Christ has always been actively engaged in what has happened historically.

Let us turn from this to another example from a later time. For this we need to recall something that I have already explained to you. As regards the time associated with the coming of materialism, it is important to know that if people want to focus their attention upon the spiritual world, it is best to do this in the winter. For this reason it was always considered that those whose natures are especially gifted for this are endowed with inspirations from the spiritual world during the midwinter nights that have been referred to. Everywhere in folk legends and sagas it is related how particularly gifted people who do not undergo initiation but are inspired through their own nature, through elemental forces working within them, are inspired during the nights between Christmas Eve and Three Kings Day, during the thirteen winter nights.

There is a very beautiful legend[74] that was discovered in Norway not long ago, the legend of Olaf Åsteson, who goes to church on Christmas Eve and begins to sleep. He sleeps until 6 January; and when he awakes he is able to tell in imaginations of what has taken place in the soul-world and in the spirit-land, as we call it. He expresses this in pictures, but he has experienced it during these thirteen nights. Such legends can be found everywhere. They are not really what people think of as legends today; for there have always been gifted people who have experienced a kind of nature-initiation through elemental forces working within them which someone who faithfully follows the indications of the path of initiation can also experience through his own will. Thus we can say: During the age of materialism there have always been people who, when the spirit of the Earth is most awake in the middle of winter, have been able to unite themselves with the spirit of the Earth and receive inspirations. This was also the time when the Christ impulse that had united itself with the Earth could not work through human consciousness.

We should think of especially gifted souls who were receptive to the spiritual world. It turned out that such souls receive the impulses for what they have to accomplish from out of the spiritual world precisely in these thirteen nights before the sixth of January. This had to occur; and it could be seen again and again in both insignificant and significant examples that there have been people in the course of history who were spiritually so endowed that, when the right moment arrived for them as they were living through those thirteen nights in winter, the spiritual impulse—and in this time especially the Christ impulse—entered into them. During the time of materialism, natural initiations, initiations that therefore took place without conscious human activity, have always been most easily enacted during these thirteen nights. And whenever such initiations manifested themselves, we find that they occurred during these thirteen nights.

There is one event that even those who have the least inclination to recognize the spiritual world—and very few people are inclined to do so today—will acknowledge, that in the fifteenth century spiritual powers visibly entered into the course of history through a young woman, the Maid of Orleans. It can also be proved historically that the whole map of Europe was shaped differently through the Maid of Orleans having helped the French in the war against the English. Anyone who reflects about this can conclude that everything would have turned out differently in accordance with human intentions if the shepherd girl had not intervened—and, in this shepherd girl, forces from the spiritual world. The Maid of Orleans was merely the instrument for what was brought about at that time. The influence that was working through her was the Christ impulse.

However, there must have been a natural initiation for this—and this natural initiation would have best taken place in the thirteen nights prior to the sixth of January. The Maid of Orleans must therefore have entered at some point into a kind of sleep condition during the time between 24 December and 6 January, when she would have been particularly receptive to the spiritual influence which can be present at this time. It would therefore be presupposed that the Maid of Orleans would have experienced the time from 24 December until 6 January in a not fully conscious state and had thereby received the Christ impulse. Well, the Maid of Orleans did experience this state of being in a very marked way!

It cannot be experienced more strikingly than if one is in that sleeping condition that one is in before one's birth, in the final period that one spends as a child before birth in the body of one's mother. Outer consciousness is of course not capable of apprehending anything then, for it is a state of sleep; and when it is the end of the time in the mother's body, this is the most well-developed state of inter-uterine sleep. Now the Maid of Orleans was born on 6 January. This is the great mystery of the Maid of Orleans, that she experienced a nature-initiation in the thirteen days preceding her birth. It therefore happened that on that sixth of January when the Maid of Orleans was born, particularly sensitive people eagerly came together in the village and said that something special must have happened. They felt that something special had come into the village. The Maid of Orleans had been born; and she had undergone a natural initiation in that condition of sleep that was so significant to her which she experienced in the last period before birth in her mother's body. This shows us that behind the threshold of what is accessible to human consciousness, spiritual beings are indeed at work beneath the threshold of this consciousness.

We see from this something of the significance of a history that reckons only with what is given in documents and outer sources of information. The Gods follow the course of history in a different way. They work through other means and on other paths. They place a Maid of Orleans into existence who through her special karma is suited for this incarnation where she is able to receive the Christ impulse and to work with it. At the appropriate time, the Gods let this Christ impulse flow into human evolution. Of course both conditions had to be fulfilled for this: the special individual karma of the Maid of Orleans was an essential factor. Not every child who was born on 6 January could accomplish what she did.

Thus we can indeed say that the Christ impulse has here been working in human beings through those forces that did not come to consciousness in them. Only today are we living in a time when we must consciously receive what for centuries sought to enter history by ways other than the conscious one.

I wanted to arouse within you a feeling of how subconscious forces manifest themselves in a tangible way, and how the kind of history that can be studied through documents and outward information has something superficial about it. It is good if especially in our time we can embrace such a study; for we can see that on the one hand great, mighty and heroic events are taking place interspersed with sacrificial deeds. But we see that the magnitude of what is happening in our time is accompanied by the consequences of the most extreme materialism, with the result that there is an attempt to explain everything that takes place in our time from purely outward circumstances. This comes to expression in that one nation ascribes the blame for present events to another nation, therefore seeking to judge everything in an external way by finding someone else at fault for what is happening. But the reasons for what is happening in our time lie deeply in subconscious events. We shall speak about this the day after tomorrow.

Our time has a quite particular potential—also through all the blood that is being shed—to be able to alert human beings to spiritual impulses of knowledge. When peace is eventually restored to the countries currently at war with one another, people will make the discovery that wars on so mighty a scale in world history cannot be explained from outward causes! They will discover that they are unable to explain this. Today people, especially the clever ones, are still saying that it is not appropriate to speak about everything that has caused this war: let history give its own verdict! And they think themselves to be particularly clever when they say that only in fifty or a hundred years will history be able to give the true picture.

What people call history today will never explain the causes of present events, and it will come to be seen that these causes cannot be discovered from external observation. But there will be other means of help, as is shown from an occult study of our present time.

What is one of the most striking phenomena of this destiny-laden time? It is without doubt that so many people are crossing the threshold of death when they are still young. We know what happens with a person when he passes through the gate of death. We know that to begin with his etheric body, astral body and ego leave his physical body and that after a relatively short time he casts off this etheric body and continues his further journey with an extract from it. But is it not reasonable to think that there must be a difference between an etheric body that has been cast off between the ages of twenty and thirty which would still have been able to see to the functions of human life for decades, and an etheric body that is cast off in old age? Yes, there is a great difference. When someone dies as a result of old age or through illness, the etheric body has fulfilled its task. But in the case of a young person, of whom there are countless numbers now passing through the gate of death, the etheric body has not been able to fulfil everything that it could have fulfilled.

I should now like to show you through an actual example what happens when etheric bodies are, as it were, forcibly separated from the physical body. One could of course give numerous examples of this; but I want to mention to you today an incident that we experienced in Dornach last autumn. We experienced this at the site where the Goetheanum stands.

A family living in the vicinity of the building had a little son of seven years of age[75]—a family belonging to our anthroposophical circle. He was a very likeable seven-year-old boy, a wonderful little child. He was so good that when his father was called up for military service, the little seven-year-old Theo said to his mother that he would have to work especially hard in order to help her in areas where his father would have helped her. One evening after a lecture, someone belonging to our circle came to tell us that little Theo had been missing since that evening. Our immediate thought was that there had been some accident. Now on that very evening, through what in outer life one calls chance, a furniture or removal van had come to a place where no such van had been for years and none has been since. At a certain spot it had overturned. Little Theo had been in the small house known as the canteen, because some friends of ours who are working on the building have their meals there. He would have left there earlier, but he was detained for some reason; and whereas he would normally have left through a door that would have led him to take a certain path, on this occasion he went out through a different door that led him to pass by the van at the very moment when it overturned. The van fell on top of him. This is one of those examples when we can so clearly see how karma works.

I have often used the simple comparison in order to show how cause and effect are frequently totally muddled up. We see someone walking along a river. Suddenly we see that he has fallen into the river. We go to the place and find a stone at the spot where he fell. The person is pulled out of the water, but he is already dead. If one does not investigate the matter further, one will recount the affair with an absolutely clear conscience as follows: the man stumbled over the stone, fell into the river and was drowned. But one would only have to have investigated further to find that his death occurred not because he fell into the water but that he fell into the water because he was dead; he had had a stroke. The situation is therefore the opposite of what one thinks. So you can see how easy it is to confuse cause and effect. It happens all the time in ordinary science that causes and effects are muddled up.

In the present case, it does of course become apparent that Theo was the cause of what happened; he was the reason that the van drove past at this time; he guided it to fall on top of him. One has to keep this in mind as the solution to the mystery. But there was more to it than this. Here we have a child who dies as the result of an accident in the earliest flowering of his youth! Now if one is united with all one's heart with the whole of the building work in Dornach and at the same time has the possibility of observing the influences involved with this building, one can say that this etheric body that was so forcibly separated from little Theo is now in the atmosphere of the building, and one gains the most beautiful inspirational forces for the work that is connected with it by uniting one's soul with what lives in an extended form, as though enlarged into a small world, in the atmosphere of the building. And I shall never hesitate unreservedly to admit that there is much of what I was able to discover at that time about our building that I owe to the fact that I directed the attention of my own soul to the etheric body of little Theo that was active in the atmosphere of the building. This is how the connections in the world are made. The essential individuality of this human being goes further on its way, but the etheric body that could have supported a human life for many decades remains behind.

Now just think of the number of unspent etheric bodies that hover in the atmosphere above us and above those who will also live after us! Those etheric bodies that have remained behind derive from those who have passed through the gate of death in early life in the course of our grievous and fateful time. We are not speaking of the paths that the individualities are following; we are speaking of a special spiritual atmosphere that is created by these etheric bodies that have remained behind. The human beings here on Earth will live in this atmosphere. They will be immersed in a spiritual atmosphere which will be filled by these etheric bodies that have sacrificed their life-forces specifically in order that in the present time mankind can take a step forward as a result of these events. But it will be necessary that one senses what these etheric bodies which will be the best inspirers of future humanity indeed want. A beautiful time of spirituality will be able to awaken if people bring understanding, an inner understanding of the heart, for what these etheric bodies will want to say to them. All these etheric bodies will help towards the spiritual upsurge of the future. For this reason it is so important that there are souls that will be able to feel what is coming into the atmosphere of the future through these etheric bodies.

You will not learn something about the nature of these etheric bodies only by being able to say that man consists of a physical body, etheric body, astral body and ego but also by knowing the secret of the influence exercised by these etheric bodies and how this influence will work on in the future.

Those who already have an inclination towards the ideas of spiritual science will have prepared themselves for being receptive to what these etheric bodies want to say. If we therefore turn our souls to the spiritual world, we will prepare ourselves and those who will come after us to feel what the legacy, the etheric legacy of the dead wants from the humanity of the future. If human souls will be so stirred by spiritual science that they are able to direct their spiritual awareness towards the spiritual worlds, something great and mighty will surely spring forth as an influential power from the blood, courage, suffering and sacrifice. I should therefore like at the end of today's lecture to summarize in a few words what can now ensoul and enliven us when we focus our minds upon the great, destiny-laden events of our time:

From the courage of the fighters,
From the blood on fields of battle,
From the grief of the bereaved,
From the people's sacrifice:
There will ripen fruit of spirit,
If souls will turn in consciousness
Towards the realm of spirit.

Lecture 8

VIENNA, 9 MAY 1915

The War, a Pathological Process—Central Europe and the Slavic East—The Dead as the Helpers of Human Progress

OUR spiritual-scientific world-conception should not only be focusing its attention upon the development and ascendancy of individual souls but it must also above all else really help us to gain further insights into our outlook upon life. In our time it should be of particular concern to us to acquire such further insights for our evaluation of life. To be sure, it is a great and also meaningful task for the individual human being to further his own development through what he can gain as the fruit of spiritual-scientific self-education; and it is only because human individuals progress in their development that they are able to contribute to the development of mankind as a whole. But our attention should not be directed to this alone; we should as people who identify with the anthroposophical world-conception also be able to be aware of the great events of our time from a high perspective, from a truly spiritual perspective. We should indeed be able to shift our minds to a higher standpoint in judging what is going on. Some perspectives with regard to the great events of our time will be shared today, because our present meeting has been convened at this fateful time.

Let us begin with something that can deeply affect us as human beings. At certain times people fall ill. Illnesses are usually regarded as something harmful to our organism, as something that invades it as a hostile force. However, such a commonly held viewpoint is by no means always justified. To be sure, there are certain illnesses which must be judged from this standpoint, where the illness invades our organism in a sense as an enemy. But this is not always so. It is not even so in the majority of cases, for illness is by and large something altogether different. In most cases illness is not the enemy but actually the friend of the organism. The actual enemy of the organism precedes the illness in the majority of cases; it develops within a person before the outbreak of the outwardly visible illness. There are opposing forces in the organism, and the illness that erupts at a particular point is the organism's attempt to defend itself against these opposing forces which had not previously been noticed. The illness is often the beginning of the organism's work to bring about healing. It is what the organism undertakes to battle against the hostile influences that precede the illness; it is the last form of the process, but it signifies the struggle of the good bodily fluids against what is lurking below. Its function is to drive this out from the organism.

Only if we look upon the greatest majority of illnesses in this way do we arrive at a true conception of the process of illness. The illness is therefore an indication that something preceded its outbreak which is being expelled from the organism by the illness. If many of life's phenomena are seen in the right light, one arrives very easily at what has been just said. The causes may lie in the greatest variety of areas. The essential point is, however, that—as has been indicated—we should view illnesses as the organism's defence against things that must be expelled from it.

Now I do not think that there is a comparison that is so appropriate than the comparison of such a quantity of significant, deeply incisive events as we have now been experiencing over a large part of the Earth since the beginning of August 1914 with a pathological process affecting human development. We cannot help thinking that these events associated with the war are indeed a pathological process. But it would be wrong to think that it is good enough if we were simply to conceive of this pathological process in the false sense that many illnesses are conceived: as if it were the enemy of the organism. The underlying cause precedes the manifestation of the illness. It is especially striking in our time how little people are inclined in our time to take such truths into account which anyone who embraces the world-conception of spiritual science not merely with his intellect but also with his feelings must immediately find perfectly plausible.

In the course of the last, say, nine months, we have had to undergo an infinite amount of painful experiences, experiences that have had to do with people's faculty of judgement. Is it not indeed the case that if one reads what is conclusively disseminated through the literature that is read by most people and emanating from many different countries of the Earth, it would appear that those who pass judgements about present events would presume that everything began in July 1914? This has been the most distressing experience that we have had to undergo in addition to all the other pain, that it has become apparent that particularly the people whose views tend to prevail—especially those who write newspaper articles—and determine the official opinion actually know nothing of how events came about and only look at their most immediate context. Hence there have been endless discussions which have been completely beside the point. Where lies the cause of the present military conflicts? Again and again people ask: Is this or that party responsible? In virtually every case they do not go further back than to July, or possibly June 1914.

I mention this because it really is so characteristic of our materialistic age. People generally think that materialism only brings a materialistic way of thinking, a materialistic conception of the world. This is not so. Materialism does not only bring this about but it also brings short-sightedness: materialism brings laziness of thinking and lack of insight. A materialistic way of thinking leads to the idea that one can prove and believe anything; and it is part of that inner education that a right understanding of anthroposophy must give us that enables us to see that, if one does not venture beyond the realm of materialism, it is possible to prove and believe anything.

Let us take a simple example. When in recent years one has presented the anthroposophical view of the world and someone or other felt obliged to assert his own views in opposition to it, one could often hear it said: Yes, Kant has through his philosophy proved that man has limits to his knowledge and that the knowledge that the spiritual-scientific world-conception seeks to attain cannot be reached. They then cite some very interesting things purporting to show that Kant has proved that one cannot penetrate into the spiritual world with human faculties of knowledge. If one nevertheless upholds spiritual science, these people come and assert that one is rejecting everything that Kant has proved! And of course, the assertion that is thereby implied is that one must be a particularly foolish person to reject what has been so strictly proved.

This is not so. The spiritual scientist does not deny that what Kant has proved is absolutely correct, and it is clear that this has been well demonstrated. But suppose that at the time when the microscope had not been invented, someone had come up with a firm idea that there are minute cells in the plant which no one could find because human eyes are not adapted for this. This argument would have to be firmly accepted, and this would be absolutely correct; for the human eye, as it is constituted, can never penetrate into the plant's organism to the extent of seeing these tiniest cells. An absolutely correct conclusion that can never be overturned. Yet life evolved in such a way that the microscope was invented as an aid to the human eye, and that, despite the above conclusion, human beings have arrived at a knowledge of the most minute cells. Only when it is seen that conclusive proofs are completely useless for reaching a knowledge of the truth, that arguments can be correct but actually do not have any particular significance for the knowledge of truth, only then will one be standing upon the right foundation. One will then know that arguments and proofs may be all very well, but their task is not that of leading to the truth.

If you just think of the comparison that I have given, you will see that Kant's assertion that human knowledge cannot extend to the supersensible worlds is just as valid as the argument that the human power of vision cannot reach to the cell. The proofs and arguments were absolutely correct, but life goes beyond such means of verification. This, too, is something that one discovers on the path of spiritual research, that one broadens one's horizon by appealing to something other than the human intellect and its proofs. Anyone who limits himself to materialistic ideas is indeed led to a boundless belief in proofs. If he has a proof in his pocket, he is wholly convinced of the truth. Spiritual science will show us that one can indeed perfectly well furnish proofs of one thing or another, but that intellectual proofs have no significance for arriving at real truth. It is therefore a symptom of our materialistic age that people become short-sighted in their intellectual views. If, moreover, this intellectual short-sightedness is also imbued with passions, something comes about which we not only see in the war that European peoples are waging with weapons but in their hostile attitude to one another, where one country accuses the others of all manner of things without any prospect that one might ever—not only during the war—be able to convince the others. Moreover, anyone who thinks that a neutral state might ever be able to choose between the assertions of two hostile states is simply being naive. Of course, what is advanced from the one side is equally well represented—and furnished with all sorts of proofs—by what is said from the other side. One acquires real insight only if one enters into the deeper foundations of the whole of human evolution.

A few years before the outbreak of this war, I tried through the cycle about individual Folk-souls and their influence upon human individuals in the various European territories[76] to cast a little light upon how the different nations relate to one another, while indicating that different forces rule over the various peoples. Today we shall supplement what was said in these lectures with some further perspectives.

Our materialistic age thinks in too abstract a way. Above all, no account is taken in our materialistic age of something such as the real development that takes place in life, that a person needs to bring to maturity what is within him in order that it may gradually ripen into a real judgement. As we know from what is fully described in *The Education of the Child from the Standpoint of Spiritual Science*[77], a human being undergoes a development such that in the first seven years his physical body, from the seventh until his fourteenth year his etheric body (and so on) are especially developed. Just as there is little awareness of this progressive development of the human individual, there is even less awareness of the parallel phenomenon, a phenomenon that is of equivalent significance.

The processes that are enacted within and among the various peoples are—as we all know from spiritual science—guided and directed by beings of the higher hierarchies. We speak in the true sense of the word of Folk-souls, of Folk-spirits.* We know, for example, that the Folk-spirit of the Italian people inspires what we call the sentient soul; that the French Folk-spirit inspires what we call the intellectual or mind soul, that the inhabitants of the British Isles are inspired by the consciousness soul; while in Central Europe it is what we call the human ego that is inspired. However, this does not imply any value-judgement about the various nations; it is simply a statement that this is so. It is, for example, stated that a fundamental inspiration of the people inhabiting the British Isles is that as a nation it brings into the world everything that is brought about through the Folk-spirit by means of the inspiration of the consciousness soul. It is remarkable how nervous people become in relation to this theme.

When during the events of the war I have again mentioned things that I already spoke about in the cycle referred to, there have been people who almost regarded it as a kind of insult to the British people when I said that they had the task of inspiring the consciousness soul, whereas the German Folk-soul has to inspire the human ego. It was as though one were to take it as an insult if one were to say that salt is white and paprika is red. It is a simple characterization, the expression of an existing truth, and it has to be accepted as such. One will be able to deal much better with the prevailing issues between the various groups comprising members of humanity as a whole if one considers the qualities possessed by the various peoples in contrast to mixing everything up, as the modern materialistic conception tends to do.

Of course, the individual human being rises above what he receives through his Folk-soul; and it is the task of our Anthroposophical Society to raise the human individual out of the group-soul nature, so that he is elevated to the life of humanity as a whole. But the fact nevertheless remains that, in so far as he belongs to a particular nation, a human individual is inspired in a certain direction by these qualities of this nation, that for example the Italian Folk-spirit speaks to the sentient soul, the French Folk-spirit to the intellectual or mind

*It should be pointed out that in these lectures Rudolf Steiner seems to use these terms interchangeably. This usage is followed in the translation.—Translator

soul and the British Folk-spirit to the consciousness soul. We therefore have to imagine that the Folk-spirit is, as it were, hovering over what human individuals initiate within the various nations. But just as in the case of an individual human being there is a development such that one can say: the ego reaches a certain stage of development at a particular time of life, so can one also speak with respect to the Folk-soul of a development in relation to its people, of a real development. However, this development is somewhat different from that of the individual human being.

Let us take the Italian people as an example. Thus we have this particular nation, and then the Folk-soul that belongs to it. The Folk-soul is a being from the supersensible world and belongs to the world of the higher hierarchies. It inspires the sentient soul, and this continues to happen for as long as the Italian people (since we are speaking of this people) exists, but it inspires the sentient soul in the most various ways at different times. There are times when the Folk-souls inspire those belonging to particular nations in such a way that this inspiration occurs, as it were, on a soul level. The Folk-soul then hovers in higher regions of the spirit, and its inspiration is exerted only upon soul-qualities. Then there are times when Folk-souls reach down further and engage more strongly with the individual members of the nation, inspiring them so forcefully that not only does a person receive them into his soul-qualities but the influence is so strong that his bodily qualities are also dependent on the Folk-soul. As long as a people is influenced by the Folk-soul in such a way that the Folk-soul only inspires soul-spiritual qualities, the national type is not so pronounced. In such a case the forces of the Folk-soul do not penetrate into the blood of individual human beings. Then comes a time when even from the way that a person looks out of his eyes and from his facial features it is possible to discern the influence of the Folk-spirit. What manifests itself is that the Folk-soul has descended more deeply; it strongly and intensively takes hold of the whole human being.

In the case of the Italian people, the time of which I have spoken—when the Folk-spirit descends deeply, when its influence can be discerned through the impression that it makes on human individuals—was roughly in the middle of the sixteenth century, around

1550. Then the Folk-soul, as it were, retraced its influence, and from this time onwards it is transmitted through heredity to the descendants. The most intensive union of the Italian people with its Folk-soul was around 1550. It is then that the Italian Folk-soul descends most deeply, it is then that this people inhabiting the Italian peninsula acquires its distinctive character. If we go back to the time before 1550, we see that the characteristic features are not so pronounced. Only then does what is characteristic of the Italian character really have its beginning; it was then that what we may think of as the real marriage between the Italian Folk-soul and the sentient soul of the human beings belonging to the Italian people took place.

For the French people—I am therefore not speaking of the individual human being, who can rise above the national character—the similar moment when the Folk-spirit therefore descended most deeply and fully penetrated the whole nation occurred in approximately 1600, at the beginning of the seventeenth century. It was then that the Folk-spirit completely took hold of the intellectual or mind soul.

For the British people the comparable time was in the middle of the seventeenth century, around 1650; it was then that the British nation first acquired its characteristically British expression.

If you know such things much will begin to be understandable to you, for you can for example raise a question such as this in a completely different way: How is Shakespeare's connection with England to be understood? Shakespeare was active in England before the Folk-spirit exerted its influence most intensively upon the English people. This is why he was not properly understood in England. There are known to be editions of his plays where everything not to the taste of governesses is edited out. Shakespeare is all too often reduced to the most superficial moralizing; and we are well aware that Shakespeare was most deeply understood not in England but in the cultural development of Central Europe.

You will now be asking when the Folk-spirit came in contact with those belonging to the Central European people. The situation is as follows. Through the fact that in Central Europe the ego is the most important element and that a kind of descent of the Folk-spirit takes place and then a withdrawal, then a further descent and a further withdrawal, there are repetitions of this cycle. Thus approximately in the time when the wonderful legends of Parzival and the Grail arose we have such a descent of the Folk-spirit, its union with individual souls and a withdrawal; and a next descent roughly between the years 1750 and 1830. It was then that what lives in Central Europe was fully embraced by the Folk-spirit of Central Europe. Since then there has again been a withdrawal of the Folk-spirit.

So you see that it is perfectly understandable that, say, Jacob Boehme lived at a time when he could receive little from the German Folk-spirit. This was not the time when the Folk-spirit united itself with the individual souls of the people. Thus although he is referred to as the 'Teutonic Philosopher', Jacob Boehme is a person who as regards the time when he lived is independent of his Folk-spirit, a kind of uprooted phenomenon, a breath of eternity in his time. If we take Lessing, Schiller and Goethe, they are additionally German philosophers who are rooted in the German Folk-spirit. It is wholly characteristic that these philosophers living in the time between 1750 and 1830 are deeply rooted in their Folk-spirit.

So you see that it is not merely a question of knowing that in the Italian nation the Folk-spirit works through the sentient soul, that in the French nation the Folk-spirit works through the intellectual soul, that in the British nation the Folk-spirit works through the consciousness soul and that in the case of the Central European people the Folk-spirit works through the ego, but that one must also know that this happens at particular times. Moreover, the events that take place can only be explained historically if one really knows such things. The nonsense pursued in the form of science, where one bases everything on documents and lists the events in sequence, and says that one must lead to the next—this nonsense leads the historical researcher not to a real history, to an understanding of human evolution, but to a falsification of what works and weaves in human history.

And if one now sees how the forces which drive these national entities (and of course, other such entities could also be characterized) work in a totally different way on the various nations, one sees the contrasting elements that are present. One sees that what happens today has not only been happening in the last few years but has been prepared over centuries.

Let us look towards the East, towards the region that bears Russian culture. The whole distinctive quality of Russian culture is that it can only really develop when the Russian Folk-soul unites with the Spirit-self—this has already been spoken of in the cycle referred to. This means that a future time must come when the characteristic features of the European East will for the first time acquire a definite form. And this will be completely different from what takes place in Western or Central Europe. For the time being, however, it is understandable that what is assigned to Russian culture does not yet exist but that Russian culture—and also the individual human being—relates to the Spirit-self by always looking up to it. Individual Russians and even deep-thinking Russian philosophers do not express the loftiest thoughts as is done in Central Europe but in a completely different way.

Here we find something highly characteristic; for what is a distinctive quality of Central European life? You all know that there was a time of the great mystics, when Meister Eckhardt, Johannes Tauler and others were all active. They all sought the divine essence that is contained in the human soul. They endeavoured to find the God within them, 'the little spark within the heart', as Eckhardt expressed it. Within the soul, they said, there must be something where the Godhead is directly present. And so there arose that aspiration where the ego sought to unite itself with the Godhead within. This divine essence, the Godhead was to be striven for, it called for an active process of development. This is a characteristic feature of the whole of Central European cultural life.

Just think of the infinite depth of feeling expressed by someone who, I might say, is internationally recognized as being representative of Central European culture and spiritual life, Angelus Silesius,[78] when he says in one of the beautiful verses contained in his *Cherubinischer Wandersmann*: When I die, it is not I who dies but God dies in me. Consider how infinitely profound this is! For someone who says this has livingly grasped the idea of immortality, in that he has felt: when a human individual dies, this means that the person concerned is imbued with the Godhead—this phenomenon of death is one that has to do not with man but with God, and since God cannot die, death must only be an illusion. Death can therefore not be a destruction of life. Someone who says 'When I die, it is not I who dies but God dies in me' knows of the existence of the immortal soul. It is a feeling of infinite depth that lives in Angelus Silesius. This is a consequence of the fact that the inspiration here occurs in the ego.

When the inspiration occurs in the sentient soul, something can happen as it did, for example, in the case of Giordano Bruno.[79] This friar felt passionately engaged with the discoveries of Copernicus; he felt that the whole world was enlivened. If you read anything that Giordano Bruno has written, you will find it confirmed that, inasmuch as he derived from an Italian background, he furnishes the proof that the Folk-soul is here inspiring the sentient soul.

Cartesius (or Descartes) was born at the point of French development that has been characterized, when the French Folk-spirit fully united itself with the French people. If you read a page of Descartes, the French philosopher, you will find that on every page he confirms what spiritual science finds: that the inspiration of the Folk-spirit is influencing the intellectual soul.

If you read Locke or Hume or another English [sic] philosopher up to and including Mill and Spencer, you find throughout the inspiration of the consciousness soul.

If you read Fichte as he struggles within the ego itself, you have the inspiration of the ego through the Folk-soul. This is characteristic of the fact that this Central European Folk-soul is experienced within the ego, and that therefore the ego is the truly aspirational quality with, I may say, all its strength and errors, its mistakes and its conquests! If someone from Central Europe is to find the path to Christ, he needs to give birth to Him within his own soul.

Try to find in the cultural life of Russia—if it has not been outwardly overwhelmed by Western culture—this idea of experiencing Christ or God in one's inner being. You will not be able to find it. The expectation is always that what enters into history manifests itself, as Solovyov[80] says, as a 'miracle'. Russian cultural life is very inclined to look for the resurrection of Christ in the supersensible world; but this is as though man were down below and the source of inspiration were moving about above mankind like a cloud and not as though it was penetrating into the human ego.

This intimate fellowship of the ego with its God, or also—if has to do with Christ—with Christ, this desire for Christ to be born within one's own soul, can only be found in Central Europe. And when East-European culture arrives at the stage of development that is appropriate for it, this will become apparent through the founding of a culture that, as it were, hovers above man, that represents a kind of group-soul quality, although at a higher level than the old group-souls. At present we must find it perfectly natural that in the way that even Russian philosophers speak, there is always a sense of something that as though hovers above the human world which one can never approach as intimately as someone from Central Europe wishes with his ego to approach the divine essence that works and weaves through the world. And when I have myself often spoken of the Godhead that weaves and surges through the world, this emanates from the feeling-world of a Central European and would not be understood by any other European nation in the same way that it can be received by the feeling-life of Central Europe. This is the characteristic quality of the people of Central Europe.

These are the forces that live in the different peoples and that confront one another, and which therefore again and again have to engage in conflicts involving powerful discharges and explosions, just as clouds release their burden of rain and cause lightning and storms.

But do we not see, one might now say, that words have resounded in the East as a kind of rallying-cry with the intention that the culture of Eastern Europe should begin now, that it should extend over the unworthy West of Europe and overwhelm it? Do we not see that the Slavophils,[81] the Panslavists and Panslavism[82] have appeared, exemplified especially in figures such as Dostoyevsky[83] and others; and that in his programme Dostoyevsky put forward particular points where he says: All you Western Europeans, you have a degenerate culture which must be replaced by Eastern Europe. A whole theory was then established, a theory which culminated essentially by saying:

In the West everything has become decadent, and it must be replaced by the fresh forces of the East. We have the good Orthodox religion which we do not oppose; we have accepted it as the cloud of the Folk-spirit hovering over people, and so forth. And then some brilliant theories were built up as to what might be the principles and intentions of the ancient Slavic world and how from the East truth should now extend its sway over Central and Western Europe.

I said that the individual can rise above his national identity. In a certain sphere, the great Russian philosopher Solovyov was such an individual. Although one can discern in every line that he writes as a Russian, he stands above his national character. In the first period of his life Solovyov was a Panslavist. But he then penetrated more deeply into what the Panslavists and Slavophils presented as a kind of philosophy or world-conception of nations. And what did Solovyov, as a Russian, find? He asked himself: Does that which constitutes the Russian nature exist in the present time? Is this, perhaps, already contained in what is advocated by those who represent Panslavism and the Slavophils? He did not rest until he discovered the truth.[84] And what did he find?

He investigated the assertions of the Slavophils (to whom he had previously belonged) in a very thorough way, and he found that a large part of the thought-forms, assertions and intentions were taken from the French philosopher de Maistre[85] who sympathized with the Jesuits, that he was the great teacher of the Slavophils as regards their world-conception. Solovyov himself demonstrated that Slavophilism did not grow out of Russian soil but was derived from de Maistre. And he also discovered something else. He unearthed a long-forgotten German book from the nineteenth century[86] which no one in Germany knows about. The Slavophils extracted whole portions from it in their literature. What is the strange phenomenon that confronts us here? People believe that something that is supposedly derived from the East comes from there, and it is a Western import. It came from the West and is being sent back again to people in the West. People in the West are made acquainted with their own thought-forms, because the thought-forms peculiar to the East do not yet exist.

When things are clearly investigated, there is always confirmation of what spiritual science has to say. Thus in what seeks to roll in from the East we are dealing with something that is still elemental, with something that will only be developed if it receives what has developed in Central Europe as lovingly as Central Europe lovingly received Greek and Latin culture from the south; for the course of human development is such that the later absorbs what came before. And the Faust mentality that I was able to characterize in yesterday's public lecture,[87] when I spoke of the year 1770, was experienced by Goethe as a Faustian aspiration when he said:

Philosophy have I digested,
The whole of Law and Medicine,
From each its secrets I have wrested,
Theology, alas, thrown in.
Poor fool, with all this sweated lore,
I stand no wiser than before.*

There then arose a rich, German cultural life, an immensely rich, intense striving in German culture. But if Goethe had written his *Faust* forty years later, he would certainly not have begun with '*Habe nun ach, Philosophie...*' ('Philosophy have I digested...' and so forth) and have become the wise man of all ages but he would nevertheless have written his *Faust* as he did in 1770. This living aspiration enters the ego from the inspiration of the Folk-soul, from that intimate connection of the ego with the Folk-spirit. This is a fundamental quality of the spiritual culture of Central Europe, and East-European culture must lovingly unite itself with it, it must accept it. That which had to flow to Central Europe was in former times absorbed from cultures of the south. When this elemental wave of development comes rolling in from the east, it is as if the pupil is angry with his teacher because he ought to be learning something from him and therefore wants to give him a good hiding. It is a somewhat trivial comparison, but it is nevertheless a comparison that presents the actual state of affairs. Large numbers of people live together in Europe with completely different

*Translation by Philip Wayne, Penguin Classics, 1999.

developmental forces. These different developmental forces must actively compete with one another; they must assert themselves in a variety of ways. The opposing forces that undoubtedly exist, forces that come in conflict with one another, have long been developing; and it is when one attends to the finer details that one finds everywhere the things that spiritual science has to say.

It is a wonderful thing that the wave of European development should concentrate itself in such a way as to present before the whole of mankind a symbolic picture of how in Central Europe the intimate connection of the ego with the spiritual world is experienced; how God may be experienced in 'the little spark within the heart', how Christ may be experienced in 'the little spark within the heart'! Christ Himself must become a living presence within the human ego. Hence as in no other European language the whole development in Central Europe tends gradually towards what is called the 'ego' or 'I' (Ich). And the German word Ich is 'I—C—H'. Ich, which is equivalent to I—CH or Jesus Christ, is in Central Europe like a mighty symbol reflecting the intimate interplay of what can be the soul's holiest possession with the soul itself. Jesus Christ and the human ego at one and the same time. Thus does the Folk-spirit work inspiring the people, in order to express in characteristic words what the underlying facts are. I well know that people laugh when something of this kind is said; when it is said that the Folk-spirit worked for centuries in order that the word Ich, which is of such symbolic significance, came about. But let people laugh! After no more than a few centuries, they will no longer laugh; they will regard this as having far more significance than what are referred to today as laws of nature.

The influence of this wave of development has been highly characteristic. Only a very small part of the truth comes to conscious expression; but what works in the unconscious depths is expressive of a far greater degree of truth. We speak, for example, of Germanic peoples. Words are formed by the active genius of language. One part of the inhabitants of Central Europe calls itself 'German'; but when one speaks of Germanic peoples, this includes Germany, Austria, Holland, the Scandinavian nations and also those living in the British Isles. The word 'Germanic' extends over a wide area. Someone living in the British Isles, however, rejects it. When he uses the word 'German', he just means those living in Germany. He does not have an equivalent for the German word 'Germane' [except in the historical sense of 'ancient German' or 'Teuton']. The German language encompasses a far wider meaning with the word. It tends as such towards putting the word at the service of selflessness; the German does not only refer to himself when he uses the word 'Germane' but includes all the others as well. The Briton rejects this. If you explore the wonders of the creative genius of language, you will see that there really is something wonderful there. With regard to what people have in their consciousness, there arises maya, the great illusion. What works in unconscious depths is far more true in its influence. Here something immensely significant and profound comes to expression.

Now compare with the way that one must sensitively set to work in order to understand the play of forces at work in Europe the utter coarseness of the way that the relationships between the European nations are viewed today, and you will be able to see the extent of the devastation that the age of materialism has wrought in the human power of judgement. The worst thing is not that people have begun to think that matter bears and supports everything but that they have become short-sighted, that they are unable to see what is fundamental and do not even take a step behind the veil that is woven over truth as maya.

Materialism has well prepared what it sought to achieve. Here too a genial spirit has been active, although it is the genius who is the leading driver of materialism, Ahriman. He has had an immense influence in recent centuries, a very considerable influence. I would like briefly to refer to a chapter which people may perhaps prefer to ignore today; and if their attention is drawn to it, they look upon this as a particular form of insanity. You see, the easiest way to influence people is to drip-feed their souls and imaginations when they are still young with what will develop within them later. In later life very few people can really be taught anything. Ahriman would never have better prospects of preparing souls in a genuinely materialistic way than if he drip-feeds the souls of young people and children with what continues to work on in the unconscious. If materialistic thought-forms are absorbed in the period when people do not yet think intellectually, they will learn to think in a thoroughly materialistic way through the materialism that has been implanted in children's souls. Ahriman achieved this by inspiring a writer of the materialistic age with the idea of *Robinson Crusoe*.[88]

Anyone who attentively reads *Robinson Crusoe* will see the extent of the influence of materialistic ideas in it. This may not be obvious at first, but the entire book—how it is constructed, how in this life of adventure he is led to everything through outward experience until finally even religion grows out of the soil like cabbages—well prepares the child's soul for materialistic thinking. And when one considers that over a certain period—the seventeenth and eighteenth centuries—there were Bohemian, Portuguese, Hungarian and other Robinson Crusoes as imitations of the original, it becomes clear that the task was thoroughly achieved, and that the contribution that the reading of *Robinson Crusoe* has made to the development of materialism is very considerable.

In contrast to such phenomena it should be indicated that there is something else that children should be given as nourishment for their understanding until late in life: these are the fairy tales that live in Central Europe, and especially the fairy tales collected by the Brothers Grimm. This is much better literature for children than *Robinson Crusoe*. And if in our time what is happening in so terrible, fateful a way between the European nations is understood as an incitement to look more closely at the way that what now manifests itself in the present has been developing beneath the surface of events, one will readily come to see that it is not ultimately a question of whether a few scholars send their titles and diplomas back to England! If the incitement afforded by this time proves to be so strong that one recognizes the materialistically inspired consciousness soul of the British people in its full significance, one will also perceive the significance of letting children read *Robinson Crusoe* and prevent this happening. If one comes to be able to take account of the warnings of our present time, one will have to set to work in a much more thorough and more radical way.

It is now thirty-five years[89] since I began to interpret Goethe's spiritual-scientific task. I tried to show that in Goethe's theory of evolution something of great spiritual magnitude was presented. The time must come when this is perceived more widely. For Goethe has given a great, powerful theory of evolution, which has spiritual stature. People found this difficult to understand. Darwin, who gave in a coarser, materialistic way what Goethe had presented in a more refined, spiritual form in his theory of evolution, was able to have greater influence in the age of materialism. Central Europe was thoroughly taken over by England. Think of the tragedy of this situation, that the most English scientist in Germany,[90] Ernst Haeckel, who swore by Darwin, should have felt such a furious hatred for everything English; and when the war broke out, he was one of the first to return to England the awards and diplomas that he had received. He was probably already too old to send back the so characteristically English theories of Darwin, but that would have been more to the point and far more important.

What is involved here is something so infinitely profound and meaningful, and it is connected with the spiritual deepening of our time that needs to happen. If one comes to see that Goethe's theory of colour has far greater depth than that of Newton, that Goethe's theory of evolution is much more profound than that of Darwin, one will be aware of what lies concealed in Central Europe also in relation to such important fields of research.

I want in this way to give you a feeling of the sense of urgency that the present, difficult and destiny-laden events need to arouse within us. An exhortation to work, which should lead us to reflect upon what lies hidden in the cultural life of Central Europe and which is in a certain sense our responsibility to draw forth. This is also what I meant when I said yesterday in the public lecture that this cultural-spiritual life of Central Europe contains seeds that must bring forth blossoms and fruit.

If we acknowledge again and again that the conscious life of the soul carries on at the surface, while beneath it lies all that has been spoken of during these days, we may also reflect upon the fact that in the impulses of many people in the present something is living which is quite different from that of which they are conscious. Do not think that those people in the West and the East whose task it is to defend the great fortress of Central Europe are fighting only for what they are aware of at the surface of consciousness. We should above all be looking at the impulses of which many of those who are dying on the battlefields are unconscious; but these impulses are there, they exist, and we should from spiritual science be able, as we look towards both East and West, to evoke the feeling that in the impulses of those who make these sacrifices something lives that will become outwardly manifest only in the future, even though those engaged in fighting have hardly any conscious idea of this. Only if we consider what is happening at present in this light will we be filled with feelings that are right and appropriate.

But just think how many souls involved in these events, with which nothing in the conscious history of mankind can be compared as regards their military scale, are suffering violent deaths, and that these souls will look down upon the death that has been thrust upon them by the great events of this time. Recall what I said the day before yesterday about the youthful etheric bodies filling the spiritual atmosphere. Consider that not only will their souls, their individualities be in the spiritual world but that impulses from these youthful etheric bodies that can be used will pervade the spiritual atmosphere. Let us try out of this situation to perceive the awakening calls which those who remain here on the Earth must be hearing. For indeed, the human individual who has passed through the gate of death calls attention to the great tasks that are to be accomplished in European culture; and people must out of the depths of spiritual life sense this urgency to engender feelings born out of knowledge with respect to the true nature of the world in which we live. If one comes to feel in this sense that each person who falls on the battlefield in the flower of his youth is the bearer of an exhortation, a call for the spiritualization of humanity in the context of European culture, one will have understood this rightly.

It is not enough that an abstract knowledge goes out from centres such as the one where we are gathered that man consists of a physical body, etheric body, astral body and an ego and that he passes through many incarnations and has a karma and so forth; one would wish that the souls who participate in our spiritual-scientific life will be stirred in their innermost depths to that feeling life of which I have spoken, to sharing in the immediate future in the experience of the awakening calls of those who have died prematurely. The most wonderful experience that we can have as people committed to spiritual science is of the living life that should pass like a breath through the ranks of those who belong to our movement. Not knowledge alone, not mere understanding, but this life, making this life a true reality.

In recent times a number of members have left the physical plane. Among them was a young fellow member, our dear Fritz Mitscher.[91] Karma brought it about that I had the task to speak at the cremation in Basel. I had to address certain words to the departing soul. Among many other things that I said to the soul was that we know that he will continue to work with us also after he has passed through the gate of death. I had to say this out of the awareness that what inspires and animates us all is no mere theory but that what we express in the form of theoretical thoughts must fill our whole soul with life. But then we must relate to those who have passed through the gate of death as to those who still live here on Earth. Indeed, we should not hesitate to say to ourselves: Those who live in a physical body are prevented through the most manifold circumstances from fully living a spiritual life. What a lot of impediments we can discern in this physical earthly life where it is a question of recognizing the really great tasks of evolution—and even more so when it is a case of fulfilling them! But the dead are far more reliable. This sense that the dead are among us, that a special mission has been entrusted to them, guided me when I spoke the words of commemoration for our friend Fritz Mitscher, who passed prematurely through the gate of death; and what was said for him relates to many others who have crossed this threshold. We see in them our most important collaborators, and it will not be misunderstood when I say that in our spiritual work we can rely far more on the dead than on the living.

But in order to be able to say this, we must be livingly engaged in what our spiritual movement can give us. My basic premiss is that, also in an outward sense, those who have crossed the threshold of death in our destiny-laden time are our most important collaborators in the spiritualizing of the human culture of the future. For the death to which those who have passed through this portal look back becomes a great teacher, and many people today need stronger teachers than life can give. One can see this through numerous examples.

I should like to give an example out of many others that could be given. A sensational article[92] opposing the spiritual science which I advocate appeared several years ago in a journal called *Hochland* that is published in South Germany. This article created a great stir. Many people were convinced by it, because it was written by a famous professor of philosophy. The editor of that journal *Hochland* (Highland) accepted this article. He has thereby propagated, as he thinks, a view of this confounded spiritual science that is worthy of consideration.

You see, it is really not a question of defending oneself against such things with outward means. It is absolutely understandable that all clever modern people find spiritual science to be utter folly. But after the outbreak of the war, something else occurred. The editor of the journal in question is a good German, a man with good German feelings. The author whose article he had published now wrote letters to that editor, who in, shall we say, his blessed 'innocence' printed them in the *Süddeutsche Monathefte* (South German Monthly). If you try to read them, you will see what that same philosopher writes to the editor of *Hochland* is full of venomous hatred of the spiritual culture of Central Europe, so that the editor feels obliged to say: Anyone who thinks like this can in Central Europe only be found in madhouses. Just think how immensely significant this criticism is! There is an editor of a South German journal. This editor accepts an article which he considers to be an authoritative means of destroying spiritual science and of which he says: This is a good article about spiritual science by a famous philosopher!

After some time the editor receives things written by the same man, which he then refers to as coming from someone who belongs in the madhouse. But should one not, in accordance with living logic, continue by saying that if this man is now a fool, was he not also a fool before, and that the good editor did not realize at the time that in the case of the critical article about spiritual science he was dealing with a fool? This is living logic. One can sometimes not wait until such living logic takes effect. Nevertheless, it is an active force in our life and one can therefore sometimes experience something further after such a reception. The article appeared at the time as a criticism of my spiritual science. People read it and said: Yes, this is written by a famous philosopher and Platonist, he must be really clever. The editor said: If someone who is so clever writes about spiritual science, this must be a good article. Some time passes, and the same editor says: The man is a fool. But the editor first needed proofs for this, as has been described. Yes, this can be a common experience. Such people who have as little ground under their feet as that editor of the South German journal need to be taught their lessons by events, which have through what we have been experiencing recently been given by the spiritual world in a far deeper sense than one would have wished.

You will therefore understand if I return to what I said earlier: our time has been the scene of many opposing forces, and if we call the war a disease (which we can do), it is a disease which was brought about by something that took place long ago, and it is a healing force which is a means of eradicating much that had gradually to lead to the damaging of the whole of cultural life. If we think of it as a disease, and if we view the disease as a means of self-defence, we will also understand this war and the destiny-laden events of the present; we will also understand the hints and exhortations that it is giving us. We will then experience it with all the inner forces of our soul, so that we can be really attentive to those who have passed through the gate of death and look towards the near future and will have learnt what they are able to inspire within the souls that wish to hear them: that a spiritual deepening that is necessary for the healing and advancement of humanity must enter into them.

If your souls are able rightly to receive what I would wish to say with these words, if you are able to make the resolve to become souls of such a kind who direct their attention to what is being whispered from above by those who have passed through the portal of death as a result of the present fateful events, you will in a very real sense be adherents and upholders of our spiritual-scientific outlook on the world.

A bridge needs to be built in the near future through spiritual science between the living and the dead, a line of communication through which the inspiring elemental forces of those who have in the present time made great sacrifices can find the path across.

For this reason, I wanted in speaking to you to awaken certain feelings within you. May these feelings be expectant feelings of what is being addressed to souls by the effects of our destiny-laden time.

In this sense, I shall again conclude with the words that I spoke the day before yesterday. They are intended to work in our souls as a mantra, so that our souls become expectant, expectant of the inspiration that will come from the dead, who are, however, quite especially alive in the spirit:

From the courage of the fighters,
From the blood on fields of battle,
From the grief of the bereaved,
From the people's sacrifice:
There will ripen fruit of spirit,
If souls will turn in consciousness
Towards the realm of spirit.

Lecture 9

PRAGUE, 13 MAY 1915

Man's Relationship to the Kingdoms of Nature and to the Hierarchies—Time-Spirits and Folk-Spirits—The Urging Voices of the Dead

IT is a difficult time in which we are living, a time of truly courageous deeds and high sacrifices on the one hand, a time of hard and difficult trials for human souls on the other. At the end of our considerations today it will therefore be my task to arouse some feelings evoked by our destiny-laden time; for since we are able to be together at such a time, it is our wish to conclude by allowing the feelings engendered at such a time to find full expression. But we should like to begin with something that can shed light upon much that must speak in a meaningful way to our souls in our time.

Since we have begun to study the world in a spiritual-scientific way, we have called the four members of our human nature the physical body, the etheric body, the astral body and the ego. And we know that the ego, or, rather, that aspect of human nature that we call I, through which we give expression to the ego, is the youngest but also for us the most significant member of the human organism. For if through the succession of Saturn, Sun and Moon-time man were to consist only of a physical body, etheric body and astral body, he would not be man. Man is the being he is through the fact that during the earthly age he has received his ego through the spirits of the higher hierarchies and that during the earthly age he now further develops this ego in the course of successive incarnations through various human communities, through various peoples and periods of time, until the Earth has reached the aim of its evolution and until, by having fully developed his ego, man has also achieved his earthly purpose. But we also know that there are higher spiritual beings—we use the word 'higher' to refer to them—who, as it were, stand above man. We speak of the hierarchy of the angels, angeloi, of the hierarchy of the archangels, archangeloi, of the archai or Time-spirits and so on in an upwards ascent. We refer to them by means of these names and we could equally well use other names, but the names are as introduced in the West.

We wish now to call to mind how we may conceive of these spiritual beings of the higher hierarchies in relation to man and his place here on the Earth. We shall begin from what man has around him here on Earth. We know that this is the mineral kingdom, the plant kingdom and the animal kingdom; and from everything that he can observe of his situation man must come to regard the human kingdom itself as the highest of these kingdoms. Above these kingdoms, as it were, as a continuation upwards, appears the realm of the angeloi, the archangeloi, the archai and so forth. We may simply visualize that these realms are not concluded with that of the human kingdom but also extend further upwards, only that the higher realms cannot be seen with the outward senses.

It might in itself appear obvious that, when we ascend from the mineral, plant and animal kingdoms to the human kingdom, invisibility begins directly as we go above the human kingdom. But it will be obvious only for as long as one does not consider that animals—as is quite clear to someone who is able to put himself wholly into the way that animals perceive the world—do not see human beings as one human being sees other human beings. If animals could speak, they would only speak of mineral, plant and animal kingdoms as being visible; they would regard themselves as the highest visible realm. That animals see human beings as one human being sees another is merely a prejudice. For animals, we human beings are actually of a supersensible, ghostly existence; and if animals only had such perceptions as we have, they would not see human beings but human beings would be as invisible to them as the realm of the angels is to us. Only because they have a certain dream-like clairvoyance do animals see man as a spectre, as a supersensible being. We cannot as such have any direct conception of the image that an animal forms of a human being.

On the other hand animals also see something in a downwards perspective, or to be more precise perceive something in a downwards direction which man no longer perceives in this sense. That is to say, animals do not merely perceive the mineral world in the way that human beings do but they—and especially the lower animals—perceive something altogether different. When an animal such as a snail crawls over the ground, it perceives the whole distinctive quality of the soil. It would constantly disturb a person if, as he walks over the floor of the Earth, he were to perceive it as does a snail or a tortoise. With the higher animals that have warm blood it is somewhat different, but especially the lower animals really do perceive the whole distinctive quality of the ground on which they are crawling. They perceive the special character of the air, they perceive everything that is around them totally differently from a human being. The animal knows whether the ground over which it is moving is peaty or sandy soil, for it inwardly perceives its essential quality. Indeed, it is rather as though we were hearing the things around us.

The whole of the mineral world is pervaded by a delicate quivering of forces that a human being does not perceive. The animal perceives this delicate quivering in such a way that it experiences the one as congenial and the other not. When, for example, an animal moves from one kind of soil to another, it is not that the animal sees it as does a human being but it does so because something is painful to it, because the delicate movements reverberate within it, because it feels a kind of affinity there. This is a kind of instinctive hearing, like a hearing of what is going on in the soil, or it is like a process of smelling. So that we can say: The animal perceives an elemental realm and from man onwards acknowledges a higher hierarchy.

We are therefore placed amidst a world that we know as the outer world of the senses, with its outwardly perceived realms or kingdoms, and the world of the higher hierarchies.

Now we also know that a being of the higher hierarchies, for example an angel, has passed through a human stage. This was while the Earth was passing through the period of Old Moon. At this time man was not yet man, for he had no ego; he was only at the preparatory stage of humanity and had the astral body as the highest member of his being. The beings who belong to the hierarchy of the angeloi had passed through their human stage during the time of Old Moon. And the spirits to whom we turn as the guardian spirits of individual human beings are these beings from the hierarchy of the angeloi to each of whom a human being is assigned. The 'spirits of your souls'* are those who are in the hierarchy directly above man, whose wings—to put it in symbolic terms—work protectively over human beings and over the single human individual.

Then we come to the hierarchy of the archangeloi. They were also once human beings. During the period of Old Sun, the beings whom we today call archangeloi were at the human stage. They did not of course take the shape that human beings have now, they were formed completely differently, but they were at that time at their human stage. We should not imagine that during the time of Old Sun the archangeloi looked like modern human beings, but as regards their development they were at their human stage. Similarly, the Spirits of Personality or Time-spirits were at their human stage during the period of Old Saturn.

Now let us single out these spirits to whom we refer as the archangeloi. Thus we have these spirits who passed through their human stage during the period of Old Sun and rose to the stage of angels during the time of Old Moon and have in our time ascended to the stage of archangeloi. We first want to place before our souls these spiritual beings who stand two stages higher than us; we shall return to them later. Then we have the spiritual beings who were human beings during the period of Old Saturn and are today Spirits of Time, who stand three stages above us. Again we want to visualize them. And now we shall consider our relationship specifically to these two kinds of spirits.

When we as human beings pass through an incarnation—we may therefore acknowledge that in our earthly bodies today we are living in an incarnation—there stand above us spirits whom we regard as

---

*This is a reference to commemorative words spoken by Rudolf Steiner before lectures that he gave during the First World War. See *Verses and Meditations*, Rudolf Steiner Press 1993, p. 205 and note 9.—Translator

belonging to the hierarchy of the angels, then spirits belonging to the hierarchy of the archangeloi and those belonging to the hierarchy of the archai, the Time-spirits or Spirits of Personality. They too are undergoing a development of their own. Let us consider specifically the archai, the Spirits of Personality or Time-spirits. Thus we pass through our incarnation, we then go through the gate of death, enter after death into a spiritual world, undergo a purely spiritual development between death and a new birth and then return to an earthly existence through a new birth. Now we may ask: On what does it depend whether after a certain number of years we again come down to the Earth? This question has often been raised in public lectures. An answer can be given from a certain point of view, but in the intimate context of our branches we can give an answer that points more to the reality of the situation.

While we are living here in the physical body, the Time-spirit has a quite particular level of development. It does something that is connected with the development of human beings on Earth and it undergoes a development of its own. When this Time-spirit has in the course of its evolution arrived at the point where we have all let what it is undergoing and has undergone flow into us, we are, as it were, ready to come down to an earthly incarnation. And when for its part it has proceeded a stage further and we have in the course of our journey through the spiritual worlds developed to a certain stage, we can again enter into an earthly phase of development. We look first from the standpoint of our own evolution. We then look at how in a very long period of time the Time-spirit undergoes its development.

If, on this basis, we view the evolution of earthly humanity by going back to the founding of Ancient Rome, eight hundred years before the Mystery of Golgotha, thus to the time when Rome was founded, we find that a certain Time-spirit began its development. Previously another Time-spirit had been guiding and directing the destiny of the Earth. And this Time-spirit who had at that time taken over the guidance of the Earth in its spiritual evolution was active right until the sixteenth century. Since that time, thus since the sixteenth century, there has been another Time-spirit. We are therefore concerned with two Time-spirits. A human individual who was, for example, incarnated in the third century before the Mystery of Golgotha underwent what this Time-spirit was bringing about for the Earth. If this person died in the third century or even in the second century, the Time-spirit cannot initially give him anything for the time after his death. What it has been able to give him it has already given him. The Time-spirit must now for its part pass through a number of years before it is able to give the person something new. Then this human individual, who has been in a spiritual world between death and a new birth, again comes down to the Earth when the Time-spirit can give him something new. Now things are so arranged that the individual human being actually on average comes several times, for the Time-spirit is not in a position always to give everything that he could give because of the imperfection of human beings. This means that a human individual comes several times in the period in which a Time-spirit is undergoing development. But the whole process depends on the fact that the Time-spirits rule over the successive incarnations of human beings.

For their part, however, the Time-spirits rule over this whole course of human destiny by virtue of their having subordinates; and these are the archangels. Such archangels in their subordinate positions have much shorter periods of rulership than the Time-spirits. Whereas the Time-spirits hold sway for as long as I have previously indicated, so that we can assume the sovereignty of one Time-spirit from the founding of Rome until the sixteenth century, the spirits whom we regard as the hierarchy of the archangels have a period of rulership lasting approximately only between three and four centuries. They therefore alternate in such a way that six or seven come one after the other during the sovereignty of one Time-spirit. So that around the time when the Mystery of Golgotha takes place, we have first the rulership over spiritual evolution of that archangel whom we associate with the name Oriphiel. Then comes the rulership of Anael, then the rulership of Zachariel, Raphael, Samael, Gabriel and now since the year 1879 we have the sovereignty of that archangel whom we call Michael.

Thus when we contemplate the spiritual worlds, we have, as it were, the higher succession of the rulerships of archangels. Because man is unable to receive everything that the Time-spirit would give him, he does not take it directly from the hand of the Time-spirit but from the hand of the archangel, of the less high power. We may therefore state: our immediate personal guardians belong to the hierarchy of the angeloi. Above them stand those who govern human beings more in connection with other human beings; and above them stand the archai or Spirits of Personality or Time-spirits.

When I speak in this way, I am referring to those beings who have pursued their development in a proper way. But not all spirits follow a rightful course of development. There are spiritual beings who were already archai during Old Saturn but who remained behind at the archai stage, thus at the stage where they were at that time. Thus now, during the Earth evolution, they have not emerged from their Saturn stage. They have not risen to the stage of rightful development. They have retained their human character; they are on the one hand supersensible Saturn beings but are at the human stage. Similarly there are beings from the hierarchy of the archangeloi who remained at the human stage on the Sun and now exist in the supersensible world as human beings. We refer to these beings collectively as luciferic beings who are therefore retarded, or as ahrimanic beings. We cannot enter today into the difference between luciferic and ahrimanic beings. They are all retarded spirits.

Now we must answer the question: How does a human being now in earthly incarnation receive the influence of the spirits who have rightfully advanced in their development, the Time-spirits or archai and the archangeloi who are their servants? These beings are of a supersensible nature—a person cannot relate to them as to the sense-perceptible world. He therefore does not, as a rule, know—if he relies wholly upon the world of the senses—that he is engaged in a development guided from above by the archai and archangeloi. He is unaware of this; but these supersensible beings are involved with everything that pertains to his being.

Now those spiritual beings whom we call Folk-spirits, who therefore guide whole peoples or nations, also belong to the rank of the archangeloi, the archangels. And in so far as we owe what we are to the people to which we belong, we must regard what the national character endows us with as a gift of the respective being from the hierarchy of the archangeloi. It is the inspiration of the archangeloi that we receive through being placed in a particular people. Now we need only to consider what it means for a human individual that he belongs to a particular people. With nationality there come spiritual qualities and also customs; a quite particular configuration of nature flows into a human individual. One can barely conceive of the difference it has made to the way one is constituted in an incarnation through the gift of the Folk-spirit—thus through the gift of an archangelic being.

Except that we have our place within a national entity and therefore, through the inspiration of an archangelic being, receive certain configurations of our whole existence, we stand within the evolution of the whole of humanity; and there we are beholden to the intuitions to which the Time-spirit from the hierarchy of the archai leads us. You must also bear in mind that in our present spiritual and intellectual culture we receive something that goes beyond all national differences; this is something that we have through the fact that we are living in the period straddling the nineteenth and twentieth centuries and would not have had if we had been living during the age of Ancient Rome or Greece. We owe this to the Time-spirit. Moreover, one can make a clear distinction between a gift of the Time-spirit and a gift of the Folk-spirit. But if it were only a matter of a regular development of man, a regular development of the angelos, the archangelos and the Time-spirit, we would in every individual case always receive the gift from our Time-spirit and from our respective Folk-spirit and would develop by receiving this gift. Human beings on the Earth would develop alongside one another. All those belonging to the various peoples over the Earth would receive the gift of the Folk-spirits on the Earth rather as if five pictures wholly distinct from one another were hanging in a room, but the one picture would not have the slightest effect on the others. Individual human beings would in this way receive the gift of their Folk-spirits alongside one another on the Earth. They would not disturb one another if all evolution were to have proceeded as it should.

But here, retarded spirits play their part. Among the archangeloi beings who guide [human affairs] are those who rightly began their evolution on the Sun and have become rightly evolved archangeloi right up to the Earth period; but there are also those who have remained at the Sun stage and are essentially only at the level of human beings. These beings are therefore at the same stage as the Folk-spirits and yet have remained behind them; they only have the qualities of invisible, supersensible human beings, not of archangeloi. These beings are retarded in their nature. In a certain sense they make the same claims on the world as the archangeloi but they have not reached the stage of the archangeloi on the Earth. Hence in a certain way they have to work with the same forces as on the Sun. The consequence of this is that the way they take hold of human beings is not as archangeloi but as human beings, as invisible human beings who enter directly into human nature, who do not guide human beings from above but invade human nature. And the impulse emanating from these spirits, who therefore act in competition with the Folk-spirits offering real guidance, is that peoples feud with one another as opposed to living together peacefully on the Earth.

A human individual would not endeavour to identify his personality, his essential humanity, with his folk but would regard this folk-element as something that nourishes him spiritually. Moreover, he would not contentiously stand up for his national character and identify himself personally with it. He would not say, I am this or that nationality, but rather: Nationality is a reality, and because I have been born into it I must derive my spiritual nourishment via this nationality. But while the archangel spurs him to think in this way, the other being intervenes who is actually on the level of humanity, is essentially a luciferic spirit and leads him into nationalism. The consequence of this is that the gift that comes down to the person concerned is not one that is archangelic in nature but that he identifies with the national character as with something of a wholly personal nature, thus leading to this conflict of nationalities on the Earth.

We must be very clear about what is involved here: because we have placed ourselves under the influence not only of the guiding archangel but also under that of the archangel who has come to a standstill and has remained behind, we identify with nationality in the way that we do on Earth. The way that we feel about these matters from a spiritual-scientific point of view is that we understand ourselves as human beings to be raised above the merely national in order to find access to the universally human. We can then be national in the most eminent sense. Just as one human individual can pursue one form of art and another person something different, and the one can practise his art without needing to be the opponent of the other, there would be no need for the one nationality to be the opponent of the other if there were no archangelic beings retarded in their evolution who cause the personal identification referred to earlier. One must keep this firmly in mind if one wants to speak of what lies at the foundation of human evolution with respect to nationality or other kinds of differentiation.

With regard to the Time-spirit you will see even more precisely how the luciferic element exerts its influence upon the rightly evolved element if you consider the following. A Time-spirit exerts an influence through a certain period. Since the sixteenth century there has been a new Time-spirit. This Time-spirit has its quite particular task. It has the task of adding the whole materialistic capacity and understanding of the world to previous evolutionary impulses. This is why the materialistic conception has made such great advances since the sixteenth century. We therefore do not need to regard materialistic understanding as something of less value than the former kind of understanding, provided that we do not identify with it one-sidedly. What will someone who looks at the matter in this way say about the rulership of the various Time-spirits? He will say: Now we are governed by a certain Time-spirit; formerly we were governed by a different Time-spirit, human beings had different conceptions, different impulses. And if he were only to be influenced by rightly evolved Time-spirits, he would say: We must now adapt to this Time-spirit, in that we immerse ourselves more in the laws of the world's evolution, of materialistic thinking. Then after a while a different Time-spirit will come who will bring a different quality to human thinking.

I have often emphasized that as practitioners of spiritual science we must say: Today we promulgate spiritual science with quite particular words and ideas and concepts, but it is not the case that we believe that what we say today applies to the whole future of the

Earth but it will change. When two thousand years will have passed, that which we call spiritual science today will be imparted with different words, just as we speak differently than in the age of Greece; nothing will remain of the manner of our words. We build not upon the foundation of something outwardly permanent but we know that one Time-spirit takes over from the other and that all stand together on equal terms.

But someone who is influenced by retarded Time-spirits from Saturn working within him and who identifies with their influence may say: Those people at that time were all stupid, this was the kindergarten of humanity. We have today gone far beyond this; we have now discovered truths that apply conclusively to the whole of the future! One becomes more modest and humble in the realm of spiritual science. Anyone who identifies with the Time-spirit will say: Copernicus has now finally discovered the truth, formerly something different was believed. People will henceforth forever say that the Earth and the planets move in an ellipse around the Sun. The Sun stands in the middle! Spiritual science today knows that this is a one-sided teaching. It is a very good way for our materialistic age to envisage the world, but in absolute terms it is wrong. It is not true that the Sun is at the focal point of an ellipse and that the Earth moves around it. In truth this is all a materialistically calculated illusory movement. The truth is that the Sun is itself moving and the Earth and the other planets follow it in a screw-like movement. And through the arising of certain positions in this screw-like movement, the Earth comes to be here or there at any one time. Through this arises the illusion of an ellipse. The line is actually a different one. The time will come when scientists will recognize this.[93]

One becomes more modest when one knows the truths expressed in a particular form are valid only for certain times. And as true practitioners of spiritual science we will never assert that from now on all people in all future times will say: Man consists of a physical body, etheric body, astral body and ego; for the future will have a very different way of expressing it. The point is that everything is in a process of development; that the ideas of yesterday are as justified as the ideas of today; that we do not only let ourselves be governed by a Time-spirit that leads us to believe that everything in former times was vain illusion and deception and that we have progressed so wonderfully beyond it. With respect to the Time-spirit you see that people are possessed by a luciferic spirit when they say: How wonderful our progress has been since then! How imperfect everything was that people used to think and say about the world! Whereas what we have now discovered will last for ever. What has been discovered since the sixteenth century will continue to exist as eternal truths.

Thus what one discerns in any particular Folk-spirit is actually a complicated being. It is the rightly evolved Folk-spirit who hovers over us and whom we, if we followed it alone, would follow in such a way that we accept its gifts, because we have been placed in its sphere. But it is constantly hampered in its activity by its luciferic companion who enters into us, causing us to identify as an individual human being with the customs and traditions of our nationality. However, individual human beings accomplish this in a variety of ways; and it is of immense importance that it is seen that in the middle of Europe a national character must develop that stands differently in relation to the being of its Folk-spirit than that which lies at the periphery of Europe. This insight is one that we must learn to acquire.

It is to the highest degree significant what goes on beneath the surface of human consciousness and which is actually dependent upon the spiritual beings of the higher hierarchies. Someone who thinks in a materialistic way will interpret it as sheer fantasy when one says that from spiritual beings there emanate such impulses that I have just specified, one of which is that in Central Europe, without people being aware of it, popular consciousness has been thrust towards such a way of experiencing the divinity or—because Christ is an active presence in Central Europe—the Christ Being; that a person from Central Europe learns to experience Christ in such a way that He speaks to the innermost depths of the soul.

This has not been the case in any territory as it has in Central Europe. For example, in the Roman period of the Christian era the Christ was indeed understood as a Being who has come to the Earth, who has been working on behalf of human beings. To be sure, those who were more advanced in their ideas and to some extent those who had already been thinking as those of us who know of spiritual science think today had a sense of the way that Paul was thinking when he wrote: 'Not I, but Christ in me!' But there is still a difference between this and an experience such as we find it in Meister Eckhardt, in Tauler, in Angelus Silesius and other similar minds. How did they relate to the Mystery of Golgotha? We need only to ask Angelus Silesius; and he will answer with the beautiful lines:

> If Christ a thousand times in Bethlehem is born
> And not in you, you will yet be eternally forlorn![94]

It is a matter of experiencing the Mystery of Golgotha within one's own soul. These individuals from Central Europe sought inwardly to experience something that is an inner picture, an inner expression of the Mystery of Golgotha. It is therefore so wonderful when Angelus Silesius speaks about death and says: Everything that fundamentally happens to me happens because God is in me and accomplishes things within me. And when I die, it is not I who dies but God actually dies in me! Think what a wonderfully intimate idea of immortality lies within the words: God dies in me! For God is of course immortal. If God dies in me, death is only apparent; then one feels how Angelus Silesius has this feeling that God only apparently dies within one, for God cannot die. Thus dying is not what it outwardly appears to be, it is only a fact of the living. And because God cannot die, but nevertheless dies within one, one has a sense of the idea of immortality.

This inner and highly intimate affinity with God, whether one experiences God as a divinity or in a Christian form, is what has long been prepared in the course of Central European evolution. And the Central European Folk-spirits have brought it about that this has found an outward, symbolic expression, a real symbolic expression. Nowhere other than in Central Europe is 'Ich' ['I'] said when one is referring to one's own ego, one's own being. Through the Folk-spirit, manifesting itself as the spirit of language, the whole of evolution has been so guided that it has gradually come to give expression to one's own being by means of the word Ich. But Ich, 'I-Ch, is Jesus Christ! Jesus Christ lies within this word. Through the fact that in the word 'Ich' Jesus Christ comes to expression in His initial letters, there is a symbolic expression of what lies in the spiritual nature of Central Europe, of how it is intimately connected with the most inward experience. Every time that one speaks the word 'Ich' one is giving expression to the initial letters of 'Jesus Christ'. If one would but cast one's spiritual eye on such things, which are indeed seen today as purely fanciful, one would have a sense of how unconsciously the spirits of the higher hierarchies are forever working into human evolution and then find something significant in the things that one merely takes for granted today.

I should like to mention one really significant fact. There is a certain group of European people who are referred to as Germanic peoples. But when in Central Europe one speaks of Germans*, one means England, Holland, Norway, Sweden and also others. One extends the concept of 'Germanness' more broadly. I am not seeking to provoke but simply wish to point out what is given in the language. When English people speak, they do not call themselves Germans; they only call the Germans [*die Deutschen*] Germans. The German [*der Deutsche*] calls himself a German [*ein Deutscher*], and when he speaks of Germans [*Germanen*] he is embracing a larger group of people. The Englishman applies the name Germans purely to the Germans [*die Deutschen*], to those who are not the same as he is. This is a hugely significant fact. It is something that is in the deepest sense significant with respect to the way that the Folk-spirit works on the one side or the other; to how in Central Europe it endeavours to encompass something wider, and the Folk-spirit of the English people endeavours to extract itself from what encompasses a wider dimension and apply it only to others.

Generally speaking, what language teaches us as the outcome of an active popular culture will gradually come to manifest itself in a wonderful way for people. When one speaks in this way about the various European peoples, there is at present little understanding of how I sought to do so several years before this war—and by no means prompted by it—in the cycle *The Mission of the Individual*

---

*Rudolf Steiner here uses the word '*Germanen*' as opposed to '*Deutschen*'.—Translator

Folk Souls in Connection with Teutonic Mythology. People interpret it as though I was wanting to express value-judgements of some kind. But the intention was not to express value-judgements but simply to give a characterization. And we can now characterize especially the West-European peoples by bringing precisely and concisely to expression what I indicated in this lecture-cycle.

We know that the human soul consists of sentient soul, intellectual or mind soul and consciousness soul, and that the ego works within these three nuances of soul. If we now consider the Italian people together with its Folk-soul, we find the distinctive quality that the Folk-soul sends its inspiration into the sentient soul. This is the characteristic element of the Italian national character, that the Folk-soul works inspirationally into the sentient soul. If something is possessed by the luciferic Folk-spirit, this is also true of the Folk-soul. And now consider that on the one hand the greatness of the Italian people consists in the fact that the sentient soul is inspired. Think of Dante, of all the great Italian artists! But also again the matter of personal identification—as it were, the superhuman aspect which is luciferically retarded in all the passionate developmental impulses that appear within the Italian people! This is not to imply a value-judgement but simply to characterize what is present.

With the French people we can see everywhere how the intellectual soul or mind soul is inspired by the Folk-soul, indeed the intellectual or mind soul.

With the British people it is the consciousness soul. Now for the present cycle of humanity the consciousness soul is that which most brings man into connection with the outer physical world. Hence that national entity which is inspired by the consciousness soul is above all entrusted with the mission of furthering and promoting materialistic culture. It is therefore again not a question of expressing a value-judgement but of simply characterizing the fact that the British nation is called upon to inspire the consciousness soul. In so far as the individual belongs to his people, thus in so far as he is inspired by the luciferic Folk-spirit, he identifies with the purely materialistic culture of the present. We indeed find this in British culture. To the extent that the individual belongs to the British nation, the materialistic spirit of the British nation becomes apparent, this distinctive spirit that between the years of 1856 and 1900 has conducted thirty-four wars of conquest and has made fifty-seven millions of earthly human beings new British subjects, and which in our time pretends to represent the freedom of individual human groups.

When we are considering a time such as ours, we must be absolutely clear that it is one that will teach people to feel what one now represents as the conflict between the various national groups of Europe or of a large part of the Earth as an awakening call. Those belonging to thirty-four nationalities are involved together in a war, wholly irrespective of minor racial differences. One should see this as an awakening call that has very little to do with what people have hitherto called history. This latter way of looking at things is especially in our time being taken to nonsensical levels. It really is so absurd what the various European nations are putting forward today, that people weigh up the various outward facts in order to discover the causes of this terrible war. But precisely this war will teach people that one will find nothing in its outward causes other than, at best, external symptoms of what lies deeply and inwardly hidden in groups of human beings as a result of the guidance of advanced and retarded spiritual beings. And in a certain sense what our present time manifests by way of trials will compel people to extend their scrutiny to the spiritual depths where lie the causes of what is outwardly happening in the world.

One can show in all sorts of ways how that which manifests itself outwardly is working in the deep foundations of consciousness. Although most of our friends are already familiar with this example, I should like again to indicate how the whole map of Europe at the end of the Middle Ages was determined by the intervention of the Maid of Orleans in the war between England and France. Anyone who views our outward history with understanding has to acknowledge that the map of Europe would have had a very different form if, as a result of the intervention of the Maid of Orleans in the war, England had not been defeated by France at that time. But the Maid of Orleans was no highly skilled strategist, she was not someone who was at the pinnacle of current training and development. She was a simple human child—a country girl. But through her, spirits of the higher hierarchies were working in the way they had to work at this time. And it has been thoroughly necessary that these spirits have been working in subconscious regions right up to our time, because people have not as yet been able to understand what must now be understood through spiritual science. We have often found it beautifully expressed in legends how higher spiritual beings intervene in the realm of the subconscious. And it is with justice, and not a matter of superstition (because it corresponds to the actual facts), that the time from Christmas until 6 January, when for the outer world the year is most withdrawn, was regarded with particular significance. If one seeks spiritual knowledge not in the way that we seek it today on the path described in *Knowledge of the Higher Worlds: How is it Achieved?* but wishes to reach it in a more elemental way, one could be inspired in these thirteen nights.

This is, for example, very beautifully expressed in the Norwegian legend of Olaf Åsteson. In this legend we are shown how Olaf Åsteson goes to church before the beginning of the Christmas festival; how before the church he enters into a state of sleep and is asleep throughout the thirteen nights; how he wakes up on Three Kings Day and is able to relate what he has experienced. And what he then pictorially relates in a visionary but primitive way corresponds to what we call the passage through the soul-world and the passage through the spirit-land. All this Olaf Åsteson has experienced in the time within which the Christmas festival is rightly placed. This should indicate to us that the clairvoyance of a child of nature could be developed in these thirteen nights between Christmas and the festival of the Three Kings.

Since the Maid of Orleans was such a child of nature, one might presuppose that in these thirteen nights she had experienced the world through a kind of dream condition, of which she said when she led the French army against the English that she had been inspired in these thirteen nights. Moreover, this happened in a quite distinctive way. Every human individual passes through a state of sleep, a condition where the senses do not yet speak; this is in the mother's body before he perceives the physical light of the Earth.

This is indeed a kind of sleeping state, and the maturest part of this state is of course in the last thirteen days before birth. What is so extraordinary, and what fills our soul with astonishment, is that the Maid of Orleans was born on 6 January. She therefore underwent an inspirational journey during the thirteen nights before her eyes had opened to the earthly light. That 6 January is the birthday of the Maid of Orleans is therefore also intentionally specified in our calendar. This is something that we need to understand in its world-historical context; for it can tell us how mysterious the connections in the world are and how mysterious powers are working in the world. Thus mysterious powers were at work then on 6 January, when the people in the little village where the Maid of Orleans was born came flocking together in the morning; when the animals behaved in so wonderful a way. On this sixth of January an inspiration could be concluded. During the thirteen nights a being could be inspired who was karmically predisposed for this. Of course, not everyone who is born on 6 January has such a predisposition, but karma must harmonize with the other circumstances.

I wanted to mention this example of the Maid of Orleans as one that well shows us how subconscious powers contribute to historical development and evolution. To be sure, there then came the materialistic developments of the ensuing centuries. They inevitably understood such a reference to the deep foundations of history as sheer lunacy. This doesn't matter; just as it matters not at all if people outside the movement still regard this spiritual science as a lot of nonsense. Spiritual science will find its way through this.

But such significant events as those within which people are living at present, and into which they have been incarnated in order to participate in them in one or another form, do not always have the same significance in historical evolution. Today these destiny-laden events signify an awakening call to human beings. Already such a wealth of literature has been written about this war, but in everything that has appeared in books, brochures and so on, we do not find what people presume will be found and which must gradually be found. One often hears: It is not really possible to speak of the causes; perhaps after the war, perhaps only after several decades will people discover from documents the true causes of the war and know who was really to blame. You can read this on every other page of the newspapers. But this is not the point; what matters is that—because of this time in which we are living—the real causes are not to be seen in these outward reasons but that one finds the cause in the spiritual world. One will find that this war has been instituted as the particular karma of materialism, which must be undergone in order that people assemble sufficient convictions to reach across from materialism to spiritualism. This is the trial that humanity has to undergo.

What, then, is actually happening around us today in so shocking a way? We know that when someone passes through the gate of death, he first leaves his physical body behind in the physical world. He initially enters the spiritual world with his etheric body, astral body and ego. He soon casts off the etheric body and this is incorporated in the rest of the world. He then passes on through the soul-land and through the spirit-land. But now consider that today a large number of people are passing through the gate of death in a relatively short period; that they cast off an etheric body that would normally have been able to support a human life for several decades. When someone between the ages of twenty and thirty dies, he casts off his etheric body which has the capacity to sustain his physical body for sixty or seventy years. The forces reside in the etheric body, for in the spiritual world nothing is lost. All those who are passing through the portal of death in the flower of their youth today surrender to the world an etheric body that would have been able to sustain this life for a long time to come. These forces are now in the spiritual world. What are these forces? I should like by means of a striking example derived from our own circle to demonstrate to you the significance of such a phenomenon.

It was last autumn when a family belonging to our anthroposophical circle lost their seven-year-old son[95] who was a very likeable boy. The outer circumstances were indeed of the most tragic nature. As a German citizen, the father had had to enlist in the war; he had just been taken ill and was in a military hospital. One evening when there had been a lecture in Dornach where our building is being erected, it was pointed out to us that the little seven-year-old boy was missing.

He had not returned home in the evening. I should not forget to mention that the family had settled in Dornach as a gardener's family. I had myself shortly beforehand travelled to Switzerland from Germany. The boy had come to meet me in front of the building and held out his hand to me; a sunny and very likeable child.

So that evening we received the news that the boy was missing. The only possible thought was that a furniture van that had brought some furniture for members had overturned in the vicinity of the building and had fallen on the child. Now you must bear in mind that for as many years as one can remember no furniture van had come that way and since then also not. You must, moreover, consider that the boy lived with his mother, who cared for the gardens. He was such a good boy that when his father had to go away he said to his mother that he would be really diligent in his help, because his father was no longer there. He had that evening been sent to the so-called canteen to fetch something for his mother. It was not far, only a short distance lies between the canteen and his mother's house. There is a fork in the track on this short stretch, so that the furniture van had to negotiate a bend.

The boy had actually wanted to leave ten minutes earlier but had been detained by someone who wanted to talk with him. Had he left earlier and by a door other than the one he left by, he would have passed the van sooner and on the left side, whereas he was now walking on the right. Because he left later by a different door and was on the right of the furniture van, when the van overturned it fell on the boy. People saw the mishap, also those who were with the horses; but no one suspected that the boy was trapped beneath the van. They then said: The van is too heavy for us to lift this evening; we'll do it in the morning. All this happened between five and six o'clock. And now we were in the position of having to get the van upright at a quarter past ten. By midnight this was done; and we lifted out the dead boy.

Now the first thing I should like to say is this, that such an example well illustrates how people think erroneously also about life. I should additionally like to cite another frequently used comparison for this erroneous thinking. Suppose that you see in the distance someone walking beside a river. You suddenly see that he has fallen into the river. You run to have a look; you find that there is a stone where he fell. You then of course say that he stumbled over the stone, fell into the water and thereby met his death. A quite different, and indeed opposite, explanation is also possible. The person may have had a heart attack. He fell into the water because he was already dead; he did not meet his death by falling into the water. This mistake is made constantly, especially in natural science. One does of course not notice it when it is so subtly concealed.

It was a similar situation with this boy. The child's karma had run its course. The spiritual beings ruling over this mystery had arranged everything so that the child could meet his death. The boy was seven years old. A really youthful etheric body that would have been able to sustain life for many decades, the forces were available. Now I shall always acknowledge what it means that for some time our Dornach building has been embedded within the enlarged etheric body of the little boy Theodor Faiß. The etheric body is indeed enlarged—it becomes bigger after death—and the etheric body of this little seven-year-old Theo has ever since formed a kind of aura for the building. And if one has anything to do with the building, if one has the need to find the ideas for the building that incorporate it rightly in the spiritual world, since the death of this boy one knows that one is inspired by the etheric body that forms together with the aura of the building, the etheric body of little Theo Faiß. No longing that I might have to appear original would lead me to deny that many of the contributions for the building have arisen and have been inspired by the circumstance that the aura of this etheric body is around the building and that one has with regard to the building this help that this unspent etheric body is working in favour of the building.

Think what significant inner facts stand behind the outer facts: a family moves its dwelling-place to the vicinity of the building; a boy is especially predisposed through his soul-being; he sacrifices his etheric body in order that the building is enshrouded in the power of this etheric body. Here we have an example through which we can see how unspent etheric bodies that have been sacrificed have their task in the world.

Only then does that which should flow by way of feeling content from our spiritual science really have its beginning. That one knows that man consists of a physical body, etheric body, astral body and ego and that he passes through various earthly lives is really not what it's all about. What matters is that something becomes part of our actual experience through these views. We also endeavour thereby to bring life into our movement, so that not only theoretically through teaching but through life itself we try to overcome the difference between the living and the dead.

When a very dear colleague of ours, Fritz Mitscher,[96] was recently taken away from us in his thirtieth year and I had to give the address at the cremation in Basel, there were some important words that I addressed to this soul with the object of requesting that it might continue working further among us also after death. For we not only need the so-called living but we need the collaboration of those who have passed through the portal of death. And they will collaborate with us in a twofold way. On the one hand, a large number of etheric bodies that those who have crossed the threshold of death in grave experiences of destiny have cast off will serve as collaborators in the near future. Youthful, unspent etheric bodies are now like a great, mighty aura in which we are now living. And then on the other hand there are the individualities themselves, who are working further from out of their etheric bodies. We can look upon these unspent etheric bodies in, for example, the case of little Theo Faiß, where his etheric body becomes an inspiration for much that is achieved through the building.

I wished to focus on the individuality in my address to Fritz Mitscher. It is an essential part of our spiritual science in this way wholly to sense and feel how the gulf separating life and death is bridged. For it must become the conscious preoccupation of our earthly lives not only theoretically to know but wholly livingly to embrace the awareness that the dead are for us as living beings, that the dead give something in the form of youthful, unspent etheric bodies. And in these etheric bodies that belonged to people who have now found death through the great destiny-laden events, there live the echoes of all that is experienced where the imminent prospect of death is—more or less consciously—seen as a sacrifice for the events demanded by the time. This enters into these etheric bodies. To seek death, or to be more precise to foresee death and nevertheless know that this death has a significance, will be the case with numerous people who are passing through the gate of death in the present time.

One can be a materialist; if one lives one's life in such a way, one may say: Folk-souls and Folk-spirits are merely names for something that abstractly links a group of human beings together with the same language and the same distinctive qualities. To speak of Folk-spirits as real beings is sheer craziness. Many of those now passing through the portal of death may themselves echo these words; but by passing in this way through death, they unconsciously give their assent to what spiritual science must say, namely that a Folk-spirit or Folk-soul is a real being. For what would it mean if Folk-spirits and Folk-souls were not real beings, and yet from all sides human beings are engaged in a bloody war? On the basis of a materialistic world-structure, this would be inconceivable. But if the individual sacrifices himself for the Folk-spirit, if to him the Folk-spirit is a real being, it is profoundly meaningful that such events befall human beings. Thus we shall come to be aware of a time when many, many unspent etheric bodies are hovering in the spiritual atmosphere, all urging that there is a spiritual world. These etheric bodies will in future be good helpers for the spiritual deepening of people's conception of the world. Human beings will simply have to experience in their souls how the dead call.

When peace again comes to reign over the fields over which terrible events are now being enacted, those who will then be living will be able to live to better effect when they hear the voice of the dead. But this is not meant merely symbolically. The unspent etheric bodies will be there and ring out their call. The world will not be able to exist in future unless people sense and feel their connection with the spiritual world. And the humanity of the future would therefore prove to be dull and impassive if they were to be unable to hear the urging of the dead. In physics, everyone accepts that no force is lost; one speaks of the transformation of forces. It is similar in the spiritual realm. The forces that the unspent etheric body carries through the gate of death do not disappear; they will continue to be there. And they can be received into the souls of the future; these souls can through this connection with the soul-residues that are left behind from unspent etheric bodies receive strength and confidence for spiritual work.

In addition to much that this war can say to us, something that is of particular importance to us as advocates of spiritual science is that we, as it were, look up into the atmosphere which will come to be an atmosphere of unspent etheric bodies; while here on the Earth there must be souls who have a feeling for the fact that these are the awakening calls of the dead. It is our task as proper advocates of spiritual science to bring this about. We must be able to find a point of view that accords with the spirit also as regards these events of our time, not the point of view that abstract thinking asserts. But we must envisage the future population of the Earth in such a way that down below there are souls who are in the physical body, while from above the unspent forces of etheric bodies send down their influences; and that these souls down below are able to say: We do not doubt that better times for spiritual awareness will come, for unspent etheric bodies are helping us with their forces. If we see this in a real way and not abstractly, we will have understood something of the exhortations that this destiny-laden time can give us especially as people who identify themselves with spiritual science. It is of such importance that this happens, for there is a need for real influences flowing into human evolution. We would have to continue working for a long time if we had to call forth through intellectual convictions what the spiritual world-conception wants to impart. In the case of the Maid of Orleans, an unconscious initiation took place. In future, the spiritual world will engage with human evolution in a different way. It will be the unspent etheric bodies that will be at our side helping us; and also those who as individualities want to bring their influences to bear upon the physical plane.

With regard to what people are able to understand, some very strange things sometimes happen also today. You will already agree that at the time of the Maid of Orleans the strategists, the army commanders did not bring about what actually happened. There is another example that I have often cited. When in the decisive moment Constantine's army was marching towards Rome, it was also not the army commanders who brought about the victory and overcame Maxentius's army—which was five times bigger—as he led it before the gates of Rome to meet Constantine. Constantine did not follow the advice of his commanders but a dream that told him to let Christ's monogram go before his army. Dreams and Sibylline oracles had led the armies together then at a certain point and decided everything. However, because Constantine was victorious the map of Europe again acquired the appearance that reflected this.

Who was it who was guiding events beneath the threshold of consciousness? It was the Christ impulse, but the impulse of Christ as He really was and not as people understood Him to be. We do not come to know the Christ impulse when we listen to the disputes of the theologians. The Christ impulse has been working not in what people have consciously formulated, in what people have understood; but He was working in linking together the events involving Constantine and Maxentius and later again with the Maid of Orleans. Likewise in our modern age there is much to be experienced, albeit sometimes in matters of minor concern. But sometimes small things can be compared with greater ones.

Thus a few years ago a famous philosopher wrote a lengthy article about the worldview of the spiritual science with which I have been associated in a South-German monthly journal.[97] This article had quite an influence; it was written in a very adversarial way, while containing a largely favourable judgement about theosophy in general and also much that one could appreciate. I was, for example, given the advice that instead of focusing on such things I should rather use my gifts in order conclusively to make it known whether Mickiewicz was the reincarnation of the Maid of Orleans and so on. But overall the article was very good at presenting what our spiritual-scientific world-conception is considered to be in such a way as to evoke an uneven impression. The philosopher who had written the article was regarded as a great Platonist, a great logician. He himself has said that the only task to which he dedicates himself is the proclamation of truth, so he should know the truth. The editor of the journal seemed very satisfied to be able to publish such a long, authoritative article about this spiritual science. That was several years ago. Then came the war.

The person concerned is not of a mind to sympathize with Central Europe but he sympathizes very strongly with England and France. Now, what happens? He writes a number of letters to the same man, the editor of the journal. The editor of the journal publishes these letters as well, but—because they are too characteristic—in a different journal, the *Süddeutsche Monatsheft.* He even points out that he is the same man—Karl Muth—who edits the journal *Hochland* and who printed the article about what he refers to as 'Steinerite Theosophy'. As for the letters, what one can say about them is that all the venom that can be expressed about Central Europeans by someone with West-European sympathies can be found there. Among other things, this man explains that in comparison to these people who are all incapable of knowing what they are fighting for, black people are free members of the nobility. In comparison to Central Europe one merely needs to consider the English world-empire, which like the Catholic Church has been instituted by God and has never done anything other than what lies in the divine ordering of the world.

Printing such a letter is something that speaks for itself! The editor in question writes of this: In the whole of Central Europe the only place where someone could be found who could write such things is a madhouse! Thus now the good Herr Muth admits that the man whom he chose to let loose on our spiritual-scientific world-conception belongs in a madhouse. Yes, this is how it stands with what had been adduced about our spiritual-scientific world-conception. Now Herr Muth should have known at the time that the man was fit for the madhouse. But he first needed the awakening call of the war. His insight had first to be stirred by what he could now easily see. There are many who wander about criticizing the world-conception that we represent who should be in the madhouse, but this does not become apparent in so grotesque a way as in the instance referred to.

I was saying that this example shows that the intellect that people have today would still have a long way to go when it comes to the world-conception of spiritual science and that it has to be said: Not only the living are necessary in order that quantum spirituality—which must come into the world—may appear but also the dead! And those who are the best source of help are those who with heart and soul had put themselves behind the course of the fateful and destiny-laden events that we are experiencing in the present. And so one would wish today that such considerations do not remain within souls as something purely theoretical but become a deeply honest feeling, the feeling that we may develop our belief in and commitment to spiritual science in such a way that our souls develop and foster the attentive awareness that there will be urging voices in the spiritual world saying to us: Let those of us who have died be a sign that a spiritual deepening must come to human beings, for we passed through this death with consciousness—not for our own souls but for what is independent of us, so that we have thereby sealed the belief in something that reaches beyond the individual, material human life.

If among those who feel a commitment to spiritual science there will be those who sense, feel and know the grave whispering of those who have thus crossed the threshold of death, something will indeed be achieved of what needs to be accomplished through spiritual science within the sensibilities of human souls; in other words, if through spiritual science there will be souls who know how to guide their conscious minds into the spirit-realm, it will be possible for much to be said to human individuals from the realm of spirit in the times to come.

This is what I wanted to indicate to you for you to ponder upon, since the arrangements are such that during this time we shall also be able to gather in a branch meeting. One would wish that at such gatherings knowledge will not merely be grasped in a seed-like form but that what is said during such gatherings may work as a living seed that is immersed in the ground of the feeling soul. The main thing will be what you will carry forward with you in your feelings as the result of such studies.

We shall therefore conclude these studies by calling to mind what is to emerge for us from the destiny-laden events of the time:

From the courage of the fighters,
From the blood on fields of battle,
From the grief of the bereaved,
From the people's sacrifice:
There will ripen fruit of spirit,
If souls will turn in consciousness
Towards the realm of spirit.

Lecture 10

PRAGUE, 15 MAY 1915

The Significance of the Position of Central Europe between East and West—Ahrimanic Inspiration and Spiritual Impulses—The Symbol of the Rose Cross

When we are gathered at such an opportunity through which a designated space is devoted to our endeavours to which we can give a spiritual stamp that accords with our spiritual-scientific feeling and sensibilities, it is good if we call to mind the wider perspective that as adherents of spiritual science we intend to adopt towards the world and its phenomena, its tasks, its great riddles. And how should our time, which is so beset with trials and tribulations, not also awaken within our souls a sense of urgency to arrive at a viewpoint that speaks to the future. There must especially in our time be the longing for a point of view that goes further than what can be discerned through outer life and outer human striving.

Thus at an important place in our new building in Dornach we shall erect a sculptural Group that directly derives from the tasks and aspirations of our spiritual-scientific world-outlook. This sculptural Group is to portray what our souls should feel in the deepest sense as deriving from our movement. This Group will include a central figure. One can designate this central figure as the Christ; one can also see it as that which in man endeavours to incorporate the divinity residing within human nature rightly in the world. One can regard this central human figure as 'man', the cosmic human being expressed in an earthly personality, as Christ was expressed in temporal, historical life through Jesus of Nazareth.

But there will be two other figures beside this central figure, one of which is as though up on a rock; it has wings but is falling down from the rock. And through the distinctive gesture of the central figure, imbued as it is not with strength but with an inner firmness, a power is engendered whereby the figure up on the rock, the winged figure, breaks its wings and plunges into the depths. This breaking of the wings—this must be well expressed in this sculptural form—is brought about not because the human being who stands in the middle, the Christ-man, breaks the wings but, because He extends His hand in His spirituality, the other—the winged being—cannot bear this and, as a result of what is going on within him and because he finds what lives below him unendurable, breaks his wings himself and plunges down. It therefore needs to be firmly stated that this being is falling of itself, that it is not being made to do so through some adversarial force.

And down below in the rock we see another figure lying bound in chains. This one has the aim of stirring up the earthly realm from below. But in this endeavour it does not prevail against what streams forth from the downwards extended hand of the central figure. It is made to coil and become bent by being repulsed and thrown back likewise in its own being through the power of the central figure.

You may have a sense that in this Group there comes to expression what we call the Christ principle of our cosmos in the central figure, the luciferic principle in the angel plunging down from the rock and the ahrimanic principle in the figure that aspires upwards from down in the cave. I have tried to form these three figures—we may speak in this way in so intimate a circle as this—as far as possible as one would a portrait, so that one will really have an impression of the form adopted by Ahriman when he appears in such a relationship to the human being and also of the physiognomy of Lucifer that he adopts when he appears in relation to man.

What the Western religious world-conception lacks even in our time and what can be conveyed to it only through our spiritual-scientific world-conception is the knowledge that Ahriman and Lucifer are involved in all that happens in the world. One can openly only hint at such things, because today people still recoil from a specific way of expressing matters of this kind. But let us recall that even in yesterday's public lecture[98] it was said that through meditation a person is on the one hand led into a region where he feels himself to be solitary and powerless in his innermost being and, on the other hand, into a region where he feels himself to be inwardly seized by fear and impotence. What threatens us when we strive one-sidedly only for freedom from material constraints, what threatens us when we aspire abstractly for the spirit, is being engulfed by the luciferic principle. What threatens us when we gravitate solely towards material things, when our lives are a constant hunger for them and we become as though hardened (as I explained yesterday in the public lecture), this is the ahrimanic principle. And man stands between the luciferic and the ahrimanic principle. This must be recognized. But it must also be recognized in the right way that it is not good enough if we simply say: We must wipe away from us everything to do with Lucifer and Ahriman. All feelings of hatred or fear that we may have about luciferic and ahrimanic influences are actually not beneficial to our human nature. We must recognize that Ahriman and Lucifer have their rightful place in the whole cosmos.

Thus in the form of the sculpture it is indicated that Christ does not want to overcome Lucifer and Ahriman through an inner hatred or from an urge emanating from Himself but that Lucifer and Ahriman overcome themselves. It is quite wrong if we develop feelings within us to the effect that Ahriman and Lucifer must be repelled by us, that we must combat them directly. The Godhead that normally prevails in the world has in its wisdom not ordered things so that the ahrimanic principles do not have their place in the world order. They have their part to play.

If we ask ourselves where the luciferic principle is today in human evolution, we must look towards the East. In the East, in Asia and in European Russia, Lucifer holds sway in cultural terms. And although, as I have explained in the cycle about the mission of Folk-souls, the Russian element has the task of developing the Spirit-self, there is in Russian culture the danger of being entangled by Lucifer. It is on its way towards this. The luciferic principle consists in that good spirits remain behind. Until the sixth and seventh centuries there was a good spirit in the Greek Orthodox Church, but what was at one time a good spirit changes into a luciferic spirit if it continues on beyond this time. Being firmly bound to the Orthodox religion is a state of 'being in the claws of Lucifer'. And this is still more intensely the case with the spiritual forms that develop in the Orient, which had their justification with respect to ancient times. By perpetuating themselves, they develop in a luciferic direction. Throughout the East, we find with very many people who are incarnated there that they have something to work through in the luciferic realm. And in the West, in accordance with the wise ordering of the world, we find souls who are immersed in the ahrimanic element. We find this most strongly in America.

In America there exists the tendency to develop a culture that is wholly immersed in materialism, in the ahrimanic element, that—even where there is an aspiration towards spiritualism—is wholly pervaded by a purely material outlook. Even where people strive towards the spirit there is a wish tangibly to conjure up spirits in a spiritistic way. This will become ever stronger, and the longing to make everything matter-of-fact will become ever greater. It will also gradually take hold of the West of Europe. Then will the mission of bringing the ahrimanic element into culture be fulfilled.

This is what I mean by the wider perspective: that we see how in Central Europe we are wedged between the luciferic principle of the East and the ahrimanic principle of the West; but how we are called upon to soar up to the forces that are represented by the Christ principle, which on the one hand causes Lucifer to break his wings through the overcoming of the feeling of powerlessness, and on the other hand develops the radiating forces against Ahriman which repel all fear that stands before any knowledge of the spiritual world. For the ahrimanic element that pulsates through the world cannot, in truth, be held back; it is a reality. The culture of Central Europe is also gripped by this ahrimanic element. But one needs to know how one should oppose it, for the course of the ahrimanic element is the passage through materialism. And this passage through materialism must be undertaken; the reason for this has a deep, wisdom-filled connection.

Just think what a one-sided religious movement—and I am referring to this 'one-sided' quality—is also currently manifested in Christianity, most strongly apparent in the element of Jesuitism.

Consider that it always opposes any real scientific progress. Only in the nineteenth century did the Catholic Church officially recognize the Copernican world-conception.[99] Conventional science will naturally be opposed by a one-sided religion, this cannot be otherwise. Two impulses reside in this opposition on the part of religion to ordinary science. One of these is that the one-sided religion feels that in a science that focuses solely upon the outer world, Ahriman makes himself manifest. This is the justified aspect of the Church's battle. Ahriman's hold over ordinary science so that it does not extend to a spiritual world-view is a justified area of attention.

On the other hand, there is an unjustified impulse in a one-sided religion's opposition to science. This one-sided religious world-outlook is itself ensouled, one might say wholly pervaded, especially by a luciferic element; for to strive for a deepening of religious life and to hate the diffusion of scientific influence into spiritual worlds is what Lucifer wants of man. Lucifer could not better achieve his aim than if all people were religious. This religiosity has an immensely strong egotistic impulse. Just think how people who do not strive for spiritual knowledge conceive of their religion. It is out of egotism that they want to develop a blissful state, to lead a life that—as they picture it—culminates in death. It is out of egotism that they want to be incarnated only once in the world! In a one-sided religion, egotism is taken to the highest level: an egotism of the soul, not only of the body. The best religious aspirations that surround us are firmly rooted in egotism. And indeed, the most pious people who move us through their piety are ruled in their religious feelings by Lucifer. It is greatly preferable to Lucifer when he acquires pious souls who have a sense for the spiritual, the good to which they aspire out of egotism. He does not want merely criminal souls, he wants to lead pious souls into his domain.

Thus on the one side stands the rightful, scientific element that would on the threshold tend towards the ahrimanic aspect if it does not look up to the spiritual world, and on the other side the luciferic element, which would also in Central Europe fall prey to egotistical religiosity if the spiritual outlook on the world were not to lead to a spiritual knowledge. This will represent a step forward in Christianity.

Thus it becomes an infinitely precious feeling if we imbue ourselves with the knowledge that we knowingly stand between what must be, the luciferic and ahrimanic element, which one cannot avoid but which loses its power when one recognizes it. This is the distinctive quality of the spiritual world: when one recognizes this element, it loses the power through which it is able to possess human beings. Lucifer and Ahriman are invisible. If we acquire a conception of them in space and time, they lose their power over us.

You should not believe that when an evil spirit is intuited by someone through clairvoyant power but is not beheld, the person concerned does something bad if this spirit is pictorially portrayed or represented sculpturally. This is right: through becoming visible to the senses, the spirit thereby loses its power. People will no longer become nervous through the spiritual representing of a figure, but the spirit thereby loses its significance as an invisible power and we place ourselves consciously into it.

Just as the Godhead itself needed Lucifer and Ahriman to bring the world into the right alignment from East and West in order that the world does not undergo an irregular development but advances as though in a pendulum-like movement, the world rulership lets the luciferic work from the East and the ahrimanic from the West. But it presents us in Central Europe with the difficult and considerable task of contemplating this pendulum movement in the right way. This pendulum is actually a boat, as if a boat were hung on a pendulum clock. And in this boat sit the souls who are striving with the right impulses in Central Europe. These souls must really dive down and must know that they must seize the right point of balance. They must recognize what lies behind the threshold, they must take it into their consciousness. And these days that are now so difficult are above all else an awakening call to those who already have a sense of what is in store for the world in future.

It does not only matter that in the course of the war one or the other side will win an outward victory but how life will continue after the victory. If it were to happen that the Central European peoples were victorious, consider that together with this victory the purely materialistic, ahrimanic world-view would predominate and would fix this further through the luciferic element and, hence, on the one hand the East and on the other hand also the West would infiltrate into Central European spirituality, an outward victory would not bring healing or salvation to Central Europe. And without people being aware of it, the ahrimanic and luciferic element has for centuries been making very powerful interventions. Just think how necessary it was to reject the Oriental, luciferic element in our Central European theosophical movement; for that which we received as theosophy from the East was pervaded by Lucifer and led in its extreme form to the recognition of an outward human idol, a physically reincarnated Christ. This was the battle that we had to wage against the unjustified interpretation of the theosophical world-conception.

But we must be clear about the need for us in Central Europe to recognize in the right way how we must involve ourselves in what is in store for humanity in the future. Through what spiritual science can be for us we will learn to see that materialism, the materialistic world-conception, should not extend over the realm that is prepared for Central Europe. Those who have an intimation that a spiritual world-conception streaming over Central Europe and from there radiating out over the entire Earth is being prepared will have to do their best to prevent this. And it would be conceivable, outwardly conceivable as a hypothesis, that after a victory this Central Europe would serve a materialistic culture. Then Ahriman would rake in the fruits of this victory. And this must be prevented.

Just think of a tragic figure such as Ernst Haeckel![100] Goethe has written a theory of evolution. Since 1884[101] I have been labouring to make it understandable to people that it is a theory of evolution that is thoroughly worthy of attention. But they cannot understand the profound manner in which Goethe has expressed it. When it is brought in a trivial way by Darwin, people understand it; the teachings have then been able to flow into their hearts and souls: thus the teaching had acquired a materialistic hue. And then take such a tragic figure as Ernst Haeckel: every thought, every fibre of his scientific life he has brought over from England. Huxley, Locke and Darwin have been his teachers. And today Ernst Haeckel is one of those who have most turned against England; he is one of the most angry combatants—in so far as he can be so as an old man; he has stood in the forefront of those who are sending back all orders, diplomas and decorations to England, although the distinctively English import of Darwinism is not being returned.

Much else can also be said. Souls are most receptive to materialism if as regards their outer lives they are, I would say, half asleep, if their souls are of a childlike quality. It passes by unnoticed that ideas are introduced to souls that prepare them later to accept materialistic interpretations as a matter of course. Ahriman has achieved this by causing a very influential figure to arise among the British people through whom the urge towards materialism is imperceptibly inculcated in the souls of children without this being suspected by anyone. This is the brilliant author of *Robinson Crusoe*. If one impresses the ideas with which *Robinson Crusoe* is filled upon the souls of children, they acquire the inclination for materialism. In the book religion arises out of itself, in the way that cabbages grow. Nothing is there which reflects something that should flow from the spiritual world. And just see how *Robinson Crusoe* spreads through the world! There was a time in the literary development of Central Europe when there were imitations of *Robinson Crusoe* in all languages. And there were many translations of the book itself! It is barely possible to count the number of *Robinson Crusoes* appearing in every nation! It lies at so deep a level. But the spiritual path must again be indicated by the greatness and meaningfulness of Central European culture, which truly has a spiritual orientation. The Brothers Grimm were indeed under higher guidance and collected the German fairy tales. And if we bring the German fairy tales to our young people instead of the ahrimanic *Robinson Crusoe*, we shall be bringing them the inclination towards spiritualism.

It gives one a deeply melancholic feeling when one—and this is related as a symptom—experiences the following. A very notable Austrian philosopher, Professor Dr Ernst Mach,[102] has written a book which was very far-reaching for many who wish to think philosophically, *Analyse der Empfindungen* (Analysis of Feelings). On the third page we find the following. He is speaking of self-knowledge. We know that self-knowledge is so extraordinarily important; I have often explained this. Ernst Mach now gives a proof for why self-knowledge is highly problematical even for the outer world. He relates the following experience: I was passing by a shop-window when I saw my own image, my own form coming towards me. I thought: What an unpleasant, repugnant person is approaching me! It was I myself.—This is how he spoke. This was also someone whom he had known so little that he said to his reflection: What an unpleasant, repugnant person this is! And in order to make this thoroughly clear, he adds that when he was already a professor, he was returning at night from a journey and was boarding an omnibus. As he boarded it he saw in the mirror a man also getting on board and he again said to himself: What is this down-at-heel schoolmaster doing here? And he adds: Thus my class demeanour was more familiar to me than my own particular appearance and bearing. Now if it is so difficult for someone who does not often look in the mirror—it says something for Ernst Mach that this happened to him—to recognize his outer form, one will get some idea of how difficult it is to acquire self-knowledge in one's soul.

And I have to say that I find it almost tragic when I read later on in the same book what Ernst Mach says about the education of his son and remarks with utter seriousness: Praise God—he doesn't say this but something like it—that my children never read any fairy tales. They have therefore not been led through having fantastical ideas into a spiritual world by reading fairy tales. We see from this how what seeks to lead Central European culture to Ahriman is implanted in souls of the present. And so one must say that what matters is not to win a victory but that on the foundation of the victory what is right may prevail.

In Central Europe we also have a powerful influence to deal with, even in the case of a victory; for we have a connection with something that is strongly pervaded by Lucifer. It was once Europe's blessing that the Arab culture of the Moors was disseminated throughout southern Europe. What has today become ahrimanic [sic] was fully justified at that time. We are burdened by the weight of the bond with the Ottoman Empire. We must find the proper standpoint and not, as it were, believe that we can let our feelings be determined by outward political points of view. That which lives in the outer world is truly not capable of keeping the ahrimanic element at bay. Journalistic literature plies its course towards the ahrimanic principle and floods what seeks to see beyond the powers interacting in our world with mockery and scorn. It is for this reason that what in our time appears under the sign of blood and sorrow should be seen as the great awakening call to make souls receptive to what wants to flow to the present from the life of spirit. And our souls must develop the inclination for what has been prepared in Central European culture, especially in the way that it really brings to expression how we are placed between two forces that pervade the world in a pendulum-like fashion and how we must find the balance.

It must be clear to us that on the one hand the world strives towards an ahrimanic hardening, becoming ossified in the fire of the purely material; that on the other hand it strives egotistically to rise to an abstract conception of the spirit. To follow either the one or the other would be the undoing of people in Central Europe. Merely to follow the science bound to the outer senses would bring us to the point of tearing the roses from the cross and contemplating only what has become lifeless. We would gradually acquire a world-conception which would completely stop people having any perception of the spiritual world, which would enable them to behold only what is ahrimanically ossified. Try to envisage the ideals of ahrimanic science: it is a world of whirling atoms, a purely material world-structure. Everything of a spiritual nature is to be rejected from this picture of the world.

The conception that people have, and it is taught already to children at school, is that there was once a swirling movement of gaseous cosmic masses out of which the Sun was formed and the planets in their turn were expelled. This is made clear to children at school by putting a drop of oil in water,[103] placing a small round piece of paper at the position of the equator, piercing it in the middle with a pin and turning the pin. Through this, little drops split off and a little planetary system arises. Of course this proves what is being shown, but the most important thing is forgotten: that the teacher has to turn it. Thus if one is honest one in truth has to imagine a great master teacher who turns the whole system in space. But the thoughts, feelings and sensations that aspire towards Ahriman are those very ones that conceive of the arising of the Sun and the planets in the manner just described.

And in this lay what led to the prevailing historical conception. Herman Grimm once said:[104] A piece of carrion around which a hungry dog is circling is a more appetizing sight than this world-conception, which is based solely on this Copernican world-conception.

This is one danger, to tear the roses from the cross and to have only the black, charred cross. The other danger is to tear the cross from the roses and to want to aspire only to the spirit, to despise that which the Godhead itself has placed within world-evolution, not to want lovingly to embrace the thought that what is here in the sense-world is an expression of the divinity. This is the one-sidedly religious view of the world which despises science, which wants only the roses and unconsciously aspires towards the luciferic element of the East—just as the science that wants to tear the roses from the cross and wants merely to retain the charred cross aspires towards the West. But we in Central Europe are called upon to have the roses on the cross, to have what is expressed only through the connection of the roses with the cross. And as we look upon the bare, inflexible cross we feel that what has come into the world as rigid matter has come into the world through the Gods. It is as if the spiritual world has created for itself a circle within the material world: *Ex Deo nascimur.*

We feel, too, that—if we understand it rightly—we should not merely enter with Lucifer into the spiritual world but that we die, in that we are connected with what has come down into the world from the divine higher Self: *In Christo morimur.*

And in combining the cross with the roses, the material world-conception with the spiritual world-conception, we feel how the soul of man can awaken in the Spirit: *Per Spiritum Sanctum reviviscimus.*

Thus the cross engirdled by roses was the symbol of someone who entered deeply into the spirituality of Central European culture: Goethe. It must therefore be our symbol. And so as we gather in this space, we want—in so far as we can be present in the future—to be mindful of what our ideal must be out of the great tasks of earthly evolution: to entwine roses around the cross, neither to tear the roses from the cross and only keep hold of the cross nor to value the roses alone and through only the roses to rush abstractly into blossoming, sprouting spiritual life. This is what is expressed in our symbol, in the Rose Cross, which we want to take ever more and more into our hearts and our feelings when we gather in a space devoted to our strivings. We can then be sure that the spirits who guide earthly evolution in a good sense will be working invisibly amongst us; that our words, that all that which we think and feel as we devote ourselves to spiritual-scientific endeavours, that all this will find the support of the spiritual powers and forces guiding our efforts in such a space. And as we engage in our spiritual-scientific contemplations, we can feel ourselves constantly inspired by the spirits who invisibly hold sway in such a space. It is these spiritual powers whom I wish to call upon, that they may always be with those striving souls who give expression in an honest, loving way in this space to their aspirations with full sincerity! If this can happen, we may be sure that this spiritual-scientific world-conception will be a means of finding the path which the Gods have always made accessible to human beings.

We gather today in such spaces. They are isolated from the intentions of what is happening in the world. The powers lying behind these intentions view what goes on in our spaces as sectarian, as superstitious. We are, in a certain sense, therefore gathered underground with respect to present-day culture. Above on the Earth is this present-day culture, which in the East is deeply pervaded by Lucifer and in the West by Ahriman. Then in order to strengthen our hearts, to enliven our souls, we again and again recall that at a different stage the Western world-conception has ascended from what was underground to what came to be above it. There was the world-conception of the Roman Empire, the world-conception that had been the recipient of the noble philosophy and artistic world-conception of the Greeks. Brilliant minds featured among those who lived in Ancient Rome and its surroundings with this old world-conception. And those who cultivated a wholly new teaching underground in the catacombs were deeply despised.

But those who were cultivating the new teaching in the catacombs, isolated from what was at that time regarded as the right world-conception above ground, knew that they had to hold fast to what has come into the world through the Christ impulse. They cultivated their endeavours in the catacombs and knew: Up above there were living those who had designs upon their lives, who persecuted them, who did not understand them. Once we have brought before our minds these conditions of the Roman Empire, let us consider human evolution as it has developed a few centuries later. What had been above has disappeared. What was living down in the catacombs has risen up; it lives victoriously throughout the Western world. It lived already in the souls of those who, outcast, scorned and despised down in the catacombs, aspired to what was to conquer the world.

So must we, my dear friends, feel, as it were, spiritually outcast, derided and persecuted by those who in our time cultivate the so-called right world-conception. But just as how it turned out in the first stage of Western Christian evolution, so will it develop further. That which people would most like to destroy—not as it was done formerly by being encased in pitch and burnt but by being scorned and despised—will come to gain acceptance. That which scorns and despises and seeks to gain mastery of the ground of the Earth solely with an ahrimanic and luciferic world-conception will be done away with, just as the old Roman culture, the old world-conception was eliminated in the form that it took at the time. But what is cultivated in our catacombs (they are spiritual catacombs, for the world has, after all, made some progress), what is being thought, contemplated and felt in these catacombs of ours and is pervading our hearts and souls will rise up and make its triumphant progress manifest in a future culture.

We may be mindful of this in every moment when we cross the threshold of such a space. As we dwell there, we may be mindful that we are still as though in a boat under the sea, which will nevertheless take an upward course and will surely do so if we strongly and powerfully immerse ourselves in the connections that our souls have formed. It is with this pledge that we wish strongly to imbue ourselves with the spiritual Christ impulse that seeks to take a further step in its development; it is with this conviction, this pledge that we want to enter this space; we want to enter it in the sense of these feelings that everything must be regarded as consecrated to the spiritual powers, to the spiritual individualities who, as we can know, weave powerfully through our movement, who protectively extend their hands of blessing over us. This is what we wish to be mindful of when we gather here in future.

Lecture 11

LINZ, 18 MAY 1915

Christ in Relation to Lucifer and Ahriman—The Threefold Nature of this Form

When our building in Dornach that is dedicated to spiritual science is completed, it will in a significant place contain a sculptural Group[105] which will depict, in particular, three figures. At the centre of this Group there will be a figure who may be seen as the representative of the highest human essence that could develop on the Earth. One will therefore also be able to experience this figure of the highest human essence in earthly evolution as the Christ who dwelt within earthly evolution for three years in the body of Jesus of Nazareth. It will be a special task to portray this Christ figure in such a way that one will on the one hand be able to see how the Being in question is living in an earthly human body but nevertheless how in every expression, in everything relating to it, this earthly body is spiritually pervaded by that which entered from cosmic, spiritual heights into this earthly body as the Christ in the thirtieth year of its life.

Then there will be two other figures: the one to the left and the other to the right of the Christ figure, if I may call this figure that I have indicated with a few words the Christ figure. This Christ figure appears to be standing in front of a rock which rises up especially in the vicinity of Christ's left side, so that its top extends over His head. Up on the rock there is another figure, a winged figure, but its wings are broken; and because its wings are broken this figure is falling into the abyss. What will have to be artistically fashioned with particular acuity is the way in which this Christ figure raises His left arm; for through this raising of the left arm of the Christ figure this falling being breaks its wings. But it should not seem as though Christ had broken the wings of this being; for the whole must be artistically fashioned in such a way that in Christ's raising of His arm it is apparent already in the whole movement of His hand that He has nothing but infinite compassion for this being. But this being cannot bear what is flowing upwards through the arm and the hand and which additionally becomes visible through the indentations that the fingers of the outstretched hand seem to leave in the rock itself. What this being feels as it comes into the proximity of the Being who represents the Christ may be expressed in words such as these: I cannot bear it that something of such purity is flowing up towards me.

This is what is living in this being and in so fundamental a way that its wings are broken and as a result it plunges into the abyss. Herein lies a particularly significant artistic task. You can see what could be lacking if Christ were to be sculpturally portrayed so that simply by raising His hand a power would stream forth from Him that breaks this being's wings and causes it to fall. It should not be portrayed like this but so that the being should itself bring about its fall; for the being that is depicted plunging down with broken wings is Lucifer.

And on the other side, on the right of the Christ figure where a ledge juts out from the rock, there is a concave cavity. In this cavity there is also a form that has wings; and this winged form is with its arm-like organs directing its attention towards the ledge above. You should therefore visualize the cavity in the rock on the right and in this cavity a winged being, whose wings are, however, formed quite differently from those of the figure up on the rock. This latter figure has more eagle-like wings, whereas the figure in the cavity has bat-like wings. The figure in the cave has the appearance of being encased within it; one sees it working down there in its fettered state hollowing out the earthly realm.

The figure standing in the middle, the Christ figure, reaches down with His right hand. Thus whereas His left hand extends upwards, His right hand is directed downwards. Again, it will be a significant artistic task to portray this not as though Christ wanted to keep this figure—which is Ahriman—in bondage but He has infinite compassion for Ahriman. But Ahriman cannot endure this; he writhes with pain through what radiates from the hand of Christ. And this radiating quality causes the golden veins down below in the cavity to wind around Ahriman's body like cords and bind him. The same that occurs with Lucifer also happens with Ahriman. We shall then try to depict this same motif, which is conceived as a work of sculpture which will stand at a significant place in the building, in the form of a painting which will express it in a completely different way. And so there will be this Group of three figures: Christ, Lucifer and Ahriman in the form of a sculpture, and above it a painting representing the same motif.

We are portraying this relationship between Christ, Lucifer and Ahriman in our building in Dornach because spiritual science really does show us in a certain sense that the next task with regard to an understanding of the Christ impulse consists in that man comes to know the nature of the relationship in the world between these three powers of Christ, Lucifer and Ahriman. For much has hitherto been said about Christianity and the Christ impulse; but what came into the world through the Christ impulse as a result of the Mystery of Golgotha is something that has not become completely clear to people.

They speak of the existence of Lucifer and also Ahriman, but in speaking of them they often speak as though one must flee from them, as though it would be appropriate to say: I want to have nothing to do with Lucifer and Ahriman! If the divine-spiritual powers which can be sought in the way I described in yesterday's public lecture[106] also did not want to have anything to do with Lucifer and Ahriman, the world would not be able to exist. One stands in the right relationship to them not by saying, 'Lucifer! I shall flee from him. Ahriman! I shall flee from him' but by regarding what man has to strive towards as a result of the Christ impulse as the state of equilibrium of a pendulum. The pendulum is in the middle in a state of balance, but it must oscillate to the one side and to the other. It is the same with man's earthly evolution. Man has to oscillate to the one side in accordance with the luciferic principle and to the other in accordance with the ahrimanic principle, but he must maintain his equilibrium by developing what Paul has expressed in the words: 'Not I, but Christ in me'.

We must conceive of Christ in His essential activity as being a reality, as a living force. This means that we must be clear that what flowed into our earthly evolution through the Mystery of Golgotha was indeed an actual happening. It does not so much matter how well or inadequately people have understood this until now but, rather, that it has been a present reality in the earthly evolution of humanity. Much could be said about what human beings have not hitherto understood about the Christ impulse; and spiritual science will need to make its contribution to the understanding of what flowed from spiritual heights into earthly evolution in the form of the Christ impulse through the Mystery of Golgotha. In order to evoke an awareness of how Christ has been actively involved, I shall—and I have also spoken of this elsewhere—draw attention to two moments in the earthly evolution of humanity which are important for the whole development of the Western world.

You will know from history what an important moment it was when Constantine,[107] the son of Constantius Chlorus, overcame Maxentius and Christianity was, through him, introduced into the further evolution of the West. That this could happen, Constantine had to win that important battle against Maxentius which then led to him making Christianity the state religion of the Western Empire. The whole map of Europe would have become different if this battle of Constantine against Maxentius had not happened. But military strategy, that which the people of that time could achieve with their powers of reason, was not the decisive element in this battle; something quite different was at work.

Maxentius had consulted the so-called Sibylline Books, the prophetic oracles of Rome, which caused him to lead his army, which had been well protected within the walls of Rome, into the open field to confront that of Constantine. Constantine, however, had had a dream before the battle in which it was indicated to him that if he marched towards Maxentius in the sign of the Mystery of Golgotha, he would achieve something great. And so Constantine—whose army was a quarter of the size of his adversary's—advanced into battle with the sign of the Mystery of Golgotha, the cross, at its head; and inspired by the power emanating from the Mystery of Golgotha,

Constantine won that significant battle through which Christianity was outwardly introduced to Europe.

If we call to mind what people at that time understood intellectually of the Christ impulse, we find an endless string of theological quarrels. They argued over whether Christ is eternally equal with the Father and over other similar matters. It has to be said that it does not so much matter what people knew at that time of the Christ impulse but, rather, that it was a present reality then, that through Constantine, through a dream that Constantine had, it guided what was to happen. It is the reality of Christ, the real power of Christ, that is important. We only begin to understand what the Christ impulse is from within spiritual science.

Another moment was the one when Europe again took a formative step in its development in the struggle between France and England. Of this one can say that if France had not been victorious against England, all the circumstances would have become different. But how did this happen? Until our time, when it must become more and more conscious, the Christ impulse has been working in the subconscious regions of the soul; and in the spiritual evolution of the West we see how the Christ impulse seeks out those states in the souls of human beings through which it can exert an influence through particular individuals. Legends have preserved for us the way that the Christ impulse can assert itself within the spiritual evolution of the West. In some cases these legends point back to those ancient pagan times when an understanding of Christianity was beginning to germinate.

If the soul does not consciously strive for initiation on the path indicated in *Knowledge of the Higher Worlds: How is it Achieved?* but, as it were, on a natural path and has been imbued with the Christ impulse through a natural initiation, the most favourable time in which this Christ impulse can inspire the soul is the time from Christmas Eve until Three Kings Day, the time from 25 December until 6 January.

We can understand this if we clearly understand that for occult knowledge it is totally apparent that our Earth is not only what geologists speak about. What geologists speak about is equivalent to man's skeletal structure. But our Earth also has the spiritual aspect that belongs to it; and it is into the Earth's aura that the Christ has entered. This Earth sleeps and is awake, just as we sleep and are awake in the course of twenty-four hours. We must also be aware that the Earth's state of sleep is during the summer, while its state of wakefulness occurs during the winter. Moreover, the spirit of the Earth is most awake during these twelve or thirteen nights from Christmas until Three Kings Day. In olden times, when—as you know from many indications in my lecture-cycles—people elevated themselves to the spiritual principle of the world more in a kind of dream-like clairvoyance, the most favourable time for this was the summer. It is perfectly natural that anyone wanting to raise themselves to the spirit in a more dream-like clairvoyance found it easier during the Earth's sleep, during the summer. Hence the St John's festival was in these ancient times the most favourable period for raising the power of the soul to the spirit. But in the place of the old way in which the spirit-realm influenced the Earth, a new, more conscious way has emerged; and now the best time for this is when the Earth is awake.

Thus the legends tell us that particularly gifted human individuals, people who are especially suited by virtue of their karma, enter around Christmas time into a particular state of consciousness which is only similar to sleep but which is inwardly such that it can be inspired by the forces that elevate human beings to the realm that we call the spirit-land.

There is a very beautiful legend, a Norwegian legend of Olaf Åsteson,[108] where we are told that he goes to church on Christmas Eve, falls into a sleep-like condition and then awakes on 6 January and is able to relate what he has experienced in this sleep-like state. And this Norwegian legend indeed tells us how Olaf Åsteson experiences something that one first perceives to be the soul world and then something that one feels to be the spirit-land, but everything is expressed pictorially in the form of imaginations.

This time was the most favourable in that era when human beings were not yet so advanced as in our time. The time is now past when the Christ impulse is able to stream into human souls through a natural initiation. People today have to be just as conscious of their path of ascent towards initiation as is described in *Knowledge of the Higher*

Worlds. We live at a time when natural initiations are becoming ever rarer and will eventually disappear altogether, so that we should no longer be counting upon them. But an initiation which can essentially be called a natural initiation was that through which the Christ impulse influenced the inner being of the simple country girl known as the Maid of Orleans, through whom the victory of the French over the English, which in so fundamental a way transformed the map of Europe, was brought about. Again, it was not what could be achieved by human reason but what guided the Maid of Orleans at that time over and above all the strategies of the army generals and through which Europe acquired a new form, namely the Christ impulse, which worked right into the subconscious of a single individual but in such a way that from this individual there radiated forth what exerts an influence upon the whole of history.

Now we would need to consider whether there could have been something similar to a natural initiation in the case of the Maid of Orleans, whether the soul of the Maid of Orleans had been inspired during the nights between 25 December and 6 January. In biographical terms it seems difficult to prove something such as the Maid of Orleans having been in a sleep-like state in the twelve or thirteen days from 25 December until 6 January in which especially the Christ impulse might have been able to exert its influence upon her, so that as a human being she could have been the vessel of purely the Christ impulse on the battlefields of France. Nevertheless, this is what happened.

There is a time that—if the karma of the individuality concerned renders this particularly possible—can indeed be suitable for such a sleep-like state to come about. This is the time of the last days in which a human individual is still in the mother's body before he perceives the physical, earthly light. He is then living in a dream-like, sleep-like state. He has not yet perceived with his senses what is taking place outwardly in the world. If by virtue of his karma a person were especially suited to receive the Christ impulse in these last days when he is dwelling in his mother's body, these days would also be days of natural initiation. Such a person would then already be strengthened and fortified by the Christ impulse residing within him by the time that his eyes open for the first time after the initiation, that is, in this case after birth; and such a person would have to be born on 6 January.

The Maid of Orleans was born on 6 January. This is the mystery of the Maid of Orleans, that she was born on 6 January, that she spent the time from Christmas until Three Kings Day in that particular sleep-like state in the body of her mother and received her natural initiation. Now consider the deep connections that stand behind the external developments that we normally refer to as history. What is expounded from documents in history is by and large the least important aspect. The simple date indicated in our calendar, that the Maid of Orleans was sent into the world on 6 January, is of immense historical significance. This is how the forces from the supersensible world work right into the sense-perceptible world; and we must read this occult script through which this influence of the supersensible world upon the world of the senses is made manifest. Thus what was at work in the Maid of Orleans was an in-streaming of the Christ impulse by way of a natural initiation already before her physical birth.

I want to explain these things in order to evoke within your souls a feeling for the fact that behind the scenes of what one ordinarily calls history, powers and associations of which outward perception has no knowledge are involved. Since the Mystery of Golgotha, however, the Christ impulse has in particular been guiding the history of European humanity. Whereas in the Orient, in Asia a worldview has been retained of which it can be said that in its feelings and sensibilities it has not yet arrived at the Christ impulse. To be sure, Europeans have allowed themselves to be tempted to regard Indian wisdom as something especially profound. But it is characteristic of this Indian wisdom—and the whole religious sensibility of Asia—that all its attention is devoted to the time preceding the Christ impulse, while in addition it has preserved the state that was present in the religious sensibility of earthly humanity before the Christ impulse.

To remain behind in evolution always signifies embracing something of a luciferic nature; and therefore Asian religious development is the bearer of a luciferic element. As we consider the religious development of Asia we cannot but be aware of seeing much in it that mankind once previously had but which it has had to abandon. But in Western culture we must cleanse all this from the luciferic element and in part raise it up in such a way that the Christ principle can flow into it.

If we move from Asia to Europe, we find disseminated throughout Eastern Europe in Russian culture an Orthodox Christianity that has remained at an earlier stage of Christian evolution, that did not want to advance further and wanted to retain something of a luciferic quality. In short, as we look towards the East we have what, I might say, the wise spirits guiding the world in the whole evolution of mankind left behind as the luciferic element.

As we look towards the West, we have a different distinctive quality. The characteristic of this American culture is that everything is sought in externalities. Great and significant achievements result from this; but the answer to everything is sought in the outer world. Let us take an example.

When we in Europe, and especially Central Europe, see that someone who had not hitherto had the opportunity to focus his heart and mind upon Christ and the spiritual, cosmic forces has suddenly made a complete change in his life, we have an interest in what happened within him to bring this about. We are not so much interested in that he experienced a leap in his development, for one finds this everywhere. Indeed, there is something wholly inappropriate about the claim formulated by modern science that nature does not make leaps.[109]

From the green leaf of a plant to a red petal is a mighty leap; from the flower to the calyx is likewise a mighty leap. It is a totally false claim, and the truth of evolution rests on the fact that leaps are a regular occurrence. Thus if someone who has for a while been taken up with external matters is suddenly able to have an inclination towards the spirit, this is not what we find especially interesting; but the inner power and industry that cause what one might call a conversion to a spiritual awareness do indeed interest us. We shall want to look into the deepest feelings of such a person; we want to know what brought him to such a radical change. It is the inner soul-aspect that we find interesting.

What does an American make of this? He does something quite peculiar. In America one would have plenty of opportunity to observe such 'conversions' taking place. An American would ask those who have undergone such a conversion to write letters. He would then gather all these letters together into a bundle and say: I have received letters from a number of people; approximately two hundred people have written letters. Fourteen per cent of all these souls who experienced such a conversion wrote that it was caused by a fear of death or hell that suddenly came over them; five per cent claimed altruistic motives; seventeen per cent ascribed it to an aspiration for moral ideals; fifteen per cent to pangs of conscience; ten per cent to following teachings that they had been given; thirteen per cent to imitating others whom they had seen being converted; nineteen per cent because it was thought that they should be given a good hiding, and so on. In this way one selects the most extreme cases, sorts and tallies them and arrives at a result that is based on 'scientific fact'. This is then compiled in books that are published on the theme of 'soul science'. All other ways of arriving at conclusions are unsound, according to these people, and are based on subjective notions (so they say). There you have an example of the externalization of what is most intimate; and it is the same with many other aspects of life in America. At a time that calls for a particular degree of spiritual deepening, spiritism of the most external kind is rampant in America! People want to make everything tangible and matter-of-fact there.

This is a materialistic conception of spiritual and cultural life. We could point towards many other things through which you would see that the culture of the West is gripped by ahrimanic influences. When the pendulum swings to the other side and we look to the East, we have the luciferic element; if we look towards the West we have the ahrimanic element. And the infinitely significant task that we in Central Europe have between East and West is to find the balance. Thus it is our wish to represent in the form of the sculptural Group[110] the greatest of the spiritual demands of our age: finding the balance between the relationship to Lucifer and the relationship to Ahriman. One will recognize what the Christ impulse wanted of earthly evolution only if one portrays Christ not simply as an entity but if one knows that Christ is that power that exemplifies for us the balance in the relationship to Lucifer and Ahriman.

That there is as yet no clarity with respect to the relationship of man and of Christ to Lucifer and Ahriman may be illustrated by means of the following example. Even the greatest things or things containing a measure of greatness are not free from the one-sidedness associated with a particular time. It is impossible to overestimate the significance of that picture that Michelangelo painted in the Sistine Chapel in Rome, *The Last Judgement*, a truly wonderful picture depicting Christ in triumph, directing the good to the one side and the evil to the other.

Let us focus our attention upon this Christ. He does not have the kind of features that we want to emphasize in the Christ who is to be represented in our building in Dornach. Here it must become visible that Christ raises His hand in compassion to Lucifer above Him. Lucifer should not be depicted as falling because of the power of Christ; he falls of his own accord because he cannot bear what streams forth from Christ as He approaches him. And Christ looks up as He gestures with His brow towards Lucifer. Moreover, Ahriman is not overcome by Christ's hatred; he feels that he cannot endure what streams forth from Christ. Christ stands in the middle as the one who brings the Parsifal element into the modern age, who through His very being and not through His power induces the others to overcome themselves, so that the others overcome themselves rather than being overcome by Him.

With Michelangelo we still see that Christ through His power sends the one to heaven and the other to hell. This will in future not be the real Christ but a Christ who is very luciferic. Such an observation does not, of course, detract from the greatness of the painting. This can be recognized, but one has to admit that Michelangelo was not yet able to paint Christ, because world evolution had not advanced sufficiently far. It must be clearly understood that one should not direct one's attention only to the Christ but, rather, to the threefold form of Christ, Lucifer and Ahriman. I can only hint at this. Spiritual science will eventually bring to light the full content of this mystery of Christ in relation to Lucifer and Ahriman.

But now consider the following. If we look towards the East we see luciferic powers in our near proximity; and in the West we see ahrimanic powers. In our spiritual-scientific studies it must be our way to look at things not with sympathy and antipathy and also to consider nations and Folk-souls not with sympathy and antipathy but as they actually are. What one refers to as the national heritage of a person who identifies himself with the character of his people is mainly dependent upon what lives within the physical and etheric body. When we are dwelling as a being of soul and spirit in the form of our astral body and ego between going to sleep and waking up, we live outside our familiar national identity. Only between waking up and going to sleep, when we are immersed in the physical body, do we partake in our nationality. Thus nationality is also something that a person gradually overcomes during his stay in kamaloka; and as he overcomes his national identity in kamaloka he aspires to the universally human in order then to live for the greater part of the time between death and a new birth in the realm of the universally human. Thus among the qualities that are laid aside in kamaloka is that which specializes us in terms of our nationality.

In this respect the various nationalities are very different from one another. Let us, for example, compare someone from France with someone from Russia. The Frenchman has the distinctive quality that he quite particularly adheres to and dwells within what the Folk-soul imparts to his physical and etheric body during his life between birth and death. This comes to expression in that the Frenchman—not as an individual but as a Frenchman—has a definite picture of what it is to be French; that it is of primal importance to think of himself as French. But these thoughts that Frenchmen, and speakers of Romance languages in general, form of their nationality lead to the idea that they have about their nationality being firmly imprinted upon the etheric body. When a Frenchman has passed through the gate of death, he discards his etheric body after a few days; and it then becomes a firmly closed entity that remains for a long time in the etheric world. This etheric body is for a long time unable to dissolve, because it is firmly impregnated with the conception that he has of his nationality; and these ideas keep the etheric body intact. Thus if we look towards the West, we see the field of death filled with firmly defined etheric bodies.

If we look more closely at the East, at the Russians, the distinctive quality of Russians is that when souls pass through the gate of death bearing such an etheric body, it dissolves relatively very quickly. This is the difference between the West and the East. The etheric bodies of Western Europeans that are separated out after death have the quality of wanting to maintain their rigidity. What the Frenchman calls '*gloire*' imprints itself firmly upon his etheric body as a national '*gloire*', so that he is condemned to direct his attention to this etheric body, to look at himself for a long time after his death. A Russian, on the other hand, looks at himself very little after his death. Through all of this a person from Western Europe is exposed to the ahrimanic influence; this materialization process of the etheric body is under the sway of the ahrimanic principle. The diffusion and rapid ascent of the etheric body is accompanied by a feeling of pleasure in the nationality concerned. How does this come to expression in the East?

Central Europe does not understand this, just as it does not have an inner feeling for it. If one studies Dostoyevsky and even Tolstoy or other leading writers who are always speaking about the 'Russian man', this comes over as a feeling of pleasure in the national character which cannot in itself be defined. We even find with Solovyov how something oppressive lives in his philosophy which Central Europeans cannot reconcile with everything that is active in Europe as a spiritual power. In Central Europe there is an intermediate state, something that could be explained further than was possible in yesterday's public lecture.

I said that something exists in Central Europe that is of an inner aspirational nature. Goethe would have written his *Faust* no differently in the 1840s: Strive ever onwards, he would have said! But this striving is deeply inward in nature. It was in Central Europe where the mystics appeared who wanted not only to recognize the divine-spiritual world but to experience it in their own souls. They wanted to experience the Christ event inwardly.

Now if one takes Solovyov, one finds that before all else he proceeds from the thought that Christ historically died once for mankind. This is perfectly correct, but there lives in Solovyov a soul that sees spiritual life rather as a cloud outside himself, a soul that sees that everything has, so to speak, already happened; whereas the Central European demands that each one experiences the Christ event anew within himself. Meister Eckhardt would have said something on the following lines to someone like Solovyov. Where Solovyov emphasizes repeatedly that Christ had to undergo death in order that man can find his true potential, Meister Eckhardt would say: You are viewing Christ as one looks upon something external. What matters is not that we always focus our attention upon historical events but we must experience Christ within ourselves; we must discover something inwardly that passes through states similar to Christ, at least spiritually, so that the Christ event is experienced anew on a spiritual plane.

Now it may surely seem contrived and fantastic if people today are told that evolution as a whole and specifically the Folk-spirit living in the language of Central Europe has brought it about that this connection of the ego with the Christ principle (I-CH = Iesus Christus or Jesus Christ) is imprinted within the German language. I-CH is conjoined so that it became 'Ich' ['I']. And as one speaks this word in Central Europe, one is pronouncing the name of Christ. This is how closely one feels the ego or 'I' to be inwardly connected with Christ. This intimate association with the spiritual world in the way that it must be striven for in all areas of cultural and intellectual life in Central Europe is not known either in the West or in the East. Therefore something needs to happen in the twentieth century in order that the Christ principle can, correspondingly, gradually spread throughout the whole continent of Europe.

I have frequently stated in various lecture-cycles[111] that that spiritual being whom we call Michael became, so to speak, the leading spirit. This leading spirit is now preparing the event which in the first of my Mystery Plays[112] is referred to as the appearance of the etheric Christ on Earth, an event that must occur in the twentieth century. It will then happen that at first a few individual souls and then an ever-increasing number will know that Christ is really here, that He is an earthly presence but in an etheric and not in an earthly form. This must be prepared.

If in the course of the twentieth century certain souls were to open their spiritual eyes clairvoyantly—and this will happen—to what is living in the etheric world, they would be disturbed by those etheric bodies that emanate from Western Europe. Their spirit-vision would rest first on them, and they would have a distorted perception of the figure of Christ. Michael therefore has to fight a battle in Europe. He must contribute something towards the diffusion of these inflexible etheric bodies from Western Europe in the etheric world. To this end, he must take those etheric bodies that readily diffuse, those from the East, and battle with them against the West. The result of this is that since 1879 there has been a mighty battle in the astral world between Russian and West-European etheric bodies, and this battle rages through the whole astral world. A mighty battle is indeed going on in the astral world, led by Michael, between Russia and France. This is what in the astral world lies at the foundation of the battle now raging in Europe. And just as we are often so staggered to find that something taking place here in the physical world has its counterpart in the spiritual world, so is it the case here.

The alliance between France and Russia,[113] which was concluded at the instigation of Ahriman and resides in the first instance within the ahrimanic realm, as is betokened by the twenty billion francs that France gave to Russia, is the physical expression of a battle that now rages between French and Russian souls, a battle that directly involves Central Europe as it strives in its innermost soul towards an encounter with the Christ. And Europe has fallen victim to the karma that precisely in Central Europe there has, tragically, to be an experience of what the East and the West, and the West with the East, must resolve between one another. The matters that the German element has outwardly to sort out with the French element can be understood only through the fact that the German element lies in the middle between the East and the West and serves as an anvil for both sides; for what is colliding from both sides in Germany is in truth the affair of these two sides. This is the spiritual truth, which is totally different from what is going on outwardly in the physical world. Just think how different the spiritual truth is from what is taking place outwardly in the physical world! This must surely sound grotesque to people today; but it is the truth, even if we find it shocking.

But there is something else that is of extraordinary interest. It surely contradicts everything that we can learn from history that England, having been united with Turkey against Russia, now suddenly must fight with Russia against Turkey. One can understand this contradiction only if one makes the following occult observation. Whereas here on the physical plane England allied with Russia is fighting against Turkey, what presents itself to occult observation is the following. If one studies this battle from an occult standpoint and views it first on the physical plane and then on the astral plane, it emerges that from a northern perspective Russia appears to be allied with England, while from a south-eastern perspective there appears to be an alliance of Turkey with England. This is due to the fact that the bond between England and Russia only has a significance on the physical plane but is not reflected in the spiritual world, since it rests wholly on material interests. From below one sees that England and Russia are allied in the north only on the physical plane. In the south-east, looking through the physical plane, one perceives on the astral plane that the English are in a soul sense allied with the Turks against Russia. Thus on the physical plane England is fighting on the same side as Russia, while on the other hand Russia is being fought by England. This is how we must view the events taking place outwardly, in so far as they manifest themselves as outward history; for what lies behind it is something entirely different.

A time will come when people will speak quite differently about present events than happens now. It must be said that there is something thoroughly unpleasant about war literature in general. And one aspect of it is particularly unpleasant. It is constantly said that one cannot speak at present about who is to blame for the war and so forth. People like to delude themselves about such things. They say that we shall learn from archived documents who was at fault! With respect to the outward events, however, it is not so difficult to resolve this if one judges dispassionately. And even if he is wrong about certain details, Chamberlain in his *War Essays*[114] is right when he says that it is possible to know the key issues about this war. It is true that there is no doubt about that, but one needs to ask the right question.

There is, for example, one question which, if it is rightly posed, can be answered quite unequivocally. It is the question: Who could have prevented this war? The constantly recurring question: Who bears the blame for this war? and many other questions are not the right ones. Who could have prevented this war? The obvious answer would be that the Russian government could have prevented it. Only in this way will one be able to find the way to define the impulses that are at work in each situation. Of course, the war that the East has been wanting for decades would not have been able to come about if there had not been a certain relationship between England, Russia and France, so that one can also, if one wants, ascribe the greater blame to England. But all these conjectures do not take into account the underlying causes that made the whole world war a necessity. It is naive to think that the war could have failed to materialize. People speak now as if this war did not need to happen when it was, of course, part of European karma.

I wanted to indicate this by speaking about the contrasts between East and West. It does not so much matter that we raise questions about the outer causes, for these are not important. We simply need to realize that this war is a historical necessity. The specific causes are then unimportant.

What is important, however, are all the various effects, towards which we must develop the right attitude; and one effect can impress us in a highly significant way. One remarkable, characteristic phenomenon is that through such a war many unspent etheric bodies are engendered. And since this is the greatest war that humanity has engaged in since historical records began, this has featured in a major way. Unspent etheric bodies accumulate. After all, a person's etheric body can nurture him for a long time, until he is seventy, eighty or ninety years old.

But in time of war human beings are sacrificed in the prime of their lives. When someone passes through the gate of death, the etheric body (as you know) is expelled after a short time; but in the case of those who have fallen in battle the etheric bodies that are expelled would have been able to sustain these human lives in the physical body for several decades. In physics it is recognized that no force is lost. It is similar in a spiritual context. These etheric bodies that pass prematurely into the etheric world continue to have their forces intact. Just think of the countless number of unspent etheric bodies that there are of those who are passing through the gate of death as young men. Moreover, there is something distinctive about these etheric bodies. I should like to illustrate this by means of an example closely connected with our movement and then go on to consider the etheric bodies of the fighters who have passed through death, which will become part of the etheric world in the near future.

Last autumn we experienced in Dornach the death of the little son of a family belonging to the Anthroposophical Society and currently employed in the vicinity of the building, the death of seven-year-old Theodor Faiß.[115] The father had previously lived in Stuttgart; he then came as a gardener to Dornach and lived near the building together with his family. He had himself been called up soon after the outbreak of the war and was at the time of the incident that I want to speak about in a military hospital.

Little seven-year-old Theo was a really sunny child, a wonderful, lovely boy. Now one day the following occurred. We had just had a lecture in accordance with my practice of speaking in Dornach in relation to what was happening with the building. After the lecture someone came to say that little Theodore Faiß had not returned to his mother since the late afternoon. It was then ten o'clock in the evening, and it was impossible to avoid thinking that a great misfortune had occurred.

On this same afternoon a furniture van had arrived and had taken a direction near the so-called canteen where there was a bend that it had to negotiate. The van had reached this spot where, it can be said in all confidence, no van of such a size—and perhaps no furniture van of any description—had ever come and none has come since. Now before the van had reached this bend little Theo had been in the canteen. He had been delayed there, otherwise he would have returned home earlier with the food that he had fetched from the canteen for supper. He then set off home—and it is only a very short distance—at such a time that he was at the very spot where the van overturned and fell on him. No one had noticed the accident, not even the coachman; for his main concern had been for his horses when the van had overturned, and he did not know that the child was underneath it. When we were notified of the child's absence, we had to try to lift the van. Friends fetched tools, and the Swiss soldiers who had been alerted helped us with this. Of course the child had already been dead since 5.30 in the afternoon. The furniture van had immediately crushed the boy, who had died of suffocation.

This is a case that can be used as an example of what I have often tried to clarify through a comparison, namely that causes and effects are confused. I have often used the following familiar instance. Suppose that we see someone walking beside a river. This person then falls into the river. Those who see this happening hurry along and find a stone at the spot where he fell into the river and think that he must have stumbled, fallen into the river and died as a result. They therefore say that he died because he fell into the river. But if an autopsy is conducted on him, one may perhaps find that he had had a heart attack and that he fell into the river as a result. He therefore did not die because he fell into the river, but he fell into the river because he was dead. You quite frequently find such confusions of cause and effect in the assessing of life situations and even more so in ordinary science.

The situation with little Theo was that his karma had run its course, so that one can indeed say that he had ordered the van to go where it did. I mention the whole case, which was outwardly tragic in the extreme, for the reason that we have here to do with the etheric body of a child which could have sustained the life of this child for decades. This etheric body has passed into the spiritual world with all its unused forces. Where is it? Since then anyone obliged to work with artistic intentions on the building in Dornach or is simply quietly pursuing thoughts within its confines knows—if at the same time he is gifted with occult perception—that the whole of this etheric body has expanded in the aura of the Dornach building. We must make the distinction that the individuality is elsewhere, it goes its own way; but the etheric body that was expelled after a few days is now present in the building. And I shall never hesitate to say that among the forces that one needs for intuition are the forces of this etheric body which was sacrificed for the building. The relationships behind ordinary life are often totally different than one supposes. This etheric body has become a protective power for the building. There is something of immense significance in such a relationship.

And now consider what a vast amount of power rises up into the spiritual world in the unspent etheric bodies of those who are now passing through the gate of death on account of the events of the war.

Things are connected quite differently than people may imagine; the karma in the world is fulfilled in a wholly different way. Spiritual science has to be prepared to put spiritually true ideas in place of fantastical imaginings. We can—to give just one example—barely conceive of anything more fantastic and untrue than something that has occurred in the last few decades.

One may well ask what has been accomplished as a result of the establishing of a special 'Peace Society',[116] in order to replace war with law, with 'international law' as it was called! At no time in human history have such terrible wars occurred since the 'Peace Society' has existed; and in the last few years this peace movement has had among special patrons the monarch who has waged the bloodiest and most terrible wars that have ever been conducted in world history. Thus the initiating of the peace movement on the part of the tsar must appear as the greatest farce that has ever been perpetrated in world history, the greatest farce and at the same time the most abominable! This is what should be called the luciferic temptation of the East.

One can say that it makes a shocking impression on the soul when one sees—however one may wish to view the situation—that at the outset, when the war impulse was making its presence felt in Europe, people had assembled in Central Europe and, moreover, in the German Parliament in Berlin and hardly said anything at all. Little was said, but events spoke for themselves. There was, however, endless talk both in the West and in the East. But in a certain sense one receives the most shocking impression from what was said by the various parties in the St Petersburg Duma. The representatives in the Duma uttered all manner of meaningless clichés with the greatest fire of enthusiasm. It was shocking. But the luciferic temptation was at work here. All this indicates to us that the fire that is burning in this war is a warning that people must truly heed.

Everything that is now happening points towards the need for a few souls to say to themselves: Things cannot continue in the world as they are at present, a spiritual element must flow into human evolution! Materialism has found its karma in this most terrible of wars. In a certain sense this war is the karma of materialism. The more human souls perceive this, so much the more will they stop discussing whether this or that faction is to blame for the war and will say to themselves: This war has been sent into world history as a warning that we should turn towards a spiritual conception of human life as a whole.

Materialism does not only make the souls of human beings materially oriented but it also perverts logic and dulls the feelings. Within Central Europe people are still far from fully understanding the implications of what I have been saying: that in Central Europe there needs to be an intimate understanding of the continuing development of the Christ impulse. But this means, among other things, that a start must be made with understanding those individuals who have already sown the seeds for this. Just one example: Goethe wrote a theory of colour. Physicists regard this as something that they smile sympathetically about when they say: What did the poet understand about colour? He was a dilettante! Since the 1880s[117] I have been labouring to gain acceptance for Goethe's theory of colour against the tide of modern physics. People cannot understand it. Why can they not understand it? Because the materialistic principle, which emanates from the British Folk-soul, has gained its entry into Central Europe. Newton, whom Goethe had to oppose, has gained the victory over what in Goethe derived from the spirit. Goethe also established a theory of evolution, in which it is shown how through the embracing of spiritual laws beings advance from the least to the most perfected state. This has been too difficult for people to understand. When Darwin brought his theory of evolution expressing this in a simplified form, people understood this. Darwin was victorious over Goethe. The materialistic thinker who is inspired by the British Folk-soul has prevailed over Goethe, who derived his insights from the most intimate dialogue with the German Folk-soul.

Ernst Haeckel's experience was a tragic one. He was intellectually nourished throughout his life by what Huxley and Darwin have given him. Ernst Haeckel's materialism is fundamentally an English product.[118] Now when the war broke out, Haeckel was furious about what emerged from the British Isles. He was one of the first to return British medals, diplomas and honours. However, what should be returned are not these decorations and insignia but British Darwinism and physics. One needs to come to this point of view in order to see how Central Europe can strive towards an intimate dialogue with the laws of the world.

The greatest damage is done when one fills a child's soul with what goes on to develop further in a purely materialistic way. This has been on the increase for centuries. Ahriman has inspired a British author of considerable standing to write a book that was specifically calculated to influence the soul materialistically from childhood in such a way that one does not notice, because one does not see all this as preparing for a materialistic view. This is *Robinson Crusoe*. The whole manner in which Robinson is described is so ingenious that once the ideas underlying this saga have been imbibed they prepare the mind in such a way that it can later only think materialistically.

Humanity has not yet been healed from the inventors of such tales; they existed before and are still with us now. This is not to say anything derogatory about the peoples of the West, who have to be as they are; my intention is, rather, to indicate how people in Central Europe must find the connection with the great values with respect to future developments that are as yet only in germinal form. Austria has a quite particular part to play in this regard. In recent decades one could see how individuals such as Hamerling in the realm of literature have aspired to the highest ideals, as has Carneri, who wanted to extend Darwinism to encompass the moral realm, and also Bruckner and other artists working in a variety of different fields.[119] It is important that a people has an awareness of such things.

Now let us consider the unspent etheric bodies that are in existence. These etheric bodies have been cast off by those who had learned in the course of a great event to sacrifice themselves for something that—at any rate ostensibly—no longer exists for them:

for their people. If as a spiritual scientist today one speaks of a Folk-soul in terms of an archangel, one will be ridiculed. What a materialist calls a Folk-soul is merely the abstract sum of the qualities that the people belonging to a particular folk share. When he refers to a people or folk, he has in mind simply the totality of human beings living together in the same geographical area and with a common outlook.

When we speak of a people or nation, we do so out of the knowledge that the Folk-spirit is present as a real being of the rank of an archangel. Even if someone who sacrifices himself by going through death for his people has no proper awareness on the field of battle of a real Folk-spirit, he confirms through the manner in which he dies that he believes in an existence that continues beyond death, that he believes that there is more to a people and its culture than what meets the eye, namely its connection and its interplay with the supersensible world. Thus regardless of their awareness of this, all those who pass through death are confirming as they do so that there is a supersensible world; and this is imprinted upon their etheric bodies. Thus when peace has become re-established, in addition to those who will be living in the physical earthly world there will be the unspent etheric bodies continually sending forth tones to the music of the spheres declaiming that there is more in the world than what can merely be seen with physical eyes! Spiritual truth will sound forth into the music of the spheres through what the dead leave behind in their etheric bodies, wholly irrespective of what they take with them with their individuality that they retain throughout their life between death and a new birth.

But what lives in and resounds from these etheric bodies must be heard, because these etheric bodies have been laid aside by those who have passed through death affirming the truth of the spiritual world. It will be mankind's greatest sin not to listen to what those who have died call out to us by means of the awakening cries of their etheric bodies. And as one looks up to the spiritual world, how infinitely one's perception will be enlivened if one considers that the fathers and mothers, the sisters and brothers, sons and daughters who have lost their loved ones must be saying to themselves: What has been sacrificed continues to live for the whole of humanity as an awakening call for what is to come!

If one were to rely merely upon what is taking place in the physical world, one might not have much hope for the successful continuation of the spiritual movement that is being nurtured out of our spiritual-scientific world-conception. When a good, faithful colleague died recently aged around thirty, in the words that I directed towards this soul that crossed the threshold of death I asked that it might work with us in our spiritual-scientific endeavours as faithfully and courageously as it had here on Earth, utilizing everything that it had come to know. This colleague has worked industriously with us on the physical plane. In my words to him in his life between death and a new birth, I asked that he might work with us after death as he has done before he died, for we count upon these dead people—the so-called dead—as we do on the living. Our spiritual-scientific world-conception must be so alive as to bridge the gulf between the so-called dead and the living, that we feel the dead among us as if they were alive.

We want not theory but life. Thus we also want to point out that when peace is resumed there will be a living bond between those living on the Earth and those who have passed through the gate of death. People will be able to learn from the dead how they are collaborating in the manner indicated in the great spiritual progress that must encompass the Earth.

It sometimes happens in life that one sees that human logic does not alone suffice. I should like to offer an example, not for personal reasons but in order to characterize the way that people relate to our movement. Some years ago one could read an article in a well-respected South German journal[120] that a famous modern philosopher had written about our spiritual science; and because the article was written by a great philosopher, spiritual science was portrayed in such a way as to make a certain impression on the readers of the journal. The editor of the journal took great pride in the fact that he was able to publish an article about spiritual science by such a famous man. Of course, the picture that he presented of spiritual science was unfavourable and the facts were distorted. But what did it take for the editor to see what kind of a judgement he had conveyed in his monthly journal about our movement? The war broke out.

The man who had written the article wrote some letters to the editor. These letters contained some of the most repulsive things that it is possible to say about Central European culture, upon which he poured his mockery and scorn. The editor now published these letters as an example of how foolishly it is possible to think about this culture, adding that the only place for a man who writes like this is a lunatic asylum. So the fact is that something of this kind was necessary for the good editor to see that the man who several years before had written this article about spiritual science, which had severely damaged the movement's public image, belongs in a madhouse. But if he now belongs in a madhouse, so did he also belong in one when he wrote an article about spiritual science!

This is the way of the world! Additional help is needed beyond what is available to people today to form a judgement. The spiritual scientist stands firmly on the ground that clearly shows that the truth eventually finds its path. But spiritual science must exert its influence within human evolution in order that what is necessary occurs. And so as at that time when the Emperor Constantine had his task to fulfil the Christ impulse had subconsciously to intervene from the spiritual world, as with the Maid of Orleans the Christ impulse had to bring its influence to bear in order that what had to happen did indeed happen, so must the Christ impulse continue to work further though now more consciously. There must in future be souls who will know that up there in the spiritual world those who have sacrificed themselves as individuals are calling us to follow them in the belief in the efficacy of the spiritual world which they have attained in death.

And the forces from unspent etheric bodies are sending their call into the future, a call that one only needs to understand in order to receive it into one's own soul. But there must be souls down below that hear this call. There must be souls that prepare themselves through the right, living understanding of our spiritual science. Our spiritual science must foster souls here on Earth that are able to sense what the etheric bodies of the dead will speak in the future; souls that know that up there reside the forces that are able to evoke a sense of urgency within human beings who had to be left to themselves on Earth. And when spirit-conscious souls direct their attention to the hidden sounds of the spiritual world, the right fruits will arise from all the blood that has flowed, the sacrifices that have been made and the sorrow that had to be borne and will continue to be borne.

In the hope that many, many souls may come together through spiritual science and hear the voices that will sound forth from the spiritual world especially through this war, I should like to speak words that summarize the concluding part of what has been said today and which express the feelings that I wish to evoke within your souls:

> From the courage of the fighters,
> From the blood on fields of battle,
> From the grief of the bereaved,
> From the people's sacrifice—
> There will ripen fruit of spirit,
> If souls will turn in consciousness
> Towards the realm of spirit.

With such feelings in our hearts we want constantly to imbue ourselves with the meaning of the Rose Cross, so that we may rightly view it as the motto for our working, weaving and feeling. Not the black cross alone. Anyone who would tear the roses from the black cross and has only the black cross would fall prey to Ahriman. The black cross represents life in its aspiration towards lifeless matter. Nor will anyone who tears the cross from the roses and wishes to keep only the roses find the right path; for the roses when separated from the cross want to elevate us to the spirit, but this life would seek egotistically to strive only towards the spirit and not make the spirit manifest within the material realm. Not the cross alone, not the roses alone, but the roses on the cross, the cross bearing the roses, both in harmonious interplay: that is what our true symbol should be.

LECTURE 12

ELBERFELD, 13 JUNE 1915

Spiritual Science as a Conviction—The Etheric Body as a Reflection of the Universe

WE are at present living in the midst of an era when there are events that arouse all manner of feelings in the human soul of the deepest and most meaningful kind. We are involved with events which lead to that which is forever regarded by spiritual science as a riddle, namely death, occurring many, many times over a relatively short period throughout the Earth. We live at a time when countless souls are having to bear pain and sorrow, and at a time when it would be our hope that significant forces for the furtherance of the evolution of mankind may be engendered. If so much has to be born out of pain and sorrow, and if indeed spiritual science teaches us that much has to be born out of pain and sorrow, spiritual-scientific studies may in this fateful time be especially suitable for awakening within us wellsprings of confidence and hope. Thus some thoughts will be presented to you today that are not directly but nonetheless indirectly connected with such feelings as may be evoked within us in this sorrowful, storm-tossed time.

What we see and feel so often taking place at present is that human beings are leaving the physical plane at a relatively early stage of their physical existence. The distinctive aspect of such experiences as these is that young lives are called away from the physical plane. We know that when someone passes through the portal of death he has to give his physical body over to the elements of the Earth, that as he crosses this threshold he is at first still united with his etheric body, his astral body and his ego. We know that after a relatively short time this etheric body is separated from the person concerned and that he undertakes his further journey that he has to make between death and a new birth in the ego and astral body, united with those members of his spiritual nature that he is initially able to acquire only in the spiritual world; whereas for his further journey during the time between death and a new birth the etheric body is separated from the human individuality and follows its own path.

Now it must strike us that when someone dies young this etheric body must be in a completely different state from when a person dies who has reached a normal stage of life. We know that scientists speak of how forces can be transformed but not lost. Thus it is recognized as a truth of physical existence that forces are never lost but are merely transformed. Spiritual science teaches that this must also be applied to the spiritual world. When an etheric body is cast off from someone who has passed through the gate of death at a young age, this is an etheric body that would have been able to sustain this person on the physical plane for many decades. After all, an etheric body must be so constituted that it can provide all those life-forces that he will require until old age. If someone crosses the threshold of death in, say, his twenty-fifth, twenty-sixth, or thirtieth year, his etheric body parts company from him; but this etheric body still has forces through which he would have been enabled to maintain physical, human life perhaps into his sixties, seventies or eighties. These forces are in the etheric body; they are not lost. And precisely at such a time as the present, when so many such etheric bodies are being, as it were, entrusted to the spiritual worlds, we need to concern ourselves with the question: What happens with the etheric bodies of those people who have passed at so young an age through the gate of death? It will be good if, in order to answer such a question really properly, we familiarize ourselves with the path followed by the etheric body of a human being during his life between birth and death.

The outward physical body of a human being constantly becomes older. This is not the case with the etheric body. However difficult it may seem to be to grasp this, it is not at all the case with the etheric body that it is always getting older; for in the same measure that the physical body grows older, the etheric body becomes ever younger and it reaches what one might call a certain child-like stage of etheric existence at the time when the human individual is of an age when he would normally cross the threshold of death. Thus we must say to ourselves: When we enter physical, earthly existence through birth, the etheric body that has united itself with our physical body is, comparatively speaking, old and becomes ever younger in the course of life and reaches its childhood stage when we pass through the gate of death. We could therefore also say that when someone dies when he is young, his etheric body is not young enough but retains a certain quality of age. But what does this actually mean? We may find the following example instructive in this respect. It is one that a number of you will already be familiar with, but I must nevertheless mention it again here in that it is a concrete instance from recent times which a number of friends may have experiemced.

This concrete example relates to a young child, the little son of one our members. It happened that on an evening when there was a lecture in Dornach we learnt after the lecture that a seven-year-old boy, the son of our friend Faiß,[121] was missing. It was soon clear that a great misfortune must have occurred. Late that afternoon a furniture van had come to the vicinity of the building in Dornach, curiously to an area where such a van had not ventured for a long time or perhaps never and where none have most likely come since. This furniture van had overturned at a certain place. This had happened towards evening, and nothing further had been noticed; but the boy was missing. And when between ten and twelve o'clock in the evening our friends together with others made every effort to lift the furniture van, which those to whom it belonged had decided to leave until the following morning because it had fallen very awkwardly, thus making the task very difficult, it emerged that the child, little Theodor Faiß, had passed by at the very moment when the van had overturned and that it had fallen on the child. This child—who was only seven years old—was a very likeable boy, a child with remarkably fine qualities.

In order to place such a fact in the light of spiritual-scientific consciousness, I should like to recall a logical train of thoughts that I have often cited in our circles. I have often said that people can confuse causes and effects through ordinary thinking, through undisciplined thinking, and that such confusions between cause and effect are actually very frequently encountered. I have tried to show this by means of an example, an example that is only intended as a means of illustration.

Suppose that you see in the distance someone walking beside a stream. You then see that he falls into the stream, and in your efforts to arrive at the spot you see that at the very place where the person fell into the water there is a stone. You try to pull him out of the water, but he is dead. What could be more natural than to say that he stumbled over the stone, fell into the stream and was drowned. But this need not be the case; for a simple physical investigation may perhaps tell us that at the moment when he had come to this place—and without his destiny having had anything to do with the stone or with anything else—he had suffered a heart attack and fell into the water as a result (so that the heart attack was the cause of his falling into the water), whereas if one does not go to the trouble of finding out what really happened one would say that his falling into the water was the cause of his death. One would therefore assume the opposite of what actually occurred.

It is more difficult to discern the relationship between cause and effect when one is concerned with events connected with the spiritual world. Thus one must say that in a case such as that of this child, who meets his death through such extraordinary circumstances (and they were extraordinary in several other respects) one has from a higher standpoint not to think that this happened because the furniture van came along and overturned and the child was by some chance underneath it and that, therefore, the van was the cause of the child's death. The right way to think about such a case spiritual-scientifically is that the child's karma had run its course, and that the reason for the van arriving at that place was actually that the child was to meet its death; that therefore the van merely provided the outward circumstances to enable the death that was prefigured by the child's karma to take place. To express it trivially one could say that the child's higher self's wish that the child pass through the gate of death had arranged the whole situation, the whole series of events.

To be sure, when someone who thinks in accordance with our present time hears such an idea expressed, he will find it perfectly crazy. However, spiritual science has to show us that much that people consider crazy today is actually true.

The significant point is, however, that in this particular case the etheric body of a seven-year-old child separated itself from the child's individuality, from what goes further with the ego and astral body through the spiritual worlds. It is not now my intention to speak about the further path taken by the individuality of little Theodor Faiß; my task is, rather, to draw attention to the fact that in this case the etheric body was one that had nurtured physical life with its life-forces for only seven years, even though the forces residing within it could have sustained a long life between birth and death. These forces remained within the etheric body. And the significant thing is that anyone who had a spiritual connection with the building that we intend to erect in Dornach in the service of spiritual science could know directly from little Theodor Faiß's death[122] what had become of his etheric body.

So much needs to be done in connection with the building. We shall be speaking further about the inspirations that need to be brought down from the spiritual world today. Helping forces are needed if all that must be brought from the spiritual world indeed becomes available to us. And it became apparent that since the death of little Theodor Faiß, our building in Dornach has been enveloped to quite a wide extent by the enlarged etheric body of this child as by an aura. It is possible to determine how widely it extends.

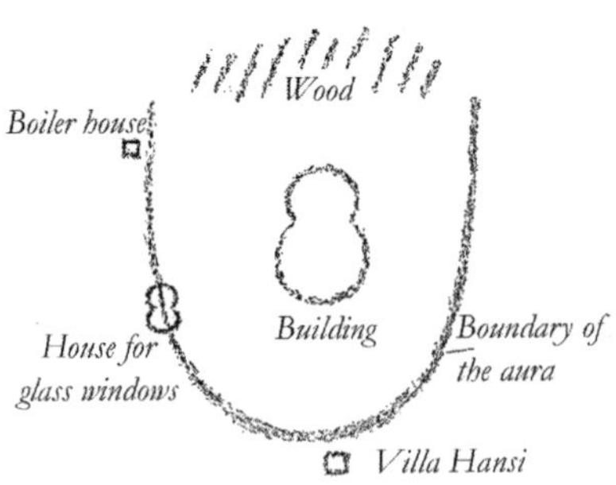

If you see the Dornach building (and those who have already seen it are aware of this), it is a circular building with two cupolas. Here we have a boiler house shaped in a particular way in accordance with spiritual-scientific principles, and here we have another house where the glass windows for the building are cut. I might mention, by the way, that somewhere here is the so-called 'Haus Hansi', where we live. Now it is remarkable that this aura of little Theodor Faiß envelops the whole building as far as this spot where the wood begins, then past the boiler house and then, after passing directly through this building where the windows are being cut, passes by Haus Hansi without enclosing it. Thus as one enters the building, one actually steps within this etheric aura.

I have often drawn attention to the fact that the etheric body becomes larger when it frees itself from the physical body. We should not therefore be surprised that this etheric body appears in so an enlarged a state. In this etheric body are the forces of mediation that enable one to receive certain impressions from the spiritual world that one needs in order to incorporate them in the forms and artistic structure of the building; and anyone whose task it is to work on the building knows what he owes to this etheric aura. I shall never hesitate to admit that since the death of little Theodor Faiß the work has been made possible for me through the mediating forces for inspirations that have been made available by this boy's etheric body which has been enveloping the building. One could well pride oneself in not needing such mediating forces; but what really matters is to acknowledge the truth of the situation.

If we bring the facts that have just been described before our minds, we will gain an impression of how it is with an etheric body that has to be separated from a human life when this life is brought to an end when the person is still young. Now it is important to be aware that the etheric body of a human being does not continue to be some kind of nebulous formation within which the physical body is embedded. Indeed, we also do not come to know the nature of a physical human body by describing it merely as a mass of muscles and bones and so on but by recognizing it as a kind of temple of the divinity, as a microcosm. We only rightly come to know what a physical body is if we become aware that the forms that it takes on are indeed derived from the whole universe; that man is by virtue of his physical body a form of miraculous proportions. Whoever is able to sense the feelings expressed in the first conversation of the second Mystery Play *The Soul's Probation* will form some idea of how an individual human being is, with respect to his physical body, placed into his physical existence by all the hierarchies; the whole world of the Gods sees it as its aim to incorporate man in physical existence. We can come to a full awareness of the significance of this physical body if we take account of the observations of clairvoyant knowledge.

Clairvoyant knowledge comes about when a person draws his soul-spiritual nature forth from his physical body and is then able to become a consciously perceiving agent in the realm of soul and spirit outside his body. There is essentially no fundamental difference between someone who perceives clairvoyantly and someone who is asleep, whose soul-spiritual nature has also withdrawn from the physical body. By virtue of the fact that clairvoyant consciousness is able to perceive outside the physical body, it can form an idea of what is happening with someone who is asleep. The following schematic drawing may make this easier to understand.

Let us suppose that this is the physical, bodily nature and this is the soul-spiritual nature of someone who is asleep. Of course, when someone is awake the soul-spiritual part is within the physical, bodily part; we are therefore visualizing a person who is asleep. The physical body and the etheric body are then in the bed, but they do not contain the astral body and the ego as they do in the waking state. But one could say that what the astral body and the ego bring about within the physical body during the waking state does not entirely cease during sleep. As far as any initial observation is concerned, the person lying in the bed is as though devoid of soul; but this is not the case for a clairvoyant consciousness. The clairvoyant must give an entirely different interpretation of this sleeping physical and etheric human being. He must say: During the entire day the region of the Earth where people are now sleeping was bathed in sunlight. (I am speaking of normal circumstances where one sleeps during the night and is awake during the day, not of those prevailing in the city and metropolitan environments of today.) Darkness descends over

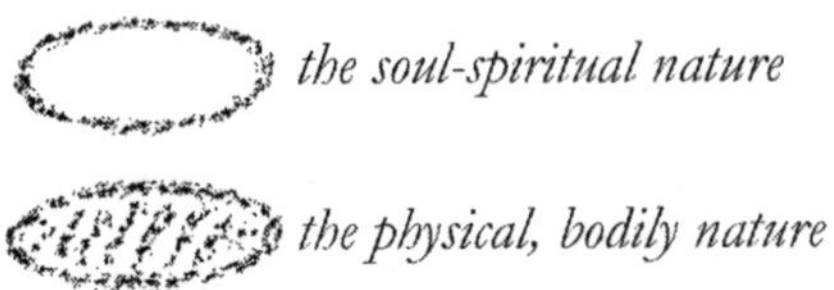

the region where the Sun was shining during the day. Remarkably, one notices that the Earth as a living being begins to think, and the organs through which the Earth thinks are these sleeping human bodies.

Just as human beings think by means of their brain, so does the Earth think through these sleeping human bodies. It is constantly perceiving during the day—its perception consists in its being illumined by the Sun from cosmic space, that is the Earth's perception; while during the night it assimilates in thought what it has perceived. The Earth thinks, says the clairvoyant; and it thinks by making use of sleeping human beings. Every sleeping human being is in a certain sense a brain-molecule of the Earth. Our physical body is so ordered that, when we are not ourselves using it, it can enable the Earth to think through it.

But just as the Earth thinks through the physical body, so does it imagine (and you know what imaginative knowledge is) everything that is not earthly on the Earth itself, that which belongs to the Earth from the whole cosmos. In man's sleeping physical body one discerns parts of the Earth's brain, and in man's etheric body (when he is asleep) one discerns an imaginative picture of that part of the universe that initially belongs to the Earth. In wonderful pictures there stream into the etheric body all the forces that must flow to the Earth from the etheric world in order that the events of this Earth can take place. Just as man belongs as a physical being to the Earth, it is equally true that as an etheric being he belongs to the heavens. Moreover, we can only use our physical body as an organ of thinking because it is organized for this purpose, because in a certain sense the Earth sets it free while we are awake. Equally, we can only use our etheric body in such a way that it gives us life-forces because the heavens make it available to us during our waking hours and because the heavenly forces of imagination are transformed within us into life-forces while we are awake. Thus we would wish to speak of our etheric body not merely as a vague nebulous form but as a microcosmic structure reflecting the heavens.

Our etheric body is given to us at our birth as a specially perfected structure. When we are born our etheric body inwardly glistens and shines with pure imaginations that come to it from the great universe. It is a magnificent reflection of the universe. And whatever a person is able to acquire during his life by way of education, knowledge and forces of will and feeling as he approaches old age between birth and death is derived from this same etheric body. The cosmic forces of the heavens make available to us what they have to give to us during life between birth and death. Hence as etheric beings we are once again young if we have pursued a normal life between birth and death, because we have drawn everything forth from this etheric body. But if an etheric body belonging to a youthful body goes through the portal of death, there is still much, much heavenly light within it. It therefore becomes a mediator of such forces as I have been describing. Quite irrespective of what becomes of the individuality of such a human soul as the one of whom we have been speaking, its etheric body becomes something of the nature of a heavenly gift, a gift of the spiritual worlds. This etheric body is therefore able to have the inspiring influence that I have indicated.

It would be going much too far to speak of the particular karma that such a human soul must have to be able to make such a sacrifice; for this cannot be brought about artificially but must be connected with the whole karma of such a person who is called upon to make a sacrifice and who has something to do that is destined to play a part in the spiritual advancement of mankind, as indeed lies behind our intentions for this building in Dornach that is to house our spiritual-scientific endeavours.

But now bring to your awareness that we are living at a time when many, many such etheric bodies, not from people of so young an age but nevertheless from those who are still young, will be in the spiritual atmosphere. Those who have passed through the gate of death on the bloody fields of battle all pass differently through the gate of death from someone who dies in his bed or through an ordinary accident or misfortune. The way that they cross the threshold of death is that in a certain sense they reckon with their death, even though more or less subconsciously—their astral body reckons to a certain degree with death. Indeed, one can always speak of a sacrifice in the case of such a death. All the etheric bodies of young people that thus ascend into the spiritual world will have unused forces; and we are living in a period of human evolution when human souls will be able consciously to look up into the spiritual world and say to themselves: A time has gone by that has sent many, many unspent etheric bodies into the spiritual world. And unspent etheric bodies contain forces of which we can already say today from a spiritual-scientific standpoint what significance they will have for the evolution of mankind.

When things of this nature are discussed, one must emphasize that what can be said in this regard does not apply to every war that has taken place on Earth in the course of human evolution. What is going on spiritually and can be discerned with the help of spiritual science is not as simple as natural science would make it. Other wars in former times demanded that they be spoken of differently. What I have to say now applies to our present fateful times. Just consider the following. I have on various occasions and at various opportunities had to emphasize that there is nothing arbitrary about whether we pursue spiritual science today but that it is really part of the evolutionary process of mankind that people gradually familiarize themselves with spiritual science. We know that every epoch of human evolution has a particular task. We can discover this from several of my lecture-cycles. And we may be aware that the blossoming of the future and immediately impending evolution of humanity can be ensured only if what can be revealed through spiritual science may become the spiritual and intellectual property of an ever greater number of souls.

But now let all of you who are for the most part full of a heart-felt enthusiasm for spiritual science consider what difficulties are associated with the propagation of spiritual-scientific truths at the present time. Consider the extent to which people out in the world oppose these spiritual-scientific truths. Consider, too, how these truths are slandered, how people look upon them as daft, crazy and insane and as sheer fantasy. I could give some striking examples, but all examples would form only a small part of what everyone who has enthusiasm for spiritual science can feel when he confronts a world that he would so dearly want to take an interest in spiritual science and that has so little wish to do so today.

The spiritual scientist may now say that what the mere earthly forces of mankind are able to attain seems so weak, utterly weak in comparison to the tasks of spiritual science. But in the near future, the unspent etheric bodies of those who have had to carry their lives and souls through the portal of death on the battlefields of our time will be there; and these etheric bodies with their unused forces will be forces of inspiration and help in the near future. We only need to develop the attitude of looking up—not in a theoretical, intellectual way but with our hearts and souls—to the heavenly etheric bodies of those who have in our destiny-laden time passed through the gate of death in their early youth and to direct our souls as in a mood of prayer to these etheric bodies; and those who are filled with enthusiasm for spiritual science need only to direct their souls towards these forces and they will receive help from these etheric bodies.

Thus if an ardent spiritual engagement with these etheric bodies becomes possible through a real embracing of spiritual-scientific ideas, among the many fruits that may be engendered by our destiny-laden time will be that the forces residing in these etheric bodies sacrificed by young people will flow into the souls of those people of the future who have an enthusiasm for spiritual science. The forces of sacrificed etheric bodies will therefore be able to stream through the souls of those who will be living in a physical body in the near future, if these souls are pervaded by a genuine understanding for this. And these will be heavenly forces, that is, forces of the spiritual world! Entirely different forces will then hold sway in the world in order to be able to bring to this world the spiritual-scientific convictions that need to come to it. If we can but find the possibility of recognizing what is taking place now in accordance with the explanations that have been given, these fateful times will acquire a deep significance also for those who are involved with spiritual science.

As we have said, the imaginative forms that indwell man's etheric body are magnificent. Nevertheless, they would present a different aspect if they had not passed through a human etheric body. But the proposition 'out of nothing comes nothing' is also valid in this realm.

This is not an absolute truth, but it is valid in this particular realm. Thus the etheric body that a person receives through the fact of a human soul entering physical existence through birth gathers forces of the spiritual world that are used during physical life. These forces are not derived from nothing, they exist in the spiritual world. They may, of course, be discovered in the spiritual world, but it is difficult to find them directly there; far greater powers would be needed for this. If, however, they have passed through a physical human being who died young and appear to one together with what they have within them through passing through that human being, it is easier to avail oneself of their help.

All the forces that lived in the youthful etheric body of little Theodor Faiß would otherwise be in the spiritual world, but it would in a spiritual sense be a Herculean task to draw them forth without him. Because they have become available through the boy, it has become significantly easier—and also a different process—to be inspired by them. Think how enormously significant it is for the whole further evolution of mankind that such a great number of etheric bodies with unused forces is being made available to it in the immediate future! But through the circumstance, through the fact that these heavenly—and I must emphasize the word 'heavenly'—forces have passed through human beings, these forces have, as it were, been freed from the laws within which they belong in the cosmos. It is impossible for these forces that are drawn directly from the cosmos to be used in an evil way.

We may regard it as a fact that, without the war, all those people who are now passing through the gate of death as a result of the war or through other related circumstances would not be providing such a quantity of etheric bodies. All these forces would of course anyway exist in the cosmos; but they could not be used by human beings on Earth because it would be too difficult to use them. Another reason why they could not be used would be that they would be being used in the lives of those reaching their normal age. It is of great significance that these heavenly forces have passed through human bodies. They thereby become free from the ordinary process of evolution; and this freedom makes it possible for these forces to be used for purposes other than the good of humanity.

They can also be used in a different way. Human life has to evolve in the light of freedom. Let us suppose that Ahriman would succeed in darkening the thoughts and reasoning power of human beings to such an extent that they would reject spiritual science. These etheric bodies would then be there, but there would be no souls inspired by spiritual science to place these forces at the service of earthly progress. Lucifer and Ahriman would then intervene and would be able to use them to further the kingdom of either Lucifer or Ahriman. Just think how immensely significant this is! It means that it has been entrusted to human hands, as it were, to determine in what way the forces that have been made available to the world through sacrificial deaths are incorporated in earthly evolution. There is the possibility that if they bring inspiration to what has been kindled through spiritual science, they will serve the evolutionary progress of the Earth.

But it could also be that—if materialism were to extend its grip over all minds or if nationalism were to be disseminated in a purely passionate way—Lucifer or Ahriman would put these forces to the service of their own ends; and these forces would then be unable to further the advancement of earthly evolution. Only if one becomes aware of these connections does one realize the whole deep significance of spiritual science for the evolution of humanity and the Earth. Only then will one be enabled to say how necessary it is that, if sacrificial forces are to be used in the right way in evolution, there are human individuals who are capable of understanding the insights that can emanate from spiritual science! Thus if one considers spiritual science in the context of the spiritual background to these destiny-laden days of ours, it becomes something immeasurably great and sacred. The intellectual awareness that we can develop from spiritual science will thereby become something that can be compared to a prayer that can be summarized in the words: O cosmic spirit, let us be wholly imbued with these convictions emanating from spiritual science, so that we may not fail in the right sense to wrest from Lucifer and Ahriman what can bring salvation and genuine progress to the Earth!

Our building is intended to serve as a symbol of the ideas and convictions that spiritual science wishes to make manifest to mankind. Hence it is constructed in such a way that in its forms there comes artistically to expression what spiritual science can give. I would have to say much if I were to explain to you what is contained in every detail of this building. You will become familiar with all this when you come to see the building over the next few years and participate in what takes place within it. I wish today to speak of only one aspect in connection with what I have just explained.

At a significant place in the building, at the point where it is directed towards the East, there will be a sculptural Group.[123] This sculptural Group is intended to give expression in particular to what the consciousness of our time must imbue itself with in the right measure. Apart from what will be added to it, this Group will essentially consist of three figures. Three beings will come to expression in this Group. A kind of rock will feature in it. This rock has a ledge that projects forward, and beneath this projection is a cavity. The central figure will stand upon the projecting rock. One may call it whatever one wishes, but one will need to see in it the representative of earthly humanity in the highest sense of the word. And if one sees the ideal of earthly humanity in that human being who for three years of his earthly life bore the Christ Being within himself, one will also be able to see the Christ in this central figure. But this should not happen in such a way that one comes before this Group with the consciousness that it is meant to be the Christ; for everything must be felt artistically. This means that it should not be interpreted in an outwardly symbolic way but everything must follow from the forms.

Up here is a second being. This being has a head that resembles—I can only say that it resembles—a human head. One might say that a human head is reminiscent of this head; for it is formed in such a way that the skull is powerfully developed and especially the forehead. Whereas in man these parts are relatively fixed, in this being everything is mobile. That is, everything is expressive of the soul. Just as we can move our hands and fingers but not the upper part of our head, this being can move everything in this region. One can see from the work that has been done on the sculpture that everything there is mobile. The lower part of this being's face recedes quite markedly. One could say that the mighty form of the skull dominates the rest of the face. I can only speak about certain aspects, for each individual line of this figure is of great significance. A characteristic feature is that there is in this being a connection between what in man has atrophied and become the larynx and the ear. The lobe of the larynx extends upwards and becomes the lower part of the ears, while their upper part is formed by the brow. On the other side there are two structures resembling birds' wings, between which there is a form that as a whole gives the impression of a transformed human countenance. Wings and larynx and ear are formed as one entity, so that one can see that with its wings this being lives in the music of the spheres, and this is localized in the ear. In man all this has atrophied. Through the raising of the left hand of the Representaive of Humanity, the wings of this figure are broken on the rock and as a result it plunges down from the rock. You would be right to suppose that this figure falling down from the rock with its broken wings is meant to portray Lucifer.

Down here in the cave there is another figure. Instead of bird-like wings it has wings resembling those of a bat, a kind of dragon-like or worm-like body and a head that is again reminiscent of a human head. But the mighty development of the brow possessed by Lucifer has totally receded in this figure; it has atrophied. The lower parts as far as the mouth are strongly developed in this figure; and it is entwined by what within the Earth is gold. The gold of the Earth becomes bonds that chain this figure. It is bent beneath the influence emanating from the hand of the Representative of Humanity, the Christ, as it extends downwards. This figure down below is Ahriman, fettered by the gold of the Earth.

With what I have just said, you will have some idea of the whole; but this idea only gives some indication of what it is about. We would never want to imitate the bad habit of the old theosophists who always worked with symbols; what matters to us is that everything emanating from spiritual science that tends towards human feeling is transformed into something artistic. One should therefore not say that these forms express this or that but that through what they are artistically and through what one sees in them they portray the relationship of man, or of Christ, to Lucifer and Ahriman. This therefore also cannot come to expression with the old artistic means.

Every movement of the fingers and of the hands, and the way that the hands are formed, will be significant; for they need to express something significant. One could initially have the idea that Christ raises His left hand and, through what He wills, transmits forces that break Lucifer's wings so that he falls; and that through the hand that He extends downwards, forces are again released that bind Ahriman. And yet it would be quite incorrect to think like this.

In order to explain the full significance of this, I should like to remind you of something that is one of the greatest works of art hitherto produced: *The Last Judgement* by Michelangelo in the Sistine Chapel in Rome. Here one sees Christ sending the good to heaven and the wicked to hell. Christ appears as one who dispatches some to the good world and others to somewhere less pleasant. This Christ as He is portrayed is not the Christ whom we may understand in His true nature only through spiritual science. Christ who is the true Christ does not condemn, does not delight in applying anger or ordinary love, but He works through what He is. Lucifer's wings are not broken, but he breaks them himself through his own soul-condition as he comes close to Christ; and Ahriman binds himself through what goes on in his soul as he is in the proximity of Christ. Hence Christ's hands as they are raised and extended downwards must express nothing but the purest compassion for the world. Lucifer in his lofty vantage-point cannot bear the hand of Christ coming close to him; and because of what he is inwardly experiencing he breaks his wings; it is not that Christ breaks them but he breaks them himself. It is similar with Ahriman.

Michelangelo did not yet understand how to portray Christ as He really is. The Christ Being is so significant, the understanding of the Christ Being is so difficult, that this can only be achieved in the course of time. Only in future will the Christ who causes beings to condemn or redeem themselves by virtue of what He is be understood. The way that Michelangelo has portrayed Him still has something luciferic and ahrimanic about it, because through His anger He leads the evil to hell and the good to heaven and is therefore governed by His passions. Whereas here the Christ's stance is not a personal one; and the beings who come near to Him judge themselves.

You see from this that man's position in the world, which includes the luciferic and ahrimanic forces, will come to expression in a prominent place in our building; that beings must be depicted who can be found only in the spiritual world. All naturalism in art, everything towards which art has aspired in recent times as a result of the materialism that has taken hold of human beings, must be overcome by the art that is being nurtured here. Something so entirely new must, also artistically, enter the world through spiritual science that it will also transcend even the greatest of artistic achievements: Michelangelo's figure of Christ in *The Last Judgement*.

It is permissible to say such things if on the one hand one emphasizes something that should not be forgotten: that our building can of course be no more than a primitive beginning for all this. Everything is imperfect, everything is elementary, everything is only a beginning, but it is the beginning of something totally new. We can of course be aware that everything is imperfect, but it is essential to draw attention to something that is an impulse which will enter into the whole of human life.

Consider how easy it would be to pass by with indifference a gift of human life consisting of the unspent etheric bodies of human beings. Consider that the forces of these etheric bodies could fall prey to Lucifer and Ahriman if it is not possible for us to use them as a healing impulse for earthly evolution. We are touching here upon a great mystery associated with the evolution of humanity on Earth: the mystery of the relationship of the Christ impulse to those of Lucifer and of Ahriman. It will increasingly become possible to understand this relationship of the Christ impulse to that of Lucifer and to that of Ahriman in the near future. Luciferic and ahrimanic forces exert their influence in the world, and through his consciousness of Christ man must become like a being who is, as it were, sitting in a boat that has to navigate its path amidst the storms stirred up by Lucifer and Ahriman. It will find its way through the sea whose living substance consists of Lucifer and Ahriman but through which man can nevertheless ply his Christ boat.

We do not come together in our branches in order to learn in a theoretical way something that spiritual science can reveal to us;

rather do we gather here so that what lives in our souls is filled with an inner orientation that can flow from this spiritual science. What matters is not what we think out of spiritual science but how we think, feel and will. And whether we focus our attention on the most insignificant or the greatest things that we can observe in the earthly evolution of humanity, everything shows us how necessary it is for the people of the future to familiarize themselves with the significance of the threefoldness of Christ, Lucifer and Ahriman. Not only Michelangelo but also the times that are now past have not been able rightly to see how this threefoldness has its place in the world. But one will also only rightly come to know Christ in His essential reality if one sees Him in His relationship to the beings of Lucifer and Ahriman who work in the world as its South and North Poles.

Much will be said about these matters in the coming days for those who are able to be present. It has been my wish today to place before your souls thoughts that enable one to see that the ideas of spiritual science also have an importance for significant events that someone who can perceive what is happening physically in its spiritual context will be able to discern taking place in the spiritual world in the near future.

One would in this sense entreat the good Gods and spirits who protect the Earth and humanity to give human beings the strength so that what must happen for the healing and well-being of mankind can take place!

Up there in the realms of spirit will be the unused etheric forces of young people who have passed through death. But there must on Earth be human hearts and human souls that look up to these forces so that they can be led by them in the right evolutionary direction. It is not only essential that these forces—which can fall prey to Lucifer and Ahriman—are there but it is of essential importance that in physical bodies there are human souls who send their reverent thoughts up to these sacrificial etheric bodies. On this will it depend how the forces that have been forged on the bloody battlefields where these sacrifices are made and suffering is borne flow into the evolution of mankind.

This more or less indicates the contribution that can be made from spiritual science to the future course of human evolution if there are a number of people who understand what can be recognized only by spiritual science.

I should like in conclusion once again to express to you in a few pragmatic words what can potentially arise out of these present, destiny-laden times:

From the courage of the fighters,
From the blood on fields of battle,
From the grief of the bereaved,
From the people's sacrifice—
There will ripen fruit of spirit,
If souls will turn in consciousness
Towards the realm of spirit.

Lecture 13

DÜSSELDORF, 15 JUNE 1915

Community above us, Christ within us

WE have gathered here today, my dear friends, primarily in order to celebrate the festival of the inauguration of the branch* founded by our dear friend Professor Craemer, which seeks to dedicate its forces to the spiritual and cultural life of the present and future in the manner adopted by our spiritual-scientific movement. On such an occasion it is always good to call to mind the essential significance of our meeting together in individual groups and to ask ourselves why we form working groups and why we focus upon the wealth of spiritual insights that mean so much to us in such groups. In order rightly to answer this question, we must be clear that in a certain sense we make a distinction—even if only in thought—between the work that we do here and the way that we pursue our other work in the world.

Those people in our present time who are unwilling to acquaint themselves in more than a rudimentary way with certain more intimate truths concerning the spiritual progress of humanity might well ask whether we could not engage with spiritual science without gathering together in self-contained groups by simply finding lecturers and enabling people who do not have any particular knowledge of one

---

* In English-speaking contexts one would normally refer to a 'group' rather than a 'branch'. However, this is the term used by Rudolf Steiner throughout this lecture; and as the whole content of the lecture emphasizes the tree-like interconnection between the various groups of the Anthroposophical Society not only in Germany but throughout the world, it seems not inappropriate to retain the word 'branch' here.—Translator

another to come together quite freely to have access to the spiritual riches of which we speak. We could of course also do this. But as long as it is in some way possible for us to establish, in the wider and narrower sense, associations of people who know one another and who come together in a spirit of friendship and brotherliness in these working groups, we want to do this in full consciousness of the attitude of soul that links us with spiritual science. For it is not for nothing that in our circles people meet to focus their attention upon the more intimate part of our spiritual knowledge and make a solemn resolve to be together in brotherly love and harmony.

It is not only that there is a certain significance in the way that we relate to one another and how we associate with one another, that we are speaking with kindred spirits, with souls who are consciously connected with us; it is not only that this is so but something else is also involved. With such associations in individual groups we are actually establishing something that is intimately connected with the whole conception that we should have of our spiritual movement if we understand it in the deepest sense. Our spiritual movement must enable us all to be fully aware that it does not only have a significance for the existence that the senses are able to encompass and for the existence that the human intellect that is directed towards outward things can embrace; it must be pervaded with the clarity that our souls are seeking through it in a real, genuine connection with the spiritual worlds. We must again and again say to ourselves with full consciousness that when we pursue spiritual science we are in a certain sense shifting the focus of our souls to those worlds which are not only inhabited by earthly beings but which the beings of the higher hierarchies, the beings of invisible worlds, inhabit as their place of existence. In the work that we do we must be fully aware that we are indeed within these invisible worlds and that our work is of significance for them.

Now the fact is that for the spiritual world, the spiritual work that we undertake when we work together in working groups with people who know one another has a completely different significance than if such work were to be carried out not within such working groups but outside them and dispersed in various places in the world. Thus the work that we accomplish together in brotherly harmony within our groups has a wholly different significance for the spiritual worlds from work that we might do otherwise. In order to understand this fully, we need to recall something of importance that has featured in a variety of ways in our spiritual-scientific work during recent years.

Let us recall that the course of our earthly evolution for us human beings has been such that in the post-Atlantean age it was carried firstly by that cultural community that we associate with the Ancient Indian period. This cultural period was then continued by what—to use an expression that is more or less appropriate (we do not need to enter into the details of this now)—we may call the Ancient Persian cultural period. Then came the Egypto-Chaldaean-Babylonian cultural period, then the Graeco-Latin, then our fifth post-Atlantean cultural period. Each such cultural period has in particular to cultivate the culture and spiritual lie as is assigned to it initially with respect to the outward, visible world. But at the same time it has to bear within itself by way of preparation what is to come in the next cultural period.

The first post-Atlantean cultural period, that of Ancient India, had to prepare the Ancient Persian epoch, the Ancient Persian the Egypto-Chaldaean and so on; and our fifth post-Atlantean cultural must prepare the sixth culture period of the immediate future. I have often said that our spiritual-scientific task is to use what we make our own not only for something that while being completely right is not the only thing that matters, namely to acquire spiritual riches for ourselves, for the eternal life of our soul, but to prepare what will constitute the content, the particular outward endeavours of the sixth cultural period. This is how it has been in each of the post-Atlantean cultural periods. And those places where the particular outward aspect for the next cultural period was always prepared were the mystery places. These were those associations of human beings in which something other was cultivated than in the outer world.

You will also know that in the case of the first post-Atlantean cultural period, that of Ancient India, it was primarily the human etheric body that was cultivated by this Ancient Indian culture, while the culture of Ancient Persia was mainly concerned with the astral body, that of Egypt and Chaldaea with the sentient soul and that of Greece and

Rome with the intellectual or mind soul. Our cultural period cultivates and will bring to its full development that which one calls the consciousness soul. But preparation must also be made for what in the sixth cultural period will give to outward culture its particular content and character. This sixth cultural period will have many features which will be radically different from the characteristic features of our time. We can emphasize three characteristics which, as we must realize, we should carry in our hearts as our ideals for the sixth post-Atlantean cultural period in preparation for this sixth cultural period.

There is at present lacking in human society a quality that will exist in the sixth cultural period among those people who may be reckoned as having reached the aim of the sixth cultural period and have not fallen short of it, thus among those who in the sixth cultural period have not remained at a mere primitive or barbaric stage. One of the most important characteristics of these inhabitants of the Earth in the sixth cultural period—thus those who will be at the peak of culture at that time—will be a certain moral quality. There is at present little evidence of this characteristic amongst mankind. A person today has to be delicately organized if he is to feel pain when quite apart from his own existence he has to look upon, observe or simply see other people in the world who are worse off than he is. To be sure, sensitive natures even today feel sorrow when confronted by the suffering that many people in the world have to bear; but these must be highly sensitive individuals.

In the sixth cultural period, those who will be at the height of cultural development will not only have that feeling that we experience today as pain with respect to poverty, suffering and misery in the world but such a person in the sixth post-Atlantean cultural period will experience the other's suffering as his own. If he sees a hungry person he will feel the hunger so acutely right down into his physical organism that this hunger of the other will be unbearable to him. What is being indicated here is that in the sixth cultural period, to a far greater extent than in the fifth, it will be a moral characteristic that the well-being of the individual will be dependent upon the well-being of the whole. So just as now the well-being of a single human limb depends upon the health of the whole body, and if the person as a whole is not healthy the individual limb will not be in a good shape either, in the sixth cultural period a common consciousness will embrace the civilized, cultivated people of that time and the individual will—as does a limb of the whole body—feel the suffering, need and poverty or the wealth of the whole to a far greater degree. This is the first, pre-eminently moral trait which will characterize the sixth cultural period.

A second fundamental characteristic will be that everything that we refer to today as beliefs and religious convictions will depend to a far, far greater extent upon the individuality of a particular person than is the case today. Spiritual science expresses this by saying that in every sphere of religion in the sixth cultural period a total freedom of thought will prevail amongst people, so that what someone wants to believe and wants to be convinced about in a religious sense will rest wholly within the power of his own individuality. Religious compulsion as is still so widespread today and is in so many different ways a dominant force in various human communities will no longer be a prevailing element in the part of humanity in the sixth cultural period which will then be civilized. Everyone will feel that complete freedom of thought in the sphere of religion is a necessary human quality.

And the third characteristic will be that people in the sixth cultural period will think they have real knowledge only if there is a spiritual dimension in it, when they recognize that a spiritual quality pervades the world and that the human soul must connect itself with it. What people call science today, and what as science bears a materialistic stamp, will no longer be called science. It will be regarded as an old superstition to which only those people who have remained behind at the stage of the superseded fifth post-Atlantean cultural period adhere.

Today we consider it to be an old superstition if someone with primitive beliefs thinks that no limb should be separated from his body after his death because he would then be unable to enter the spiritual world as a whole human being. Such a person today still connects the idea of immortality with pure materialism, with the belief that an impression of his entire form must pass into the spiritual world. He therefore thinks materialistically while believing in immortality; and as we know today from spiritual science that the spiritual aspect of our being has to be separated from the body and that only the spiritual element enters the supersensible world, we must therefore regard that materialistic belief in immortality as superstition. Similarly, all materialistic beliefs also in the scientific domain will in the sixth post-Atlantean cultural period be regarded as outmoded superstition. People will purely as a matter of course accept as science only what—as spiritual science indicates—has pneumatology or a spiritual conception as its foundation.

You see, the whole purpose of spiritual science is to prepare the qualities that have been specified for the sixth cultural period. We try to cultivate spiritual science in order to overcome materialism so as to prepare the kind of science that must exist in the sixth cultural period. We establish human communities where there is absolutely no trace of a belief in authority, of a tendency to accept a teaching merely because it emanates from some particular person. We establish human communities in which everything must be based on the soul's free assent to the teachings. We thereby prepare what spiritual science calls freedom of thought; and by joining together in brotherly associations in order to develop spiritual science, we are preparing the kind of culture and civilization which shall pervade the sixth post-Atlantean cultural period.

But we must look still deeper into the course of human evolution if we want wholly to understand what will be the real concern of our brotherly associations. In the first post-Atlantean cultural period, people cultivated what then came to prevail in the second cultural period also in communities which had their particular mystery-character. That is, in the associations peculiar to the first post-Atlantean or Ancient Indian cultural period, there was already an endeavour to focus upon the cultivation of the astral body which was to be the dominant concern of the second epoch. It would take us much too far to describe today what was practised in these associations peculiar to Ancient India (as distinct from what constituted Ancient Indian culture itself) in order to prepare the cultural epoch of Ancient Persia. But it can be said that when these people of the Ancient Indian cultural period came together in order to prepare what needed to be made ready for the second cultural period, they felt: This has not yet been achieved, we do not yet have within us what will come to be ours when our souls will have reincarnated in the next cultural period. It, as it were, still hovers over us. And so it was too.

In this first cultural period, that which was only to come down from heaven to the Earth in the second was still hovering over human souls; and through the work that people on Earth accomplished in intimate associations connected with the mysteries, forces had flowed upwards enabling the spirits of the higher hierarchies to nurture what was then to stream down into the souls of human beings in the second, Ancient Persian cultural period. One could say that the forces that, having gained greater maturity, descended into the souls who were incarnated in Ancient Persian bodies were like little children in the first epoch. These souls received up in the spiritual world the forces from the work of human beings that streamed upwards from below in preparation for the next cultural epoch; and through these forces there was nurtured what was then to stream down. And so it must be in every further cultural period.

In our cultural period we need to be aware that it is the consciousness soul that has developed within us through ordinary civilization, through ordinary culture; it is that which began in the fourteenth, fifteenth and sixteenth centuries to take hold of people as science, as outer materialistic consciousness, and it will have arrived at its full development once the fifth cultural period has run its course.

In the sixth cultural period, however, it must be the Spirit-self that takes hold. The Spirit-self must be developed in human souls in the way that the consciousness soul is being developed now; and it is the distinctive quality of the Spirit-self that it presupposes the existence of these three characteristics of which I have spoken: brotherly social life, freedom of thought and pneumatology. A human community within which the Spirit-self is developed as the consciousness soul is developed in our souls of the fifth post-Atlantean cultural period through outer culture needs these very characteristics. We may therefore picture to ourselves that through the fact that we meet together in a brotherly way in working groups, what we may conceive of as the child of those forces of the Spirit-self being nurtured by the beings of the higher hierarchies hovers invisibly over our work, so that the Spirit-self can stream down into our souls when they will again be there in the sixth cultural period. We carry out work in our brotherly working groups that streams up to the forces that are being prepared for the Spirit-self.

So you see that it is only essentially out of the wisdom imparted by our spiritual science that we are able to understand what we are really doing with respect to the higher, spiritual worlds when we gather together in such working groups; and the thought that we are doing this, that we undertake the work that we do in our working groups not only to benefit ourselves but in order that it may stream up to spiritual worlds, the thought of this work in connection with the spiritual worlds gives the right consecration to a branch undertaking such work. As we cherish such a thought, we imbue ourselves with the mood of consecration that founds such a working group within our spiritual movement. It is therefore of particular significance that we grasp this fact in its true spiritual sense. We come together in working groups which in addition to studying spiritual or pneumatological science, in addition to wanting to be based on freedom of thought and having nothing to do with dogma or ideology, imbue their work with brotherly collaboration. What matters is that we really take this idea of community rightly into our consciousness, that, as it were, we say to ourselves: Apart from the fact that as souls of the present day we belong to the fifth post-Atlantean cultural period and therefore follow a very individual path of development whereby individual, personal life is increasingly drawn forth from the life of the community, we must again develop a sense for a higher community that we establish out of free brotherly love in the form of the breath of magic that we breathe in our working groups.

The deep significance of West-European culture is that the consciousness soul is being sought within the fifth post-Atlantean epoch. It is the task of West-European and quite especially of Central-European culture that human beings increasingly develop within themselves an individual culture, an individual consciousness. This is what matters at present. We can compare this cultural period of ours with that of Greece and Rome. In the Greek cultural period we see it especially clearly: there is still a prevalence of a group-soul quality, a quality which is specifically evident in civilized Greeks.

A person who lived and was born in Athens felt himself above all to be an Athenian. This sense of community between the city and what belonged to it had a different significance for the human individual than a human community has today. In our time a person wants to grow out from the community, and that is the right task of the fifth post-Atlantean cultural period. In Rome a person was first and foremost a Roman citizen; this is what he was primarily. But in the fifth post-Atlantean cultural period we want above all else to be human individuals, to aspire in our innermost being to our true humanity.

What we experience as being so painful today when we see people battling it out with one another on the Earth is simply a reflection of the ceaseless striving of the fifth cultural period towards the free development of the universally human. Because of the hostile way in which the various countries and peoples are shutting themselves from one another, all the more strength will need to be developed as a counterweight which above all enables people to be anchored in their true humanity and grow as individuals beyond any form of community. But on the other hand they must in turn prepare communities based on full consciousness and established on their own independent initiative into which they will enter freely in the sixth cultural period. There hovers before us as a high ideal a form of community that will so encompass the sixth cultural period that civilized human beings will quite naturally meet one another as brothers and sisters.

One thing that we know from the many lectures that have been given in recent years is that in the East of Europe a people is living whose particular task will be to bring the elemental forces residing within it to clear manifestation only in the sixth cultural period. We know that the Russian people will have developed the maturity only in the sixth cultural period to bring the forces that are currently present within it in an elemental form to the point where they can make their mark upon the world.

Western and Central Europe have the task of bringing to human souls what can be brought through the consciousness soul. This is not what the East is called upon to do. Eastern Europe will have to wait until the Spirit-self comes down to the Earth and is able to pervade the souls of human beings. This has often been mentioned; it can very easily lead to arrogance and supercilious pride specifically in the East. The height of post-Atlantean culture is being reached already in the fifth cultural period. What is to follow in the sixth and seventh cultural periods will be a descending evolutionary path. Nevertheless, this descending cultural development in the sixth cultural period will be inspired and pervaded by the Spirit-self.

Today the man of the East, who is called 'the Russian man' by leading representatives of the East themselves, feels instinctively—albeit often in a perverted way—that this is so, even if his consciousness of it is for the most part thoroughly hazy. It is thoroughly characteristic that this expression 'the Russian man' occurs so frequently. There is genius in language, as when something of this kind is derived from it and people say not as they do in the West, the British, the French, an Italian, a German but 'the Russian man'. Many members of the Russian intelligentsia attach importance to the constant use of the expression 'the Russian man'. This is deeply rooted in the whole genius of this culture. The term refers to a quality of universal humanity that extends over a community as brotherliness. This is indicated by emphasizing this human aspect in the expression. But it also shows that the full height of what is to be attained in the far future has not been reached, in that the term includes something that is sharply at variance with the noun. The adjectival word 'Russian' nullifies what is expressed in the noun; for when true humanity has been attained, there should be no such adjective that renders this humanness as in any way exclusive.

But the idea that a certain conception of community, of brotherliness, must prevail in future lies at a far, far deeper level at present among members of the Russian intelligentsia. In this respect the Russian soul already feels that the Spirit-self is to descend, but it can only do so if there is a human community that is imbued with brotherliness. It can never be disseminated in a community of human beings that is not pervaded by brotherliness. For this reason, the Russian intelligentsia, as they call themselves, make the following reproach to Western and also Central Europe. They say: You pay no heed to anything resembling true community life; you are only concerned with individualism. Everyone wants to be someone in his own right, everyone wants only to be an individual. You take the personal element whereby every human individual feels himself to be a self, an individuality, to its highest extreme. This is what sounds forth from the East to Central and Western Europe in very many reproaches with respect to barbarism and the like. And those who want to become conscious of what is actually going on say that the whole of Western and Central Europe has already lost all feeling for human connections. Confusing the present with the future, they say that true human connections, where everyone feels himself to be the brother of the other, where each person relates to the other as his 'little father' or 'little mother', exist only in Russia. So speak the Russian intelligentsia. They therefore say that Western Christianity has not succeeded in developing any true human community; but, so they say, Russians still know what community is.

Alexander Herzen[124] brought this to its ultimate conclusion when he said that no one in Western Europe will ever be really happy, however hard one may try in the context of Western European culture and civilization. Humanity will never find contentment there. Only chaos can ever prevail there. The only possible salvation lies in Russia, where people have still not become separate from community, where in their village communities they still have something of the nature of a group-soul quality which they firmly hold on to.

What we call the group-soul, in which animals still wholly live but from which mankind has gradually been emerging, is revered by the Russian intelligentsia as something great and significant amongst their people. They cannot rise to the thought that the notion of the community of the future should hover as a high ideal that has yet to be realized. They hold firmly to the thought: We are the last people in Europe to retain this! The others have already abandoned this group-soul quality, which we have preserved; and we must continue to do so.

This kind of group-soul life has no place in the future, for it is the old group-soul quality. It would only be a luciferic group-soul, one that has remained behind at an earlier stage, whereas the true group-soul life that is to be aspired to is that which we seek in our spiritual science. But the extent to which one needs the spirit of community for the descent of the Spirit-self can be recognized in the urge and longing of Russian people. Just as it is being sought there along a false path, so in our spiritual-scientific stream must it be sought on a true path.

And we would want to call out to the East: Precisely what you are to preserve, namely, the old luciferic-ahrimanic community, is the thing that we must utterly overcome. A community of a luciferic and ahrimanic nature will have just as firm a religious compulsion as the Catholic Church in its Orthodox form had to exhibit in Russia. This kind of community will not understand what freedom of thought is, and it will least of all be able to rise to the point where complete individuality is nevertheless combined with a social brotherly life in community. It would therefore want to preserve what has remained of a blood brotherhood, of relationships governed purely through blood. A community that is based not upon blood but upon the spirit, on the community of souls, is what must be striven for on the path of spiritual science. This is what we are aspiring towards when we say to ourselves that we must create communities in which the blood no longer has a voice. Blood will, of course, continue to be a significant factor, it will come to expression in family relationships; what must remain will not be eradicated, but something new must emerge! What is significant in the child will be preserved in the forces of old age, but a person needs to develop something new in later life.

The factor of blood should not be interpreted as encompassing the great human communities of the future. This is the great error that plays from the East into the bloody events of the present, that a war has broken out under the heading of a community of blood amongst the Slavic peoples. What has just been discussed is indeed entering into the fateful events of our present time, but the true kernel of it all is the instinctive feeling that the Spirit-self can only appear in a brotherly community. However, it should not be a community of blood but it must be a community of souls. What will then grow as a community of souls and what should be developed there is something that we are cultivating in its childhood phase in our working groups, in our branches. Whereas what binds Eastern Europe so firmly to the group-soul nature, in that for example it regards the Slavic group-soul as something that it does not want to abandon but, on the contrary, wants to view it as the all-encompassing principle underlying the whole development of the state, is what must be overcome.

It is hugely symbolic that of the two states from whence the war originated, Russia together with the whole Slavic world gives blood-related brotherhood as the reason for the war, while Austria, as the opposing force, has thirteen official nationalities and thirteen different languages. The order for mobilization in Austria had to be issued in thirteen languages, because thirteen nationalities are represented in Austria: Germans, Czechs, Poles, Ruthenians, Rumanians, Magyars, Slovaks, Serbs, Croats, Slovenians (among whom there is a distinct Slovenian dialect), Bosnians, Dalmatians and Italians. Thus there are thirteen different races (if one disregards further minor differentiations) united in Austria. Whether one sees this or not, it shows that Austria consists of a collection of people where community can never be based upon a brotherhood of blood, for this bizarrely formed border contains thirteen different bloodlines. One could say that the most diverse, composite state in Europe stands in opposition to the state that most aspires to the group-soul or to conformity.

But this aspiration to a group-soul quality brings much else in its wake; and this leads us to something else that has a significant bearing on our theme today. Yesterday in the public lecture[125] I referred to the great philosopher Solovyov as one of the most eminent figures of all Russia. Solovyov is a truly remarkable thinker, but he is thoroughly Russian; and he is very difficult to understand from a West-European point of view. But anthroposophists should become familiar with him; those whose thinking is based on spiritual science should come to understand him at least to a certain extent.

I now want to speak from our more intimate standpoint about Solovyov's main, central idea.[126] Solovyov is far too much of a philosopher to accept without further ado the idea of a group-soul. He has difficulties with it, and he contradicts it on several occasions. But there is one idea that predominates in him even though not fully consciously, so that one would wish that Solovyov were fully clairvoyant and could foresee what his soul will only see on the Earth when it is incarnated in the sixth cultural period!

The idea that is from the outset very difficult for the Western European, and of course also for the Central European, to understand and which became the main, central idea in Solovyov's mind is the following. We in Western Europe try among many other things, not least as a means of preparing for the sixth cultural period, to understand death in its significance for life. We try to understand that death is the manifestation of a form of existence, that in death the soul is transformed into a different form of existence. We describe how man lives in his body, and what kind of a life he leads between death and a new birth. We endeavour to understand death; we endeavour to overcome death by understanding it, by showing that it is only a semblance, that the soul in truth lives on when it passes through death. It is for us a primal aim that we seek to overcome death through understanding.

We are dealing here with one of the points, indeed one of the main points, where the ideas of spiritual science radically differ from the conception that Solovyov, the great Russian thinker, has of this matter. His idea is this: There is evil in the world, it is a part of reality. If we behold evil, wickedness, with our senses, we cannot deny that the world is full of evil. This, says Solovyov, refutes the idea that the world is divine; for when we behold the world with our senses, how can we believe in a divine world since a divine world cannot be evil! But the senses see evil everywhere, and its most extreme form is death. Because there is death in the world, the world is revealed in all its evil. Death is the ultimate form of evil.

This is how Solovyov characterizes the world. He says—and I quote almost verbatim—that you should simply look at the world with your ordinary senses! Just try to understand the world with your ordinary intellect. You can never deny the fact of evil in the world; and it would be absurd to want to understand death! Death is a reality. It makes itself everywhere apparent. Knowledge acquired through the senses can never acknowledge death; it therefore reveals a world of wickedness, a world of evil. Can we believe, asks Solovyov, that this world is divine when it shows us that it is full of evil, when it shows us death wherever we go? We can never believe that this world is divine if it shows us death. For in God there can be no evil, no wickedness, and above all no evil in its ultimate form. In God there can be no death. If, therefore, God were to come into the world—I am repeating what Solovyov says almost word-for-word—if He were to appear in the world, could we readily believe Him to be God? No, we could not so easily believe that He was God! He would first have to prove Himself! If a being came who claimed to be God, we would not believe Him and He would first have to prove His identity. He would, says Solovyov, first have to produce some sort of a document enabling us to know that He is God! Nothing of this kind can be found in the world. Through what is in the world God cannot prove His identity, for everything that is in the world contradicts the very notion of divinity. By what means, therefore, can He demonstrate who He is? He can do so only if, when He comes into the world, He shows that He has conquered death, that death can have no power over Him. We would never believe that Christ is God if He did not prove His identity; and He has done this through His Resurrection, by showing that death, the ultimate evil, is not in Him. Thus here we have a consciousness of God based solely upon a real, historical Resurrection of Christ that proves God to be God. Nothing in the world other than the Resurrection enables us to know that there is a God. If Christ had not risen (Solovyov quotes these words of Paul[127] again and again), all our belief would be in vain; and everything that we can say about a divine process in the world would also be in vain.

Hence Solovyov formulates the following proposition. If we behold the world, we see in it everywhere only wickedness and evil and decay and meaninglessness. If Christ had not been resurrected, the world would be meaningless; therefore Christ has risen! Solovyov has said that there may be people who believe that it would not be logical for one to say that had Christ not been resurrected, the world would be meaningless; therefore He has risen! But, he goes on to say, this is a far better logic than anything that you might say to the contrary!

In this strange demand for a document to prove God's divinity which we find in Solovyov's writings, I have given you a specific instance of the distinctive aspect of thoughts as they exist in the East, of how curiously thoughts accumulate in order to understand the means whereby God directly demonstrates that He is God. How different it is in the West and in Central Europe! What is the aim of our spiritual-scientific endeavours? Try to compare and survey everything that we pursue out of spiritual science! What is its aim, what do we want to achieve? We want to recognize from knowledge—so that we can have insight into it—that the world has meaning and significance, that it is not only full of evil and decay. We want to understand directly through knowledge that the world has meaning; and by understanding that the world has meaning, we want to prepare ourselves for experiencing the Christ Being. We want to comprehend the living Christ. We want to accept all these things as a gift of Christ. We know that what can be given to us in accordance with the worlds, 'I am with you always even unto the end of the world',[128] is indeed so. We want to accept all that Christ unceasingly promises us; for He speaks not only through the Gospels but also within our souls. This is what He means by the words: 'I am with you always even unto the end of the world'. He can always be found as the living Christ. We want to live in Him, to receive Him into ourselves. 'Not I, but Christ in me'[129]—this is the most significant of Paul's sayings for us. 'Not I, but Christ in me.' Thus through Him we see: wherever we may turn, there is meaning! Faust wanted to say the same thing when he expressed his whole conception of the world in these words:

> Spirit sublime, you gave me, gave me all
> For which I asked. Not unto me in vain
> Did you turn your visage in the fire.
> Gave me nature's splendour to be mine,
> Power to feel her touch and to enjoy.
> No cold amazed encounter do you grant,
> You teach me in her deepest heart to gaze,
> As dwelling in the bosom of a friend.
> The ranks of living creatures do you lead
> Before me, teaching me to know my brothers
> In air and water and the silent glade.
> And when the storm in forests roars and rages,
> And giant pines in toppling cause their weight
> To bring their neighbour trees down to the ground,
> And in falling make the mountain shake,
> Then to a sheltering cavern do you lead me,
> Showing me my self, and to my heart
> Deep mysterious wonders are revealed.

[From *Faust*, Part one, Scene XIV, 'Forest and Cavern']

Thus gaining a spiritual understanding of the outer and inner worlds, meaningfully understanding death itself and realizing that it is the transition from one form of life to another! And in therefore seeking the living Christ, we also follow Him through death and through the Resurrection. We do not begin from the Resurrection, as do those from Eastern Europe. We follow Christ by whom we are inspired, Christ whom we receive into our imaginations. We follow Christ until death. We follow Him not only by saying: *Ex Deo nascimur* but by saying: *In Christo morimur.* We scrutinize the world and know that the world is the document through which God gives expression to His divinity. In that we experience and try to understand the weaving and working of spiritual realities, we in the West cannot say that we need a document for God to establish His identity if He should come into the world, but we seek God everywhere. We seek God in nature and in the souls of human beings.

The fifth post-Atlantean cultural epoch therefore also needs what we cultivate in the brotherly associations of our branches. It needs the conscious cultivation of the spiritual aura nurtured by the higher hierarchies that still hovers over us, which will flow into human souls when they come to live in the sixth cultural period. We do not want to cling to something that is dead, as does the East with respect to the group-soul, to an outdated form of community. We want to cultivate the early stages of a living reality, which is the community-spirit of our branches. We have no wish to look for what speaks from the blood in order to summon together those in whom something in common is addressed by the blood and cultivate some kind of community on this basis. We want to call together people who resolve to be brothers and sisters and who have hovering over them what they want to develop by cultivating spiritual science and by feeling the good spirit of brotherhood hovering over them.

This is what we want to receive into ourselves as a dedicatory thought at the inauguration of one of our branches. With such a thought we consecrate a branch when we found it. Community and quickening life! We seek community above us, the living Christ within us Who needs no document, Who does not first have to be authenticated by the Resurrection, Who is worthy of belief because we experience Him within ourselves. Community above us, Christ within us: this is what we make our motto, our motto of consecration when we found a branch. Whether two or three or seven or many, many people are gathered in Christ's name, Christ lives in them. And all those who acknowledge Christ as their brother in this sense are themselves sisters and brothers.

If we are able to receive such words of consecration and carry out our work with such an attitude, the right spirit of our spiritual-scientific movement will hold sway in whatever we do. Even in these difficult times, our spiritual-scientific friends from elsewhere have gathered together with those who have founded their branch here. This is always a good practice; for those who work in other branches will thereby also carry the dedicatory thought, the motto of consecration. And they pledge themselves to think constantly of those in a branch who have undertaken to work with one another on behalf of our movement. In this way, the invisible community that we want to establish through the nature of our work will grow and grow. If such an attitude connected with our work becomes more and more widespread, we will do justice to the demands placed upon us by spiritual science with respect to the progress of mankind. And then we may believe that those who guide human progress and human knowledge as the great Masters of Wisdom will be with us. To the extent that you are working here in accordance with our spiritual-scientific ideals, I know that the high Masters who guide our movement from the spiritual worlds will also be in the midst of your work.

From this point of view I call today upon the power, the grace and love of these Masters of Wisdom who direct and guide the work that we do in brotherly associations in our branches; I call upon the grace, the power and the love of these Masters of Wisdom who are directly connected with the forces of the higher hierarchies that they may descend upon the work of this branch. May your good spirit, you great Masters, and may the good spirit of our spiritual-scientific movement be with this branch. May they hold sway in its work!

Lecture 14

DÜSSELDORF, 17 JUNE 1915

Man's Experiences after passing through the Gate of Death

I HAVE often said in relation to many spiritual-scientific observations that the concern of our spiritual-scientific movement and what it endeavours to achieve is not primarily one of theoretically absorbing those concepts and ideas that one may acquire through spiritual science but that the fruits of spiritual science should become part of the most intimate stirrings and impulses of our life of soul. To be sure, we must proceed from the results of spiritual-scientific knowledge, and one can only acquire such knowledge if one studies it and concerns oneself with it. But spiritual science should not be apprehended like any other science, so that one knows merely in hindsight that one has heard something or other, that this or that is true with respect to some established fact; rather should spiritual science work upon our soul in such a way that the soul becomes different in a certain aspect of its feeling life, that it becomes different as a result of receiving what can flow through spiritual science. The concepts, ideas and images that we acquire through spiritual science should stir our soul in the most intimate way; they should unite with our feeling life so that we learn through spiritual science not only to see the world differently but also to feel differently about it than we would otherwise. The spiritual scientist should enter into certain life-situations quite differently than is possible without spiritual science; and only if he can do this has he really achieved what spiritual science has to offer us.

We are living at present at a difficult time, when an aspect of the most important questions of spiritual science, that of death, is appearing in so innumerable instances before our eyes, souls and hearts, for some in a very immediate sense, for others somewhat more remotely. The spiritual scientist should also in this grievous time be able to keep spiritual science alive in his heart. He should be able to relate differently to the events of the time—even when he is very close to them—than someone else. One person may need consoling, another may need cheering up; but both should find these in spiritual science. Only when this can be the case have we understood spiritual science in its true sense.

The intensity with which the ideas of spiritual science affect us enables us to experience that we learn to feel quite differently about many things than we can feel about anything in the world without spiritual science. If you peruse much of what has already been said in the context of our spiritual science about the riddle of death, you will be able to understand much of what I should like to say today. This will augment what I have already explained and will not merely be a repetition of previous statements. We must learn not only to think differently about death but we must learn to feel differently about it; for the riddle of death is indeed connected with the deepest mysteries of the spiritual world. We must be quite clear that we lay aside all that enables us to form perceptions and acquire knowledge in the physical world and, hence, to experience anything of the outer world when we pass through the gate of death. We form ourselves in the physical world through our sensory impressions of the world. We lay these senses aside when we enter the spiritual world; we have them no longer. This should already serve us as a proof that we must make efforts to think in a different way from how we have learned to think through our senses when we think about the supersensory world.

It is true that we have a kind of reference point, in that something analogous, something of a similar kind to the experiences in the spiritual world, manifests itself also in the ordinary life that we spend between birth and death. This comes in the form of the dream experiences that enter into ordinary life. We do not apprehend dream experiences through our senses; and indeed, our senses have nothing to do with them. Nevertheless, they are clothed in images that are sometimes reminiscent of sensory life. In these dream-images, albeit in a weak form, we have a reflection of the manner in which spiritual existence approaches us as a world of imagination between death and a new birth. We have imaginative perceptions after death; experience manifests itself in images.

But if, for example, you see a red colour in the world of the senses and feel moved to ask what lies behind this red colour, you will say that it is something that fills the space, something of a material nature. The red colour also appears to you in the spiritual world, but there is nothing material behind it, nothing that would give a material impression in the ordinary sense. Behind the red is a soul-spiritual being; behind the red is the same that you feel with your soul as your world. One could say that from the sense-impression of the colour we descend in the outward, physical sense to the material world, whereas from imaginative perceptions we rise up ever higher into spiritual regions in the spiritual world.

Now we must be quite clear—and this is especially emphasized in the new edition of *Theosophy*[130]—that these imaginative perceptions do not present themselves to us as do sense-impressions of the physical world. These imaginations are certainly there, but we encounter them as experiences: the red, the blue are in that context experiences. One may justifiably refer to these imaginations as red or blue, but they are of a somewhat different nature than the sense-impressions of the physical world. They are far more intimate; we are connected with them in a far more intimate way. In the outward context you are separate from the red colour of the rose; but you feel yourself to be within the red colour in the spiritual world, you are connected with the red colour. When you perceive something red in the spiritual world, the powerful will of a spiritual being is unfolding. This will rays forth, and what it radiates forth is red. Yet you feel yourself to be within this will; and this experience of being within, of feeling oneself within, you then quite naturally characterize as red. It could be said that the physical colour is like a frozen spiritual experience, a congealed spiritual experience. This is just one example of how we must develop the capacity in many areas to think somewhat differently, to give different values and meanings to our concepts, if we really want to rise to an understanding of the spiritual world.

Then we also need to be aware that in the spiritual world the relationship of what we call imaginations to the spiritual beings who express themselves in, for example, colours is not like the relationship of a colour to a sense-perceptible being. The rose is red, that is a quality of the rose. But when a spirit comes near to us and, in accordance with what has just been said, we are aware that the spirit radiates red, the red is not a quality of the spirit in the way that the red is a quality of the rose; this red is, rather, a revelation of the inner aspect of the spirit; it is more like a script that the spirit inscribes into the spiritual world. One has but to discern what lies behind the imaginations.

The activity that one develops here is only to be compared in the physical world with its ahrimanic reflection, that is, with reading. We behold the rose's red colour and we know that red is a quality of the rose. The red in the spiritual world is something that we do not merely behold but we interpret it, though not in a fanciful way (I must forever be warning against this); our soul discovers out of itself that it has been presented with a sound, a letter, something that needs to be deciphered or read, enabling one to know what is meant. The spirit means something when it manifests itself as red or blue or green or as C or G sharp. The spirit means something by this; one begins to speak with the spirit, one begins to read its script.

Our ordinary cultural life depends on the fact that such things which have their deep wisdom in the spiritual world are then also transplanted into the outer world. We speak rightly of an occult reading, for someone who acquires a clairvoyant consciousness, who enters into the spiritual world, who perceives the imaginations and learns to decipher them, beholds the essential nature of the souls that live in the spiritual world, not only through colours but also through other impressions which are reminiscent of sense-impressions and those that have newly arisen in the spiritual domain.

This activity, which is purely of a soul-spiritual nature, is under the sway of rightly evolved spiritual beings. Here in the physical world, Ahriman forms a reflection of what I have been characterizing. Ordinary reading of characters in the physical world is an ahrimanic reflection of this occult reading; for all reading in the physical world through signs that are formed artificially is an ahrimanic activity. Not without justice has the invention of printing been experienced as a 'black art', as it has been called. One ought not to think that one might be able to escape from the clutches of Lucifer and Ahriman through expedients of whatever kind. Lucifer and Ahriman must have their place in outward culture. It is only necessary to find the point of balance, of finding the middle way when life inclines constantly towards the luciferic and ahrimanic side. If someone were not to want to be affected by Ahriman, he would never learn to read. But it is not a question of fleeing from Ahriman and Lucifer but that we enter into a right relationship with them; that in spite of the fact that we are surrounded by their forces, we are able to relate in the right way to them. When we know that we follow what we have so often referred to as the Christ impulse that dwells within us, and when we embrace the spiritual feelings that inspire the will to follow Christ at every moment of our lives, we can also read. We may then learn—and we will do so if it is karmically right for us—that Ahriman initiated reading, and we will view this ahrimanic art in the right light. If we do not discover this, we will be verbally giving praises to ahrimanic culture, to the progress, to the glory of ahrimanic culture as exemplified by reading.

But all such things also entail obligations, and it is a question of honouring them. Especially at our present time much can be said by way of defending or opposing one thing or another. Indeed, we have what we may call a flood of war literature. Every day brings not only brochures but also books. Among these one can also often read statements such as: This country has such and such a number of illiterate people, of people who read and write, and so on. It would not be consistent with what someone familiar with spiritual science might say out of his sense of responsibility to accept such a statement at face value. Were I, for example, to want with respect to what I have to say about our present time to adduce all sorts of bad things about a particular nation and in order to make my point say that there are such a number of people in this country who cannot read and such a number who cannot write, I would not be speaking rightly from a spiritual-scientific point of view. Only those things should be put forward for which one can bear responsibility in terms of one's occult obligations.

From this you see—I merely wished to cite this as an example—that spiritual science must really also enter into life in this deeper sense and honour its obligations. And if the spirit-researcher says things that others also say, you will always be able to see that they are said in a completely different context, which is what matters. To someone who is unfamiliar with spiritual science, much of what is said within spiritual science will therefore quite naturally often seem very strange, since he is used to having different conceptions and will sometimes feel obliged to say to himself: This spiritual science calls black white and white black! And in fact this is sometimes necessary, for if one reaches up into the spiritual world with the ordinary concepts and ideas that one acquires in the physical world, many concepts have to be fundamentally altered.

Let us from this standpoint consider one of the most enigmatic concepts that we are faced with from the impressions of the physical world, that of death. In the physical world, a person always sees death from one side, from the side whereby he sees human life developing to the point where a person dies, that is, where the physical body initially falls away from the higher members of human nature and then decomposes within the physical world. One can truly say that what the person sees concerning death from the perspective of the physical world means that he is viewing it from the one side. Viewing it from the other side means seeing it in an opposite light, seeing it completely differently.

When we enter through birth into physical life, our experience is such that we have not yet fully attained the high-point of physical consciousness. You know that we do not remember the first years of our life with our ordinary physical consciousness. No one can with his ordinary physical consciousness remember his birth. At any rate, there is no one who will maintain that he can remember with his ordinary consciousness how he was born. We may say that it is a matter of physical consciousness that the moment of a person's birth must be forgotten. It is forgotten, just as the first years of life are also forgotten. When in our physical life between birth and death we look back at our life, we remember back to a certain point. Then our memory breaks off. The point where it breaks off is not our physical birth but includes a period subsequent to it. No one can know by experience that he was born. He can only conclude that he was. We conclude that we were born by—and only by—observing people being born after us. When scientists assert that they will only accept what they can see, none of them—if they were logically consistent—would be able to assert in accordance with this principle that they had been born, for unless one is clairvoyant it is impossible to perceive one's own birth; one can only infer it.

Precisely the opposite happens with regard to death. The moment of the death that the person has previously undergone stands before the eyes of his soul as the most vivid and most light-filled impression throughout the time between death and a new birth. But do not think that this is a painful impression. You would then be imagining that the dead person looks back upon what you see of death in the physical world, the decline and dissolution. Rather does he see death from the other side; he sees in death something that one must call the most beautiful of experiences even in the spiritual world, for in what man is normally able to experience in the spiritual world there is nothing more beautiful than the sight of death. To behold this victory of the spirit over matter, this radiating of the spiritual light of the soul from the dim darkness of the material world, is the greatest, most significant thing that can be perceived on the other side of the life through which man passes between death and a new birth.

When a person lays aside the etheric body between death and a new birth and has gradually fully re-established his consciousness, which occurs not very long after death, the situation is such that he no longer has the same relationship to himself that he has here in the physical world. When someone is asleep here in the physical world, he is unaware of himself; and when he awakes he becomes aware that he has a self, an ego or I. In the spiritual world after death it is somewhat different (since his self-consciousness is at a higher stage), it is not quite like that. I shall speak shortly about how it is. But there is essentially something like a reflective awareness of the ego, the self. Just as one needs to engage in self-reflection in the morning when one awakes, so is this also the case in the spiritual world. But this self-contemplation is a matter of looking back to the moment of death. It is always as if, in order to perceive our ego between death and a new birth, we were to say to ourselves: You have really died, therefore you are I, you are an ego!

This is the most significant point: one looks back at the victory of the spirit over the body, one looks back to the moment of death which is the most beautiful experience that one can have in the spiritual world; and in this looking back one becomes aware of one's self in the spiritual world. This is always not exactly like an awakening—this would be a one-sided way of interpreting it—but it is a case of becoming self-aware through looking back at one's death. It is therefore so important that a person has the possibility of really looking back at the moment of death with the full consciousness that emerges after death, so that he does not in any way merely dream what he beholds then but can fully understand what he perceives; this is enormously important. We can, moreover, prepare ourselves for this already during life by trying to practise self-knowledge. It is a fundamental task of spiritual science to give people the self-knowledge that they need; for spiritual science is essentially a means of leading a person into his wider self, that self through which one belongs fundamentally to the whole world. I said that consciousness after death is somewhat different from here in the physical world. If I were to give you a pictorial impression of the nature of consciousness after death, I would do so in the following way:

Here we have an eye, and here an object. How do we become aware that there is an object outside us? By the impression that the object makes upon our eye. The object makes an impression on our eye, and we come to know something about it. The object is out in

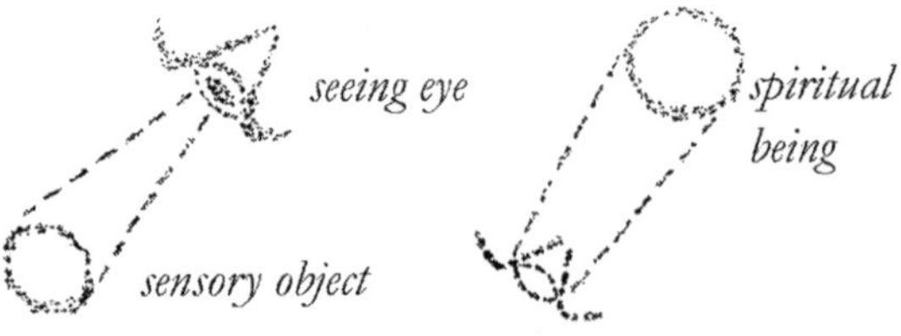

the world, it makes an impression on our senses, and we take the mental picture that we are able to form of the object into ourselves, into our soul. The object is outside us. The idea that we then form is given to us by it.

In the spiritual world it is different. Because I cannot draw it differently, I should like to draw what I always refer to as an eye of the soul in the form of an eye, although it is not strictly correct. This eye of the soul which a person has after death is not so constituted that he, for instance, sees an angel or another human soul which is also in the spiritual world in the way that he sees a flower in the physical world; rather does this eye of the soul have the characteristic—and we shall not at first think in terms of seeing a human soul but, rather, a being of the higher hierarchies—that when an angel or archangel is present, the eye is not conscious of seeing an angel outside itself but is, instead, aware of being seen by an angelic being. It is the exact opposite of the physical world. We live into the spiritual world in such a way that with respect to the beings of the higher hierarchies we become aware that we are known by them, that they think us. We feel ourselves embedded in them, we feel ourselves comprehended by the angels, archangels and Spirits of Personality just as the realms of minerals, plants and animals feel themselves comprehended by us.

Only with respect to human souls is it the case that we can both be seen by them—so that we have the feeling that they see us—and we also have the feeling that our perception enters into them. It is a seeing that both we and other human souls undertake. With respect to all other beings of the higher hierarchies, we have the feeling that we are perceived, thought and visualized by them; and in that we are perceived, thought and visualized by them, we are in the spiritual world. Suppose, therefore, that we are dwelling as a soul in the spiritual world, just as we abide in the physical world. We will constantly have the feeling of relating to the beings of the higher hierarchies, just as here in the physical world we have the feeling of entering into connection with the mineral, plant and animal kingdoms. The only difference is that we need constantly to be aware that we have a self. Then we look back to our death and say to ourselves: This is who you are! This awareness is on-going; it is a constant component of our consciousness.

What I am saying today represents an addition to various descriptions that you can derive from my cycles and books. What is expressed more inwardly here is described more from an external viewpoint in, for example, my book *Theosophy*. But only by perceiving something of this nature in more of a soul sense does one enter rightly into the experiences that one must have with respect to these matters and to the spiritual world as a whole.

It is, therefore, self-knowledge that leads us forward, that makes us strong for the life between death and a new birth. This was brought home to me recently in a particularly vivid way when I had the task of speaking on several occasions at the cremations of friends of our movement. I always felt the necessity of saying something intimately connected with the character, with the self of the one who had gone through the portal of death. Whence came this inspiration or intuition to convey to those who had died something connected with their being? It derived from the life of those individuals after their death. Anything that strengthens the forces of their self-knowledge is helpful to them. By speaking immediately after their death, when their consciousness has not yet awakened, of those qualities that they feel within themselves, it was possible, as it were, to liberate something of the strength that they need in order gradually to be able to develop the capacity to look back at the moment of death, when their whole being—in the way that it has developed between birth and death—appears in a concentrated form. One therefore helps the deceased person if one enables some aspect of what they remember of the qualities and experiences that belonged to them to flow to them directly after their death. In this way one strengthens the power of self-knowledge. And if one is able clairvoyantly to enter into the soul of such a dead person, one feels in one's soul the urge especially at this time to hear something about the way he was, about things that he experienced or about his main attributes.

As you may understand, just as here on Earth the life of one person is not like that of another but the lives of all people differ one from another, so it is with those who have passed through the gate of death. No one soul-life is like another between death and a new birth. It could be said that every soul-life that one can observe is a new revelation, and one can only emphasize certain particular qualities. I should like both today and the day after tomorrow in Cologne to speak about such things. I shall now speak of one specific example.

Some time ago in Dornach, we witnessed the departure from the physical plane of a member who had reached a fairly advanced age.[131] A member whose life had been spent in diligent, thoughtful work but who in her last years had for some time been closely aligned with our spiritual-scientific view of the world and had impressed it deeply into her heart, into her own soul. So one can say that this person had arrived at the point where in the latter part of her physical existence she was as regards her feelings and sensibilities completely at one with our world-conception. Now as you know, when a person goes through the portal of death he first lays aside his physical body, continues for a while to bear his etheric body and then lays this aside as well. Then comes a time when the person must first gradually acquire the consciousness that will be his between death and a new birth. As we know, he then experiences a full review of his life as a great life's tableau. At this time the powerful impulses residing within his soul emerge all of a sudden, so that much that is of significance in this respect may appear quite differently than during his life. While he is alive, a person is to a large extent bound by the limits that his physical body places upon him. Immediately after death one overcomes the heaviness, burdensome nature and solidity of the physical body which weaken the clarity of many soul-impulses. If the soul has during life strongly absorbed the impulses of spiritual science, if it has embraced these impulses with its innermost feelings, it can also unfold these impressions after death in a quite different way since it has the availability of the supple, flexible etheric body that is no longer constrained by the physical body.

One could especially see this in that individual of whom I have just spoken, who shortly after her death, after I had managed to enter fully into her soul, poured forth from her soul what had lived within her by way of spiritual-scientific impulses. She would not, of course, have expressed herself in such words during physical life; but because the etheric body was still there, she was able to clothe it in physical words. What she had taken into herself through spiritual science became the expression of her soul while she still retained her supple etheric body. And the necessity then arose that, a few days later at the cremation of the person concerned, I had to speak these very words that had sounded forth from her being, which therefore belonged not to me but to her:

In world expanses I will to bear
My feeling heart, that warm it may become
In the fire of the working of holy forces;

In world thoughts I will to weave
My own thinking, that clear it may become
In the light of the eternal life-in-becoming;

In soul-foundations I will to immerse
The sense of what has been, that strong it may become
For true aims of human working;

In God's peace I so aspire
'Midst life's struggles and concerns,
My self for the higher self preparing;

Striving for peace in joyous work,
Sensing world-being in my own being,
I would fulfil man's highest duty;

May I live expectantly in the light
Of destiny's star, that grants me
The place in the realm of spirit.

In these words, which express a soul's feelings after death, there resides what this soul has become through spiritual science. Then came the time which everyone has to pass through more or less after death, a time that cannot really be called a time of sleep; for when one has laid aside the etheric body, one is indeed immediately fully within the spiritual world but one is blinded by its rich abundance. One cannot take it all in; one first has to adapt the forces that one has brought with one to the spiritual world and thereby attune oneself to it. One sees too much after death; there is indeed consciousness, and it must first be adjusted to the level of the forces that one has acquired. One then begins to be able to orientate oneself and really live in the spiritual world. It is not actually quite correct to say that one awakes to consciousness after a certain time; one should say that one has too much consciousness and would need to tone it down to the level where it becomes bearable. This is then the moment of awakening.

The soul of whom I have just been speaking therefore entered into this state, when the etheric body has been laid aside, of not being able to bear the spiritual light. But it had a great deal of strength—you can see this from the words that I have read; and this strength had gradually been wholly permeated by the influence that spiritual science is able to bring to bear upon a person's feeling and willing. Some time after death it therefore happened that this being, this soul, arrived at a state of consciousness which it could bear. One could, of course, say much about the time that then begins for a soul if one were to describe everything that such a soul experiences. Only parts of this can be described; and in that we stand within our movement, the most significant thing to be observed in souls is what connects them to our movement. One can learn from what connects human souls in general after death with the whole world; but one can best observe the life of the soul after death through souls that are as closely affiliated to one as this soul of whom I am now speaking.

And so it happened that it could first be observed that this soul came to a self-orientating consciousness by participating in our meetings, by actually taking part in our meetings. This involvement fully manifested itself at this year's Easter festival in Dornach, where the attempt was made to explain to our dear friends in Dornach something of the profound meaning of Easter. This soul was present. It took part; just as she had formerly participated with an inner warmth, just as many who still inhabit their physical body have the need to add something to what they have heard. It wanted to say something; and the remarkable thing is that it formulated in words—because through this it had the possibility of understanding their meaning—how it was now living and especially with regard to what it had experienced at this Easter lecture. And what then came was something like an addition to the verses communicated shortly after her death. These additional words which now emerged from her consciousness are as follows:

To human souls I would direct
Spirit-feeling, that wills to awaken
The word of Easter in the heart;

With human spirits I would think
Warmth of soul, that powerfully
They can feel the Risen One;

One can see that this soul wants to work further with those with whom it was connected in our spiritual-scientific movement. It wants to dedicate itself to them so that the message of Easter awakens in their hearts, as the Easter lecture had sought to achieve, so that they may develop a right feeling for what in spiritual science we call the Risen One. But something that came to expression in the following three lines was of particular significance. This was especially beautiful and deeply moving.

I had in those Easter lectures and in many other lectures that I gave at that time made a repeated effort to do what I have already done, namely, to draw attention to the significance that spiritual science has not only for this present earthly life but for the whole world. Someone who passes through the gate of death can have a direct experience of this and have an understanding of what is happening within spiritual science. I therefore advise so many people whose loved ones have passed through the portal of death to read or speak to them about spiritual-scientific teachings, for what has been formulated in spiritual-scientific words has significance not only for souls living in the physical body but is deeply meaningful for souls that are disembodied. It comes to them as a spiritual breath of life, as a spiritual water of life, or, to put it another way, they perceive light emanating from us who are down below. For us this light is, one might say, symbolic, for we hear words and receive them as thoughts into our soul; but the dead really see it as a spiritual light.

Now it is highly significant that this soul, who has often heard such things, wanted formally to say: I have understood this, it is really so! For its words in this connection were:

Earth-flame of spirit-knowledge brightly
Irradiates death's dark appearance...

It is a reality for the soul. It wishes to say: What you speak in those nether regions shines upwards like a flame. And it expressed this by saying 'Earth-flame': '[It] brightly irradiates death's dark appearance...' Why does it speak of 'death's dark appearance'? If you think about it, you will understand. It said this because it has often heard us referring to the world as maya: on the Earth it lives in the senses' world of appearances; now it is also in a world of appearances through which it must for the first time perceive real being:

> Earth-flame of spirit-knowledge brightly
> Irradiates death's dark appearance;

and then something that strengthens the soul:

> The self becomes world-eye and ear.

'World-ear' is what is meant. It means that the whole self now becomes like a mighty sense-organ; it becomes an organ of perception for the whole world. There is a beauty in the way in which the dead person shows how she is aware that what spiritual science says is true. For this soul it is characteristic that immediately after death it wants to express itself and say: Yes, I have reached the point where that which I have learnt on Earth is presented to me as true.

These words had a certain importance for me because they came from the spiritual world, from that soul of whom I have been speaking, a few weeks after another deeply satisfying event had occurred.

Friends of our movement lost a fairly young son in the present war who had voluntarily enlisted. The young man fell in battle. He had begun to show an interest in spiritual science shortly before his death. He was only seventeen or eighteen. He had died after falling in battle. After some time it could be seen that the soul of this young man—and it is often the case that souls who have crossed the threshold of death in battle come fairly quickly to consciousness—approached his parents, really came close to them. And it was possible to hear him say to them: I should like you to understand that it is becoming clear to me that what I have been hearing in your house about spiritual science, about spiritual light and spiritual beings, is true, and that what I have been hearing is helping me.

I mention this not because there is anything special about this but because it shows the nature of the connection between earthly life and spiritual life. There is also something else remarkable that I want to mention in this connection. After a lecture that I gave in one of our branches, I went to the parents in question and told them this—I had at the time written down the words that had come through—and also informed them of the night when it had occurred that the young man approached his parents and had addressed their souls in the manner described. The father then said, 'This is quite extraordinary. I very seldom have dreams; but that same night I dreamt of my boy, I dreamt that he appeared to me and that he wanted to say something to me but I had not understood it.'

People outside our spiritual movement today will find it strange if such things are related to them; and so it is best to keep them as far as possible to ourselves. But it is nonetheless important that we explore these things more fully, for our knowledge is formed out of these individual building-stones of experiences from the spiritual world. And we will only be able to arrive at a clear picture if we do not merely confine ourselves to listening to beautiful theories about the spiritual world but if we are able to make spiritual science so vitally alive within our souls that we are able to bear it when the spiritual world is spoken of in the way that reasonable people speak of what they experience in the world of the senses. Spiritual science will only become alive within us in the right way—and it should indeed become fully alive within us—if we derive life from it and not merely knowledge or a teaching. This will enable it to bridge for us the gulf that through materialism—which in the absence of spiritual science will inevitably spread ever more widely—exists between the physical, sense-perceptible world through which we pass between birth and death and the spiritual world in which we live between death and a new birth, so that we gradually learn to become citizens also of the spiritual world. It is this that matters: that we learn to feel that a person who has passed through the gate of death has merely taken on a different form of life and for our feeling may be regarded after death as someone who through the events of life has had to emigrate to a distant country where we shall be able to follow him at some later date; so all that we have to bear is a time of separation. But this must be livingly felt and experienced through spiritual science. If you do but form a picture formed of various specific facts, you will see that—even for someone who cannot perceive the spiritual world—these facts harmonize and are in accord with one another, that the belief that one has before perceiving the spiritual world is no blind belief, no belief in authority, but a belief carried by a feeling that is deeper than critical knowledge, by the human soul's innate feeling for truth.

We are living at a time when the outer destiny-laden events indicate that we need to enter more deeply into human life. It would be much better if, instead of discussing who is to blame for this war and who is doing this or that, people would consider the events of the war as an awakening call to gain a deeper understanding of human souls than the overwhelming majority of people have achieved so far. Among the most important things that I have said is that I have indicated that we must learn through spiritual science to transform, to review our conceptions and ideas. Among these conceptions we can now—and this will be added today to our considerations of this highly important subject of death—include that of the war. One would be right, also from a spiritual-scientific point of view, to regard the war as an illness of evolution. It is certainly an illness, but you should bear in mind that you do not do justice to an illness if you judge it for what it is. What manifests itself through an illness is also largely what preceded the illness in the human body: the lack of order, the disharmony. Then comes the illness, which often arises in order to counteract what was disorderly in the body. Even when someone has an illness before death, this is so. He is carrying certain disharmonies which make it impossible for him to enter directly into the spiritual world. The spiritual world would perhaps be imperceptible to him for too long or there would be other hindrances, because there are disharmonies within him that cannot be brought into the spiritual world. This is why an illness may befall someone before death. This makes his soul sufficiently free from disharmony that he can enter the spiritual world.

If it is an illness that leads to recovery, the reason for this illness is that what preceded it, what was determined by the karma of former lives, perhaps by thousands of years, may be balanced out. It is, for example, not a good thing to say that if a child has measles, it should not have had this illness! One cannot know what might have happened to the child if it had not had the measles to deal with, for what was living deeply within the child came out through the illness and found its balance.

So it is also good to observe the war and to see what is wrong not so much in what now has to be undergone in blood and iron but also to contemplate what has been taking place within cultural streams over long, long periods of time. People must learn to look more deeply into these connections! After this war a time will come when people will begin to reflect about it. They will then come to realize how many empty words have been spoken in the course of assigning blame to one party or another. And even if it is fairly long after the war, something will surely emerge; and people will speak quite differently than they do now. There will be people who will say: If history continues to be studied as it has been studied hitherto, one will find this or that in this or that act of diplomacy; these things are recorded in one place or another. But if one proceeds in the way that history has hitherto dealt with everything and seeks 'objectively to judge' everything (as one says), one will never discover why this war arose. One will then become aware that it is necessary to look beyond the outward causes to the deeper reasons that spiritual science will have to explain. Unfortunately, it is only possible today to give some hints about these things. One will find that in many places at the time of the outbreak of the war, some event happened where consciousness did not play a significant part but something unconscious took place beneath the threshold of outer events; so that those things which the historian is accustomed to look upon as factors pertinent to discovering the causes of the events are not of any relevance. One will learn from this example that history in its customary form does not tell us anything at all. It will be an awakening call to look for deeper reasons.

Just as in virtually each one of the lectures that I have given recently I had to direct a kind of awakening call to our souls by way of a conclusion, I should like to do so again today.

One has to bear a certain responsibility simply through having developed some relationship to spiritual science. The spiritual-scientific conception of the world must at least enable one to become capable of thinking that those superficial judgements which—because of the hold that materialism has over the world—are everywhere favoured should not be the judgements that we make as advocates of spiritual science. What is taking place today is a superficial hatred from nation to nation. I have spoken much about this in our branch lectures. It does not need to fill us in the same way, but we should also not become unfair; and we can learn from the old Theosophical Society how to become really unfair!

What they impressed upon their members with respect to religions was that all religions are the same. This is more or less the equivalent of telling people that there are some condiments or food supplements on the table: pepper, salt, sugar, paprika; they are all food supplements of some kind, one should not give preference to one over another. Thus if I have a cup of coffee and add pepper to it, that's all one and the same! The same logic applies when one says that the same kernel of truth underlies all religions. This logic does, to be sure, save one the trouble of studying the great, wonderful evolution of the world in all its details, for one arrives at the proposition that one kernel of truth is at the foundation of everything. But with respect to this, we have long freed ourselves from the most superficial judgements. Thus the wish to enter with loving understanding into the distinctive quality of every nationality, which we rightly acknowledge, should not prevent us from seeing where our hearts need to stand when guided by our understanding. It will not be possible for all our friends to agree in this respect. This, however, is not the point; what matters is that our souls endeavour to detach themselves from the standpoint of the outer world and enter into the distinctive qualities of the various Folk-souls. We shall then see that those who identify themselves with our spiritual-scientific world-conception have in many respects a certain responsibility, the responsibility towards a thoroughness and a deeper insight into actualities that spiritual science makes possible.

One then sometimes makes some painful discoveries. One learns that the great awakening call that confronts us through the fateful events that surround us does not make all souls feel obliged to enter with their hearts more deeply and more thoroughly into what is going on in the form of the superficial judgements of materialism, which we wish to overcome. In this respect, one would wish and yearn for souls who are within our movement to form a host of people who adopt a certain thoroughness also with respect to the questions that stir us deeply today. And thoroughness is necessary today in so many ways. One has no idea of all that is possible in our time.

I could say a great deal about things that can deeply stir the heart of anyone who really follows with human love what is going on in our time. Much in the way of thoughts and views is being disseminated, sometimes with the best of intentions, out of an unhealthy world-conception ensnared by Ahriman. But especially with regard to the flood of literature about the war, we must in many ways deepen our thoughts about the tasks of cultural development. Such an attempt is now being made in our lectures by indicating the real position of the various peoples; for it is in many respects a matter of defending thoroughness against superficiality.

It has, for example, in recent weeks been possible to experience something very remarkable. For understandable reasons I would not want to give the title of a book that appeared outside Germany,[132] although in the German language, which, it is maintained, was written by a German. I should expressly like to emphasize that one can bring oneself to understand any possible viewpoint. One can, perhaps, understand the most anti-German viewpoint when it is presented by someone or other. One will try to understand it; one does not need to share it, but one can perhaps understand it. But this book to which I am referring has features which have nothing to do with the fact that it adopts a thoroughly anti-German standpoint, pouring venom in every line upon Germany and the German nature. One could even understand the fact that it is poisonously written. But nevertheless, no one should come and say that if a German speaks in this way about the book, we can understand this to mean that he is saying something disparaging about Germany and its culture.

However, there is something else that really matters here. The book is written in such a way that anyone who has a little feeling for inner objectivity and inner thoroughness and who has had some education must find that it is the most dreadful imitation of the worst kind of trash. Quite irrespective of the viewpoint that it expresses, it is in a literary sense so abysmal that if anyone finds something worth having in the book, this shows that he is taking what is from a literary point of view mere trash, a book that has been cobbled together and written out of sheer, utterly overt ignorance, as something that should be taken seriously. Thus it is not a question of the author's standpoint; it is that one sees from the manner in which it is written, such as no one who has learnt to think—even in a formal sense—would write, that one is dealing here with a book of very limited value. Nevertheless, I have had to hear judgements that this book, whose title I shall not give for particular reasons, is taken seriously. When such things occur, it is up to us not to shrink back but to form a judgement on the basis of a certain comprehensiveness. Even if someone may perhaps agree with certain sentences expressed in this book, he still does not need to take the book seriously for the very reason that it is a dreadful, shoddy piece of work and one does not take such a shoddy piece of work seriously, because one would not wish that something that is itself true should be expressed in such a dreadful manner, with the worst possible feeling and in an uncultured way. I wanted to characterize such an example purely for the reason that I wanted to draw attention to the fact that many things are involved when the spiritual scientist tries to form a judgement about the world.

If it were really possible to consider a book to be good even if it is stylistically a disaster, this would be a sign that one has not made spiritual-scientific feeling sufficiently alive in one's heart, in one's soul. It is certainly not for any reason other than to draw attention to the way in which spiritual science must livingly penetrate our feeling and thinking to the most radical degree that such specific examples are cited in this realm. And it is indeed necessary that such specific impulses are sought within our souls. I must admit that the dreadful rejoicing that has hitherto brought people a particular sense of satisfaction when journeying through Germany is not now in evidence even after great victories. One has observed something of the way that in every soul there has at the same time been pain and grief concerning the immense losses. I believe that it is so. The vain rejoicing at victory is not the only sound to ring forth; for these fateful, destiny-laden days that we are now experiencing demand not only immense sacrifices but they open up an enormous number of wounds, also spiritual wounds if one considers the behaviour of many people. It is therefore necessary that we now and again recall, especially when we are considering important elements from the realm of spiritual science, what responsibility has been placed upon our souls and how we must be longing for times when the influences of the young, unspent etheric bodies and those of the souls who are still on Earth in the bodies of human beings and are able to send up their feelings and soul-capacities can indeed meet one another.

A time will come after this war when the unspent etheric bodies of those who have passed through the portal of death and have developed forces from the sacrifices that they have made, and who are now able to send them down for the spiritualization of mankind, will exert their influence. But down below there must be souls who are able to receive this, souls who will look up in living faith to what has ascended into the spiritual world from those who have passed prematurely through death in order to radiate down to the Earth forces for the spiritualization of mankind.

In order that what I have been saying at the conclusion of this lecture may come clearly before our minds, I should like again to speak these words:

From the courage of the fighters,
From the blood on fields of battle,
From the grief of the bereaved,
From the people's sacrifice—
There will ripen fruit of spirit,
If souls will turn in consciousness
Towards the realm of spirit.

Lecture 15

COLOGNE, 19 JUNE 1915

The Overcoming of Death through Cognitive Insight—Experiences of the Soul before Birth and after Death

THE day before yesterday at the branch in Düsseldorf, we gave consideration to what in the context of life one refers to as man's passage through the gate of death. The essential point here is that Western spiritual development gradually evolves towards a knowledge such that death is overcome through cognitive insight, by recognizing it as a transformation of life itself.

It is quite natural that in our age, pervaded as it is by materialistic views, death must increasingly appear as a boundary of the world wherein man lives. We can easily imagine that in olden times this was significantly different; it was of course different because, as we know, people in these former times still had a kind of remnant of ancient dream-like clairvoyance. This dream-like clairvoyance was associated with a state of dwelling in the spiritual world; and in those times, our souls were incarnated in bodies that made it possible to live clairvoyantly in the spiritual worlds, our souls were connected with the spiritual world, thus making death at that time not so significant or final a phenomenon as it is in our times. But this present consciousness would become ever more pronounced if in our time the knowledge made available through spiritual science were not gradually to manifest itself; for one should not think that this spiritual science that we make our own does not have the greatest significance as a spiritual science also for the whole of human experience.

To be sure, many of us will say that we are progressing on our path through the spiritual-scientific movement in a twofold way. Firstly, by penetrating with our understanding and reasoning powers what spiritual science gives us. Secondly, by applying to our own soul the spiritual-scientific methods that are outlined in, for example, the book *Knowledge of the Higher Worlds: How is it Achieved?*, we are endeavouring to arrive at a perception of the spiritual world already during our physical incarnation. But there will be many who say that only a very few are enabled through their karma to enter the spiritual world in a fully conscious way in this incarnation. It is certainly true that someone might enter it merely by applying these rules; but noticing that one is within it and being attentive to the fact is more difficult than the process of entering it. And there are many who, even though they are within the spiritual world, find it impossible to devote their sensitive, intimate attentiveness to what they experience so as really to be conscious of their position within it. It could be said that for someone who applies the rules given in the book *Knowledge of the Higher Worlds,* it does indeed happen after a relatively short time that as regards his own self he is within the spiritual world but he does not notice it. In this regard it must again and again be emphasized that an intelligent grasp of what is given in spiritual science does not in any way depend on whether one can oneself have insight into the spiritual world. We have often said that presenting the facts of the spiritual world is something that does of course require spiritual-scientific perception. But if what has been found has been transmitted, anyone can understand it provided that he applies his healthy intelligence unobscured by materialistic prejudices in an open-minded way.

We must be clear that it is not enough to claim or persuade ourselves that we have gone far beyond the preconceptions manifested by the materialistic age. To be sure, we will have gone far beyond these prejudices in our will and our aspirations if we seriously devote ourselves to the spiritual-scientific movement; for the fact is that no one will honestly and sincerely ally himself with this spiritual-scientific movement who does not have the deepest inner longing to rise above materialistic prejudices. But our habits of thought are influenced so fundamentally by these materialistic prejudices, and especially by what is not directly a materialistic prejudice but is connected with such a prejudice. It is because of such an underlying materialistic prejudice or preconception that people are in a certain sense unable to develop the capacity to think in an all-embracing way. However much our time is based on reason and logic, there is little evidence in our time of a sharp intelligence and reasoning power among those whose endeavour it is to be at the forefront of the scientific or other cultural aspirations of our present time.

People do not in our time strive towards clarity of thinking. If clarity of thinking was something towards which they fully aspired, they would also be able fully to understand spiritual science. Anyone who thinks with full clarity does not find anything to object to in what spiritual science has to say, at any rate in general terms—for the spiritual scientist can err over details, just as anyone else can. Countless examples could be given to show us how little our time is inclined to devote itself to clear, precise thinking.

I should like to give you an example from what we are now experiencing. It has again been possible to read of a very familiar judgement on the part of a really great person, someone of considerable importance. This judgement has been repeated, and one of the German publicists has made much of the fact that this judgement has again been put forward. Thus a great person once said that war is the continuation of politics by other means.[133] To many thinkers who think in accordance with our time, this appears to be so infinitely logical: war is a continuation of politics. Of course, nothing should be said against the greatness of the man who expressed this observation. He means to say that nations conduct certain political negotiations between one another and thereby order their mutual affairs; if these negotiations arrive at a certain point where they cannot, so to speak, be taken any further, what, then, should happen? Well, war comes in their place. In this way the judgement of all people can be taken into account and directly acknowledged. But if one gives this a little thought, one comes to see how one-sided this judgement is.

For it is, for example, equivalent to saying that there are two individuals who are friends or who have such a relationship with one another that they get on well together and perhaps love one another, and that they then start quarrelling. One could also say that quarrelling is the continuation of love. Viewed outwardly, quarrelling is the continuation of love. But one will not have said anything special about the nature of the quarrel if one knows that this quarrel is the continuation of love. One has therefore not achieved anything or said anything even remotely illuminating about the war if one sees it as the continuation of politics.

It is indeed the case that judgements in our time may appear hugely meaningful but are nevertheless thoroughly one-sided. Many judgements today are greatly valued that have no particular bearing on the matter at hand. Nevertheless, such a judgement does not necessarily always need to be fruitless, and it can even have a significance of some value. But those who acknowledge the value of our world-conception should be able to penetrate the veil of maya also with regard to outer life. Of course, it is not a question of objecting in the least to the judgement that appears in every other newspaper article, for it certainly has some merit; but one would have some strange inner experiences if one were wanting to examine it with clear thinking.

Thus one finds today in almost every newspaper article statements such as: We will be victorious because we must be victorious! As said, nothing shall be said against the justice of this statement, against the fruitfulness and worthiness of this statement; but if someone is standing before a river which he has to cross says: I will swim because I have to, the correctness of the statement is dependent on whether he can swim. And one can in this case attest with clear thinking as to the correctness of the statement of the non-swimmer: I want to swim across because I must swim across. What kind of value does such a statement have? Well, it has a great value, for it gives forces, it gives courage and confidence, it pervades the will; it is a statement that spurs on the will. It is not a statement that recognizes something but one through which the will is steeled. The statement is thereby significant and important. Do not misunderstand such things. They are put forward in order to show that a clear thinking that penetrates things is something altogether different from what is so often held to be valid. In our time, materialistic habits of thought are extraordinarily great and powerful.

However, our judgement is most dulled if we were to become drawn into verifying what the spirit-researcher says. It is the case that everything that the spirit-researcher says can—even if one has never cast one's eye into the spiritual world—be understood if one really applies sound, right thinking. There is no one who, even without being clairvoyant, would be obliged to oppose spiritual science if only he has a sound faculty of judgement. To be an opponent of spiritual science signifies that quite other reasons reside in a person's nature, in his soul. One of these is the following.

When a human being stands in the physical world with his perceptive faculties, he has the constant availability for this purpose of his physical body, his etheric body and also his astral body. These—the physical body, etheric body and astral body—have long been involved in the world's evolutionary process through the ages of Saturn, Sun and Moon and have been built up within man out of the forces of the divine hierarchies. They are today what they have become in the past. When a human individual enters his physical body, he is placed with what has been prepared for him in the course of long ages. All this supports him when he is engaged in physical perception. Every time that we have a perception and form an idea, an impression is made upon our physical body. We know nothing of this, but this impression indeed happens within the physical body. And that it happens is the reason why we have memory during physical life. One needs, however, to have a right picture of this.

If we ask ourselves why we have memory in physical life, we must say that every time that we form an idea or mental picture an impression is made upon the physical body. This impression is, indeed, more or less human-like. But every mental picture that we form does not, as someone who thinks in a materialistic or fanciful way may suppose, make an impression only somewhere or other in the brain but upon the whole human being. Moreover, every such mental picture impresses itself in a manner depending on the nature of the formation of the head, and also the upper part of the chest.

It is really true that as I am speaking to you now, perhaps a hundred syllables a minute, you will during these minutes have fifty human beings forming themselves within you, so that fifty human beings are quickly removed, the one rapidly exchanging places with the other. You can work out for yourself how many such human images will have been formed within you by the time that the hour of the lecture is over. These human images are more or less similar in their outward form, but not entirely so; none is totally like another. Each is different from the others, even though only a little different. As a child might imagine it, one could have the idea that an impression that one is now having of the outer world and which one recalls tomorrow has taken up residence within one in some form. It has not done so but an image which is human-like has remained within one. Indeed, from every impression of the outer world an image remains which is human-like. And when you recall the impression again the following day, you transpose your soul into this human image that is within you. And the reason why you do not see this human image the following day but recall the impression is that you are reading in your astral body. It is a right reading activity, an unconscious reading activity; just as when you write something down and want to read it you do not describe the letters but what the letters signify, so is it tomorrow when you recall what you have experienced today.

You do not behold the image which arose within you, the human phantom that lives within you, but you interpret it. In your soul you put yourself into this human phantom, and your soul experiences something quite different from this human phantom. It experiences again what it has experienced yesterday. This should come as no surprise, for if today you read Goethe's *Faust*, what do you have within you? Masses of paper and printer's ink in whatever form. In an outwardly material sense, this is all that *Faust* is; and you would never have the *Faust* that Goethe wrote if you were not able to do something with the paper and printer's ink that you have in front of you. If you could not decipher it, it would be nothing but paper and printer's ink.

With respect to the outer world, materialists are forever saying that what the spiritual scientist claims to be a reality is nothing of the kind. But these materialists are just as clever as someone who would say: Why do you go on about Goethe's *Faust* when it is, after all, nothing but paper and printer's ink? This judgement about *Faust* is just the same as the judgement that materialists pronounce today about the world. But the same is also true in the case of our memories. Tomorrow nothing will remain in our human nature of today's impression of the phantom, the image, and everything beyond this must be left to the soul's work on this phantom. And just as from the paper and printer's ink the whole structure of Goethe's *Faust* emerges, so from what has remained within us of the phantom does the re-enlivening of today's impression appear when we recall it tomorrow.

But this activity that must be carried out in order that we can remember is brought about by our wonderfully formed physical body and then our etheric body which have been prepared by the ages of Saturn, Sun and Moon. They accomplish, they do this work for us. And a person who thinks materialistically senses and feels this. Now consider: the spiritual truths that are arrived at are gained without this help, so that the help of the outer physical body is not demanded. In this case, forces that otherwise work in the body must be derived from the inner nature of the soul; the soul must be the source of this activity. When one has a spiritual perception that is not brought about through the outer world, we cannot when we want to recall it take ourselves back to an inner phantom that has remained and which is, after all, in the body. We have here to engender everything again from within, without this support, by means of a much stronger power. This, too, is nothing so very surprising. You only have to think of the difference when what I have in mind is reflected on a small scale.

Suppose that someone reads a poem today, and this poem that he has read today he still has tomorrow in printed form. Then he can read it again tomorrow and again the day after. But suppose that he does not have a copy of it and must then speak it from memory. You see the difference. The one time we do something which involves no activity on our part; what we would otherwise have to do, the external piece of paper brings from the one time to the other; we have a support in the paper. We have to make more of an effort if we want to reconstruct the poem from our soul, from within.

Thus someone who lives in the spiritual world has to make a greater effort with his will than one who depends on the support of his body. But this is connected with the fact that everything that is discovered in spiritual science or is only understood requires a considerable inner effort. One can be far lazier and more lethargic if one is a materialist than if one is a spiritual scientist. This is the reason why people are materialists, or at least one of the reasons. They are not materialists for the reason that they are compelled by some kind of logic; they are materialists through fear and also through lethargy, because they want everything that takes place within the soul not to be enacted through the inner forces of the soul but, rather, through what is inscribed and recorded within the body. These are things that we need to be thoroughly aware of if we want to understand the reasons why so many people oppose spiritual science. But it is particularly difficult to embrace with one's thinking capacity something that will and indeed must be arrived at when a person passes through the gate of death.

The day before yesterday I referred to what is essential when someone crosses the threshold of death, namely, self-knowledge. Now of course this self-knowledge is not a simple matter. Some of you will have already heard me speaking about the extent to which people are prone to the greatest errors even in connection with their outward form.

There is a philosopher to whom I have often referred who lived in Vienna; this is Ernst Mach,[134] a serious-minded philosopher (and I am not speaking of the Hamburg mocker of theosophy by the name of Maack). He wrote an *Analysis of Feelings*, where with great naivety he says the following: I was walking along the street when I suddenly had to stop, for I met a person of whom I thought: this is someone with a very unpleasant face, indeed with a repugnant face. And then I discovered that I had passed by a shop window, and the reflection was such that I had seen myself. This made me aware how unfamiliar I was with my own form.

When he saw himself, he accordingly considered himself to be an unpleasant-looking person with a repugnant face. This is a professor of philosophy, a famous present-day professor. And in order to intensify the point he is making, he adds something else: When he had been a professor for some time, he arrived in a town after a long train journey and got on to a bus. He then saw a man who was also boarding the bus from the other direction and he thought: Here's a down-at-heel schoolmaster getting on board! But then he saw that there was again a mirror on the other side, and he discovered that he had mentally referred to himself as a down-at-heel schoolmaster. He points out that he was more familiar with his generic type than his own particular form.

Now if it is already so difficult to recognize oneself with respect to one's outer appearance (it may perhaps be easier with women, because they tend to look more often in the mirror), it is quite another thing when it comes to matters of the soul. There is not really another possibility for our present time of coming to know oneself than to sharpen our cognitive powers through what one can receive within spiritual science. The concepts and ideas that we receive through spiritual science are suited in the best sense for sharpening our self-knowledge. Everything that we may receive through the book *An Outline of Occult Science* is fundamentally based upon self-knowledge in a universal sense. All the thoughts and ideas that we receive through this book really lead us to the point of coming to know ourselves, of knowing what man really is. As we study how the human physical body, etheric body and astral body have come into being through Saturn, Sun and Moon evolution, we come to know what is within us. And by coming to know what is within us in a universal sense, our powers of imagination are sharpened in order that we may know ourselves in a particular, individual sense far better than is otherwise possible.

To what extent does this self-knowledge have a significance for the moment of death? For as long as we dwell here in the physical body, self-knowledge is simply knowledge. But when we pass through the gate of death, all the self-knowledge that we have acquired is transformed into will-forces. The better we know ourselves, the stronger will be this kind of will-force when we have laid aside our physical body.

Let us suppose, for example, that we have in our earthly life come to see that in certain respects we were a person with a violent temper. Well, you know how difficult it is wholly to transform ourselves in physical life and to overcome something like a violent temper even if we are aware of it. But in the moment when we lay aside our physical body, the mere knowledge that we had a hot temper becomes a force of will. And this will is directed towards excluding violence from our being. Every judgement involving insight becomes a will-judgement when we pass through the gate of death; it becomes a force of will.

And then something very significant arises which we can in a certain sense call the reversal of something that is experienced before a person's birth but which is forgotten, because he is unable to look back to the period before his birth. But let us imagine that he could already now accomplish what he will develop in Jupiter existence: when he is gradually preparing out of the spiritual world to enter once more into an incarnation, he would in a highly remarkable way experience something like a perception of his future form, his future life. He would also behold something of his physical form. But there is one thing that he would never perceive in this physical form, which would appear to him as two points.

Let us imagine that as we advance towards birth we would have our physical form hovering before us as though in a mist. We would see it as light, but within it we would see dark, impenetrable points, dark spheres, also much else besides but also these dark spheres. Long before a human individual advances towards his physical birth, he sees—as it were in time, not in space—before him: This is what you will be! And he sees, in a certain sense, how his physical organism is fashioned out of the essence of the Spirits of Form. This appears to him more or less as a figure of light, but hovering within it two dark spheres. When the person approaches physical life, this happens in part already in the body of the mother; he takes certain forces from these surroundings which the mother then forms. He gradually feels connected with this figure of light, and then he feels as if he were especially within these two spheres. Previously they seemed to him to be impenetrable, now he is within them and then feels the forces that come towards him from all sides that enter in to him. Then he pierces these two spheres, the space of the spheres; the space loses its impenetrability. And these are the spaces where the eyes will be.

Thus when one is approaching physical, earthly incarnation, what one does not immediately see is what enables us to see, namely the eyes. They are like impenetrable spheres that accompany our approach to life. Then one penetrates them in the last phase before one enters the physical world. If one were to experience this consciously, it would indeed be a wonderful phenomenon. Just think that as one makes one's way from the spiritual world to the physical world, one says to oneself: Now your soul is approaching this physical form. You will find there two dark spheres. You cannot look through them with your present soul-vision; they are full of spiritual substance! Then one acquires the power to make what is spiritually impenetrable transparent. And when one then, as one says, 'perceives the light of the world', these spaces that were impenetrable to sight are the very reason why one sees. One cannot oneself see the eyes; were one to see them, one would not see the world.

When one passes through the portal of death, the subsequent sight of death is also, therefore, such a wonderful phenomenon in the spiritual life of a human being after death because something similar is happening with the whole human being as occurred here with the eyes. Only what now occurs with the whole human being is experienced consciously. One must after death acquire the feeling in one's inner experience: You have departed from the world. Hitherto one had in the eye the physical world as a physical experience, that which the etheric body finally still shows as a tableau. Now one comes through the portal of death with what one has engendered by way of self-knowledge, and this becomes a power of will.

Now imagine that here [referring to a drawing] is a dead person. He leaves his physical experiences behind. He radiates his power of will, this power of will that he has acquired through self-knowledge; and this radiant power of will that he has acquired through self-knowledge clears away that which prevents us from perceiving our spiritual surroundings. Just as when we approach our birth we clear away the obscuring aspect of the eye, so do we remove what prevents us from perceiving the spiritual world through this power of will. After death we make ourselves transparent. This is the significant event.

When someone passes through the gate of death, for as long as he still has his etheric body he surveys the whole of his life as a mighty tableau. This stands before him. But he also has the feeling: You are seeing yourself! This is you as you were living between birth and death, this is all you were! Now there stirs within him all the power of self-knowledge that he has acquired, and it has the penetrating power that I have described which enables the etheric body to depart. It is then as if a veil were to fall away, and what is behind comes for the first time to manifestation, and this is the spiritual world. It is an immense experience to go through the gate of death and to have the whole last life before one through the etheric body having become free and to receive the feeling: This last life is a veil that covers up a vast world that you were not able to see during life. Now the power of will deriving from self-knowledge battles against this veil and removes it; and when the veil is torn the spiritual world appears behind it.

One does not need to have anxiety for the reason that someone might say: In our present time so many people have done absolutely nothing to arrive at a certain self-knowledge. According to the judgement of many people, one can hardly be cleverer and more intelligent than a contemporary university professor of philosophy; this is, after all, the ideal of intelligence at present. And yet one cannot be so little cut out for self-knowledge as a really famous man who is even a philosopher, Ernst Mach, who really is a person of some significance!

Thus someone might become troubled and say that self-knowledge is in a poor state at present. Admittedly, if the situation were such that it would be indicated to people that they would only have the power of will deriving from the self-knowledge ensuing from their present life, things would look bad for them! Present-day people are very proud of the immense advances in knowledge that have been achieved, and from a certain aspect also rightly. Just think how a modern doctor who knows everything about current medical practice proudly looks down upon those who haven't been doctors for very long. They are all fools, he naturally thinks.

With respect to outward knowledge, human beings have over the course of recent centuries achieved and come to know many things about the outer world: how external phenomena relate and so on.

In this sense, great advances have been made. But with respect to self-knowledge, the olden times when we were involved with former incarnations were far ahead of the present; so far, indeed, that a person of today, if he thinks materialistically, has absolutely no understanding of what derives from olden times. For what people today view as old prejudices was, in that it was experienced by the souls of these former times, basically self-knowledge; and what has been recorded are only the last remnants of self-knowledge.

As regards earthly life, it is the case that someone with an ordinary sense-bound consciousness has no knowledge of his former incarnations. It is true that among the theosophists there are people who manage after a relatively short time to know terribly much about their former incarnations.

In a European city I once became acquainted with a society where Seneca, Frederick the Great, the Emperor Joseph, the Duke of Reichstadt, Madame Pompadour, Marie Antoinette and certain others were sitting together at one coffee table. But apart from those who know so much about their former incarnations after they have learnt a little theosophy, people generally know not very much or nothing at all about their former incarnation through ordinary outward knowledge; for just as it is true that a person knows nothing of his previous incarnation through what the present cycle of human experience gives him, so is it equally true that he is dependent for his will-development after death upon what has remained to him from former lives.

Whereas between birth and death people know nothing of their former incarnations, in the life between death and a new birth they have all the forces of their previous incarnations within them and also that which is always lived through between death and a new birth. Thus when someone passes through the gate of death, he not only has that power of will that derives from the self-knowledge that people generally do not have today but all the will-forces that come not from the self-knowledge in this life but from the self-knowledge that he has acquired in former lives. He is therefore not bereft of that power of will that clears away the fabric that has been woven through his own life. However, if in the course of the coming millennia a person wants to acquire new will-forces, even this self-knowledge from olden times would become ever weaker; and this is why spiritual science is needed for the further evolution of mankind. For such is the course of human evolution that the power of human will is still sufficient for today; but the time is now beginning when this power of will can be strengthened through man's coming to know the spiritual world during earthly development.

The earthly evolution of mankind would be exposed to a danger if people were to resist in every respect receiving something from spiritual science from now onwards until the end of earthly evolution. They would then increasingly come to the point of being little able to perceive anything of spiritual phenomena and happenings in the world of spirit. This would be ever less and less possible for them. They would have increasing difficulty in penetrating the veil of which I spoke. You see, therefore, what significance self-knowledge transformed into a power of will has. Here this knowledge is self-perception, there it is self-will which is directed towards removing the veil from the spiritual world. Especially in those who pass through the portal of death one perceives how important it is for them that they are strengthened in their power of will as it has now been characterized, in the power of will that derives from self-knowledge.

It is therefore really meaningful that when a person passes through the portal of death he concerns himself through these various stages with what is within him, with what is within his self, with what he was during his earthly life. And if someone has communion with a dead person, it is of great, essential significance to make this communion especially fruitful by helping the person who has thus departed in strengthening his self-awareness, in the fulfilment of this self-awareness. This is meant in a very real sense.

Let us think of someone who was with us here in physical life and who has passed through the portal of death. As we have lived with him, we know how he was, we know what he particularly liked doing and so on. When he has passed through the portal of death, it is necessary—urgently necessary—for him, as it were, to summon up everything that he wills through strong inner forces; and this must flow from his review of his life. We can help him in this if we think of him in such a way as he appeared to us in life; if we endeavour to send him thoughts that characterize him as he was. In addition to the various things that have been said about our concern with the dead who have departed from us, we can also make our help available to them by bringing them a kind of picture of their essential being. In this way we relieve them of some of the effort in the unfolding of that will which needs to tear away the veil that has been characterized. It therefore happened that the situation of which I spoke to you the day before yesterday arose for me. Thus when I had to speak recently at the funerals of friends, I felt myself confronted with the need to express at the funeral itself what lives in these friends as regards their essential nature. What I had said was spoken not out of memories but emerged from my own soul in such a way that this soul of mine put itself wholly into the other soul after it had crossed the threshold of death.

When one has to do with a soul that has crossed the threshold of death, it is a matter of putting oneself in the place of this soul. Here in the physical world one is directly confronted by the object, one beholds it from without. In the spirit-realm, one is with one's whole being within this soul-spiritual essence. And so it was that, in the particular case of which I spoke the day before yesterday, it was possible for me to put myself into the soul of this person who had passed through the portal of death and who has been characterized by me as someone who had for many years before her death greatly concerned herself with this world-conception of ours, so that for as long as she was still within her etheric body she was—through her having immersed herself in spiritual science and having received certain forces—able to express in words something of her own essence, what she was as a being. I managed to catch these words from the dead person who had passed through the portal of death, and I had to speak them at her funeral.

In other cases it was different. When I had to speak at the funeral of our dear Fritz Mitscher,[135] who must be remembered with particular fondness by the members of our branch, the situation was that I felt the need fully to put myself within this soul who had gone through the gate of death. But now the need arose to put in words what this soul was in life for those who had befriended it and were around it also as members of our anthroposophical movement, in order together with this soul after its death to ponder and share in all that self-knowledge had contributed to encouraging the development of its will. It then became necessary to say things at this funeral that were in harmony with what our dead friend Fritz Mitscher experienced in the times of his development after he had joined forces with our spiritual-scientific movement; what he had assimilated; how his inner karma had led him.

And the words that I had to speak are, as I said, not my words; they emanated from the forces of his own soul, but formed in such a way that they expressed the essence of the years which had preceded his death. This is what I had to say—it was not a case of wanting to say what I myself had to say. They were, of course, not directly his own words; the soul in question would never have said this out of itself in life. It is what the other soul has felt, a soul that is linked with the soul of the one who has departed as can be sensed only in the case of a soul that is already disembodied. I would like to share with you these words that I had to speak at the funeral.

As a hope that gladdens us,
So do you venture upon the field
Where spirit-blossoms of the Earth
Would, through the power of soul-being,
Manifest themselves to the questing spirit.

Your longing had its deep affinity
With a pure love of truth;
The goal to which you tirelessly
Aspired throughout your life
Was creation from the spirit-light.

You cultivated your fine gifts
To follow with sure step
The radiant path of spirit-knowledge,
Unswayed by outward opposition
As a true servant of the truth.

Your spirit-organs you enhanced
That they boldly and persistently
Thrust error from you
To both sides of the path
And create for you a realm for truth.

To fashion your self that it reveal
The purity of light,
That the Sun-power of the soul
Might radiate its strength within you,
Was your concern and joy.

Other cares, other joys,
They barely touched your soul,
For knowledge, as the light that
To existence meaning gives,
Held for you life's truest worth.

As a hope that gladdens us
So do you venture upon the field
Where spirit-blossoms of the Earth
Would, through the power of soul-being,
Manifest themselves to the questing spirit.

A loss that deeply us aggrieves,
So do you venture from the field
Where earthly seeds of spirit
Have matured for your senses' spheres
In the womb of soul-being.

Feel how we look lovingly
Up to the heights that called you now
Away for other creating.
Extend your strength from realms of spirit
To the friends you've left behind.

Hear the entreaty of our souls,
Sent to you in confidence:
We need here for earthly work
Strong power from spirit-lands
Which to our dead friends we owe.

As a hope that gladdens us,
A loss that deeply us grieves:
Let us hope that from far and near,
Unforsaken for our life,
You shine as starry soul in spirit-realms.

Although these words should not be regarded as having been spoken by the soul itself, they were nevertheless spoken in such community with it that after a relatively short time something was manifested from this soul that now came from it alone; thus not from my soul but only from the soul that had gone through the gate of death. And this then sounded forth, and since that time these words have repeatedly resounded to me:

To fashion my self that it reveal
The purity of light,
That the Sun-power of the soul
Might radiate its strength within me,
Was my concern and joy.

Other cares, other joys,
They barely touched my soul,
For knowledge, as the light that
To existence meaning gives,
Held for me life's truest worth.

And when for the first time—it has often happened since—I heard these words from this soul that had passed through death, it occurred to me—for what I have read out was indeed written down word-for-word as I heard it in connection with this soul—that a dialogue could arise. At the cremation the words spoken were:

To fashion your self that it reveal
The purity of light...

In these verses the second person is used. But this was not my doing. I only noticed when the words came back from the dead soul that these words were formed in such a way that they were given back in the first person:

To fashion my self that it reveal
The purity of light...

You see there a dialogue, a kind of mutual understanding, extending beyond the grave.

In connection with this I should like to speak of something that is often mentioned in our spiritual-scientific movement but which cannot be spoken of enough. In the verses that were addressed to a soul that had passed through the portal of death, you find that something resounds which comes particularly to expression where it is said:

Here the entreaty of our souls,
Sent to you in confidence:
We need here for earthly work
Strong power from spirit-lands
Which to our dead friends we owe.

Do not regard such a plea as mere words. This speaks of something that is in the deepest sense significantly connected with the whole nature of our spiritual-scientific movement.

When a soul has endeavoured, as has the one in question, to imbue all the knowledge and experiences that it has assimilated with spiritual-scientific impulses and it goes prematurely through the gate of death, it is indeed the case that such a soul can continue to be a faithful collaborator. Thus when I spoke these words for this soul, it was something of the nature of a plea that it may become a helper for what must be our will to accomplish for the future of the Earth. For you can regard it as an absolute certainty that the gulf between the living and the dead must be livingly spanned through our spiritual science over the course of earthly evolution. We must learn to regard the dead not as people who are dead but as those who live and act creatively among us, just as we live together with those who live in a physical body. Those who are the so-called dead will then work with us with those forces that are available to them.

We must try to understand in a living way and not as a theory the impulses that spiritual science would have us translate into the living life that we want to contribute out of the future to cultural development. And it must truly be said that, if one takes account of the present circumstances of our outward culture, the help of those in the spiritual world will be needed in the future. Those who truly provide access here on Earth to the spiritual-scientific movement will need the souls of the dead. Hence it was said that for earthly work we need the strength from the lands of spirit that we owe to dead friends. It is a plea that these souls that are working further with the forces which have been strengthened by what they have received here, and imbued with what they have received in spirit-lands, may work together with us on Earth; that they be imbued with that which is of the same nature as what we will.

There are so often symptoms of the considerable difficulties and hindrances that confront what we refer to as our earthly anthroposophical task. Among many others that can be observed, one may now be cited. Some years ago an article appeared in a South German journal that created a sensation,[136] because it was made known that its author was a leading philosopher. The editor of the journal was called Karl Muth. This Karl Muth had at the time accepted a lengthy article; when my book *Occult Science* appeared, he published this article in connection with the book. It would not perhaps have been particularly difficult for me to repudiate at any rate the most hostile aspects of the article and its most foolish assertions. For the truth about that great philosopher is, while for many he is indeed a great philosopher, there are many others who have encountered him in life—he does not need to have come particularly close to them or to have sat opposite to them—to whom he appears as a kind of bur that sticks to them. This is also how he appeared to me, and I have had to keep myself away from him.

But after he had written postcard after postcard, letter after letter, to me, he also sent me this article in manuscript form. I could not bring myself to read the article because it began in such a silly way. Thus he says, for example, that Steiner calls what he has written in his book occult science. But there cannot be such a thing as an occult science, for it is the essential nature of science that it is not occult but public. Thus an occult science contradicts the nature of science itself! This is how the article began. And as I skimmed through it, I came upon such shameless nonsense that it was totally beyond me to read the manuscript any further. It is still lying around somewhere. It is ridiculous to say such a thing about *Occult Science*, for one merely needs to have some knowledge of German to sense how silly it is. It is just as though someone were to say: No science is natural. But there is natural science! It is true that there is no science that is secret, but there is an occult science. It was therefore too silly for words; but the editor of the journal found that it was a particularly significant article. The article has been much read, and what he said about occult science, where he subjected it to thorough criticism, was considered to be very clever.

Now the war came. The philosopher is no German, and he now considers himself to be among the most hostile enemies of Germany. He now writes a series of letters to the same Karl Muth, who at the time—please forgive the hackneyed expression—had licked his lips at the thought of having received the article from the famous philosopher. Much venom and poison has been disseminated about Germany and the German people, but nothing has been written that is as awful as what this famous philosopher wrote in his letters to Karl Muth. His judgements and criticisms about Germany and the German nature are of the most atrocious kind. What then ensued can even be regarded as a good sign.

After spitting out this venom and poison, the philosopher in question wrote—unfortunately not with 'secret science', because the censor did not prevent him from overstepping the mark—so that it even arrived in Munich, and Muth found the courage* to print more of it; but now not in order to publish the 'significant article of a significant man' but some years later the same Karl Muth prints these writings about Germany and writes: Of course a man who writes like this must be someone who belongs in a mad-house! You see, for Karl Muth these writings about the German nature were necessary in order to make him realize that the man is a fool. A few years ago he let the same fool loose on our spiritual science. A sensible person could have known this already, but fools are also often reckoned to

*'Mut(h)' is the usual German word for courage.—Translator

be famous philosophers; and this should not trouble anyone! But you see from this what dangers spiritual science is exposed to. Had the war not come and Karl Muth had not been taught that the good man, this Professor Wincenty Lutoslawski, is actually a fool, he would have had occasion to accept another article from the pen of this 'famous philosopher' seeking to destroy spiritual science.

You also see from this that in our time people are often not inclined to determine through their power of judgement what standpoint they should adopt towards spiritual science. I only mention this in order to show by means of an example—and one could cite many such examples—what hindrances our spiritual-scientific movement is exposed to; that even those who are later necessarily regarded as fools are let loose upon it. It may perhaps also be justified to point out that much else that is said against this same spiritual science is not much cleverer than this; for where something is demonstrated in a really striking way, there must surely be some truth in it.

We must make it clear to ourselves that in order to make spiritual-scientific impulses truly alive, we also need the forces of those who have gone through the gate of death and who, before they crossed this threshold, have received what is embraced within the light of spiritual science. The gulf between the living and the dead must above all else first be removed in the domain of our spiritual science itself. This must, therefore, be our constant watchword: to keep alive the awareness that we had of the souls who were close to us while they were living among us in a physical body wholly as they were then, though oriented towards a different form of life; this is something that we want to do, even if the souls in question have passed through the gate of death. One of the most beautiful and significant things that we can achieve out of spiritual science is that we are able to regard those who have passed through the gate of death as people who live among us and give us blessings; just as we meet with those who are living in a physical body. And this will find some essential support through the fact that on the battlefields where something new is being prepared out of blood and death, so many souls are now passing at an early point in their physical life through the portal of death and making available unspent etheric bodies to the spiritual world.

Man's etheric body is prepared in such a way that it can supply a person with life-forces until old age. If someone passes through the portal of death when he is still young, the forces that could still have been used if he had reached old age are unspent. And we can now look up into the etheric realm of the spiritual world where such a person still remains for a time once he has left the physical plane; from those who have fallen on the fields where battles are being waged and who have passed through the gate of death, there are many youthful etheric bodies that do not immediately dissolve but continue to hold together and contain forces that could have sustained life for a long time.

These etheric bodies will be forces that are able to help human beings when they look up longingly with the consciousness of spiritual science to where what is contained in unspent etheric bodies will reside. Those forces from above will join with those who wish consciously to unite themselves with these forces out of a spiritual-scientific consciousness. As we feel and sense this, we may direct our attention to them. We may commit ourselves to the spiritual world in a living way. We may say to ourselves that there must in the future, in the time that will follow this war, be people here on this Earth of ours who have within them souls that are able to look up into the spiritual world in such a way that these unspent etheric bodies will be realities for them; that through knowledge of the spiritual world this becomes a reality for them. Then spiritual science will show that it has grown beyond mere knowledge to real life; a life that, moreover, has its reality through the destiny-laden events of our time. One will then be able to say that because there will be souls in the world that look up to the etheric bodies in yonder world that develop their unspent forces, those human souls on the Earth will be able to receive these forces and will be able to work with ever greater strength. And the forces of these unspent etheric bodies of those who have made their sacrifices on the fields of blood and death will be fruitful for earthly souls in the future.

For this reason, we wish also today to be mindful of the collaboration that can arise between souls that—pervaded in a soul-spiritual sense by spiritual-scientific knowledge—will in future look up to what remains of the etheric bodies from this war, to what can arise from this inner, soul collaboration. We wish also today to inscribe in our souls those words that I have been speaking at the end of the studies conducted in our branches out of the whole context of the events of our time:

From the courage of the fighters,
From the blood on fields of battle,
From the grief of the bereaved,
From the people's sacrifice—
There will ripen fruit of spirit
If souls will turn in consciousness
Towards the realm of spirit.

Notes

TEXT *sources*: The single lectures collected in the present volume were taken down by various listeners who, while not being professional stenographers, had a fair command of shorthand. The printed text is based upon their own transcriptions. In the case of the Düsseldorf lecture on 17 June 1915, it was possible to compare the printed text of the first German edition of 1967 with the original shorthand version; and some changes were as a result incorporated in the second edition of 1980. For the lecture in Bremen on 21 February 1915 there is only a summary based on notes; nevertheless, the lecture was included where it chronologically belongs.

The seven lectures given in 1915 in Munich and Stuttgart originally envisaged for GA 159/160 have been transferred to GA 174a and GA 174b respectively, thus giving a stronger thematic identity to the present volume.

The verses that Rudolf Steiner read for deceased members of the Anthroposophical Society in the various lectures have always been reproduced in the text of the lectures so as not to detract from the coherence of their inner structure.

The drawings in the text have been made from sketches in the transcriptions, which in turn were based on Rudolf Steiner's blackboard drawings.

The titles of the lectures derive from Marie Steiner or Wolfram Groddeck (editor of the second German edition of 1980).

Details of publications of some of the lectures as separate publications or as supplements to the weekly journal *Das Goetheanum* prior to the first publication of the complete volume (notably the lectures of 19 February, 15 May and 15 June in 1941) can be found in the German edition.

The following lectures have previously been published in English translation: 31 January 1915 in the 1969 *Golden Blade* under the title 'The Great Virtues'; 13 March 1915 in the *Anthroposophic News Sheet* dated 12 and 26 December 1948 under the title 'Spiritual Science, a Necessity for the Present Time; 7 and 9 May 1915 in the *Anthroposophic News Sheet* dated 10 February and 30 June 1946 under the respective titles 'Effects of the Christ Impulse on the Historical Course of Evolution' and 'The Subconscious Forces'; 18 May 1915, *Christ in Relation to Lucifer and Ahriman,* Anthroposophic Press 1978; 13 June 1915 in the *Anthroposophical News Sheet* vol. 8, nos. 39–42 under the title 'The Etheric Body as a Reflection of the Universe'; 15 June 1915, *How Anthroposophical Groups Prepare for the Sixth Epoch/Preparing for the Sixth Epoch*, Anthroposophic Press 1976; and 17 June 1915 (in part), included in the anthology *Life Beyond Death* Rudolf Steiner Press 1995 under the title 'The Human Being's Experiences beyond the Gates of Death'. The other seven lectures have not previously been translated.

1 See *Our Dead. Memorial, Funeral and Cremation Addresses 1906–1924* (GA 261), English edition SteinerBooks 2011, p. 104 f.

2 Ibid., p. 110 f.

3 Regarding Plato's teaching about the virtues see, for example, the dialogues in *Republic* and *Laws.*

4 Rudolf Steiner spoke only on a few occasions about this theme, and very strikingly, for example, in the lecture of 10 September 1923 in Dornach (GA 350), English edition entitled *From Mammoths to Mediums*, Rudolf Steiner Press, London 2000.

5 Giordano Bruno (1548–1600), Italian philosopher and Dominican monk. Opposed the geocentric conception of the world and developed a cosmic teaching of the infinity of the universe. See his book *De l'infinito universo et mondi* (1584). Giordano Bruno was condemned as a heretic by the Catholic Inquisition and burnt at the stake.

6 *Christ and the Spiritual World. The Search for the Holy Grail*, 6 lectures given in Leipzig between 28 December 1913 and 2 January 1914 (GA 149), the sixth lecture.

7 Jeanne d'Arc (1412–1431). Led the French in the Hundred Years War against the English. In many of the present lectures, Rudolf Steiner refers to the special nature of her influence. Readers who are interested in further exploring this figure from an anthroposophical

point of view are referred to *The Mission of Joan of Arc* by Joan M. Edmunds, Temple Lodge, Forest Row 2008.

8 'The Rejuvenating Forces of the German Folk-Soul'. See the lecture with the same title given on 4 March 1915, GA 64 (neither lecture is available in English).

9 The Souls' Awakening, Scene 6; in *Four Mystery Dramas/The Four Mystery Plays* (GA 14).

10 Lina Grosheintz-Rohrer. See Rudolf Steiner, *Our Dead. Memorial, Funeral and Cremation Addresses 1906–1924* (GA 261), p. 96 f.

11 Rudolf Steiner, ibid., p. 90 f. Rudolf Steiner speaks very often in these lectures about the destiny of Theo Faiß, from which a visibly exact picture of the sequence of events leading to an accident arises.

12 See Rudolf Steiner, ibid., p. 110 f.

13 The Battle at Milvian Bridge in 312.

14 Lecture in Hanover, 1 January 1912 entitled 'The Dream Song of Olaf Åsteson'. In Rudolf Steiner, *Our Connection with the Elemental World* (GA 158), English edition, Rudolf Steiner Press 2016.

15 See note 12.

16 There are especially at this point and in the following paragraph gaps in the summary of what was said.

17 The Norsemen, also known as Vikings, undertook bold expeditions of conquest from Scandinavia and Denmark. Under their leader Rollo they established themselves at the Seine estuary; the territory that they annexed became the French duchy of Normandy. A descendant of Rollo, William the Conqueror, invaded England in 1066.

18 According to the oldest Russian source, the Nestor Chronicle, the Novgorod Slavs called upon three brothers, Rurik, Sineus and Truvor, from the Varangian Norse race to be their princes. The name Ros or Rus, probably related to Ruotsi, the name that the Finns applied to the Swedes, was later transferred to the Slavs.

19 Old-Norse Hrörekr. The ruling race descended from Rurik came to an end with the extinction of the Vladimir dynasty (1598).

20 Cf. the lecture of 20 October 1918 (GA 185), *From Symptom to Reality in Modern History*, Rudolf Steiner Press, London 1976.

21 See the lecture referred to in note 8.

22 See *The Anthroposophic Movement* (GA 258), 8 lectures given in Dornach in June 1923.

23 The Indian boy Krishnamurti was put forward by Annie Besant and her followers as the reborn Christ.

24 *The Inner Nature of Man and Our Life between Death and a New Birth*, Vienna, April 1914 (GA 153).

25 Ernst Mach (1838–1916), Austrian physicist, historian of science and philosopher. Mach advocated a sensualistic monism with an anti-metaphysical orientation and can be regarded as one of the precursors of logical positivism.

26 Ferdinand Maack (1861–1930). German physician and the author of esoteric works. In 1923 he founded a 'Rosicrucian' Society, concerned himself intensively with alchemy and invented the 'manuradioscope', a device for investigating the radiations of the hands. Maack brought up the so-called 'Jesuit myth', which portrayed Rudolf Steiner as a pupil of the Jesuits (see *Die Anthroposophie und ihre Gegner, 1919–1921*, GA 255b, p. 435).

27 'As a young man I once saw on the street a face in profile that I experienced as highly unpleasant and repugnant. I received a real shock when I recognized that it was my own, which I had perceived through two pieces of mirror inclined towards one another as I passed by a broken mirror. Not long before, I boarded a bus very tired after an exhausting night's train journey just as a man was approaching from the other direction. "What is this down-at-heel schoolmaster doing here?", I thought. It was myself, for a big mirror was hanging opposite me. The class demeanour was, therefore, far more at the forefront of my mind than my own.'

28 The date of the rejection of the Austrian ultimatum by Serbia.

29 Edward VII (1841–1910) took a leading part in Britain's alliance-forming policy against Germany.

30 See notes 17–20.

31 Conversation with Eckermann on 1 September 1829.

32 Letter to Zelter of 20 February 1828.

33 Michael Bernays, *Schriften zur Kritik und Literaturgeschichte*, vol. I, *Zur neueren Kulturgeschichte*, Stuttgart 1895, p. 70 f.

34 Cf. Rudolf Steiner, lecture of 19 December 1911 (GA 127), *The Mission of the New Spirit Revelation*, Rudolf Steiner Press, Forest Row 2021.

35 C.S. Picht specifies as an example the translation by Emille Vedel, Paris 1913: 'C'est le charme éternel de la femme qui nous élève aux cieux'. See Rudolf Steiner's lecture in Straßburg on 23 January 1910 (GA 272).

36 *The Threshold of the Spiritual World* (1913), GA 17.

37 Ludwig Feuerbach, 1804–1872. German philosopher who studied with Hegel but visibly rejected his views. Feuerbach was known mainly for his anthropological theory of religion (*Das Wesen des Christentums*, 1841). The book referred to here, (*Gedanken über Tod und Unsterblichkeit*, 1830), still derived from the first, pantheistic phase of his philosophy; it was confiscated by the censor. For the quotation see *Sämtliche Werke*, Stuttgart 1903–11, p. 46. See also Rudolf Steiner's description of Feuerbach in his book *The Riddles of Philosophy* (GA 18), English edition, Anthroposophic Press 1973.

38 'The laws of absolutely free movement are known to have been discovered by Kepler; a discovery deserving immortal fame. Kepler proved this in the sense that he found the general expression for the empirical data (section 227). Since then it has become an empty generalisation that Newton was the first to discover the proofs of these laws. It would not be easy to identify a glory more wrongfully transferred from a first discoverer to someone else... The difference is merely that what Kepler expressed in a simple and sublime manner in the form of laws of celestial movements Newton transformed into the reflected form of force and gravity, of that which in the event yields the law of their magnitude.' Hegel, *Enzyklopädie der philosophischen Wissenschaften*, Part two, 'Naturphilosophie', section 270.

39 'As, for example, from England, whose constitution is regarded as the freest, because private individuals play a predominant part in the affairs of the State, experience shows that this country is, in its civil and penal legislation, the right and freedom of property, organisations for art and science, the furthest behind the other civilized States of Europe, and objective freedom, i.e. proper rights, has largely been sacrificed to formal freedom and particular private interests (especially in the organisations and estates ostensibly devoted to religion).' Hegel, ibid., Part three, 'Die Philosophie des Geistes', section 544.

40 'Die tragende Kraft des deutschen Geistes' (The Leading Strength of the German Spirit). See the lecture with the same title given in Berlin on 25 February 1915 (GA 64). (Not translated)

41 GA 7.

42 In July 1902 for the convention of the Federation of European Sections of the Theosophical Society.

43 George R. S. Mead (1863–1933). The last private secretary of H. P. Blavatsky, for a time General Secretary of the European Section of the Theosophical Society. Author of the book *Fragments of Faith Forgotten, Some Short Sketches Among the Gnostics, Mainly of the First Two Centuries*, which Rudolf Steiner greatly appreciated. In 1913 Mead resigned from the Theosophical Society in connection with the exclusion of the German Section.

44 See Ernst Haeckel, *Ewigkeit, Weltkriegsgedanken über Leben und Tod, Religion und Entwicklungslehre*, Berlin 1915, p. 65 and 114; *Englands Blutschuld am Weltkriege*, Eisenach 1914.

45 Johann Gottlieb Fichte, *Reden an die deutsche Nation*, Berlin 1908, first address.

46 Fourteenth address. '...quite apart from the rightful resolve in matters of conscience not to let ourselves be commanded by an outer authority, a higher spirit who has never wholly revealed itself to us has been the moving force behind us. This spirit is revealed to you if you have a visionary capacity for the spirit-world, and looks at you with clear and lofty eyes. The multifarious and confused mixture of sensory and spiritual impulses shall become altogether abhorrent to the world-rulership, and the spirit alone, pure and stripped of all sensory impulses, shall take the helm of human affairs. Our blood has flowed so that this spirit may become free to develop itself and to grow towards an independent existence. It is up to you to give this sacrifice its significance and justification by granting this spirit access to the world-rulership for which it is destined.'

47 *The Inner Nature of Man and the Life between Death and a New Birth* (GA 153).

48 See notes 25–27.

49 See note 2.

50 Galatians 2:20.

51 See note 14.

52 See note 11.

53 Sybil Colazza. See note 1.

54 See note 24.

55 See note 2.

56 GA 121, lectures held in June 1910.

57 See note 18.

58 The quotation from the dramatic poem by Maxim Gorky (1868–1936) entitled 'The Night Hostel'—also a play with the title *The Two Barefooted Ones*—was derived by Rudolf Steiner from Dmitri Merezhkovsky's *The Long March of the Rabble*, which was published in German translation in 1907.

59 'The chain of culture alone makes out of these ruins a whole in which human figures indeed disappear but the human spirit lives on immortally... Ever rejuvenated in its representatives, the genius of humanity blossoms and is regenerated further in peoples and generations.' Herder, *Ideen zur Philosophie der Geschichte der Menschheit*, ninth book I.

60 *The Mission of the Individual Folk Souls*, given in Christiania (Oslo) in June 1910 (GA 121), Rudolf Steiner Press, London 1970. (New edition: SteinerBooks 2023.)

61 'I have personally always willingly recognized the immense contributions that the little British island kingdom—thanks to the advantages of its insular situation and its geographical connections—has made to human culture. Moreover, through my labours concerning Darwinism over the past 50 years, through my personal acquaintance with Darwin and Huxley, with Huxley and John Murray, and also with many other famous scientists in England and Scotland, I have formed the most congenial and fruitful personal connections.' Haeckel, *Ewigkeit, Weltkriegsgedanken über Leben und Tod* (see note 44).

62 Meister Eckhardt (c. 1260–1328), German Dominican monk, learned mystic, whose teachings were condemned as heretical by the Inquisition. In contrast to most scholars of his time he also wrote in German (*Deutsche Predigten*, German Sermons). See also Rudolf Steiner's description of Eckhardt in *Mysticism at the Dawn of the Modern Age and its Relationship to the Modern World-Conception* (GA 7).

63 'Everyone has an idea of becoming and will likewise admit that it is *one* idea; moreover, that if one analyzes it, the definition of *being*, but also of its exact opposite, *nothing*, is contained within it; moreover, that these two definitions are undivided in this one idea; so that becoming is therefore a unity comprising being and nothing.' Hegel, *Enzyklopädie der philosophischen Wissenschaften*, first part: 'Die Wissenschaft der Logik' (The Science of Logic), section 88, 3.

64 '...where there is a belief in spirituality and in the freedom of this spirituality, and a wish to continue developing this spirituality through freedom, this—wherever it originates and in whatever language it is spoken in—is our territory, it belongs to us and it will make itself ours.' *Reden an die deutsche Nation*, seventh address.

65 See note 23.

66 *The Portal of Initiation,* Scene 1 (GA 14).

67 *The Theosophist*, London 1914, vol. XXXVI, no. 3.

68 GA 7.

69 See Rudolf Steiner, *Eurythmy. Its Birth and Development* (GA 277a), English edition, Anatasi Ltd., Weobley 2002, p. 173.

70 Emile Dalcroze (1865–1950) was a composer and music teacher, a pupil of Anton Bruckner and Mathis Lussy, who established a rhythmic form of gymnastics and a rhythmic, musical training.

71 I Cor. 15:14.

72 'Die übersinnliche Erkenntnis und ihre stärkende Seelenkraft in unserer schicksaltragenden Zeit' (Supersensible Knowledge and its strengthening Soul-Power in our Destiny-laden Time). Corresponding indications were given in two public lectures given in Berlin on 16 and 23 April 1915 (GA 64, not translated).

73 See note 13.

74 See note 14.

75 See note 11.

76 *The Mission of the Individual Folk Souls in Relation to Teutonic Mythology* (GA121), English edition, Rudolf Steiner Press, London 1970.

77 A lecture given in Berlin on 14 May 1906 (GA 96). Included in the collection of early lectures on education, *The Education of the Child*, Anthroposophic Press, New York, as well as in the volume containing all the lectures in GA 96, *Original Impulses for the Science of the Spirit*, Completion Press, Australia 2001.

78 Angelus Silesius, 1624–1677. *Cherubinischer Wandersmann*, Book 1, verse 32. This is an approximate rendering of the actual words:

I die and live no more,
The Godhead dies in me,
And what my life shall be
His life doth it imbue.

79 See note 5.

80 Vladimir Solovyov (1853–1900), Russian philosopher of religion, publicist and poet. Rudolf Steiner often speaks in his lectures about the being and work of Solovyov, whose publications he had translated into German by Harry Köhler (Harriet von Vacano) and contributed an Introduction (*Ausgewählte Werke*, Jena 1914, Stuttgart 1921–22). Rudolf Steiner considered Solovyov to be a thinker who mediates between the spirituality of West and East (see the essay, 'Wladimir Solowjoff, ein Vermittler zwischen Ost und West' in Rudolf Steiner, *Der Goetheanumgedanke*, collected articles and essays 1921–1925, GA 36).

81 This name is associated with a series of nineteenth-century Russian philosophers who, in contrast to the 'Westernisers', advocated the emancipation of Russian culture.

82 Originally a scientific designation for the relationship of Slavic languages. The nationalistic ideas of the Slavophils led to the demand that all Slavic peoples be united under Russian sovereignty.

83 Fyodor Mikhailovich Dostoyevsky (1821–1881). His journeys to Western Europe strengthened in him the conviction that the aspiration for power had alienated the West from Christianity. The thoughts paraphrased here can be found in his *Diary of a Writer*, first published in 1873 in the Petersburg weekly journal *Grazhdanin* (The Citizen).

84 See Solovyov, edition referred to in note 80, volume 4: 'Die nationale Frage in Russland' (The National Question in Russia), Part 2, p. 315f.

85 Joseph-Marie Comte de Maistre (1753–1821) in his political philosophy advocated absolutism and the feudal ordering of society. He saw the foundation of political and social life in Catholicism and in the primacy of the pope.

86 This is a reference to Heinrich Rückert's book *Lehrbuch der Weltgeschichte in organischer Entwicklung* (Textbook of World History in its Organic Development), 1857.

87 'Das Schicksal des Menschen im Lichte der Erkenntnis geistiger Welten' (Man's Destiny in the Light of Knowledge of the Spiritual Worlds), 8 May 1915. Hitherto unpublished (envisaged for GA 70) and not translated.

88 Daniel Defoe (1660–1731) became world-famous in 1719 through his novel *The Life and Surprising Adventures of Robinson Crusoe of York* (first German translation 1720). This book was based on the true story of the adventurer Alexander Selkirk, who spent four years on the uninhabited Pacific island of Juan Fernandez (1704–9) before he was rescued. The idea for a story of this kind—a favourite literary subject—could, on the other hand, also go back to the Andalusian Arabic philosopher Ibn Tufail, who wrote a comparable philosophical novel in the twelfth century.

89 In 1882 Rudolf Steiner was assigned the task of editing Goethe's scientific writings in Kürschner's *Deutsche National Literatur*. Volume one, writings about the formation and transformation of organic natures, appeared in 1883. The Introductions and elucidations by Rudolf Steiner for the four volumes appeared as a special edition under the title of *Goethes Naturwissenschaftliche Schriften*, Dornach, GA 1, 1987. See in this connection the correspondence between Karl Julius Schröer, Joseph Kürschner and Rudolf Steiner in *Blätter für Anthroposophie*, 13/2, February 1961.

90 See notes 44 and 61.

91 See note 2.

92 This was written by Wincenty Lutoslawski (1863–1954), a Polish philosopher and Plato specialist, who advocated a messianic world-conception based on Catholicism. He was a professor in Krakow and Geneva. At the International Congress for Philosophy in Bologna in 1911 he took part in the discussion after Rudolf Steiner's lecture (see GA 35, p. 466). In *Kriegshefte der Süddeutschen Monathefte*, February 1915, p. 623–631, Muth writes with reference to his correspondence with Lutoslawski: 'In addition to several smaller articles in *Hochland*, Lutoslawski has published three major articles about Rudolf Steiner's theosophy, about will exercises and about his conversion [to the Catholic Church], which were widely respected. The notes contain some remarkable biographical information... Where in the whole of Ger-

many could a single person be found—outside lunatic asylums—who is so forsaken by good spirits and confronts a great world-historical situation such as the present one so blindly and lacking in ideas as this Reader of Philosophy at Geneva University! For it is not enough to have unburdened his overwrought brain in an epistolary outpouring; he also wants this letter itself to be published.'

93 Modern astronomy takes as its starting point the idea that one can adopt a standpoint in the cosmos whereby the Sun moves in a double screw-like movement (apex movement combined with the movement of the galaxy).

94 *Cherubinischer Wandersmann*, Book 1, verse 61.

95 See note 11.

96 See note 2.

97 See note 92.

98 'Die übersinnliche Erkenntnis und ihre stärkende Seelenkraft in unserer schicksaltragenden Zeit'. See note 72.

99 Until 1822 studies that referred to the Earth's movement around the Sun were on the index of books forbidden by the Catholic Church.

100 See notes 44 and 61.

101 See note 89.

102 See notes 25 and 27.

103 Rudolf Steiner often cites this so-called 'Plateau experiment' as a striking example. 'A mixture of water and alcohol is prepared which has precisely the specific gravity of pure olive oil, and into this mixture a fairly large drop of oil is poured. This does not float on the fluid medium but sinks to the middle of it and in the form of a sphere. In order to set this in movement, a small disc made of card-paper is pierced with a long needle and carefully immersed in the middle of the spherical drop of oil so that the outermost edge of the disc forms the equator of the sphere. This disc is now rotated, at first fairly slowly then ever faster and faster. The movement naturally takes the drop of oil along with it, and as a consequence of the centrifugal force parts of it separate off which after they have become separate entities still continue rotating for a considerable time, first as circles then as little spheres. In this way a formation arises which is often surprisingly similar to our planetary system; in the middle the biggest

sphere representing our Sun and moving around it smaller spheres and rings which can symbolize for us the planets together with their moons.' Quoted from Vinzenz Knauer, *Die Hauptprobleme der Philosophie* (The Main Problems of Philosophy), Vienna and Leipzig 1892, p. 281. J.A.F. Plateau, physicist (1801–1883).

104 'Long ago when I was a young man the great Kant-Laplace fantasy of the arising and eventual demise of the Earth had become current... No more barren perspective for the future can be imagined than that which is thrust upon us as something that we should scientifically expect today. A piece of carrion around which a hungry dog is circling would be a refreshing, appetising morsel in comparison to this ultimate excrement of creation in the form of which our Earth would eventually be engulfed by the Sun; and the thirst for knowledge with which our generation embraces and claims to believe such a notion is a sign of a sick imagination, which learned people of future ages will apply much astuteness to explain as a historical phenomenon of the age.' Herman Grimm, *Goethe-Vorlesungen* (Lectures on Goethe), vol. 2, Stuttgart and Berlin 1913, p. 171 f.

105 The sculptural Group carved by Rudolf Steiner, 'The Representative of Humanity between Lucifer and Ahriman' and often simply referred to as the 'Group', today occupies its own separate space in the Goetheanum.

106 'Die übersinnliche Erkenntinis und ihre stärkende Seelenkraft in unserer schicksaltragenden Zeit'. See note 72.

107 See note 13.

108 See note 14.

109 This was first made in this form by Carl von Linnaeus in *Philosophia botanica*, Stockholm 1751, no. 77.

110 See note 105.

111 See especially *The Fall of the Spirits of Darkness*, 14 lectures given in Dornach between 29 September and 28 October 1917 (GA 177).

112 See note 66.

113 This alliance was negotiated in 1897 between President Faure and Tsar Nicholas II.

114 Houston Stewart Chamberlain (1855–1927, an Englishman living in Germany), *Neue Kriegaufsätze* (New War Essays), Munich 1915, p. 36.

115 See note 11.

116 This is a reference to the Hague Peace Conferences of 1899 and 1907, both of which were convened at the instigation of the Russian tsar, Nicholas II.

117 See note 89.

118 See notes 44 and 61.

119 Robert Hamerling (1830–1889). Cf. Rudolf Steiner, *Gesammelte Aufsätze zur Literatur 1886–1902* (GA 32); see also *The Riddle of Man* (GA 20); *The Course of My Life* (GA 28); 'Robert Hamerling, ein Dichter und ein Denker und ein Mensch', Dornach 1939. Batholomäus Ritter von Carneri (1821–1909). Cf. Rudolf Steiner, 'Carneri, der Ethiker des Darwinismus' in *Methodische Grundlagen der Anthroposophie 1884–1901*, GA 30; also in *The Riddle of Man* and *The Course of My Life.*

120 See note 92.

121 See note 11.

122 See above.

123 See note 105.

124 Alexander Herzen, 1812–1870, writer and publicist. Exiled because of his participation in an oppositional student circle, lived from 1846 onwards in Paris and later in London, Geneva and Brussels. *From the Other Shore*, Hamburg 1850, published in Russia in 1858.

125 'Warum nennen sie das Volk Schillers und Fichtes ein Barbarenvolk?' (Why do they call the people of Schiller and Fichte a bunch of barbarians?). See the lecture given in Berlin on 5 November 1914 (GA 64). (See note 8.)

126 Rudolf Steiner based the following passage on the German translations of Solovyov's works cited in note 80, vol. I, 1, *The Spiritual Foundations of Life* (1884), p. 68 f.; vol. I, 2, Sunday and Easter letters, p. 45 f.

127 See note 71.

128 Matthew 28:20.

129 See note 50.

130 This is a reference to the sixth revised and enlarged edition, Leipzig 1914. Compare also *'Theosophy', Die Textentwicklung der Auflagen 1904–1922 in vollständiger Lesefassung*, Rudolf Steiner Verlag, Dornach 2004. (The first English edition of the book appeared in 1922.)

131 Lina Grosheintz-Rohrer, see note 10.

132 Dr iur. Richard Grelling, *J'accuse. Von einem Deutschen* (I accuse. By a German), third edition, Lausanne 1915.

133 Paraphrased quotation from the book by the Prussian General Karl von Clausewitz entitled *Vom Kriege* (On War), 1832.

134 See note 25.

135 See note 2.

136 See note 92.

Rudolf Steiner's Collected Works

The German Edition of Rudolf Steiner's Collected Works (the *Gesamtausgabe* [GA] published by Rudolf Steiner Verlag, Dornach, Switzerland) presently runs to 354 titles, organized either by type of work (written or spoken), chronology, audience (public or other), or subject (education, art, etc.). For ease of comparison, the Collected Works in English [CW] follows the German organization exactly. A complete listing of the CWs follows with literal translations of the German titles. Other than in the case of the books published in his lifetime, titles were rarely given by Rudolf Steiner himself, and were often provided by the editors of the German editions. The titles in English are not necessarily the same as the German; and, indeed, over the past 75 years have frequently been different, with the same book sometimes appearing under different titles.

For ease of identification and to avoid confusion, we suggest that readers looking for a title should do so by CW number. Because the work of creating the Collected Works of Rudolf Steiner is an ongoing process, with new titles being published every year, we have not indicated in this listing which books are presently available. To find out what titles in the Collected Works are currently in print, please check our website at www.rudolfsteinerpress.com (or www.steinerbooks.org for US readers).

Written Work

CW 1 Goethe: Natural-Scientific Writings, Introduction, with Footnotes and Explanations in the text by Rudolf Steiner
CW 2 Outlines of an Epistemology of the Goethean World View, with Special Consideration of Schiller
CW 3 Truth and Science
CW 4 The Philosophy of Freedom
CW 4a Documents to 'The Philosophy of Freedom'
CW 5 Friedrich Nietzsche, A Fighter against His Time

CW 6 Goethe's Worldview
CW 6a Now in CW 30
CW 7 Mysticism at the Dawn of Modern Spiritual Life and Its Relationship with Modern Worldviews
CW 8 Christianity as Mystical Fact and the Mysteries of Antiquity
CW 9 Theosophy: An Introduction into Supersensible World Knowledge and Human Purpose
CW 10 How Does One Attain Knowledge of Higher Worlds?
CW 11 From the Akasha-Chronicle
CW 12 Levels of Higher Knowledge
CW 13 Occult Science in Outline
CW 14 Four Mystery Dramas
CW 15 The Spiritual Guidance of the Individual and Humanity
CW 16 A Way to Human Self-Knowledge: Eight Meditations
CW 17 The Threshold of the Spiritual World. Aphoristic Comments
CW 18 The Riddles of Philosophy in Their History, Presented as an Outline
CW 19 Contained in CW 24
CW 20 The Riddles of the Human Being: Articulated and Unarticulated in the Thinking, Views and Opinions of a Series of German and Austrian Personalities
CW 21 The Riddles of the Soul
CW 22 Goethe's Spiritual Nature and its Revelation in 'Faust' and through the 'Fairy Tale of the Snake and the Lily'
CW 23 The Central Points of the Social Question in the Necessities of Life in the Present and the Future
CW 24 Essays Concerning the Threefold Division of the Social Organism and the Period 1915-1921
CW 25 Cosmology, Religion and Philosophy
CW 26 Anthroposophical Leading Thoughts
CW 27 Fundamentals for Expansion of the Art of Healing according to Spiritual-Scientific Insights
CW28 The Course of My Life
CW 29 Collected Essays on Dramaturgy, 1889-1900
CW 30 Methodical Foundations of Anthroposophy: Collected Essays on Philosophy, Natural Science, Aesthetics and Psychology, 1884-1901
CW 31 Collected Essays on Culture and Current Events, 1887-1901
CW 32 Collected Essays on Literature, 1884-1902
CW 33 Biographies and Biographical Sketches, 1894-1905
CW 34 Lucifer-Gnosis: Foundational Essays on Anthroposophy and Reports from the Periodicals 'Lucifer' and 'Lucifer-Gnosis,' 1903-1908
CW 35 Philosophy and Anthroposophy: Collected Essays, 1904-1923
CW 36 The Goetheanum-Idea in the Middle of the Cultural Crisis of the Present: Collected Essays from the Periodical 'Das Goetheanum,' 1921-1925

CW 37 Now in CWs 260a and 251
CW 38 Letters, Vol. 1: 1881-1890
CW 39 Letters, Vol. 2: 1890-1925
CW 40 Truth-Wrought Words
CW 40a Sayings, Poems and Mantras; Supplementary Volume
CW 42 Now in CWs 264-266
CW 43 Stage Adaptations
CW 44 On the Four Mystery Dramas. Sketches, Fragments and Paralipomena on the Four Mystery Dramas
CW 45 Anthroposophy: A Fragment from the Year 1910

Public Lectures

CW 51 On Philosophy, History and Literature
CW 52 Spiritual Teachings Concerning the Soul and Observation of the World
CW 53 The Origin and Goal of the Human Being
CW 54 The Riddles of the World and Anthroposophy
CW 55 Knowledge of the Supersensible in Our Times and Its Meaning for Life Today
CW 56 Knowledge of the Soul and of the Spirit
CW 57 Where and How Does One Find the Spirit?
CW 58 The Metamorphoses of the Soul Life. Paths of Soul Experiences: Part One
CW 59 The Metamorphoses of the Soul Life. Paths of Soul Experiences: Part Two
CW 60 The Answers of Spiritual Science to the Biggest Questions of Existence
CW 61 Human History in the Light of Spiritual Research
CW 62 Results of Spiritual Research
CW 63 Spiritual Science as a Treasure for Life
CW 64 Out of Destiny-Burdened Times
CW 65 Out of Central European Spiritual Life
CW 66 Spirit and Matter, Life and Death
CW 67 The Eternal in the Human Soul. Immortality and Freedom
CW 68 Public lectures in various cities, 1906-1918
CW 69 Public lectures in various cities, 1906-1918
CW 70 Public lectures in various cities, 1906-1918
CW 71 Public lectures in various cities, 1906-1918
CW 72 Freedom—Immortality—Social Life
CW 73 The Supplementing of the Modern Sciences through Anthroposophy
CW 73a Specialized Fields of Knowledge and Anthroposophy
CW 74 The Philosophy of Thomas Aquinas
CW 75 Public lectures in various cities, 1906-1918
CW 76 The Fructifying Effect of Anthroposophy on Specialized Fields
CW 77a The Task of Anthroposophy in Relation to Science and Life: The Darmstadt College Course
CW 77b Art and Anthroposophy. The Goetheanum-Impulse

CW 78 Anthroposophy, Its Roots of Knowledge and Fruits for Life
CW 79 The Reality of the Higher Worlds
CW 80 Public lectures in various cities, 1922
CW 81 Renewal-Impulses for Culture and Science—Berlin College Course
CW 82 So that the Human Being Can Become a Complete Human Being
CW 83 Western and Eastern World-Contrast. Paths to Understanding It through Anthroposophy
CW 84 What Did the Goetheanum Intend and What Should Anthroposophy Do?

Lectures to the Members of the Anthroposophical Society

CW 88 Concerning the Astral World and Devachan
CW 89 Consciousness—Life—Form. Fundamental Principles of a Spiritual-Scientific Cosmology
CW 90 Participant Notes from the Lectures during the Years 1903-1905
CW 91 Participant Notes from the Lectures during the Years 1903-1905
CW 92 The Occult Truths of Ancient Myths and Sagas
CW 93 The Temple Legend and the Golden Legend
CW 93a Fundamentals of Esotericism
CW 94 Cosmogony. Popular Occultism. The Gospel of John. The Theosophy in the Gospel of John
CW 95 At the Gates of Theosophy
CW 96 Origin-Impulses of Spiritual Science. Christian Esotericism in the Light of New Spirit-Knowledge
CW 97 The Christian Mystery
CW 98 Nature Beings and Spirit Beings—Their Effects in Our Visible World
CW 99 The Theosophy of the Rosicrucians
CW 100 Human Development and Christ-Knowledge
CW 101 Myths and Legends. Occult Signs and Symbols
CW 102 The Working into Human Beings by Spiritual Beings
CW 103 The Gospel of John
CW 104 The Apocalypse of John
CW 104a From the Picture-Script of the Apocalypse of John
CW 105 Universe, Earth, the Human Being: Their Being and Development, as well as Their Reflection in the Connection between Egyptian Mythology and Modern Culture
CW 106 Egyptian Myths and Mysteries in Relation to the Active Spiritual Forces of the Present
CW 107 Spiritual-Scientific Knowledge of the Human Being
CW 108 Answering the Questions of Life and the World through Anthroposophy
CW 109 The Principle of Spiritual Economy in Connection with the Question of Reincarnation. An Aspect of the Spiritual Guidance of Humanity
CW 110 The Spiritual Hierarchies and Their Reflection in the Physical World. Zodiac, Planets and Cosmos

CW 111	Contained in CW 109
CW 112	The Gospel of John in Relation to the Three Other Gospels, Especially the Gospel of Luke
CW 113	The Orient in the Light of the Occident. The Children of Lucifer and the Brothers of Christ
CW 114	The Gospel of Luke
CW 115	Anthroposophy—Psychosophy—Pneumatosophy
CW 116	The Christ-Impulse and the Development of I-Consciousness
CW 117	The Deeper Secrets of the Development of Humanity in Light of the Gospels
CW 118	The Event of the Christ-Appearance in the Etheric World
CW 119	Macrocosm and Microcosm. The Large World and the Small World. Soul-Questions, Life-Questions, Spirit-Questions
CW 120	The Revelation of Karma
CW 121	The Mission of Individual Folk-Souls in Connection with Germanic-Nordic Mythology
CW 122	The Secrets of the Biblical Creation-Story. The Six-Day Work in the First Book of Moses
CW 123	The Gospel of Matthew
CW 124	Excursus in the Area of the Gospel of Mark
CW 125	Paths and Goals of the Spiritual Human Being. Life Questions in the Light of Spiritual Science
CW 126	Occult History. Esoteric Observations of the Karmic Relationships of Personalities and Events of World History
CW 127	The Mission of the New Spiritual Revelation. The Christ-Event as the Middle-Point of Earth Evolution
CW 128	An Occult Physiology
CW 129	Wonders of the World, Trials of the Soul, and Revelations of the Spirit
CW 130	Esoteric Christianity and the Spiritual Guidance of Humanity
CW 131	From Jesus to Christ
CW 132	Evolution from the View Point of the Truth
CW 133	The Earthly and the Cosmic Human Being
CW 134	The World of the Senses and the World of the Spirit
CW 135	Reincarnation and Karma and their Meaning for the Culture of the Present
CW 136	The Spiritual Beings in Celestial Bodies and the Realms of Nature
CW 137	The Human Being in the Light of Occultism, Theosophy and Philosophy
CW 138	On Initiation. On Eternity and the Passing Moment. On the Light of the Spirit and the Darkness of Life
CW 139	The Gospel of Mark
CW 140	Occult Investigation into the Life between Death and New Birth. The Living Interaction between Life and Death
CW 141	Life between Death and New Birth in Relationship to Cosmic Facts

CW 171 Inner Development-Impulses of Humanity. Goethe and the Crisis of the 19th Century. Cosmic and Human History, Vol. 2
CW 172 The Karma of the Vocation of the Human Being in Connection with Goethe's Life. Cosmic and Human History, Vol. 3
CW 173 Contemporary-Historical Considerations: The Karma of Untruthfulness, Part One. Cosmic and Human History, Vol. 4
CW 174 Contemporary-Historical Considerations: The Karma of Untruthfulness, Part Two. Cosmic and Human History, Vol. 5
CW 174a Middle Europe between East and West. Cosmic and Human History, Vol. 6
CW 174b The Spiritual Background of the First World War. Cosmic and Human History, Vol. 7
CW 175 Building Stones for an Understanding of the Mystery of Golgotha. Cosmic and Human Metamorphoses
CW 176 Truths of Evolution of the Individual and Humanity. The Karma of Materialism
CW 177 The Spiritual Background of the Outer World. The Fall of the Spirits of Darkness. Spiritual Beings and Their Effects, Vol. 1
CW 178 Individual Spiritual Beings and their Influence in the Soul of the Human Being. Spiritual Beings and their Effects, Vol. 2
CW 179 Spiritual Beings and Their Effects. Historical Necessity and Freedom. The Influences on Destiny from out of the World of the Dead. Spiritual Beings and Their Effects, Vol. 3
CW 180 Mystery Truths and Christmas Impulses. Ancient Myths and their Meaning. Spiritual Beings and Their Effects, Vol. 4
CW 181 Earthly Death and Cosmic Life. Anthroposophical Gifts for Life. Necessities of Consciousness for the Present and the Future.
CW 182 Death as Transformation of Life
CW 183 The Science of the Development of the Human Being
CW 184 The Polarity of Duration and Development in Human Life. The Cosmic Pre-History of Humanity
CW 185 Historical Symptomology
CW 185a Historical-Developmental Foundations for Forming a Social Judgement
CW 186 The Fundamental Social Demands of Our Time—In Changed Situations
CW 187 How Can Humanity Find the Christ Again? The Threefold Shadow-Existence of our Time and the New Christ-Light
CW 188 Goetheanism, a Transformation-Impulse and Resurrection-Thought. Science of the Human Being and Science of Sociology
CW 189 The Social Question as a Question of Consciousness. The Spiritual Background of the Social Question, Vol. 1
CW 190 Impulses of the Past and the Future in Social Occurrences. The Spiritual Background of the Social Question, Vol. 2

CW 191 Social Understanding from Spiritual-Scientific Cognition. The Spiritual Background of the Social Question, Vol. 3
CW 192 Spiritual-Scientific Treatment of Social and Pedagogical Questions
CW 193 The Inner Aspect of the Social Riddle. Luciferic Past and Ahrimanic Future
CW 194 The Mission of Michael. The Revelation of the Actual Mysteries of the Human Being
CW 195 Cosmic New Year and the New Year Idea
CW 196 Spiritual and Social Transformations in the Development of Humanity
CW 197 Polarities in the Development of Humanity: West and East Materialism and Mysticism Knowledge and Belief
CW 198 Healing Factors for the Social Organism
CW 199 Spiritual Science as Knowledge of the Foundational Impulses of Social Formation
CW 200 The New Spirituality and the Christ-Experience of the 20th Century
CW 201 The Correspondences Between Microcosm and Macrocosm. The Human Being—A Hieroglyph of the Universe. The Human Being in Relationship with the Cosmos: 1
CW 202 The Bridge between the World-Spirituality and the Physical Aspect of the Human Being. The Search for the New Isis, the Divine Sophia. The Human Being in Relationship with the Cosmos: 2
CW 203 The Responsibility of Human Beings for the Development of the World through their Spiritual Connection with the Planet Earth and the World of the Stars. The Human Being in Relationship with the Cosmos: 3
CW 204 Perspectives of the Development of Humanity. The Materialistic Knowledge-Impulse and the Task of Anthroposophy. The Human Being in Relationship with the Cosmos: 4
CW 205 Human Development, World-Soul, and World-Spirit. Part One: The Human Being as a Being of Body and Soul in Relationship to the World. The Human Being in Relationship with the Cosmos: 5
CW 206 Human Development, World-Soul, and World-Spirit. Part Two: The Human Being as a Spiritual Being in the Process of Historical Development. The Human Being in Relationship with the Cosmos: 6
CW 207 Anthroposophy as Cosmosophy. Part One: Characteristic Features of the Human Being in the Earthly and the Cosmic Realms. The Human Being in Relationship with the Cosmos: 7
CW 208 Anthroposophy as Cosmosophy. Part Two: The Forming of the Human Being as the Result of Cosmic Influence. The Human Being in Relationship with the Cosmos: 8
CW 209 Nordic and Central European Spiritual Impulses. The Festival of the Appearance of Christ. The Human Being in Relationship with the Cosmos: 9

CW 210 Old and New Methods of Initiation. Drama and Poetry in the Change of Consciousness in the Modern Age
CW 211 The Sun Mystery and the Mystery of Death and Resurrection. Exoteric and Esoteric Christianity
CW 212 Human Soul Life and Spiritual Striving in Connection with World and Earth Development
CW 213 Human Questions and World Answers
CW 214 The Mystery of the Trinity: The Human Being in Relationship with the Spiritual World in the Course of Time
CW 215 Philosophy, Cosmology, and Religion in Anthroposophy
CW 216 The Fundamental Impulses of the World-Historical Development of Humanity
CW 217 Spiritually Active Forces in the Coexistence of the Older and Younger Generations. Pedagogical Course for Youth
CW 217a Youth's Cognitive Task
CW 218 Spiritual Connections in the Forming of the Human Organism
CW 219 The Relationship of the World of the Stars to the Human Being, and of the Human Being to the World of the Stars. The Spiritual Communion of Humanity
CW 220 Living Knowledge of Nature. Intellectual Fall and Spiritual Redemption
CW 221 Earth-Knowing and Heaven-Insight
CW 222 The Imparting of Impulses to World-Historical Events through Spiritual Powers
CW 223 The Cycle of the Year as Breathing Process of the Earth and the Four Great Festival-Seasons. Anthroposophy and the Human Heart (*Gemüt*)
CW 224 The Human Soul and its Connection with Divine-Spiritual Individualities. The Internalization of the Festivals of the Year
CW 225 Three Perspectives of Anthroposophy. Cultural Phenomena observed from a Spiritual-Scientific Perspective
CW 226 Human Being, Human Destiny, and World Development
CW 227 Initiation-Knowledge
CW 228 Science of Initiation and Knowledge of the Stars. The Human Being in the Past, the Present, and the Future from the Viewpoint of the Development of Consciousness
CW 229 The Experiencing of the Course of the Year in Four Cosmic Imaginations
CW 230 The Human Being as Harmony of the Creative, Building, and Formative World-Word
CW 231 The Supersensible Human Being, Understood Anthroposophically
CW 232 The Forming of the Mysteries
CW 233 World History Illuminated by Anthroposophy and as the Foundation for Knowledge of the Human Spirit

CW 233a	Mystery Sites of the Middle Ages: Rosicrucianism and the Modern Initiation-Principle. The Festival of Easter as Part of the History of the Mysteries of Humanity
CW 234	Anthroposophy. A Summary after 21 Years
CW 235	Esoteric Observations of Karmic Relationships in 6 Volumes, Vol. 1
CW 236	Esoteric Observations of Karmic Relationships in 6 Volumes, Vol. 2
CW 237	Esoteric Observations of Karmic Relationships in 6 Volumes, Vol. 3: The Karmic Relationships of the Anthroposophical Movement
CW 238	Esoteric Observations of Karmic Relationships in 6 Volumes, Vol. 4: The Spiritual Life of the Present in Relationship to the Anthroposophical Movement
CW 239	Esoteric Observations of Karmic Relationships in 6 Volumes, Vol. 5
CW 240	Esoteric Observations of Karmic Relationships in 6 Volumes, Vol. 6
CW 243	The Consciousness of the Initiate
CW 245	Instructions for an Esoteric Schooling
CW 250	The Building-Up of the Anthroposophical Society. From the Beginning to the Outbreak of the First World War
CW 251	The History of the Goetheanum Building-Association
CW 252	Life in the Anthroposophical Society from the First World War to the Burning of the First Goetheanum
CW 253	The Problems of Living Together in the Anthroposophical Society. On the Dornach Crisis of 1915. With Highlights on Swedenborg's Clairvoyance, the Views of Freudian Psychoanalysts, and the Concept of Love in Relation to Mysticism
CW 254	The Occult Movement in the 19th Century and Its Relationship to World Culture. Significant Points from the Exoteric Cultural Life around the Middle of the 19th Century
CW 255	Rudolf Steiner during the First World War
CW 255a	Anthroposophy and the Reformation of Society. On the History of the Threefold Movement
CW 255b	Anthroposophy and Its Opponents, 1919–1921
CW 256	How Can the Anthroposophical Movement Be Financed?
CW 256a	Futurum, Inc. / International Laboratories, Inc.
CW 256b	The Coming Day, Inc.
CW 257	Anthroposophical Community-Building
CW 258	The History of and Conditions for the Anthroposophical Movement in Relationship to the Anthroposophical Society. A Stimulus to Self-Contemplation
CW 259	The Year of Destiny 1923 in the History of the Anthroposophical Society. From the Burning of the Goetheanum to the Christmas Conference
CW 260	The Christmas Conference for the Founding of the General Anthroposophical Society

CW 278	Eurythmy as Visible Song
CW 279	Eurythmy as Visible Speech
CW 280	The Method and Nature of Speech Formation
CW 281	The Art of Recitation and Declamation
CW 282	Speech Formation and Dramatic Art
CW 283	The Nature of Things Musical and the Experience of Tone in the Human Being
CW 284/285	Images of Occult Seals and Pillars. The Munich Congress of Whitsun 1907 and Its Consequences
CW 286	Paths to a New Style of Architecture. 'And the Building Becomes Human'
CW 287	The Building at Dornach as a Symbol of Historical Becoming and an Artistic Transformation Impulse
CW 288	Style-Forms in the Living Organic
CW 289	The Building-Idea of the Goetheanum: Lectures with Slides from the Years 1920–1921
CW 290	The Building-Idea of the Goetheanum: Lectures with Slides from the Years 1920–1921
CW 291	The Nature of Colours
CW 291a	Knowledge of Colours. Supplementary Volume to 'The Nature of Colours'
CW 292	Art History as Image of Inner Spiritual Impulses
CW 293	General Knowledge of the Human Being as the Foundation of Pedagogy
CW 294	The Art of Education, Methodology and Didactics
CW 295	The Art of Education: Seminar Discussions and Lectures on Lesson Planning
CW 296	The Question of Education as a Social Question
CW 297	The Idea and Practice of the Waldorf School
CW 297a	Education for Life: Self-Education and the Practice of Pedagogy
CW 298	Rudolf Steiner in the Waldorf School
CW 299	Spiritual-Scientific Observations on Speech
CW 300a	Conferences with the Teachers of the Free Waldorf School in Stuttgart, 1919 to 1924, in 3 Volumes, Vol. 1
CW 300b	Conferences with the Teachers of the Free Waldorf School in Stuttgart, 1919 to 1924, in 3 Volumes, Vol. 2
CW 300c	Conferences with the Teachers of the Free Waldorf School in Stuttgart, 1919 to 1924, in 3 Volumes, Vol. 3
CW 301	The Renewal of Pedagogical-Didactical Art through Spiritual Science
CW 302	Knowledge of the Human Being and the Forming of Class Lessons
CW 302a	Education and Teaching from a Knowledge of the Human Being
CW 303	The Healthy Development of the Human Being
CW 304	Methods of Education and Teaching Based on Anthroposophy
CW 304a	Anthroposophical Knowledge of the Human Being and Pedagogy

CW 305	The Soul-Spiritual Foundational Forces of the Art of Education. Spiritual Values in Education and Social Life
CW 306	Pedagogical Praxis from the Viewpoint of a Spiritual-Scientific Knowledge of the Human Being. The Education of the Child and Young Human Beings
CW 307	The Spiritual Life of the Present and Education
CW 308	The Method of Teaching and the Life-Requirements for Teaching
CW 309	Anthroposophical Pedagogy and Its Prerequisites
CW 310	The Pedagogical Value of a Knowledge of the Human Being and the Cultural Value of Pedagogy
CW 311	The Art of Education from an Understanding of the Being of Humanity
CW 312	Spiritual Science and Medicine
CW 313	Spiritual-Scientific Viewpoints on Therapy
CW 314	Physiology and Therapy Based on Spiritual Science
CW 315	Curative Eurythmy
CW 316	Meditative Observations and Instructions for a Deepening of the Art of Healing
CW 317	The Curative Education Course
CW 318	The Working Together of Doctors and Pastors
CW 319	Anthroposophical Knowledge of the Human Being and Medicine
CW 320	Spiritual-Scientific Impulses for the Development of Physics 1: The First Natural-Scientific Course: Light, Colour, Tone, Mass, Electricity, Magnetism
CW 321	Spiritual-Scientific Impulses for the Development of Physics 2: The Second Natural-Scientific Course: Warmth at the Border of Positive and Negative Materiality
CW 322	The Borders of the Knowledge of Nature
CW 323	The Relationship of the various Natural-Scientific Fields to Astronomy
CW 324	Nature Observation, Mathematics, and Scientific Experimentation and Results from the Viewpoint of Anthroposophy
CW 324a	The Fourth Dimension in Mathematics and Reality
CW 325	Natural Science and the World-Historical Development of Humanity since Ancient Times
CW 326	The Moment of the Coming Into Being of Natural Science in World History and Its Development Since Then
CW 327	Spiritual-Scientific Foundations for Success in Farming. The Agricultural Course
CW 328	The Social Question
CW 329	The Liberation of the Human Being as the Foundation for a New Social Form
CW 330	The Renewal of the Social Organism
CW 331	Work-Council and Socialization
CW 332	The Alliance for Threefolding and the Total Reform of Society. The Council on Culture and the Liberation of the Spiritual Life

CW 332a	The Social Future
CW 333	Freedom of Thought and Social Forces
CW 334	From the Unified State to the Threefold Social Organism
CW 335	The Crisis of the Present and the Path to Healthy Thinking
CW 336	The Great Questions of the Times and Anthroposophical Spiritual Knowledge
CW 337a	Social Ideas, Social Reality, Social Practice, Vol. 1: Question-and-Answer Evenings and Study Evenings of the Alliance for the Threefold Social Organism in Stuttgart, 1919-1920
CW 337b	Social Ideas, Social Realities, Social Practice, Vol. 2: Discussion Evenings of the Swiss Alliance for the Threefold Social Organism
CW 338	How Does One Work on Behalf of the Impulse for the Threefold Social Organism?
CW 339	Anthroposophy, Threefold Social Organism, and the Art of Public Speaking
CW 340	The National-Economics Course. The Tasks of a New Science of Economics, Volume 1
CW 341	The National-Economics Seminar. The Tasks of a New Science of Economics, Volume 2
CW 342	Lectures and Courses on Christian Religious Work, Vol. 1: Anthroposophical Foundations for a Renewed Christian Religious Working
CW 343	Lectures and Courses on Christian Religious Work, Vol. 2: Spiritual Knowledge—Religious Feeling—Cultic Doing
CW 344	Lectures and Courses on Christian Religious Work, Vol. 3: Lectures at the Founding of the Christian Community
CW 345	Lectures and Courses on Christian Religious Work, Vol. 4: Concerning the Nature of the Working Word
CW 346	Lectures and Courses on Christian Religious Work, Vol. 5: The Apocalypse and the Work of the Priest
CW 347	The Knowledge of the Nature of the Human Being According to Body, Soul and Spirit. On Earlier Conditions of the Earth
CW 348	On Health and Illness. Foundations of a Spiritual-Scientific Doctrine of the Senses
CW 349	On the Life of the Human Being and of the Earth. On the Nature of Christianity
CW 350	Rhythms in the Cosmos and in the Human Being. How Does One Come To See the Spiritual World?
CW 351	The Human Being and the World. The Influence of the Spirit in Nature. On the Nature of Bees
CW 352	Nature and the Human Being Observed Spiritual-Scientifically
CW 353	The History of Humanity and the World-Views of the Folk Cultures
CW 354	The Creation of the World and the Human Being. Life on Earth and the Influence of the Stars

SIGNIFICANT EVENTS IN THE LIFE OF RUDOLF STEINER

1829: June 23: birth of Johann Steiner (1829–1910)—Rudolf Steiner's father—in Geras, Lower Austria.

1834: May 8: birth of Franciska Blie (1834–1918)—Rudolf Steiner's mother—in Horn, Lower Austria. 'My father and mother were both children of the glorious Lower Austrian forest district north of the Danube.'

1860: May 16: marriage of Johann Steiner and Franciska Blie.

1861: February 25: birth of *Rudolf Joseph Lorenz Steiner* in Kraljevec, Croatia, near the border with Hungary, where Johann Steiner works as a telegrapher for the South Austria Railroad. Rudolf Steiner is baptized two days later, February 27, the date usually given as his birthday.

1862: Summer: the family moves to Modling, Lower Austria.

1863: The family moves to Pottschach, Lower Austria, near the Styrian border, where Johann Steiner becomes stationmaster. 'The view stretched to the mountains . . . majestic peaks in the distance and the sweet charm of nature in the immediate surroundings.'

1864: November 15: birth of Rudolf Steiner's sister, Leopoldine (d. November 1, 1927). She will become a seamstress and live with her parents for the rest of her life.

1866: July 28: birth of Rudolf Steiner's deaf-mute brother, Gustav (d. May 1, 1941).

1867: Rudolf Steiner enters the village school. Following a disagreement between his father and the schoolmaster, whose wife falsely accused the boy of causing a commotion, Rudolf Steiner is taken out of school and taught at home.

1868: A critical experience. Unknown to the family, an aunt dies in a distant town. Sitting in the station waiting room, Rudolf Steiner sees her 'form', which speaks to him, asking for help. 'Beginning with this experience, a new soul life began in the boy, one in which not only the outer trees and mountains spoke to him, but also the worlds that lay behind them. From this moment on, the boy began to live with the spirits of nature . . .'

1869: The family moves to the peaceful, rural village of Neudorfl, near Wiener Neustadt in present-day Austria. Rudolf Steiner attends the village school. Because of the 'unorthodoxy' of his writing and spelling, he has to do 'extra lessons'.

1870: Through a book lent to him by his tutor, he discovers geometry: 'To grasp something purely in the spirit brought me inner happiness. I know that I first learned happiness through geometry.' The same tutor allows him to draw, while other students still struggle with their reading and writing. 'An artistic element' thus enters his education.

1871: Though his parents are not religious, Rudolf Steiner becomes a 'church child', a favourite of the priest, who was 'an exceptional character'. 'Up to the age of ten or eleven, among those I came to know, he was far and away the most significant.' Among other things, he introduces Steiner to Copernican, heliocentric cosmology. As an altar boy, Rudolf Steiner serves at Masses, funerals, and Corpus Christi processions. At year's end, after an incident in which he escapes a thrashing, his father forbids him to go to church.

1872: Rudolf Steiner transfers to grammar school in Wiener-Neustadt, a five-mile walk from home, which must be done in all weathers.

1873–75: Through his teachers and on his own, Rudolf Steiner has many wonderful experiences with science and mathematics. Outside school, he teaches himself analytic geometry, trigonometry, differential equations, and calculus.

1876: Rudolf Steiner begins tutoring other students. He learns bookbinding from his father. He also teaches himself stenography.

1877: Rudolf Steiner discovers Kant's *Critique of Pure Reason,* which he reads and rereads. He also discovers and reads von Rotteck's *World History.*

1878: He studies extensively in contemporary psychology and philosophy.

1879: Rudolf Steiner graduates from high school with honours. His father is transferred to Inzersdorf, near Vienna. He uses his first visit to Vienna 'to purchase a great number of philosophy books'—Kant, Fichte, Schelling, and Hegel, as well as numerous histories of philosophy. His aim: to find a path from the 'I' to nature.

October
1879–1883: Rudolf Steiner attends the Technical College in Vienna—to study mathematics, chemistry, physics, mineralogy, botany, zoology,

biology, geology, and mechanics—with a scholarship. He also attends lectures in history and literature, while avidly reading philosophy on his own. His two favourite professors are Karl Julius Schröer (German language and literature) and Edmund Reitlinger (physics). He also audits lectures by Robert Zimmermann on aesthetics and Franz Brentano on philosophy. During this year he begins his friendship with Moritz Zitter (1861–1921), who will help support him financially when he is in Berlin.

1880: Rudolf Steiner attends lectures on Schiller and Goethe by Karl Julius Schröer, who becomes his mentor. Also 'through a remarkable combination of circumstances', he meets Felix Koguzki, a 'herb gatherer' and healer, who could 'see deeply into the secrets of nature'. Rudolf Steiner will meet and study with this 'emissary of the Master' throughout his time in Vienna.

1881: January: '... I didn't sleep a wink. I was busy with philosophical problems until about 12:30 a.m. Then, finally, I threw myself down on my couch. All my striving during the previous year had been to research whether the following statement by Schelling was true or not: *Within everyone dwells a secret, marvellous capacity to draw back from the stream of time—out of the self clothed in all that comes to us from outside—into our innermost being and there, in the immutable form of the Eternal, to look into ourselves.* I believe, and I am still quite certain of it, that I discovered this capacity in myself; I had long had an inkling of it. Now the whole of idealist philosophy stood before me in modified form. What's a sleepless night compared to that!'

Rudolf Steiner begins communicating with leading thinkers of the day, who send him books in return, which he reads eagerly.

July: 'I am not one of those who dives into the day like an animal in human form. I pursue a quite specific goal, an idealistic aim—knowledge of the truth! This cannot be done offhandedly. It requires the greatest striving in the world, free of all egotism, and equally of all resignation.'

August: Steiner puts down on paper for the first time thoughts for a 'Philosophy of Freedom', 'The striving for the absolute: this human yearning is freedom.' He also seeks to outline a 'peasant philosophy', describing what the worldview of a 'peasant'—one who lives close to the earth and the old ways—really is.

1881–1882: Felix Koguzki, the herb gatherer, reveals himself to be the envoy of another, higher initiatory personality, who instructs Rudolf Steiner to penetrate Fichte's philosophy and to master modern scientific thinking as a preparation for right entry into the spirit. This 'Master' also teaches him the double (evolutionary and involutionary) nature of time.

1882: Through the offices of Karl Julius Schröer, Rudolf Steiner is asked by Joseph Kürschner to edit Goethe's scientific works for the *Deutschen National-Literatur* edition. He writes 'A Possible Critique of Atomistic Concepts' and sends it to Friedrich Theodor Vischer.

1883: Rudolf Steiner completes his college studies and begins work on the Goethe project.

1884: First volume of Goethe's *Scientific Writings* (CW 1) appears (March). He lectures on Goethe and Lessing, and Goethe's approach to science. In July, he enters the household of Ladislaus and Pauline Specht as tutor to the four Specht boys. He will live there until 1890. At this time, he meets Josef Breuer (1842–1925), the co-author with Sigmund Freud of *Studies in Hysteria,* who is the Specht family doctor.

1885: While continuing to edit Goethe's writings, Rudolf Steiner reads deeply in contemporary philosophy (Eduard von Hartmann, Johannes Volkelt, and Richard Wahle, among others).

1886: May: Rudolf Steiner sends Kürschner the manuscript of *Outlines of Goethe's Theory of Knowledge* (CW 2), which appears in October, and which he sends out widely. He also meets the poet Marie Eugenie Delle Grazie and writes 'Nature and Our Ideals' for her. He attends her salon, where he meets many priests, theologians, and philosophers, who will become his friends. Meanwhile, the director of the Goethe Archive in Weimar requests his collaboration with the *Sophien* edition of Goethe's works, particularly the writings on colour.

1887: At the beginning of the year, Rudolf Steiner is very sick. As the year progresses and his health improves, he becomes increasingly 'a man of letters', lecturing, writing essays, and taking part in Austrian cultural life. In August–September, the second volume of Goethe's *Scientific Writings* appears.

1888: January–July: Rudolf Steiner assumes editorship of the 'German Weekly' *(Deutsche Wochenschrift)*. He begins lecturing more intensively, giving, for example, a lecture titled 'Goethe as Father of a New Aesthetics'. He meets and becomes soul friends with Friedrich Eckstein (1861–1939), a vegetarian, philosopher of symbolism, alchemist, and musician, who will introduce him to various spiritual currents (including Theosophy) and with whom he will meditate and interpret esoteric and alchemical texts.

1889: Rudolf Steiner first reads Nietzsche *(Beyond Good and Evil)*. He encounters Theosophy again and learns of Madame Blavatsky in the theosophical circle around Marie Lang (1858–1934). Here he also meets well-known figures of Austrian life, as well as esoteric figures like the occultist Franz Hartmann and Karl Leinigen-Billigen (translator of C.G. Harrison's *The Transcendental Universe).* During this period, Steiner first reads A.P. Sinnett's *Esoteric Buddhism* and Mabel Collins's *Light on the Path.* He also begins travelling, visiting Budapest, Weimar, and Berlin (where he meets philosopher Eduard von Hartmann).

1890: Rudolf Steiner finishes Volume 3 of Goethe's scientific writings. He begins his doctoral dissertation, which will become *Truth and Science* (CW 3). He also meets the poet and feminist Rosa Mayreder (1858–1938), with whom he can exchange his most intimate thoughts. In September, Rudolf Steiner moves to Weimar to work in the Goethe-Schiller Archive.

1891: Volume 3 of the Kürschner edition of Goethe appears. Meanwhile, Rudolf Steiner edits Goethe's studies in mineralogy and scientific writings for the *Sophien* edition. He meets Ludwig Laistner of the Cotta Publishing Company, who asks for a book on the basic question of metaphysics. From this will result, ultimately, *The Philosophy of Freedom* (CW 4), which will be published not by Cotta but by Emil Felber. In October, Rudolf Steiner takes the oral exam for a doctorate in philosophy, mathematics, and mechanics at Rostock University, receiving his doctorate on the twenty-sixth. In November, he gives his first lecture on Goethe's 'Fairy Tale' in Vienna.

1892: Rudolf Steiner continues work at the Goethe-Schiller Archive and on his *Philosophy of Freedom. Truth and Science,* his doctoral dissertation, is published. Steiner undertakes to write Introductions to books on Schopenhauer and Jean Paul for Cotta. At year's end, he finds lodging with Anna Eunike, née Schulz (1853–1911), a widow with four daughters and a son. He also develops a friendship with Otto Erich Hartleben (1864–1905) with whom he shares literary interests.

1893: Rudolf Steiner begins his habit of producing many reviews and articles. In March, he gives a lecture titled 'Hypnotism, with Reference to Spiritism'. In September, volume 4 of the Kürschner edition is completed. In November, *The Philosophy of Freedom* appears. This year, too, he meets John Henry Mackay (1864–1933), the anarchist, and Max Stirner, a scholar and biographer.

1894: Rudolf Steiner meets Elisabeth Fürster Nietzsche, the philosopher's sister, and begins to read Nietzsche in earnest, beginning with the as yet unpublished *Antichrist.* He also meets Ernst Haeckel (1834–1919). In the fall, he begins to write *Nietzsche, A Fighter against His Time* (CW 5).

1895: May, *Nietzsche, A Fighter against His Time* appears.

1896: January 22: Rudolf Steiner sees Friedrich Nietzsche for the first and only time. Moves between the Nietzsche and the Goethe-Schiller

Archives, where he completes his work before year's end. He falls out with Elisabeth Förster Nietzsche, thus ending his association with the Nietzsche Archive.

1897: Rudolf Steiner finishes the manuscript of *Goethe's Worldview* (CW 6). He moves to Berlin with Anna Eunike and begins editorship of the *Magazin für Literatur.* From now on, Steiner will write countless reviews, literary and philosophical articles, and so on. He begins lecturing at the 'Free Literary Society'. In September, he attends the Zionist Congress in Basel. He sides with Dreyfus in the Dreyfus affair.

1898: Rudolf Steiner is very active as an editor in the political, artistic, and theatrical life of Berlin. He becomes friendly with John Henry Mackay and poet Ludwig Jacobowski (1868–1900). He joins Jacobowski's circle of writers, artists, and scientists—'The Coming Ones' *(Die Kommenden)*—and contributes lectures to the group until 1903. He also lectures at the 'League for College Pedagogy'. He writes an article for Goethe's sesquicentennial, 'Goethe's Secret Revelation', on the 'Fairy Tale of the Green Snake and the Beautiful Lily'.

1898–99: 'This was a trying time for my soul as I looked at Christianity. . . . I was able to progress only by contemplating, by means of spiritual perception, the evolution of Christianity. . . . Conscious knowledge of real Christianity began to dawn in me around the turn of the century. This seed continued to develop. My soul trial occurred shortly before the beginning of the twentieth century. It was decisive for my soul's development that I stood spiritually before the Mystery of Golgotha in a deep and solemn celebration of knowledge.'

1899: Rudolf Steiner begins teaching and giving lectures and lecture cycles at the Workers' College, founded by Wilhelm Liebknecht (1826–1900). He will continue to do so until 1904. Writes: *Literature and Spiritual Life in the Nineteenth Century; Individualism in Philosophy; Haeckel and His Opponents; Poetry in the Present;* and begins what will become (fifteen years later) *The Riddles of Philosophy* (CW 18). He also meets many artists and writers, including Käthe Kollwitz, Stefan Zweig, and Rainer Maria Rilke. On October 31, he marries Anna Eunike.

1900: 'I thought that the turn of the century must bring humanity a new light. It seemed to me that the separation of human thinking and willing from the spirit had peaked. A turn or reversal of direction in human evolution seemed to me a necessity.' Rudolf Steiner finishes *World and Life Views in the Nineteenth Century* (the second part of what will become *The Riddles of Philosophy)* and dedicates it to

Ernst Haeckel. It is published in March. He continues lecturing at *Die Kommenden,* whose leadership he assumes after the death of Jacobowski. Also, he gives the Gutenberg Jubilee lecture before 7,000 typesetters and printers. In September, Rudolf Steiner is invited by Count and Countess Brockdorff to lecture in the Theosophical Library. His first lecture is on Nietzsche. His second lecture is titled 'Goethe's Secret Revelation'. October 6, he begins a lecture cycle on the mystics that will become *Mystics after Modernism* (CW 7). November–December: 'Marie von Sivers appears in the audience. . . .' Also in November, Steiner gives his first lecture at the Giordano Bruno Bund (where he will continue to lecture until May, 1905). He speaks on Bruno and modern Rome, focusing on the importance of the philosophy of Thomas Aquinas as monism.

1901: In continual financial straits, Rudolf Steiner's early friends Moritz Zitter and Rosa Mayreder help support him. In October, he begins the lecture cycle *Christianity as Mystical Fact* (CW 8) at the Theosophical Library. In November, he gives his first 'theosophical lecture' on Goethe's 'Fairy Tale' in Hamburg at the invitation of Wilhelm Hubbe-Schleiden. He also attends a gathering to celebrate the founding of the Theosophical Society at Count and Countess Brockdorff's. He gives a lecture cycle, 'From Buddha to Christ', for the circle of the *Kommenden.* November 17, Marie von Sivers asks Rudolf Steiner if Theosophy needs a Western–Christian spiritual movement (to complement Theosophy's Eastern emphasis). 'The question was posed. Now, following spiritual laws, I could begin to give an answer. . . .' In December, Rudolf Steiner writes his first article for a theosophical publication. At year's end, the Brockdorffs and possibly Wilhelm Hubbe-Schleiden ask Rudolf Steiner to join the Theosophical Society and undertake the leadership of the German section. Rudolf Steiner agrees, on the condition that Marie von Sivers (then in Italy) work with him.

1902: Beginning in January, Rudolf Steiner attends the opening of the Workers' School in Spandau with Rosa Luxemberg (1870–1919). January 17, Rudolf Steiner joins the Theosophical Society. In April, he is asked to become general secretary of the German Section of the Theosophical Society, and works on preparations for its founding. In July, he visits London for a theosophical congress. He meets Bertram Keightly, G.R.S. Mead, A.P. Sinnett, and Annie Besant, among others. In September, *Christianity as Mystical Fact* appears. In October, Rudolf Steiner gives his first public lecture on Theosophy ('Monism and Theosophy') to about three hundred people at the Giordano Bruno Bund. On October 19–21, the

German Section of the Theosophical Society has its first meeting; Rudolf Steiner is the general secretary, and Annie Besant attends. Steiner lectures on practical karma studies. On October 23, Annie Besant inducts Rudolf Steiner into the Esoteric School of the Theosophical Society. On October 25, Steiner begins a weekly series of lectures: 'The Field of Theosophy.' During this year, Rudolf Steiner also first meets Ita Wegman (1876–1943), who will become his close collaborator in his final years.

1903: Rudolf Steiner holds about 300 lectures and seminars. In May, the first issue of the periodical *Luzifer* appears. In June, Rudolf Steiner visits London for the first meeting of the Federation of the European Sections of the Theosophical Society, where he meets Colonel Olcott. He begins to write *Theosophy* (CW 9).

1904: Rudolf Steiner continues lecturing at the Workers' College and elsewhere (about 90 lectures), while lecturing intensively all over Germany among theosophists (about 140 lectures). In February, he meets Carl Unger (1878–1929), who will become a member of the board of the Anthroposophical Society (1913). In March, he meets Michael Bauer (1871–1929), a Christian mystic, who will also be on the board. In May, *Theosophy* appears, with the dedication: 'To the spirit of Giordano Bruno'. Rudolf Steiner and Marie von Sivers visit London for meetings with Annie Besant. June: Rudolf Steiner and Marie von Sivers attend the meeting of the Federation of European Sections of the Theosophical Society in Amsterdam. In July, Steiner begins the articles in *Luzifer-Gnosis* that will become *How to Know Higher Worlds* (CW 10) and *Cosmic Memory* (CW 11). In September, Annie Besant visits Germany. In December, Steiner lectures on Freemasonry. He mentions the High Grade Masonry derived from John Yarker and represented by Theodore Reuss and Karl Kellner as a blank slate 'into which a good image could be placed'.

1905: This year, Steiner ends his non-theosophical lecturing activity. Supported by Marie von Sivers, his theosophical lecturing—both in public and in the Theosophical Society—increases significantly: 'The German Theosophical Movement is of exceptional importance.' Steiner recommends reading, among others, Fichte, Jacob Boehme, and Angelus Silesius. He begins to introduce Christian themes into Theosophy. He also begins to work with doctors (Felix Peipers and Ludwig Noll). In July, he is in London for the Federation of European Sections, where he attends a lecture by Annie Besant: 'I have seldom seen Mrs Besant speak in so inward and heartfelt a manner... Through Mrs Besant I have found the way to H.P. Blavatsky.' September to October, he gives a course of 31 lectures for a small group of esoteric students. In October, the annual meeting of the German Section of the Theosophical Society, which still remains very small, takes place. Rudolf Steiner reports membership has risen from 121 to 377 members. In November, seeking to establish esoteric 'continuity', Rudolf Steiner and Marie von Sivers participate in a 'Memphis-Misraim' Masonic ceremony. They pay 45 marks for membership. 'Yesterday, you saw how little remains of former esoteric institutions.' 'We are dealing only with a "framework" ... for the present, nothing lies behind it. The occult powers have completely withdrawn.'

1906: Expansion of theosophical work. Rudolf Steiner gives about 245 lectures, only 44 of which take place in Berlin. Cycles are given in Paris, Leipzig, Stuttgart, and Munich. Esoteric work also intensifies. Rudolf Steiner begins writing *An Outline of Esoteric Science* (CW 13). In January, Rudolf Steiner receives permission (a patent) from the Great Orient of the Scottish A & A Thirty-Three Degree Rite of the Order of the Ancient Freemasons of the Memphis-Misraim Rite to direct a chapter under the name 'Mystica Aeterna.' This will become the 'Cognitive-Ritual Section' (also called 'Misraim Service') of the Esoteric School. (See: *Freemasonry and Ritual Work: The Misraim Service,* CW 265.) During this time, Steiner also meets Albert Schweitzer. In May, he is in Paris, where he visits Édouard Schuré. Many Russians attend his lectures (including Konstantin Balmont, Dimitri Mereszkovski, Zinaida Hippius, and Maximilian Woloshin). He attends the General Meeting of the European Federation of the Theosophical Society, at which Col Olcott is present for the last time. He spends the year's end in Venice and Rome, where he writes and works on his translation of H.P. Blavatsky's *Key to Theosophy.*

1907: Further expansion of the German Theosophical Movement according to the Rosicrucian directive to 'introduce spirit into the world'—in education, in social questions, in art, and in science. In February, Col Olcott dies in Adyar. Before he dies, Olcott indicates that 'the Masters' wish Annie Besant to succeed him: much politicking ensues. Rudolf Steiner supports Besant's candidacy. April–May: preparations for the Congress of the Federation of European Sections of the Theosophical Society—the great, watershed Whitsun 'Munich Congress,' attended by Annie Besant and others. Steiner decides to separate Eastern and Western (Christian–Rosicrucian) esoteric schools. He takes his esoteric school out of the Theosophical Society (Besant and Rudolf Steiner are 'in harmony' on this). Steiner makes his first lecture tours to Austria and Hungary. That summer, he is in Italy. In September, he visits Édouard Schuré, who will write the Introduction to the French edition of *Christianity as Mystical Fact* in Barr, Alsace. Rudolf Steiner writes the autobiographical statement known as the 'Barr Document.' In *Luzifer-Gnosis*, 'The Education of the Child' appears.

1908: The movement grows (membership: 1,150). Lecturing expands. Steiner makes his first extended lecture tour to Holland and Scandinavia, as well as visits to Naples and Sicily. Themes: St John's Gospel, the Apocalypse, Egypt, science, philosophy, and logic. *Luzifer-Gnosis* ceases publication. In Berlin, Marie von Sivers (with Johanna Mücke (1864–1949) forms the *Philosophisch-Theosophisch* (after 1915 *Philosophisch-Anthroposophisch) Verlag* to publish Steiner's work. Steiner gives lecture cycles titled *The Gospel of St John* (CW 103) and *The Apocalypse* (104).

1909: *An Outline of Esoteric Science* appears. Lecturing and travel continues. Rudolf Steiner's spiritual research expands to include the polarity of Lucifer and Ahriman; the work of great individualities in history; the Maitreya Buddha and the Bodhisattvas; spiritual economy (CW 109); the work of the spiritual hierarchies in heaven and on earth (CW 110). He also deepens and intensifies his research into the Gospels, giving lectures on the Gospel of St Luke (CW 114) with the first mention of two Jesus children. Meets and becomes friends with Christian Morgenstern (1871–1914). In April, he lays the foundation stone for the Malsch model—the building that will lead to the first Goetheanum. In May, the International Congress of the Federation of European Sections of the Theosophical Society takes place in Budapest. Rudolf Steiner receives the Subba Row medal for *How to Know Higher Worlds*. During this time, Charles W. Leadbeater discovers Jiddu Krishnamurti (1895–1986) and proclaims him the future 'world teacher,' the bearer of the Maitreya Buddha and the 'reappearing Christ.' In October, Steiner delivers seminal lectures on 'anthroposophy,' which he will try, unsuccessfully, to rework over the next years into the unfinished work, *Anthroposophy (A Fragment)* (CW 45).

1910: New themes: *The Reappearance of Christ in the Etheric* (CW 118); *The Fifth Gospel; The Mission of Folk Souls* (CW 121); *Occult History* (CW 126); the evolving development of etheric cognitive capacities. Rudolf Steiner continues his Gospel research with *The Gospel of St Matthew* (CW 123). In January, his father dies. In April, he takes a month-long trip to Italy, including Rome, Monte Cassino, and Sicily. He also visits Scandinavia again. July–August, he writes the first Mystery Drama, *The Portal of Initiation* (CW 14). In November, he gives 'psychosophy' lectures. In December, he submits 'On the

Psychological Foundations and Epistemological Framework of Theosophy' to the International Philosophical Congress in Bologna.

1911: The crisis in the Theosophical Society deepens. In January, 'The Order of the Rising Sun,' which will soon become 'The Order of the Star in the East,' is founded for the coming world teacher, Krishnamurti. At the same time, Marie von Sivers, Rudolf Steiner's co-worker, falls ill. Fewer lectures are given, but important new ground is broken. In Prague, in March, Steiner meets Franz Kafka (1883–1924) and Hugo Bergmann (1883–1975). In April, he delivers his paper to the Philosophical Congress. He writes the second Mystery Drama, *The Soul's Probation* (CW 14). Also, while Marie von Sivers is convalescing, Rudolf Steiner begins work on *Calendar 1912/1913*, which will contain the 'Calendar of the Soul' meditations. On March 19, Anna (Eunike) Steiner dies. In September, Rudolf Steiner visits Einsiedeln, birthplace of Paracelsus. In December, Friedrich Rittelmeyer, future founder of the Christian Community, meets Rudolf Steiner. The *Johannes-Bauverein,* the 'building committee,' which would lead to the first Goetheanum (first planned for Munich), is also founded, and a preliminary committee for the founding of an independent association is created that, in the following year, will become the Anthroposophical Society. Important lecture cycles include *Occult Physiology* (CW 128); *Wonders of the World* (CW 129); *From Jesus to Christ* (CW 131). Other themes: esoteric Christianity; Christian Rosenkreutz; the spiritual guidance of humanity; the sense world and the world of the spirit.

1912: Despite the ongoing, now increasing crisis in the Theosophical Society, much is accomplished: *Calendar 1912/1913* is published; eurythmy is created; both the third Mystery Drama, *The Guardian of the Threshold* (CW 14) and *A Way of Self-Knowledge* (CW 16) are written. New (or renewed) themes included life between death and rebirth and karma and reincarnation. Other lecture cycles: *Spiritual Beings in the Heavenly Bodies and in the Kingdoms of Nature* (CW 136); *The Human Being in the Light of Occultism, Theosophy, and Philosophy* (CW 137); *The Gospel of St Mark* (CW 139); and *The Bhagavad Gita and the Epistles of Paul* (CW 142). On May 8, Rudolf Steiner celebrates White Lotus Day, H.P. Blavatsky's death day, which he had faithfully observed for the past decade, for the last time. In August, Rudolf Steiner suggests the 'independent association' be called the 'Anthroposophical Society.' In September, the first eurythmy course takes place. In October, Rudolf Steiner declines recognition of a Theosophical Society lodge dedicated to the Star of the East and decides to expel all Theosophical Society members belonging to the order.

Also, with Marie von Sivers, he first visits Dornach, near Basel, Switzerland, and they stand on the hill where the Goetheanum will be built. In November, a Theosophical Society lodge is opened by direct mandate from Adyar (Annie Besant). In December, a meeting of the German section occurs at which it is decided that belonging to the Order of the Star of the East is incompatible with membership in the Theosophical Society. December 28: informal founding of the Anthroposophical Society in Berlin.

1913: Expulsion of the German section from the Theosophical Society. February 2–3: Foundation meeting of the Anthroposophical Society. Board members include: Marie von Sivers, Michael Bauer, and Carl Unger. September 20: Laying of the foundation stone for the *Johannes Bau* (Goetheanum) in Dornach. Building begins immediately. The fourth Mystery Drama, *The Soul's Awakening* (CW 14), is completed. Also: *The Threshold of the Spiritual World* (CW 147). Lecture cycles include: *The Bhagavad Gita and the Epistles of Paul* and *The Esoteric Meaning of the Bhagavad Gita* (CW 146), which the Russian philosopher Nikolai Berdyaev attends; *The Mysteries of the East and of Christianity* (CW 144); *The Effects of Esoteric Development* (CW 145); and *The Fifth Gospel* (CW 148). In May, Rudolf Steiner is in London and Paris, where anthroposophical work continues.

1914: Building continues on the *Johannes Bau* (Goetheanum) in Dornach, with artists and co-workers from seventeen nations. The general assembly of the Anthroposophical Society takes place. In May, Rudolf Steiner visits Paris, as well as Chartres Cathedral. June 28: assassination in Sarajevo ('Now the catastrophe has happened!'). August 1: War is declared. Rudolf Steiner returns to Germany from Dornach—he will travel back and forth. He writes the last chapter of *The Riddles of Philosophy*. Lecture cycles include: *Human and Cosmic Thought* (CW 151); *Inner Being of Humanity between Death and a New Birth* (CW 153); *Occult Reading and Occult Hearing* (CW 156). December 24: marriage of Rudolf Steiner and Marie von Sivers.

1915: Building continues. Life after death becomes a major theme, also art. Writes: *Thoughts during a Time of War* (CW 24). Lectures include: *The Secret of Death* (CW 159); *The Uniting of Humanity through the Christ Impulse* (CW 165).

1916: Rudolf Steiner begins work with Edith Maryon (1872–1924) on the sculpture 'The Representative of Humanity' ('The Group'—Christ, Lucifer, and Ahriman). He also works with the alchemist Alexander von Bernus on the quarterly *Das Reich*. He writes *The Riddle of Humanity* (CW 20). Lectures include: *Necessity and Freedom in World History and Human Action* (CW 166); *Past and Present in the*

Human Spirit (CW 167); *The Karma of Vocation* (CW 172); *The Karma of Untruthfulness* (CW 173).

1917: Russian Revolution. The U.S. enters the war. Building continues. Rudolf Steiner delineates the idea of the 'threefold nature of the human being' (in a public lecture March 15) and the 'threefold nature of the social organism' (hammered out in May–June with the help of Otto von Lerchenfeld and Ludwig Polzer-Hoditz in the form of two documents titled *Memoranda,* which were distributed in high places). August–September: Rudolf Steiner writes *The Riddles of the Soul* (CW 20). Also: commentary on 'The Chymical Wedding of Christian Rosenkreutz' for Alexander Bernus (Das *Reich*). Lectures include: *The Karma of Materialism* (CW 176); *The Spiritual Background of the Outer World: The Fall of the Spirits of Darkness* (CW 177).

1918: March 18: peace treaty of Brest-Litovsk—'Now everything will truly enter chaos! What is needed is cultural renewal.' June: Rudolf Steiner visits Karlstein (Grail) Castle outside Prague. Lecture cycle: *From Symptom to Reality in Modern History* (CW 185). In mid-November, Emil Molt, of the Waldorf-Astoria Cigarette Company, has the idea of founding a school for his workers' children.

1919: Focus on the threefold social organism: tireless travel, countless lectures, meetings, and publications. At the same time, a new public stage of Anthroposophy emerges as cultural renewal begins. The coming years will see initiatives in pedagogy, medicine, pharmacology, and agriculture. January 27: threefold meeting: 'We must first of all, with the money we have, found free schools that can bring people what they need.' February: first public eurythmy performance in Zurich. Also: 'Appeal to the German People' (CW 24), circulated March 6 as a newspaper insert. In April, *Towards Social Renewal* (CW 23) appears—'perhaps the most widely read of all books on politics appearing since the war'. Rudolf Steiner is asked to undertake the 'direction and leadership' of the school founded by the Waldorf-Astoria Company. Rudolf Steiner begins to talk about the 'renewal' of education. May 30: a building is selected and purchased for the future Waldorf School. August–September, Rudolf Steiner gives a lecture course for Waldorf teachers, *The Foundations of Human Experience (Study of Man)* (CW 293). September 7: Opening of the first Waldorf School. December (into January): first science course, the *Light Course* (CW 320).

1920: The Waldorf School flourishes. New threefold initiatives. Founding of limited companies *Der Kommende Tag* and *Futurum A.G.* to infuse spiritual values into the economic realm. Rudolf Steiner also focuses on the sciences. Lectures: *Introducing Anthroposophical*

Medicine (CW 312); *The Warmth Course* (CW 321); *The Boundaries of Natural Science* (CW 322); *The Redemption of Thinking* (CW 74). February: Johannes Werner Klein—later a co-founder of The Christian Community—asks Rudolf Steiner about the possibility of a 'religious renewal,' a 'Johannine church.' In March, Rudolf Steiner gives the first course for doctors and medical students. In April, a divinity student asks Rudolf Steiner a second time about the possibility of religious renewal. September 27–October 16: anthroposophical 'university course.' December: lectures titled *The Search for the New Isis* (CW 202).

1921: Rudolf Steiner continues his intensive work on cultural renewal, including the uphill battle for the threefold social order. 'University' arts, scientific, theological, and medical courses include: *The Astronomy Course* (CW 323); *Observation, Mathematics, and Scientific Experiment* (CW 324); the *Second Medical Course* (CW 313); *Colour.* In June and September–October, Rudolf Steiner also gives the first two 'priests' courses' (CW 342 and 343). The 'youth movement' gains momentum. Magazines are founded: *Die Drei* (January), and—under the editorship of Albert Steffen (1884–1963)—the weekly, *Das Goetheanum* (August). In February–March, Rudolf Steiner takes his first trip outside Germany since the war (Holland). On April 7, Steiner receives a letter regarding 'religious renewal,' and May 22–23, he agrees to address the question in a practical way. In June, the Klinical-Therapeutic Institute opens in Arlesheim under the direction of Dr Ita Wegman. In August, the Chemical-Pharmaceutical Laboratory opens in Arlesheim (Oskar Schmiedel and Ita Wegman are directors). The Clinical Therapeutic Institute is inaugurated in Stuttgart (Dr Ludwig Noll is director); also the Research Laboratory in Dornach (Ehrenfried Pfeiffer and Gunther Wachsmuth are directors). In November–December, Rudolf Steiner visits Norway.

1922: The first half of the year involves very active public lecturing (thousands attend); in the second half, Rudolf Steiner begins to withdraw and turn toward the Society—'The Society is asleep.' It is 'too weak' to do what is asked of it. The businesses—*Der Kommende Tag* and *Futurum A.G.*—fail. In January, with the help of an agent, Steiner undertakes a twelve-city German lecture tour, accompanied by eurythmy performances. In two weeks he speaks to more than 2,000 people. In April, he gives a 'university course' in The Hague. He also visits England. In June, he is in Vienna for the East–West Congress. In August–September, he is back in England for the Oxford Conference on Education. Returning to Dornach, he gives the lectures *Philosophy, Cosmology, and Religion*

(CW 215), and gives the third priests' course (CW 344). On September 16, The Christian Community is founded. In October–November, Steiner is in Holland and England. He also speaks to the youth: *The Youth Course* (CW 217). In December, Steiner gives lectures titled *The Origins of Natural Science* (CW 326), and *Humanity and the World of Stars: The Spiritual Communion of Humanity* (CW 219). December 31: Fire at the Goetheanum, which is destroyed.

1923: Despite the fire, Rudolf Steiner continues his work unabated. A very hard year. Internal dispersion, dissension, and apathy abound. There is conflict—between old and new visions—within the Society. A wake-up call is needed, and Rudolf Steiner responds with renewed lecturing vitality. His focus: the spiritual context of human life; initiation science; the course of the year; and community building. As a foundation for an artistic school, he creates a series of pastel sketches. Lecture cycles: *The Anthroposophical Movement; Initiation Science* (CW 227) (in Wales at the Penmaenmawr Summer School); *The Four Seasons and the Archangels* (CW 229); *Harmony of the Creative Word* (CW 230); *The Supersensible Human* (CW 231), given in Holland for the founding of the Dutch Society. On November 10, in response to the failed Hitler-Ludendorff putsch in Munich, Steiner closes his Berlin residence and moves the *Philosophisch-Anthroposophisch Verlag* (Press) to Dornach. On December 9, Steiner begins the serialization of his *Autobiography: The Course of My Life* (CW 28) in *Das Goetheanum*. It will continue to appear weekly, without a break, until his death. Late December–early January: Rudolf Steiner re-founds the Anthroposophical Society (about 12,000 members internationally) and takes over its leadership. The new board members are: Marie Steiner, Ita Wegman, Albert Steffen, Elisabeth Vreede, and Gunther Wachsmuth. (See *The Christmas Meeting for the Founding of the General Anthroposophical Society*, CW 260.) Accompanying lectures: *Mystery Knowledge and Mystery Centres* (CW 232); *World History in the Light of Anthroposophy* (CW 233). December 25: the Foundation Stone is laid (in the hearts of members) in the form of the 'Foundation Stone Meditation.'

1924: January 1: having founded the Anthroposophical Society and taken over its leadership, Rudolf Steiner has the task of 'reforming' it. The process begins with a weekly newssheet ('What's Happening in the Anthroposophical Society') in which Rudolf Steiner's 'Letters to Members' and 'Anthroposophical Leading Thoughts' appear (CW 26). The next step is the creation of a new esoteric class, the 'first class' of the 'University of Spiritual Science' (which was to have been followed, had Rudolf Steiner lived longer, by two more advanced classes). Then comes a new language for

Anthroposophy—practical, phenomenological, and direct; and Rudolf Steiner creates the model for the second Goetheanum. He begins the series of extensive 'karma' lectures (CW 235–40); and finally, responding to needs, he creates two new initiatives: biodynamic agriculture and curative education. After the middle of the year, rumours begin to circulate regarding Steiner's health. Lectures: January–February, *Anthroposophy* (CW 234); February: *Tone Eurythmy* (CW 278); June: *The Agriculture Course* (CW 327); June–July: *Speech Eurythmy* (CW 279); *Curative Education* (CW 317); August: (England, 'Second International Summer School'), *Initiation Consciousness: True and False Paths in Spiritual Investigation* (CW 243); September: *Pastoral Medicine* (CW 318). On September 26, for the first time, Rudolf Steiner cancels a lecture. On September 28, he gives his last lecture. On September 29, he withdraws to his studio in the carpenter's shop; now he is definitively ill. Cared for by Ita Wegman, he continues working, however, and writing the weekly installments of his *Autobiography* and *Letters to the Members/Leading Thoughts* (CW 26).

1925: Rudolf Steiner, while continuing to work, continues to weaken. He finishes *Extending Practical Medicine* (CW 27) with Ita Wegman. On March 30, around ten in the morning, Rudolf Steiner dies.

Index

P

R

S

Steiner

A NOTE FROM RUDOLF STEINER PRESS

We are an independent publisher and registered charity (non-profit organisation) dedicated to making available the work of Rudolf Steiner in English translation. We care a great deal about the content of our books and have hundreds of titles available – as printed books, ebooks and in audio formats.

As a publisher devoted to anthroposophy…

- We continually commission translations of previously unpublished works by Rudolf Steiner and invest in re-translating, editing and improving our editions.
- We are committed to making anthroposophy available to all by publishing introductory books as well as contemporary research.
- Our new print editions and ebooks are carefully checked and proofread for accuracy, and converted into all formats for all platforms.
- Our translations are officially authorised by Rudolf Steiner's estate in Dornach, Switzerland, to whom we pay royalties on sales, thus assisting their critical work.

So, look out for Rudolf Steiner Press as a mark of quality and support us today by buying our books, or contact us should you wish to sponsor specific titles or to support the charity with a gift or legacy.

office@rudolfsteinerpress.com
Join our e-mailing list at www.rudolfsteinerpress.com

RUDOLF STEINER PRESS